THE NEW KOREA

Books by Alleyne Ireland

Mr.Ireland, one of the foremost living authorities on government,is particularly well known
for his works on Colonial Administration.

"Nothing in the English language in the
same field can compare with them for monu-
mental fullness of design and execution."
-The Springfield Republican.

Democracy and the Human Equation

Mr. Ireland earnestly considers the problem of
making Government responsive to the needs of
modern civilization.

"Every book like this which is sincere and
honestly thought out is of value to all who
are thinking at all upon the great problems
of today."*-The Boston Post.*

An Adventure with a Genius

Recollections of Joseph Pulitzer.

"One of the most graphic portraits of a man
that could be created."
-The Boston Evening Transcript.

"The book holds its readers like a vise and
haunts them like a vision. "*-Life.*

アイルランドの著作について
政治（行政）分野で現存する最高位の権威の一人である
アイルランド氏は植民地統治の作品で特によく知られる。
　「同分野の英語による書籍で、その途方もなく豊かな
　　構成と内容に匹敵するものはない」

　　　　　　　　　　　　―スプリングフィールド・リパブリカン紙

"Democracy and the Human Equation"
（民主主義と人類の平衡化）
アイルランド氏は現代文明が必要とするものに応じられる
政府を作ることの難しさを真剣に考察している。
　「この本のように、誠実にそして正直に考え抜いた本
　　というのは、今日の重大な諸問題 を考える者たち皆に
　　とって価値のあるものだ」

　　　　　　　　　　　　　　　　　　―ボストン・ポスト紙

"An Adventure with a Genius"
Recollections of Joseph Pulitzer.
（天才との冒険－ジョーゼフ・ピューリツァーの回想）

　「人間が創造しえる最も写実的な描写の一つ」
　　　　　　　　　　― ボストン・イブニング・トランスクリプト紙

　「この本は読者を万力のように捕え、幻のように付きまとう」
　　　　　　　　　　　　　　　　　　　　― ライフ誌

THE
NEW KOREA

By

ALLEYNE IRELAND, F.R.G.S.,

Author of "Democracy and the Human Equation,"
"An Adventure with a Genius,"etc

NEW YORK
E.P.DUTTON & COMOPANY
681 FIFTH AVENUE

PREFACE

About twenty years ago I published three volumes dealing with colonial administration in the Far East. They related to British rule in Burma, the Federated Malay States, the Straits Settlements, Sarawak, British North Borneo, and Hong Kong, American rule in the Philippines, Dutch rule in Java, and French rule in Indo-China.

It had been my intention to include an account of Japanese rule in Formosa; but by the time I had turned back east after two years of westerly travel the Russo-Japanese war was in progress, and a visit to Formosa was out of the question. When, in 1922, the opportunity presented itself to spend the greater part of the year in the Far East, I decided that a volume describing Japanese administration in Korea would make a more interesting contribution to the study of Government than a similar work about Formosa.

Formosa is merely one example among many of a civilized race ruling a people in a very low stage of development. Korea, on the other hand, presents the rare spectacle of one civilized race ruling another civilized race. It is true that at the time Japan annexed Korea, in 1910, the actual conditions of life in the Peninsula were extremely bad. This was not due, however, to any lack of inherent intelligence and ability in the Korean race, but to the stupidity and corruption which for five hundred years had, almost continuously, characterized the government of the Korean dynasty, and to the existence during that period of a royal court which maintained throughout Korea a system of licensed cruelty and corruption.

はじめに

　私は約 20 年程前に極東の植民地運営について 3 冊の本を出版した。それらの内容は、イギリスによるビルマ、マラヤ連邦、海峡植民地、サラワク、北ボルネオ会社、香港の支配、そして、アメリカによるフィリピン支配、オランダによるジャワ支配、フランスによるインドシナ支配に関するものである。

　私は、日本による台湾支配も考慮に入れようと思っていたが、2 年に及ぶ西洋への旅を終えて東洋へ戻った時には、日露戦争が始まっており、台湾の訪問など考えられなかった。1922 年に、その年の大半を極東で過ごす機会が訪れた時、私は、日本による朝鮮統治について執筆する方が、台湾に関する同種の研究よりも、政治に関する研究として、より興味深い貢献が出来るだろうと考えた。

　台湾は、文明化された民族が、発展途上の非常に低いステージにいた民族を統治した多くのケースの中の単なる一例に過ぎない。一方、朝鮮では、ある文明化された民族がもう 1 つの文明化された民族を統治したという稀な光景を見せてくれる。1910 年に日本が大韓帝国を併合した当時、半島の人々の生活実態が極めて悲惨だったというのは真実である。

　しかしながら、それは、朝鮮民族の元々の知性や能力が欠落していたからではなく、過去 500 年にわたってほぼ絶え間なく朝鮮王朝を特徴づけてきた愚かさと腐敗によるものであり、その間に存在し

Such was the misrule under which the Koreans had suffered for generation after generation that all incentive to industry, thrift, and social progress had been destroyed, because none of the common people had been allowed to enjoy the fruits of their own efforts.

The title of the present volume gives the key to its contents. What I have attempted is to present in some detail the aims, the methods, and the results of Japanese administration in Korea. Of the right of the Koreans to govern themselves, of the right of the Japanese to govern them I have said but little, for the subject has been discussed exhaustively by other writers, both from the point of view of the Korean nationalists and from that of the Japanese imperialists, and is in any case of such a nature that a judgment one way or the other can reflect nothing but the individual temperament of the judge.

There is already in existence a voluminous literature relating to Korea, much of it of great interest and importance. Most of it, however, falls under one of two heads—writing descriptive of the country and of the people, or polemical writing in which Japanese administration in Korea is attacked or eulogized on the basis of material specially selected to serve one purpose or the other.

To the English-reading public there is available at present only one source of statistically-based information covering every phase of Japanese rule in Korea—the *Annual Report on Reforms and Progress in Chosen*, compiled and published by the Government-General. Although these

た王朝の残虐な行為と汚職にまみれた体制が朝鮮全域で蔓延っていたせいであった。

　一般大衆は誰もが、努力してもその結果を享受することを許されなかった。そのため、産業や倹約、社会進歩などに対する意欲は悉く破壊された。こうした悪政によって朝鮮人は何世代にもわたって苦しみ続けたのである。

　本書の題名は内容を読み解く鍵となっている。私は日本による朝鮮統治の目的、方法、そして結果についてある程度詳しく紹介しようと試みた。また、朝鮮人が自らを統治する権利や、日本人が朝鮮を統治する権利については僅かを述べるに留めた。それは他の著者によって、朝鮮民族主義者と日本帝国主義者の両方の視点から既に徹底的に論じられており、こうした意見は、どのみち、判断する者の個人的な気質に左右されるものだからだ。

　朝鮮に関する著述は既に山のように存在し、その多くは非常に興味深く重要な内容である。しかしながら、その殆どは次の２つのうちのどちらかに該当する。即ち、国や人々について描写したものと、何らかの目的のために選ばれた資料に基く日本の朝鮮統治に関する攻撃または賞賛といった論争とである。

　英語を読む一般大衆にとって、統計に基づいて日本による朝鮮支配の全段階を網羅した情報で、唯一現在入手可能なものは、總督府から編纂出版されている *"Annual Report on Reforms and Progress in Chosen"* である。これらの報告は非常に多くの価値ある論評と、

reports contain a great deal of valuable comment and a considerable body of statistical data, a careful perusal of the volumes covering the past ten years convinced me that a work such as I had in mind could not be written from that material alone. It was clear that a good deal of the matter appearing in the reports had been condensed from departmental reports in which various subjects had been treated in full detail. Both as to data and to comment a large proportion of the contents of the present volume is taken from translations of official material which has not hitherto been accessible in English.

Where I have expressed my own opinion of Japanese administration in Korea, it has been derived from the consideration of what I saw in the country, what I have read about it in official and in unofficial publications, and from discussions with persons—Japanese, Korean, and foreign—who were living in the Peninsula at the time of my visit.

ALLEYNE IRELAND.

多大な統計データを含んではいるが、過去10年間の報告書を注意深く熟読した結果、私が思い描いていたような著作は、こうした資料からだけでは書けないと思うに到った。この報告に登場することの大半は、各部局が様々な問題について詳細をまとめたレポートの要約である。本書に収められた内容のデータや論評の大部分も、従来は英語では読めなかった公的な資料の翻訳からまとめられている。

　本書で私が日本の朝鮮統治について私自身の意見を表明している部分は、私自身が朝鮮で見たことや、公的・私的両方の出版物で読んだこと、そして、私が訪れた際に半島に住んでいた、様々な人々―日本人、朝鮮人、外国人―との議論などから導き出されたものである。

　アレン・アイルランド

CONTENTS

目次

CONTENTS

Preface 6

CHAPTER

I . INTRODUCTORY   28

Korea's Position in Far Eastern Affairs   28
Annexation by Japan   28
Imperialism and Nationalism Contrasted   30
Self-rule and Dependent Rule Contrasted   42
Japanese Rule in Korea Characterised   52

II . DESCRIPTIVE AND HISTORICAL 58

Descriptive 58
Population 66
Railways 72
Roads 78
Streets 80
Maritime Transportation 82
Postal, Telegraph, and Telephone Communications 84
Historical 88

III . SUMMARY 130

Relations between Japan and Korea 130
Governor-General Saito Appointed 140
New Spirit Introduced in Administration 140
Material Progress 150
Reorganization of Government 156
General Progress of the Country 160

IV. GOVERNMENT ORGANIZATION 168

I. THE GOVERNMENT-GENERAL 168
Provincial Government 176
The Present Organization of the Government of Korea 190
The Civil Service 204
Appointment and Salary 204
Pensions 206

目　次

はじめに　7

第一章　序論　29
　　　　極東情勢における朝鮮の立場　　　29
　　　　日本による併合　　　29
　　　　帝国主義と民族主義の対比　　　31
　　　　自治と属国統治の対比　　　43
　　　　日本統治の特徴　　　53

第二章　朝鮮の描写と歴史　59
　　　　朝鮮の描写　　　59
　　　　人口　67
　　　　鉄道　73
　　　　道路　79
　　　　街路　81
　　　　海運　83
　　　　郵便・電信・電話通信　　　85
　　　　朝鮮の歴史　　　89

第三章　概論　131
　　　　日本と朝鮮の関係　　　131
　　　　齋藤總督の任命　　　141
　　　　統治への新しい精神　　　141
　　　　物質的発展　　　151
　　　　政府の再編成　　　157
　　　　全体的な進歩　　　161

第四章　政府組織　169
　　　　I 總督府　　　169
　　　　地方政府　　　177
　　　　朝鮮總督府組織　　　191
　　　　官吏としての職務　　　205
　　　　任命と給与　　　205
　　　　年金　　　207

V. GOVERNMENT ORGANIZATION 212

II. LOCAL ADMINISTRATION 212

Introductory 212
Formation of Local Councils 222
Inspection of Local Administration 230
Local Finance 232
Municipalities 240
Villages 244
School Associations for Japanese 248
District Educational Bodies for Koreans 252
Water-utilization Associations 254

VI. THE LAWS AND COURTS OF KOREA 260

Historical 260
The Sources of Law in Korea 270
Civil Procedure 274
Criminal Procedure 276
The Judiciary 282
Courts of Law 284

VII. POLICE AND PRISONS 290

I. Police Administration 290

Historical 290
After the Annexation 296
Summary Police Jurisdiction 300
Cost of the Police Force 302

II. Prison Administration 304

Control and Administration of 304
Number of prisoners 306
First Offenders 308
Recidivism 310
Pardons 310
Prisoners' Labor 312
Morbidity and Mortality of Prisoners 314

VIII. GOVERNMENT FINANCE 318

Historical 318
Subsequent to the Annexation of 1910 324
Sources of Government Revenue 328

第五章　政府組織　213
　　　Ⅱ地方政府　　　　　　213
　　　　概説　　　　　　　　213
　　　　地方議会の編成　　　　　　223
　　　　地方行政の監察　　　　　　231
　　　　地方財政　　　　　233
　　　　府　　　　241
　　　　面　　　　245
　　　　日本の学校組合　　　　　　249
　　　　朝鮮人の地方教育機関　　　　253
　　　　水利組合　　　　　　255

第六章　司法制度と裁判所　　261
　　　　司法制度の歴史　　　　　　261
　　　　法源について　　　　271
　　　　民事訴訟の手続き　　　　275
　　　　刑事訴訟の手続き　　　　277
　　　　裁判官　　　　　283
　　　　裁判所　　　　　285

第七章　警察と監獄　　291
　　　Ⅰ警察行政　　　　291
　　　　歴史的背景　　　　　291
　　　　併合後　　　　　297
　　　　簡易司法警察権　　　　301
　　　　警察の経費　　　　303
　　　Ⅱ監獄行政　　　　305
　　　　監獄の管理体制　　　　　305
　　　　受刑者数　　　　307
　　　　初犯の受刑者　　　　309
　　　　常習的犯行　　　　311
　　　　恩赦　　　311
　　　　獄中労働　　　　313
　　　　囚人の罹患率および死亡率　　　315

第八章　政府の財政　　319
　　　　財政の歴史　　　　319
　　　　1910年の併合に続いて　　　325
　　　　政府歳入の収入源　　　329

Monopolies and Other Government Undertakings 332
Lumber Undertaking Station 334
Objects of Government Expenditure 338
The Korean National Debt 342

IX. EDUCATION 352

Principles of 352
Objects of 354
Rules for Guidance of Teachers 356
Historical Development 358
Present State of the Educational System 368
The School Curriculum 378
Salaries of Teachers 380
Religion in the Schools 382
Educational Finance 386

X. MEDICAL, SANITARY, AND SOCIAL SERVICE 394

Historical 394
Epidemic Diseases 404
General Causes of Death 404
Sanitary Equipment 406
Expansion of Medical Organs 410
The Central Health Society 412
Hygienic Inspection 414
Bacteriological Service 414
Opium Control 414
Relief Work for Lepers 418
Hospitals 418
The Severance Union Medical College 420
Health Practitioners 424
Vital Statistics 426
Social Service 428

XI. THE ECONOMIC DEVELOPMENT OF KOREA 438

I. AGRICULTURE 438

Historical 438
Yield of Principal Crops 448
Value of Agricultural Products 450
Sericulture 450
Land Tenure 454

専売事業とその他の政府事業　　　333
営林廠　　　335
政府支出の対象　　　339
朝鮮国債　　　343

第九章　教育　　353

教育の基本理念　　　353
教育の目的　　　355
教師への指針　　　357
教育制度の歴史的発展　　　359
現在の教育制度の状況　　　369
学校教科課程　　　379
教師の給料　　　381
学校における宗教　　　383
教育の財政　　　387

第十章　医療・公衆衛生・社会福祉　　395

公衆衛生の歴史　　　395
伝染病　　　405
一般的な死因　　　405
衛生設備　　　407
医療機関の拡張　　　411
中央衛生會　　　413
衛生検査　　　415
細菌研究　　　415
アヘン取締　　　415
ハンセン病患者救済事業　　　419
病院　　　419
セブランス連合医学専門学校　　　421
医療関係者　　　425
人口動態統計　　　427
社会福祉事業　　　429

第十一章　経済発展　　439

Ⅰ　農業　　439
農業の歴史　　　439
主要作物の生産　　　449
農産物の価格　　　451
養蚕　　　451
土地制度　　　455

Financing the Farmer 460
Official Encouragement of Agriculture 462
Irrigation 468
Agricultural Labor 472

XII. ECONOMIC DEVELOPMENT OF KOREA 480

II. FORESTRY, FISHERY, AND MINING 480

Forestry 480
Historical 480
Condition of the Forests 484
Afforestation 486
Fishery 490
Experiments in Aquatic Products 494
Development of the Fishing Industry 496
Economic Progress of the Fishing Industry 498
Mining 500
Historical 500
Present State of the Mining Industry 504

XIII. ECONOMIC DEVELOPMENT OF KOREA 510

III. COMMERCE, MANUFACTURES, AND BANKING 510

Currency 510
Economic Development 518
Commerce 518
The Foreign Trade of Korea 518
Distribution of Foreign Trade 522
Gold and Silver Bullion 522
General Character of the Export Trade 526
General Character of the Import Trade 528
Manufactures 532
Banking 538
Historical 538
Banking Statistics 544
The Bank of Chosen 546
The Chosen Industrial Bank 550
Ordinary Banks 550
People's Banking Associations 552
The Oriental Development Company 552
Mutual Credit Associations (Mujin-Ko) 554

農民への融資　461
公的機関による農業の奨励　463
灌漑　469
農業労働　473

第十二章　経済発展　481

Ⅱ 林業, 水産業, 鉱業　481
林業　481
林業の歴史　481
山林の状態　485
造林事業　487
水産業　491
水産試験　495
水産業の発展　497
水産業の経済成長　499
鉱業　501
鉱業の歴史　501
鉱業の現状　505

第十三章　経済発展　511

Ⅲ 貿易, 製造業, 銀行業　511
貨幣　511
経済開発　519
貿易　519
朝鮮の対外貿易　519
対外貿易の割合　523
金と銀　523
輸出貿易の一般的特徴　527
輸入貿易の一般的特徴　529
製造業　533
銀行業　539
銀行業の歴史　539
銀行統計　545
朝鮮銀行　547
朝鮮殖産銀行　551
普通銀行　551
金融組合　553
東洋拓殖株式会社　553
相互信用組合（無盡講）　555

APPENDICES: 564

Appendix A. Treaty of Annexation 566

Appendix B. Imperial Rescript on Annexation 570

Appendix C. The Late Korean Emperor's Rescript on Cession of Sovereignty 574

Appendix D. Imperial Rescript Concerning the Reorganization of the Government-General of Chosen 578

Appendix E. Governor-General's Instruction to High Officials Concerning Administrative Reforms 580

Appendix F. Governor-General's Proclamation to the People of Chosen 586

Appendix G. Governor-General's Address to Provincial Governors 590

Appendix H. Administrative Superintendent's Instructions to Provincial Governors 596

Appendix I. Rules for Teachers 614

MAP OF KOREA (CHOSEN) 628

附録　　565

A 韓国併合に関する条約　　567

B 韓国併合に付下し給える詔書　　571

C 日韓併合に関する旧韓国皇帝の勅諭　　575

D 朝鮮總督府官制改正の詔書　　579

E 總督府および所属官署に対する總督の施政方針訓示　　581

F 總督による朝鮮人民への声明　　587

G 總督による道知事への演説　　591

H 道知事会議に於ける政務総監の訓示要旨　　597

I 朝鮮總督府訓令　教員心得　　615

朝鮮地図　　628

THE NEW KOREA

THE NEW KOREA

CHAPTER I

第一章

CHAPTER I

INTRODUCTORY

Korea is destined to occupy a position of constantly increasing importance with reference to the general problem of the Far East. Her geographical situation predetermines for her a future indissolubly linked with that of China, of Asiatic Russia, and of Japan, with two of which she has land frontiers, and from the third is separated only by a narrow strait. It is impossible to foresee any political, social, or economic developments in northeastern Asia in which Korea will not fill a role as significant as that of Turkey in respect of the Near East, of Egypt in respect of the British Empire, or of the Panama Canal Zone in respect of the United States.

The annexation of Korea by Japan in 1910 made waste paper out of bales of laboriously compiled reports and of ingenious predictions about Far Eastern affairs. It reflected, in brief, the determination of Japan to forestall any attempt which might be contemplated by China to reassert, and to make active, its former suzerainty over Korea, or on the part of Russia to secure in the Korean Peninsula a position of such dominance as would create the temptation, and furnish the instrument, to take the control of the country out of the hands of its weak, incompetent, and corrupt rulers.

第一章

序論

朝鮮半島は極東の諸問題にとって絶えず重要な位置にあることを運命づけられていた。その立地条件により、朝鮮の未来は周辺諸国の未来と切っても切れない結びつきを運命づけられているのである。中国、ロシアとは国境を挟んで隣接し、日本とは狭い海峡で隔てられているだけである。北東アジアのいかなる政治的、社会的、あるいは経済的発展において朝鮮が重要な役割を果たさなくなると予測することは不可能だ。それは、近東におけるトルコ、大英帝国におけるエジプト、あるいは米国におけるパナマ運河地域が重要なのと同じである。

1910 年の日本による併合は、極東情勢について苦心の末まとめられていた大量の報告書や精密な予測といったものをごみ同然にしてしまった。端的に言えば、この併合は日本の決断を反映したものであった。すなわち、かつて朝鮮の宗主国であった中国が、再びその権利を主張し行動に移すことを未然に防ぐためであり、またロシアが朝鮮半島において、その脆弱で無能で腐敗した支配者の手から朝鮮半島の支配権を奪おうとする衝動を起こし、その手段を備えるような優位な地位を確保することを前もって封じ込めようというものであった。

Looking forward from 1910, one thing was clear where many things were obscure, namely that Japan, having decided to make Korea part of her Empire, would deem the permanence of her occupation to be a major element of her national policy, to be held intact, at whatever cost, against internal revolt or foreign intrigue.

In the field of international policy the Japanese annexation of Korea is perfectly suited to serve as a demarcating issue between two schools of political conviction—the imperialist and the nationalist—and according to whether the reader belongs to one or to the other of these schools, so will he convince himself that Japan has the "right" to rule Korea, or that the Koreans have a "right" to independent nationhood.

The common employment of the word "right" in this connection has done much to befog the actual matter in controversy between the imperialists and the nationalists, since the "rightness" of either doctrine when applied to a particular case can only be measured with reference to the particular circumstances.

The most extreme imperialist would balk at the suggestion that the United States should, on account of its great power and of its advanced social development, annex every backward and undeveloped country south of the Rio Grande. The most extreme nationalist would ridicule the idea that the "right" of the Australian aborigines to self-determination justified an effort to emancipate the island-continent from white rule. The pinnacle of absurdity would be reached if anyone should start a movement to restore the control of the North American Continent to the Indian tribes. Grotesque as these instances appear when viewed from the practical standpoint, they

併合以降の出来事を見るに、多くの事が曖昧模糊とする中で１つ
だけ明らかなことがあった。日本は朝鮮を自らの帝国の一部に編入
し、その永久支配を国家政策の中枢に据え、どのような犠牲を払っ
ても内乱や諸外国の陰謀から守り続けようとしていることだ。

　国際政策の分野において、日本の朝鮮併合は政治信条を二分する
争点、すなわち帝国主義派か民族主義派かで論争するにはうってつ
けである。読者は自分がどちらの派に属しているかによって「日本
は朝鮮を支配する権利を有する」、または「朝鮮人は独立した国民
であることの権利を有する」と自分自身に言い聞かせるであろう。
　この文脈で「権利」という言葉を一般的に使うが、それは帝国主
義者と民族主義者、両者の論争において、実際の問題点を非常に曖
昧にしてしまっている。何故なら特定の状況において、どちらの信
条が「正しい」かというのは、その状況を取り巻く諸事情に言及し
てはじめて判断できることだからである。
　最も過激な帝国主義者でも、社会発展を遂げた大国だからという
理由で「アメリカはリオ・グランデ以南にある、発展が遅れた未開
発なあらゆる国を併合すべきだ」とする提案には躊躇を覚えるだろ
う。また最も過激な民族主義者でも「オーストラリア原住民アボリ
ジニには民族自決の権利があり、オーストラリア大陸を白人支配か
ら解放しようとする努力は正当である」とする考え方を一笑に付す
だろう。北米大陸を原住民であるインディアンに返還しようという運
動などは、ばかばかしさの極みでしかないだろう。現実的な視点に立

32   INTRODUCTORY

suffice to expose the fallacy of basing either an imperialist or a nationalist
policy upon a principle of abstract right.

It is my purpose to examine Japanese rule in Korea as a concrete
example of colonial administration, without reference to the legal or moral
sanctions upon which it rests. The reasons for thus limiting the inquiry will
be obvious to all serious students. I state them here in the hope that they
will be accepted as valid by the general reader.

The annexation of weak countries by strong countries is a phenomenon
which has persisted since the beginning of recorded time; practically every
strong nation has practiced the habit.

The arguments for and against such a procedure have been stated and
re-stated thousands of times in every country, and have been expressed in
almost every language. They are familiar to, or accessible to, every person
who will read this volume. I have nothing to add to them. A discussion of
the moral, ethical, legal, political, social, and economic problems raised
by an act of annexation, as such, is irrelevant to a presentation of the
facts descriptive of a working system of colonial government, since the
character of an administration is what it is, and can be fairly judged only
on the basis of the data of its operation.

To combine a description of a colonial government with an essay
on the moral quality of the imperialist principle would be to invite
confusion of thought. Thus, in any given case, if the administration of
an imperial government is found to be bad in fact, this badness will be
used by nationalists as an argument against imperialism, whereas if bad
administration is found in a popular government, nationalists will not

てば奇怪に見えるものだが、こうした事例は、帝国主義者であろうが、民族主義者であろうが、権利という抽象的な原則の上に自らの指針を建てることが如何に間違いであるかを明らかにしてくれている。

日本の朝鮮統治を植民地統治の具体例として検証するのが本書の目的であり、それが法的あるいは倫理的に認めうるものであるかは問題としない。この様に限定された検証を行うことの理由については、熱心な研究家諸氏には明らかであろうし、また一般の読者にもその理由を納得して頂けるものと期待している。

強国による弱小国の併合は有史以来存続している歴史的事実であり、実際、全ての強国が繰り返し行ってきたことである。

そのような行為に対して、あらゆる国で、ほとんどあらゆる言語で、賛否両論が言い尽されてきた。本書の読者はこうした賛否両論についてはよくご存じであり理解されているものと思うので、本書で付け加えることは何もない。また、併合によって湧き起こった議論が道徳上、倫理上、法律上、政治的、社会的そして経済的な問題であっても、植民地政府内で稼働しているシステムについて、ありのままの事実を述べるにあたっては意味のないものである。政権の特徴はありのままに捉えるべきもので、事業内容に関する客観的資料を基にして初めて公正な判断が出来るのである。

ある植民地政府についての客観的な記述に対して、帝国主義者の政治信条の道徳性を論じる評論を組み合わせることは思考の混乱を招くことになる。どんな場合でも、検証によって帝国政府の悪政が露見した場合には、民族主義者は帝国主義そのものへの反論として

tolerate any use of this badness as an argument against popular rule.

Conversely, with reference to good administration; if nationalists find that it exists in fact under a system of popular self-government, they will welcome the finding as a justification of that system; but if good administration is found in an imperial dependency, nationalists will not allow the finding to stand to the credit of the imperialist system; they will then shift the issue from the quality of the administration to the quality of the sanctions from which the government derives its authority.

In a word, to the nationalists good government is good government if it is self-government, and even bad government is good government if it is self-government—in the first case because both good government and self-government are good; in the second case because, under self-government, bad government will certainly lead to a demand for, and to the instituting of, good government. Thus, so runs the argument, bad self-government is merely a passing phase in the evolution of good self-government.

This attitude of the nationalists is perfectly logical so far as it affects their desire for nationhood, since it enables them to use bad colonial administration as an argument in support of an independence agitation, and at the same time undercuts the position of those imperialists who seek to justify colonial rule by appealing to the visible evidences of what good colonial administration can do for the safety, health, cultural advancement, and prosperity of a colonial domain.

It is clear, then, that with reference to an accepted group of facts, a totally different evaluation will be made by a nationalist and by an

その悪政をたたくだろうが、その一方で国民政府の下での悪政が判明した場合なら、これを人民統治そのものへの反論として帝国主義者が利用することを民族主義者は断じて許さないだろう。

　反対に善政の場合ではどうだろうか。もし国民による自治政府の下で善政が行われていると判明したなら、民族主義者たちはそのシステムの正しさが証明されたとして検証結果を歓迎するだろう。しかし同様に帝国属国での善政が伝えられても、その検証が帝国主義システムの功績を讃えるものであるならば、これを是としないだろう。彼ら民族主義者はその論点を行政の質の問題から、政府がその権力のよりどころとする拘束力の質の問題に向けようとするだろう。

　要するに、良い政府も自治政府も「善」であるので、自治政府であれば良い政府であり、悪い政府であっても、自治政府である限り必ず良い政府への要求そして樹立へと向かうので、良い政府である、というのが民族主義者の主張なのだ。彼らの論理で行くと、悪い自治政府は、良い自治政府へと進化する過程の一段階であるということになる。

　こうした民族主義者の考え方は、独立国家建設の想いを達成する目的の限りにおいて極めて理に叶っているであろう。なぜなら、植民地行政の悪政は独立運動を支持する論点となり得るからである。それと同時に、植民地支配を正当化しようとする帝国主義者の立場を貶めるからである。帝国主義者が植民地政府の善政、つまり行政が治安、保健衛生、文化面での発展および植民地の繁栄にどのように貢献出来るかを、目に見える形で証明し訴えても、である。

　従って、事実と認められた資料に関しても、民族主義者と帝国主

imperialist. Japanese rule in Korea, and the opposition to it on the part of the Korean nationalists, furnish an excellent illustration of the point. The Japanese refer with pride to their road-building, to their great extension of educational facilities, to their effective protection of life and property throughout a country but recently overrun by bandits, to their rapid development of agriculture, trade and industry, to their technical training schools, to their scientific experiment stations which serve the farmer, the fisherman, the stock-breeder, and the manufacturer, to the enormous increase during the past fifteen years in every branch of production, with its connotation of increased employment for Koreans, to the constantly mounting number of Koreans appointed to the Government service.

The foregoing facts cannot be gainsaid, as will be proved by the data contained in subsequent chapters. But the Korean nationalists attribute to them a sinister significance. The roads, they say, are built solely for the purpose of facilitating the movement of Japanese troops; the educational system is nothing more than an ingenious scheme for destroying Korean nationality; the protection of life and property is merely an excuse for maintaining a large Japanese police force; the economic development of the country is simply a device for swelling the profits of Japanese capitalists; the technical schools and the scientific bureaus have no other aim than to make Japanese rule profitable to the Japanese; the employment of Koreans in the Government service is an insidious form of bribery calculated to secure support for the Japanese occupation of the country.

The situation thus created is familiar to all students of colonial

義者で全く評価が違ってくるのは明らかである。朝鮮における日本の統治と、それに反対する民族主義者の対立の構図はこの点を物語る優れた実例であろう。日本人は自分たちが成してきたことに対し、誇りをもってこれを功績としている。すなわち道路工事、教育施設の拡大、最近匪賊（ひぞく）に蹂躙されたとはいえ、この国全体の生命と財産を効果的に守ってきたこと、農業および貿易・産業の急激な開発、各種技術訓練学校の設立、国内の農民、漁師、牧畜業者、製造業者のための科学実験施設の設立など、全て日本人が行ってきたことである。またこの15年間の各種製造業の生産量の著しい増加—これは朝鮮人雇用率の増加も意味している。官公庁への朝鮮人雇用数の絶え間ない増加なども彼ら日本人が誇らしく口にする事例である。

　以上は反対しようのない事実であり、それは後の章に記載された資料によって立証されるだろう。しかし朝鮮の民族主義者たちはこうした事実に対しても悪意ある意味付けをするのである。彼らによると、道路建設の目的は日本の軍隊の移動を迅速に行うためであり、教育制度は朝鮮の民族性を破壊するために仕掛けられた巧妙な罠でしかない。また生命と財産の保護は巨大な日本の警察力を維持するための単なる言い訳であり、経済発展は日本人資本家に膨大な利益をもたらす道具立てでしかない。さらに技術学校などの設立目的は日本統治により日本人が利益を得ることであり、官公庁への朝鮮人雇用は、日本による国土占領をしっかりと支えるために計算された狡猾な形の賄賂である、といったような具合である。

　こうして生み出される状況は、植民地政府の研究に携わる者には

38   INTRODUCTORY

government. If the local administration builds roads, erects schools, and so on, it is wrong, because the motive is base; if it fails to do these things it is wrong, because it is the obvious duty of an imperial ruler to confer such benefits upon a dependency. So also in relation to developing the resources of a dependency; if the sovereign power invests money in the colony, it is wrong because all it amounts to is capitalist exploitation; if it does not invest money in the colony, it is wrong because the failure to do so reflects a determination to keep the people poor and weak in the interest of an easy domination; if it employs natives in the government service it is wrong because such a policy tends to weaken nationalist sentiment; if it fails to do so it is wrong because such a course discloses the purpose of making the colony the happy hunting ground of imperial officials.

To all colonial governors this is an old story. All sincere and humane colonial governors—and none is more worthy of such a description than is Viscount Saito, Governor-General of Korea since 1919—are compelled to close their ears to the mutually destructive criticisms to which I have alluded, and must content themselves with carrying out from day to day measures designed to improve the general conditions of their dependencies.

The bulk of the present volume is devoted to a description of the administrative system of the Japanese in Korea, and to a statistical account of its results. The author feels it incumbent upon him to furnish his readers with a brief statement of the point of view from which he has approached his task.

周知のものである。つまり、現地政府が道路や学校の建設などを行うのは誤りである。なぜなら、動機が不純だからである。しかし、建設を怠るのも誤りである、何故なら属国に恩恵を与えるのは帝国支配者の明白な義務だからである。属国の資源開発に関しても同様である。主権国が植民地に投資をすることは間違いである。何故ならとどのつまり資本的搾取に繋がるからである。投資しないのも間違いである、何故ならそれは安易な支配をするために民衆を貧しき弱者にとどめようとする意図が見えるからである、となる。官公庁への雇用については、先住民を官公庁に雇用することは間違いである、なぜならそれは民族主義的感情を弱めるためだからである。また、そうしないことも間違いである。なぜならそれは植民地を帝国官僚の役人天国にしようとしているからである、となる。

これは植民地總督にとっては耳新しい話ではない。しかし、誠実で人間味あふれる總督たち、その中でも1919年以来朝鮮總督府總督に就任している齋藤子爵ほど、この表現に相応しい人物はいない。彼らはこれまで私が述べて来たような水掛け論には耳を貸さず、日々属国の状況改善のためにあらゆる手だてを講じることに専念しなくてはならないのである。

本書はその大部分を朝鮮における日本の統治制度の解説と、業績に関する統計的報告に割いている。この課題に取り組むにあたって、著者の観点について簡潔に述べることは、読者に対する著者としての責務であると感じている。

過去40年間、著者はその約半分を独立国—イギリス、アメリカ、

During the past forty years he has lived about half the time in self-governing countries—England, the United States, Canada, Australia, Japan, France, Germany, and Denmark—and the other half in colonial dependencies—India, the British West Indies, the French West Indies, British and Dutch Malaya, French Indo-China, British Borneo, the Philippine Islands, and in a few scattered dependencies of various powers.

This experience has left him without any trace of prejudice in respect of forms of government, for he has seen government wisely and honestly administered under every form, and stupidly and dishonestly administered under every form; he has seen freedom cherished under a monarchy and destroyed under a republic, and vice versa; he has seen justice dispensed with an even hand under popular rule and under autocratic rule; he has seen judicial decisions bought and sold in self-governing countries and in the dependencies of imperial powers. In each class of territory he has seen, living side by side, persons content with their government (whilst favoring reforms in this or in that particular) and persons who are so discontented with the same government that nothing short of its complete destruction appears to offer an adequate guaranty of desired reforms.

When the strongly dissatisfied group exists in a sovereign state, its members become socialists of one kind or another, or communists, or syndicalists, or fascists, or anarchists, according to their individual temperaments; when the group exists in a dependency, its members create a party aiming at the achievement of independence from the sovereign state.

It is one of the most curious matters forced upon the attention of a

カナダ、オーストラリア、日本、フランス、ドイツ、デンマークで暮らし、残り半分を植民地国—インド、英領西インド諸島、仏領西インド諸島、英蘭領マレー半島、仏領インドシナ、英領ボルネオ島、フィリピン諸島、その他の散在する様々な国の植民地で暮らしてきた。

　この体験を通し、著者はどのような政府に対しても政府の形態による先入観を持つことはなくなった。なぜならどのような形態であれ、賢明にかつ誠実に統治している政府もあれば、愚かでかつ不実な統治をしている政府があることも目にしてきたからである。著者は、自由が君主制の下で大切にされ、共和制の下で潰される場合もあること、またその逆も見て来た。また、民衆政治の下でも専制政治の下でも、正義が公明正大に施されていることもあり、自治国家そして帝国属領でも、裁判所の判定が売買されていることも見て来た。社会のあらゆる階層で、自国政府に満足を覚えている人（彼らも状況に応じた改革を支持しているのだが）もいれば、同じ政府に対し強い不満を持ち、現政府が完全に破壊されなければ改革など望むべくもないと感じている人々もいることを見て来たのである。

　主権国家において強い不満を持つ集団が存在する場合、彼らはそれぞれの気質に応じてある種の社会主義者や、共産主義者、労働組合至上主義者、ファシスト、あるいは無政府主義者になるのであるが、属領にそうした集団が存在する場合、彼らは統治国家からの独立を目的とした政党を結成するのである。

　属国の民族主義政党の主たる目的は主権国家としての地位を獲得することであるが、これは比較政治学の研究者の目にはとても奇妙

student of comparative government that the chief object of the nationalist party in a dependency should be to obtain the status of an independent sovereign nation, since the obvious fact is that in most of the countries which already exist as sovereign states there are to be observed all the evil conditions for which a colonial independence party deems independent sovereignty to be the unfailing panacea.

If the opponents of imperially imposed rule could point to the self-ruled countries and say: "In these countries there are justice, toleration, honest and efficient administration, social equality, adequate protection of life and property, equal economic opportunity, and freedom from the exploitation of the weak by the strong, and of the poor by the rich," the argument against imperialism would rest upon solid foundations. But the anti-imperialists cannot say with truth that the kind of dispensation described above exists in any marked degree in the general category of self-ruled states; nor can they say with truth that, in whatever degree it does exist anywhere, this degree is higher in self-ruled countries than it is in imperial dependencies.

No informed person would be prepared to maintain that Spain, Mexico, the Central American Republics, Russia, Rumania, and Bulgaria—all of them self-governing, independent states—enjoy a superior general social condition, or are better administered, than Burma, Java, British Guiana, the Federated Malay States, Korea, and the Philippine Islands—all of them ruled as dependencies.

Self-rule and dependent rule each have inherent in them the possibility of misrule. In self-ruled countries the danger lies in the dishonesty and

に映ってしまうのだ。何故なら紛れもない事実として、主権国家の国々にもありとあらゆる悪が見受けられるのだが、それら諸悪に対し独立派の人々は独立主権を万能薬の如くに考え、いったん手にすれば全てが解決すると思っていることだ。

帝国により押し付けられた権力による統治に反対する者が、独立国に向かってこう言ったと仮定しよう、「正義、寛容、誠実かつ有能な政府、社会的平等、生命財産の保護、経済における機会の平等、強者による弱者および富裕層による貧困者の搾取からの解放—独立国にはこれらが存在しているのです」と。これならば帝国主義を否定する論拠は土台のしっかりしたものになるだろう。しかしながら反帝国主義者も真実性をもって、独立国家とみなされる国々にも、先に述べたような統治は際立っては存在しているとは言えず、仮に存在していたとしてもその度合いが独立国において属領より高いとも言えないのである。反帝国主義者も本音では真実性をもって独立国が良いと言いきれないのである。

スペイン、メキシコ、中央アメリカ共和国、ロシア、ルーマニア、ブルガリアなどの自治独立国が、ビルマ、ジャワ、英領ギアナ、マレー連邦、朝鮮、フィリピン諸島といった属領よりも、その社会状況や行政面で優れているなどということは、事情を知る者なら言わないであろう。

自治でも植民地統治でも、それぞれ悪政の可能性が内在している。自治国における危険性は不誠実さや無能さにあり、それらは党派政

incompetence of which partisan politics and political machinery are the supple instruments and the staunch defenders. As between the good of the country and the good of the party, the latter is usually—by the liberal use of patronage, and by the unrestrained employment of sophistical oratory—accorded in practice the leading position.

In dependencies the threat to good government comes from another source—the stupidity, the incompetence, or the arrogance of colonial officials. In the matter of corruption I am convinced beyond all doubt that, allowing for an occasional exception, the government of self-ruled countries is much more corrupt than that of colonial dependencies, and that, in the latter, malversation in public office is of very rare occurrence. In the twenty-five years during which I have kept in touch with the dependencies controlled by the India Office and by the Colonial Office in London I have not heard of a dozen cases of graft on the part of non-native government officials above the rank of mere clerks.

There exists, of course, in each type of government an obligation to govern well. This responsibility is rooted in morals, and where moral considerations do not operate with sufficient force to compel the ruling authority to govern well, the promptings of expediency will usually suffice to dip the scale on the side of reasonably humane and efficient administration.

It seems to me that these two factors, morality and expediency, act with greater effectiveness in colonial dependencies than in self-governing countries, and this chiefly for two reasons. In self-governing countries the moral responsibilty is split up among thousands, or millions of voters; in dependencies it is centered in a single person, the Governor-General, the

治や政治機構を意のままになる道具、強固な擁護者とする。庇護を自由に利用し、勝手気ままに詭弁を弄することで、実際のところ、国の利益より党の利益が優先されてしまうのが普通である。

　属領の場合、良い政府にとって脅威は別のところにある。すなわち植民地官僚の愚かさ、無能、あるいは傲慢さに由来するものである。政治の腐敗に関しては、多少の例外はあるにしても、自治国家政府の方が政治腐敗は深刻であり、植民地政府の官公庁内の汚職は非常に稀であると私は断言出来る。25年に亘りインド省やロンドンの植民地省が管轄する属領と連絡を取り合ってきたが、単なる事務官以上の植民地出身者でない官僚の汚職事件は、十数件も聞いたことがない。

　いかなる形態の政府であっても当然のことだが、適切な統治をする義務がある。職務への責任感は道徳観に根差したものだが、道徳的配慮が統治者に適切な統治を行わせる充分な力を持たない行政機関においては、普通、便宜主義が推進力になって適度な人道的かつ能率的な行政が行われるのである。
　道徳性と便宜主義という2つの要因は自治国家よりむしろ植民地でその効力を発揮しているように思えるが、それには主に2つの理由が考えられる。自治国家では倫理責任は何千、何百万の有権者の間で分散されるものだが、植民地では1人の人物、すなわち総督、知事、長官といった役職にある者に集中してしまう。前者では悪政

Governor, the Chief Commissioner, or whatever the title may be. In the former case every voter can shift the blame for bad government on to some one else's shoulders; each political party can shift it on to the shoulders of the other party, one branch of a legislature can make a gift of it to the other; both branches can leave it on the doorstep of the Chief Executive; the Chief Executive can hand it back to the voters with the comment that he is but the servant of the people, that they had demanded certain legislation, certain administrative measures, and that he had carried out their wishes; finally, the Chief Executive and the Legislature can combine to lay the blame upon incompetent or corrupt officials, who will presently be disciplined, reformed, dismissed, or denied re-election, as the case may be.

In a dependency the situation is totally different. A Colonial Governor, vis-a-vis his colony and his Colonial Office in the home country, occupies a position analogous to that of a ship's captain vis-a-vis his ship and his owners. He is directly responsible for the conduct of affairs; he takes the credit for success, he must accept the penalties of failure; he can never plead an alibi.

Furthermore, the Colonial Governor looks for his advancement to the distant authority of a Secretary of State at the national capital. Promotion and other rewards will depend upon the way in which he administers his charge. He is little likely to earn them if, from preventable causes, his territory fails to advance in its health, prosperity, and general social condition; he is almost certain to miss them if, in consequence of harsh and incompetent administration, the people rise in revolt against his rule, or sink into the apathy and sloth which are the assured products of prolonged

の責任について、有権者は他の者に、政党は他の政党に転嫁出来る
し、上院下院の二つの議会でお互いに責任をなすりつけたり、両院
ともが大統領に丸投げすることも出来る。そして、大統領は有権者
に向かって「自分は公僕であり、有権者が望んだとおりに立法行為、
行政措置を実行しただけである」と言うことも出来る。最終的には、
大統領と議会は結託して、その責任を無能な官僚、もしくは汚職官
吏に押し付けることも出来るし、場合によってはその官僚は処罰、
矯正、罷免もしくは再任拒否処分に遭うだろう。

　植民地の事情は、これとは全く異なる。總督と植民地および本国
の植民地省との関係は、船長と船・船主の関係とよく似ている。總
督は職務に対し直接責任を負うことになるが、それはすなわち成功
を自分の功績に出来るということであり、同時に失敗に対する処罰
も甘受しなくてはならず、自分は関与していないとの言い訳は許さ
れないのである。
　さらに總督は本国の国務長官クラスの栄転を望むことも出来る
が、昇進やその他の見返りは如何に職務を全うしたかにかかってい
る。しかし、もし回避出来る原因で彼の植民地が健全な発展、繁栄
を享受することなく、一般的な社会状況も改善されなかったとした
ら、こうした可能性は薄くなってしまうだろう。もし冷酷非情で無
能な統治の結果、民衆が反乱を起こしたり、あるいは長期に亘る失
政の末に人々が無気力怠惰に陥ったりすると、彼はほぼ確実に昇進、

48   INTRODUCTORY

misgovernment. Briefly, the success of his rule will be the measure of his personal success.

Since he is directly responsible for the conduct of his subordinates, and for the appointment of most of them, and has in addition the power of promotion and dismissal, his officials have every incentive to earn their own advancement by rendering such service as will redound to the credit of the Governor.

I do not intend to imply that a home government may not, even in modern times, be actuated by the base motive of ruthlessly exploiting a colonial dependency—the earlier history of the Belgian Congo is a case in point—or that in such circumstances the administration may not be as bad as the motive. But such a situation is, year by year, falling in the scale of statistical expectation because, international relations being what they now are, the influence of publicity being what it now is, and party tactics in home countries demanding, as they now do, a diligent assemblage of material on which to base attacks on the party in power, the ventilation of grave abuses in colonial administration presents a very serious political problem to the home government which is responsible for them or which tolerates them.

The other important factor, which has to be taken into account when estimating the probability of government being competently administered in a dependency, is one to which recent political events in Europe have imparted a striking significance. It is that as social and economic conditions increase in complexity under the combined influences traceable to industrial development, to the growing size of commercial and banking enterprises, and to the gradual substitution of the community for the

第一章　序論　49

報償の機会を失ってしまうことになる。要するに統治の成功が彼個人の成功の尺度であるということだ。

　部下に対しても、總督はその行動や任命に直接責任を負い、加えて彼らの昇進、解雇に関する権限も与えられている。であるから、部下である官僚たちは昇進の望みを一心にかけて、總督の名声が広まるようにと務めに励むのである。

　本国政府には植民地に対する冷酷非情な搾取—過去にはベルギー領コンゴの例があるが—への野心はないかもしれない、あるいはそのような動機を持っていても、実際の行政は動機ほど酷くはないかもしれない、などと言うつもりはない。しかし、こうした酷い植民統治が起こりうる確率は年々低くなってきている。国際情勢の現状や世論の関心の高まり、そして各政党が与党の攻撃材料として情報収集にやっきになっているという本国の事情もある。植民地における重大な悪政が世論に問われれば、本国政府にとってはそれについての責任、あるいはそれを黙って見過ごした責任を問われるという非常に深刻な政治問題となってくるのである。

　もう1つの重要な要因は、最近ヨーロッパで起こった政治事件によってその重要性を増したのだが、植民地政府の行政能力の可能性を計る上で考慮しなくてはいけない事柄である。それは政府の問題が従来の政治的な方法—議会での討論、国民投票、あるいは公務員を公選によって選ぶこと等—では解決し難くなっており、高度に専門化した知識を必要とする解決法に益々頼らざるを得なくなってい

individual as the unit of social progress, the problems of government are, day by day, becoming less amenable to political solutions—to legislative debate, long ballots, and the popular election of public officials—and more clamorous of solutions dependent upon highly expert technical knowledge.

The assumption that politics would be the competent and all-sufficient handmaid of social service was given authoritative currency through the propaganda associated with the American War of Independence, the French Revolution, and the fight for Parliamentary Reform in England. These movements were spread over a period of about a century and a quarter, roughly from 1760 to 1890, a period during which public sentiment was strongly averse to the idea of government regulation, and was totally blind to the possibility that Government might become, as it has since become, not only the trustee of social progress but also its most powerful instrument. What these revolutionary and reform movements were chiefly concerned with was, in fact, settling what Government should not do to people, not with what Government should do for people.

It is safe, indeed, to infer that the liberal-minded statesmen of the eighteenth and nineteenth centuries would be horrified if they could witness the extent to which Government today intrudes upon everything, and regulates almost everything which happens to a citizen, or is done by him whilst he is moving from his cradle to his grave.

Whether or not Government should undertake its vast business of regulation and of social service is a question upon which opinions may well differ; but the obstinate adhesion to the belief that politics, whose life-blood is a mixture of contention, intrigue, and self-interest, can and will furnish the spirit, the knowledge, and the technique essential to the

ることだ。これは産業が発達し、商業、金融業ともに大企業化して
きたこと、また社会の進歩が共同体単位から個人単位に徐々に移行
していることから、社会的、経済的な状況が益々複雑になって来て
いるためである。

　政治とは社会に奉仕する有能で全てを満たしてくれる召使いのよ
うなものだという思い込みが、アメリカ独立戦争、フランス革命、
イギリス議会改革などに関連したプロパガンダを通して権威あるも
のとして流布していた。これらの政治運動は大雑把に1760年から
1890年まで1世紀以上に亘って広まったが、この期間の国民感情は
政府による規制という考えに強い嫌悪感を抱いており、政府がそれ
以来そうであるように、社会進歩の受託者となるだけでなく、その
最も強力な道具となる可能性があることは全く見えていなかった。
これらの革命的、改革的運動の主たる関心事は、国民に対し政府は
「何をすべきでないか」であって、「何をすべきか」ではなかったの
である。

　もし18、19世紀のリベラル派の政治家が、今日の政府があらゆ
ることに介入し、市民に起こること、あるいは市民のゆりかごから
墓場までに行われることのほとんどすべてを規制しているのを目の
当たりにしたら、恐怖を感じるだろう。

　政府が規制や社会奉仕という膨大な事業を行うべきかどうかは、
意見が分かれるところだろう。しかし、政治にとって闘争と陰謀と
私利私欲が活力源であり、政治は社会、経済が抱える問題を効果的
に処理するにあたって不可欠な精神、知識、技術を提供することが

52 INTRODUCTORY

effective handling of social and economic problems is what has brought parliamentary government into disrepute in almost every country in which it is practiced.

The establishment of Fascism in Italy, the support which that principle is receiving in other countries, the adoption of the City-manager plan in the United States, the setting up, by the mutual consent of opposing interests, of "Czars" to administer the affairs of certain great American industries (baseball and the movies, for instance), and the recent dictatorship in Spain, are all in their essence revolts against the open-to-all system of guidance and control.

If my observation has led me to believe that in countries where authority is vested in a small group of trained public officials there will, as a rule, be found a better administration of government than in countries where administration is subject to the influence of an uninformed and, *ad hoc*, unintelligent public, I do not from that belief infer that, because a country is ruled under a system of concentrated authority and of fixed responsibility, it is, therefore well governed.

So, with reference to Korea, there can be found in its history under Japanese rule instances of the abuse of power, of official incompetence, to some extent of corruption; but whether or not Korea has on the whole been well governed can be determined only from a study of the available data. From such a study, which has occupied me for more than three years, and of which the results are presented in this volume, I have formed the opinion that Korea is today infinitely better governed than it ever was under its own native rulers, that it is better governed than most self-

できるという信念に頑なに固執することが、議会政治を実践している
るほとんどすべての国で評判を落とす原因となっている。

　イタリアにおけるファシズムの確立および他国での支持運動、ア
メリカにおける市政管理者計画、アメリカの巨大産業（例えば野球
や映画等）を取り仕切る、対立する利害の相互同意によって台頭し
た「専制君主」的企業家の存在、スペインにおける独裁者の存在、
これらは全て本質的には、誰もが参加出来る指導・管理システムへ
の反乱であった。
　訓練された少数の官僚に権限が与えられている国の方が、無知で
その場しのぎの無教養な民衆に行政が左右される国よりも、原則と
して善政が行われると私が信じるに至ったとしても、その信念から、
ある国で権力が集中し権限に対する責任が固定されたシステムの下
で支配されているが故にその国はよく統治されていると推論するも
のではない。

　従って朝鮮に関しても日本統治の歴史の中で権力の濫用、役人の
無能さやある程度の腐敗、といった事例を見つけることは可能だろ
う。しかし朝鮮が概して良く統治されていたか否かは、入手可能な
資料を基にして初めて評価出来るのである。私は３年以上に亘りこ
うした資料を基に研究しその結果を本書に記したのであるが、私が
到った結論というのは次の通りである。今日の朝鮮は李王朝時代と
は比べ物にならないくらい良く統治されており、また他の多くの独

54   INTRODUCTORY

governing countries, that it is as well governed as any of the British, American, French, Dutch, and Portuguese dependencies which I have visited, and is better governed than most of them, having in view as well the cultural and economic development of the people as the technique of administration.

立国と比較してもその統治は優れている。そして、これまで私が尋
ね歩いたイギリス、アメリカ、フランス、オランダ、ポルトガル領
のいずれの植民地と同じくらい良く統治されていたが、その多くの
植民地よりも、政府の行政手腕のみならず、民衆の文化的経済的発
展においても優れているのである。

CHAPTER II

第二章

CHAPTER II

DESCRIPTIVE AND HISTORICAL

Descriptive--

Korea* is a peninsula extending almost due south from Manchuria. Its area is approximately 85,000 square miles; its coast-line is about eleven thousand miles long, and has the peculiarity that on the west and south it is deeply indented and, for the most part, fringed with islands, whereas the east coast presents an almost unbroken front and has very few islands adjacent to it.

On the north, Korea is bounded by Manchuria, from which it is separated by the Yalu River, and by Asiatic Russia, which lies on the other side of the Tumen River; on the east by the Sea of Japan; on the west by the Yellow Sea; and on the south by the Korea Strait. The distance from Fusan, Korea's southeastern port, to Moji, the port at the southwestern entrance of Japan's Inland Sea, is only 135 miles.

The east coast of Korea has but two harbors of consequence—Seishin and Gensan—both in the northern sector, on the improvement of which the Government-General has expended more than five million yen. On the south and west coasts, however, Korea is well supplied with good ports. Of these the principal one is Fusan, at the southeastern tip of the Peninsula. Here the Government has spent more than thirteen million yen in

---

* The Japanese have adopted officially the name Chosen, by which the Peninsula was known in ancient times. Throughout this volume ' Korea' is used, as being more familiar to the world at large.

第二章

朝鮮の描写と歴史

朝鮮の描写

　朝鮮 * は半島であり、満州からほぼ真南にある。面積は、およそ
8万5000平方マイル、海岸線はほぼ1万1000マイルで、西と南は
深く入り組んでいて、多くの島々によって縁どられている。一方東
海岸の海岸線は切れ目なく続き、沿岸部には殆ど島はない。

　北はヤールー河を境に満州と国境を接しており、ロシアとは豆満
江を境に隣接している。東には日本海が広がり、西は黄海、南は朝
鮮海峡である。朝鮮の南東部にある釜山港と日本の瀬戸内海の玄関
港である門司との距離は、わずか135マイルである。

　朝鮮の東海岸には、重要な2つの港がある。清津と元山である。
いずれも北部にあり、この港の修築に總督府は500万円以上を投じ
た。朝鮮の南岸と西岸は、良い港に恵まれている。この中で最も重
要な港は、半島の南東端にある釜山である。ここに總督府は1300
万円以上を投じて近代的な設備を整えた。汽船が日に2回、日本と
の間を運行しており、乗客は桟橋から直接、南満州鉄道に乗り継ぐ

---

*　日本は「Chosen」という呼称を正式に採用している。昔から朝鮮半島はそ
の名前で知られていた。本書では、"Korea" を使っているが、その方が馴染み
があるためである。

providing modern facilities. A steamer runs twice daily to and from Japan, and passengers can transfer directly on the dock to a train of the South Manchuria Railway. This railway enables one to travel without changing cars as far as Changchun in Northern Manchuria and, with a single change there or at Mukden, to go to Peking, Dairen in Southern Manchuria, or to make connection with the Trans-Siberian. Thus, one can go by rail from Fusan to any point in Northern Asia or in Europe which is provided with a railroad.

The capital of Korea, Keijo (commonly called Seoul), is on the main line from Fusan, and is also connected by rail with the port of Jinsen (Chemulpo) on the west coast, and with Gensan on the east coast. Near the mouth of the Yalu is Shin-gishu, also on the South Manchuria Railway main line, which is becoming year by year an increasingly important depot for trade both by land and by sea. Other important ports on the west coast are Chinnampo, which serves Heijo, capital of the Province of South Heian; Kunsan, which is connected by rail with Ko-shu, the Provincial Capital of South Chusei; and Mokpo, which is the port for Kwo-shu, capital of the Province of North Zenra.

Korea may be described, topographically, as a country of constricted plains intersected by rugged mountain ranges. Along the east coast from north to south the mountains thrust themselves almost into the sea, and I have never seen a more beautiful or striking region than the Diamond Mountains, which lie to the south of Gensan. The whole of the east coast, so far as I saw it, presents an aspect of romantic wildness, which is enhanced by the extraordinary coloring of the soil and of the fantastically

ことが出来る。この鉄道を使えば乗り換えなしで、満州北部の長春
まで行ける。長春または奉天で1度乗り換えれば北京や満洲南部の
大連に行くことが出来るし、またシベリア鉄道に乗り継ぐことも出
来る。このように釜山から鉄道で、北アジアやヨーロッパの、鉄道
が整備された場所ならどこでも行けるわけである。

　朝鮮の首都、京城（通常はソウルと呼ばれる）は、釜山からの本
線にあり、また鉄道によって西岸の仁川の港および、東岸の元山と
結ばれている。鴨緑江の河口近くには新義州があり、南満州鉄道の
本線にもつながっていた。ここは、陸海両方の交易の拠点として、
年々重要性を増している。西岸にある他の重要な港と言えば、平安
南道の中心地である平壌に物資を供給していた鎮南浦港、そして鉄
道で忠清南道の中心地である公州と結ばれている群山港がある。そ
して木浦港、これは全羅南道※の中心地である光州の港である。

　　※原文で"North Zenra"と記載されているが、木浦港は全羅南道の光州の港
　　　であるので、"South　Zenra"の誤表記と解釈して翻訳した。

　朝鮮は地形的に、険しい山脈に挟まれた僅かな平地を持つ国と言
えるだろう。東海岸に沿って北から南へ、山々はほとんど海に突き
出さんばかりだ。私は、元山の南に広がる金剛山ほど美しい、或い
は、目を見張るような場所を他に見たことがない。東海岸全体が神
秘的な野生味ある景観を呈しているように私には見える。土肌や幻
想的に形作られた岩山、柱のように突き出た奇岩の独特な色合いが

62 DESCRIPTIVE AND HISTORICAL

shaped crags and isolated pillars of rock. The soil is of a rich terracotta color, the unplanted portions furnishing a rich background for the brilliant green of the young rice plants. The rocks and crags, which in some places are bare, in others clothed with creepers, range in color between deep purple and rich yellow. It would not be a difficult undertaking to make the east coast of Korea into one of the most popular tourist resorts in the Far East.

The climate of Korea, generally speaking, runs to extremes both of heat and of cold. Spring and autumn are very short seasons, and the difference in temperature between day and night is very great, sometimes reaching 25 degrees Fahrenheit in places near the Manchurian border. This difference is not so great in the south of the Peninsula, since there the climate is somewhat modified by the surrounding ocean. The cold in winter fluctuates, there being frequent short spells of mild weather, so that the people describe the winter climate as "three cold and four warm."

The mean annual temperature in southern Korea is about 55° F., in central Korea about 52°, and on the northern border about 40°. The fall of rain and of snow is abundant compared with that of Manchuria and Mongolia, but scanty compared with that of Japan proper, being from thirty to forty inches a year in most places, gradually decreasing in the direction from southeast to northwest.

The following account of the seasons is abridged from Dr. J. D. Van Buskirk *"The Climate of Korea, and Its Probable Effect on Human Efficiency,"* which was printed in the *Transactions of the Korea Branch of the Royal Asiatic Society,* Vol. 10, 1919.

Like the rest of the temperate zone, Korea has four seasons. The winter

第二章　朝鮮の描写と歴史　　　63

一層趣を増している。土は、濃いテラコッタ色で、むき出した土肌
が水田の鮮やかな緑を引き立てている。切り立った岩山は、岩肌が
むき出したところもあれば、蔓に覆われたところもあり、深い紫か
ら黄金色までの異なった色彩の表情を見せてくれる。朝鮮の東海岸
を、極東で最も人気のある避暑地の１つにすることは難しくないだ
ろう。

　朝鮮の気候は、一般的に言って、寒暑の差が激しい。春と秋は、
とても短く、日中と夜の気温の変動がとても大きい。満州との国境
に近い場所では、時に華氏25度にも達する。半島の南部は、周り
を囲む海によって気候が多少緩和されているため、気温差はそれほ
どでもない。冬の寒さは、温暖な気候が短期間続き、それが頻繁に
繰り返されるため、人々はそれを「三寒四温」と表現している。
　年平均気温は、朝鮮南部では華氏約55度、朝鮮中部では約52度、
北部国境付近では約40度である。降雨量や降雪量は殆どの場所で
年間30〜40インチ位で、南東から北西方向に向かって徐々に減っ
ていく。降雨量降雪量とも満州やモンゴルと比べると多いが、日本
本土と比べると少ない。
　以下の季節についての説明は、Transactions of the Korea Branch
of the Royal Asiatic Society, Vol. 10, 1919 に掲載された J.D. ヴァン・
バスカーク博士の" The Climate of Korea and Its Probable Effect
on Human Efficiency "からの要約である。
　他の温暖地域同様、朝鮮にも四季がある。冬の寒さはかなり厳し

64   DESCRIPTIVE AND HISTORICAL

is quite cold and in the northern part especially is severe. In the north, frost occurs in September or October; and for about five months the mean daily tem perature is below freezing point on the Manchurian border. Streams are frozen over for the whole winter, and there are severe snow storms. The station at Chukochin reports temperature as low as 41° below freezing point, Fahrenheit. Seoul has over two months with the mean daily temperature below freezing, and, during a period of five years, averaged twenty-eight days a year below freezing point every hour of the day.

Summer is the rainy season. There are not such intensely hot days as are common in the United States, but the heat is continuous, so that the summers are more trying than in places in the United States having the same mean temperature. The highest temperature reported by the Government stations is 103.2° F. from Wonsan (Gensan), but this is exceptional. Taikyu, the Provincial capital of North Keisho-do has as a rule the hottest weather, its maximum going as high as 103° F. The coast towns in the south have less extreme heat, Fusan reporting a maximum of 91.5° F. and Mokpo 95.2° F. The humidity of the summer is high, and this, with the steady heat and the rains, makes the total effect of the summers quite depressing.

Spring and autumn are nearly ideal seasons in Korea. The winter ends and spring advances almost imperceptibly—no hot days followed by severe cold, but a gradual warming up, with bright sunshine, occasional rains, and for the most part gentle winds. There is in the southern part of the country, even as far north as Seoul, a distinct short season of rains in April. This furnishes an abundant supply of water to irrigate the rice fields and makes this an ideal region for rice-farming. The heat gradually grows

第二章　朝鮮の描写と歴史　　　65

く、特に北部は厳しく、9月か10月には霜が降りる。

　そして約5カ月に亘り、満州との国境では、日の平均気温は氷点下になる。川は冬の間中凍り、激しい吹雪が襲う。中江鎮測候所では、華氏マイナス41度を記録したこともある。ソウルは約2カ月に亘り、1日の平均気温が氷点下になる。5年間で1日中気温が氷点下だった日は、年平均28日である。

　夏は雨季である。米国などでよくある酷暑の日などはないが、平均気温が同じ場所と比べると、米国の暑さより耐えがたく感じる。總督府の測候所の記録では、最高気温は元山で華氏103.2度だが、これは例外的だ。慶尚北道の中心地である大邱は、概して最も暑い時には最高気温は華氏103度ぐらいまで上がる。南の沿岸の町では極端に暑い日は少なく、釜山では最高気温華氏91.5度、木浦では95.2度を記録している。夏の湿度は高く、蒸し暑い雨の日が続くので、かなり鬱陶しい季節である。

　朝鮮の春と秋は理想的な季節と言える。厳しい寒さの後にいきなり暑い日が続くのではなく、日差しが明るくなり、時折降る雨と柔らかい風を伴い、徐々に徐々に暖かくなっていく…こうして冬が終わるといつの間にか春になっているのだ。朝鮮南部や、ソウルのような北部でも、4月に、はっきりとした短い雨季がある。これは、水田の灌漑のために充分な水を供給し、この地域を稲作に適した場

more intense and the rains more heavy, and then summer has come.

The autumn is comparatively warmer than the spring, alike sunshiny and equable. There is a more distinct marking of the beginning of autumn than of any other season. The rains rather suddenly cease in September and there is a different feeling in the air. But autumn changes to winter so gradually that one hardly knows when winter begins.

Population--

The following data in regard to the population of Chosen are taken from the *Annual Report on Administration of Chosen, 1922-1923* compiled by the Government-General, and issued in December 1924.

Under the old Korean Government no census, strictly speaking, was ever taken, or, if attempted, it was taken solely for the purpose of fixing the basis of tax assessment. The men in charge unscrupulously indulged in the vicious practice of falsifying their returns in order that they might fatten on the taxes paid by families which they had omitted to record in the official registers. The statistics compiled in this way were, of course, absolutely worthless. When Japan established its protectorate, in 1906, the Japanese police adviser to the Korean Government found this evil very detrimental to the smooth working of civil administration, and therefore caused instructions to be sent to each provincial police office to make an honest count of the entire population on a given date. This was, one may say, the first real census ever taken in Korea. As there were many difficulties to be overcome the count could not be made as accurately

所にしている。暑さが段々厳しくなり、雨が激しさを増すと、夏の到来だ。

秋は、春に比べると暖かく、そして春同様に明るく穏やかな季節である。他の季節と違い、その訪れには、はっきりとした兆しを感じる。9月になると突然雨も収まり、空気もどこか違っている。しかし、秋は少しずつ冬に変わっていくので、いつ冬が始まったのか分からないくらいだ。

人口

次にあげる朝鮮の人口に関する資料は、朝鮮總督府が編纂し、1924年12月に発行された『朝鮮總督府施政年報　大正十二年度』から取ったものである。

昔の大韓帝国政府の下では、厳密に言えば人口調査は行われたことがなく、あったとしても、課税評価の基準を定めるために行われた。それだけでなく担当役人たちは、恥知らずにも戸籍を隠蔽し、徴収した税金を着服して私腹を肥やし続けていた。そのような方法で編纂された統計は、当然ながら、全く価値がない。日本が1906年に朝鮮を保護国とした時、日本の警察顧問は、この様な不正は民政を円滑に行うにあたり大きな障害となると判断し、各道地方の警務部に、定められた日までに全人口の正確な数を出すように通達した。これは、朝鮮で行われた本当の意味での最初の人口調査だと言えるだろう。まだまだ多くの弊害があったために、総計は、望んだほどには正確には出来なかったが、それでも調査の結果、従来の人

68   DESCRIPTIVE AND HISTORICAL

as was desired, but the results showed that the population had been very much underestimated. Hitherto the population had been put at something over five million; the new count proved it to be nearly seven million. A more careful investigation, made after the annexation of 1910, placed the total population at 13,313,017; and the estimated population in 1923 was 17,626,761. Of this total the Koreans make up something over 17,000,000, the Japanese nearly 400,000, all other races about 32,000. The ratio of females to males was 94 to 100 among Koreans, 88 to 100 among Japanese, and 13.7 to 100 among foreigners.

The following table shows the distribution of the population according to occupation.

Occupation	Japanese	Korean	Foreign	Total
Agriculture, forestry, and stock-farming..	38,573	14,738,126	5.346	14,782,045
Fishing, and salt-manufacture......	10,775	213,266	25	224,066
Industries...........	63,999	358,205	3,517	425,721
Commerce, and transportation..........	126,893	984,405	16,080	1,127,378
Public service, and the professions........	117,080	325,733	1,576	444,389
Miscellaneous........	20,642	410,561	4,737	435,940
Unrecorded.........	8,531	177,843	848	187,222
Total..........	386,493	17,208,139	32,129	17,626,761

It is thus seen that slightly more than 80 per cent of the entire population of Korea is dependent for its subsistence upon direct use of land.

The exact number of Koreans living outside the Japanese Empire is not known, but the latest investigations put it at more than 1,500,000, the large majority of whom live in Manchuria and Siberia, and the remainder in China (chiefly in Shanghai), in the United States, Hawaii, and Mexico.

口はかなり低く見積もられていたことが判明した。従来は人口は
500万人を超えたぐらいだとされてきたが、新たな統計で、700万
人近くはいることが明らかとなった。1910年の併合後に行われた、
更に精密な調査では、総人口は1331万3017人だとの結果が出てい
る。1923年の予想人口は1762万6761人となった。この統計のうち、
朝鮮人が1700万人以上、日本人が40万人近く、他の人種が約3万
2000人だった。女性対男性の割合は、朝鮮人では94対100、日本
人では88対100、外国人では13.7対100だった。

　次の表は、職業による人口分布である。

職業別の人口分布

職業	日本人	朝鮮人	外国人	合計
農業 林業 牧畜	38,573	14,738,126	5,346	14,782,045
漁業 塩製造	10,775	213,266	25	224,066
工業	63,999	358,205	3,517	425,721
商業 輸出	126,893	984,405	16,080	1,127,378
公共サービス	117,080	325,733	1,576	444,389
その他	20,642	410,561	4,737	435,940
不明	8,531	177,843	848	187,222
合　計	386,493	17,208,139	32,129	17,626,761

　このように朝鮮の全人口の80パーセントを少し越えた人数が、
土地の直接利用に生計を依存していることが分かる。

　大日本帝国の外に住んでいる朝鮮人の厳密な数は分からないが、
最新の調査では150万人以上としており、その大部分が満州とシベ
リアに居住し、残りは中国（主に上海）、アメリカ、ハワイ、そし
てメキシコである。

For the protection of Koreans living abroad, particularly for those in neighboring Chinese territory, a special item was incorporated in the Korean budget for 1920; and the Governor-General, in co-operation with the Japanese consulates in Manchuria, is doing his best for their welfare by founding schools, hospitals, and monetary organs in important places, by sending doctors to treat gratis the sick in remoter parts, by encouraging the formation of Korean societies and giving them financial help, and by providing for the relief of poor Koreans in times of natural calamity.

Moreover, as the activities, open or otherwise, of agitators abroad were the first cause of the popular unrest in Chosen at the time of the Independence Movement, the Japanese authorities saw the necessity of controlling them, as well as of protecting law-abiding Koreans from the intrigues of the disaffected, by a more efficient method than had hitherto been employed. Accordingly, the Japanese consuls at Antung, Mukden, Kirin, and Chientao—all in Manchuria —were, in 1920, charged with the duty of acting as secretaries of the Government-General of Korea.

Little is known of the original inhabitants of Korea. When the Chinese statesman, Ki-tze, invaded the country in the twelfth century, B.C., he found the Peninsula occupied by cave-dwellers living in a state of savagery. The race as it exists today is clearly of Mongol stock, but it presents points of difference from both the Chinese and the Japanese. The general consensus of opinion among foreign residents is that the Koreans are an amiable and intelligent people quite capable of responding to education and to other measures designed to foster social progress. I may add that neither in Korea nor in Japan proper did I encounter any anti-Korean feeling. On the contrary I met many Japanese who were eager to

第二章　朝鮮の描写と歴史　　　71

　海外に居住する朝鮮人、特に隣接する中国の領土に居住する者の保護のために、1920年の朝鮮向けの予算の中には特別項目が組み入れられた。そして朝鮮總督府は、満州の日本領事館と協力して、重要な場所に、学校や病院、金融機関などを建設したり、僻地に医師を派遣して病気の人を無料で治療したり、朝鮮人社会の形成を奨励し、財政援助をしたり、自然災害の時に貧しい朝鮮人に救援物資を送るなどして、朝鮮人の福祉のため全力を挙げたのだ。

　その上、独立運動の時代にあっては、海外の煽動者による活動が朝鮮国内でも大きな社会不安を引き起こし、そのため日本当局は、法に従う朝鮮人を彼らから守るだけでなく、より効果的な手段で不満分子を抑えつける必要性を感じていた。それに応じて、安東、瀋陽、吉林そして、間島―全て満州にある―の日本領事は、1920年、朝鮮總督府の書記官として活動する任を負った。

　朝鮮の原住民についてはほとんど知られていない。中国の政治家・箕子が紀元前12世紀に朝鮮を侵略した際、半島の人々はまだ穴居生活を送っていたのである。今日存在する人種は、明らかにモンゴルの血統だが、中国人とも日本人とも違った点がある。多くの外国人居住者の認めるところだが、朝鮮人は愛想が良く知的で、教育や社会進歩につながることには積極的に応じている。私自身、朝鮮でも日本本土でも、反朝鮮感情には遭遇しなかった。

　その逆に、朝鮮古来の文化を賞賛し、李王朝以前何世紀にも亘り日本の芸術、宗教、そして哲学に影響を与えてきた朝鮮人に対し感

72   DESCRIPTIVE AND HISTORICAL

enlarge upon the admirable features of the early Korean culture and to express their appreciation of the contribution which Koreans had made to the art, religion, and philosophy of Japan itself, in the centuries preceding the accession of the Yi Dynasty, which, after more than five hundred years of misrule had reduced the Korean people to a cultural and economic condition deplorable in the extreme, and which came to an end when Japan annexed the country in 1910.

Railways--

The first railway construction undertaken in Korea was a line of about 25 miles between Seoul and Chemulpo. A concession for this undertaking was secured from the Government of Korea by an American citizen, Mr. James R. Morse, in 1898. The selection of this particular route was due to the circumstance that the line would connect the capital of the country with the nearest deep-water port.

Whilst the line was still under construction it was bought by a Japanese company which carried the undertaking through and opened the line to traffic in 1902. The next line to be constructed was that from Seoul to Fusan, a port at the extreme southeastern tip of the Peninsula, about 135 miles from Moji, the nearest Japanese port. The concession for the construction and operation of this line was granted in 1898 to a Japanese syndicate which began work in 1901. The line was completed in 1904 and was opened to traffic on January 1, 1905, its length being 268 miles.

The outbreak of the Russo-Japanese War in 1904 gave a strong impetus to railway construction, and by the end of 1905 the total mileage had increased to 636. In the following year the Japanese Government

第二章　朝鮮の描写と歴史　　　73

謝の意を表す多くの日本人に出会ったのである。李王朝の 500 年以
上に亘る悪政が朝鮮民衆を、文化的にも経済的にも極度に惨めな状
態に追いやってしまったが、日本が 1910 年に朝鮮を併合したこと
によって、それも終わりを告げたのである。

鉄道

　最初に朝鮮で着手された鉄道建設は、ソウルと仁川の間の約 25
マイルの路線だった。この路線の敷設権は 1898 年、朝鮮政府によっ
てアメリカ人のジェームズ・R・モースに対して保証されていた。
この路線を選んだのは、国の首都と、最寄りの水深の深い港を結ぶ
という事情によるものだった。

　路線がまだ建設中の間に、日本の会社が買い取り、そのまま事業
を完成させ、1902 年に開通させた。次に建設すべき路線は、ソウル
から半島の最南東端にある港で、最も近い日本の港である門司から
135 マイルのところにある釜山までの路線だった。

　路線敷設と運営の免許は 1898 年に日本の財閥に対して与えられ、
建設は 1901 年に始まった。線路は 1904 年に完成し、1905 年 1 月 1
日に開業した。全長 268 マイルだった。

　1904 年の日露戦争勃発は、鉄道建設の大きな推進力となり、1905
年末には全長 636 マイルまでに延長された。その後、日本政府はソ
ウルから釜山の路線、ソウルから仁川への路線を買い取り、日本軍

74   DESCRIPTIVE AND HISTORICAL

purchased the lines from Seoul to Fusan, and from Seoul to Chemulpo,
and took over the two lines (Seoul-Shingishu, and the Masan branch line)
built by the Japanese military engineers, thus bringing the whole railroad
system under government control and management. At the time of the
annexation of the country by Japan (1910) the management of the railways
was assigned to the Railroad Department of the Government-General.

From this time onward a steady increase has occurred in railroad
mileage, and a great deal has been spent on improving the lines. Among
the more important undertakings are to be noted the construction of an iron
bridge, about 3000 feet long, across the Yalu River, connecting the Korean
railroad system with that of the South Manchuria Railway Company; and
the building of branch lines connecting the ports of Gensan on the east
coast, Chinampo on the west coast, and Mokpo on the south coast with
the main line running north and south the whole length of the Peninsula.
Several other lines are projected as part of a general plan to provide Korea
with an adequate net-work of standard-guage and light railroads.

The management of all the state-owned railways in Korea was, in
1917, entrusted to the South Manchuria Railway Company—an important
and highly efficient Japanese Corporation. The terms of the arrangement
are, in brief, that the Government makes the plans for new construction
and improvements, and provides the capital for these purposes, while
the Company is responsible for carrying out these plans, for the proper
maintenance of the railways, and for their operation. With respect to the
capital advanced by the Government since the annexation the Company
must pay interest on it at the rate of 6 per cent, though the concession was
made in 1921 that for the following three years it should pay interest at

第二章　朝鮮の描写と歴史　　75

の技術者が建設した2つの路線（ソウル―新義州と、馬山支線）を引き継ぎ、このようにして全鉄道路線を政府の規制と管理の下に置いたのである。日本による朝鮮併合の際（1910年）、鉄道の管理は、朝鮮總督府の鉄道局に割り当てられた。

　それ以降、鉄道の総延長は着実に伸びており、路線改善のために多くの労力が費やされた。更に重要な事業の中でも特筆すべきは、鴨緑江を渡り、朝鮮鉄道網と南満州鉄道網とをつなぐ、長さ3000フィートの鉄橋の建設だった。また、東岸にある元山、西岸の鎮南浦そして南岸の木浦のそれぞれの港を結ぶ支線を建設して、半島を縦断する本線と連結させることだった。その他の数本の路線は基本計画の一環として朝鮮内に標準規格と軽便鉄道の鉄道網を敷くことである。

　1917年、朝鮮の国有鉄道の経営は全て日本の基幹企業である南満州鉄道会社に委託された。取り決めの条件としては要するに、總督府が新たな建設と改善計画を作成し、会社はその計画の実行、鉄道の適切な維持、そして運営の責任を負うというものであった。併合以来總督府が前払いした資本金については、会社側は6パーセントの利子を支払うことになったが、交渉の結果、1921年以降に前払いされた資金については、向こう3年間4パーセントの利子を支払うことになった。鉄道経営については、細かい点を除いては、總督府の法律と規制の範囲内で行わなければならないが、これは日本本土

76   DESCRIPTIVE AND HISTORICAL

4 per cent instead of 6 on the capital advanced in and after 1921. In the management of the railways the Company must work within the terms of the laws and regulations of the Government-General, which are, except in minor details, the same as those in force in Japan proper.

The general features of railway development during the ten years ending on March 31, 1922 are shown in the following table:

RAILWAY DEVELOPMENT IN KOREA

		1912 *	1921 *
Total amount of capital †.......	Yen.	114,720,385	214,906,215
Construction and repairs ‡.......	Yen.	8,767,647	18,287,156
Passenger receipts..............	Yen.	3,820,185	13,361,903
Freight receipts.................	Yen.	2,816,482	11,454,094
Miscellaneous receipts..........	Yen.	180,596	3,293,689
Total receipts..................	Yen.	6,817,263	28,109,695
Operating expenses.............	Yen.	5,012,712	21,629,879
Number of passengers carried....		4,399,022	13,821,144
Tons of freight carried..........		1,105,362	3,331,381
Miles of line open to traffic......		837	1,165

* The figures are for fiscal years, which end on March 31.
† Invested up to the year.
‡ During the year.

Later figures are available for some of the foregoing items. Thus at the end of March, 1925, the mileage had increased to 1300, the number of passengers carried to 17,487,874, the receipts from traffic to 29,027,866, whilst the tonnage of freight carried remained practically stationary.

In addition to the state railways there are a number of short privately owned lines. At the time of annexation there was only one private line in operation, having a length of five miles. In 1914 the Government decided to subsidise such lines, on the principle of making up any deficit in profit below a certain percentage on the paid-up capital. Up to 1917 deficiencies were made up by subsidy to the point of 6 per cent. This was raised to 7

と同様である。

1922 年 3 月末日までの 10 年間に於ける鉄道開発の主だった内容
は、次の表に示されている。

朝鮮の鉄道開発

	1912[*]	1921[*]
資本金の総額[†]	114,720,385 円	214,906,215 円
建設と修理[‡]	8,767,647 円	18,287,156 円
旅客収入	3,820,185 円	13,361,903 円
貨物収入	2,816,482 円	11,454,094 円
雑収入	180,596 円	3,293,689 円
合計収入	6,817,263 円	28,109,695 円
営業経費	5,012,712 円	21,629,879 円
乗客数	4,399,022	13,821,144
貨物総重量（トン）	1,105,362	3,331,381
開通路線（マイル）	837	1,165

[*] 数字は会計年度毎のもの　[†] 累積　[‡] 年間

継続中の事業に関してはその後の数字も入手可能である。例えば、
1925 年の 3 月末には、距離は 1300 マイルに伸び、旅客数は 1748 万
7874 人に増加、貨物総重量は事実上変化がないのに対して、合計収
入は 2902 万 7866 円に増えている。

国有鉄道に加え、短距離の私鉄がいくつもある。併合時営業して
いた私鉄は一社のみで、営業線総延長は 5 マイルであった。1914 年
に總督府は、資本金に対する私鉄の赤字を一定の割合以下に抑える
ために補助金で補填することを決めた。1917 年までは、この補助金
によって赤字は払込済資本金額の 6 パーセントまで埋め合わせされ

per cent in 1918, and to 8 per cent in 1919. This policy exerted a marked influence on private railway construction. By 1923 the length of such lines open to traffic had increased to 333 miles, whilst those under construction, or projected, totaled 1340 miles.

During the ten years 1912-1922 the number of passengers carried on private railways increased from 156,523 to 1,995,259, and the tonnage of freight carried from 4161 to 536,650, including baggage. During the same period the paid-up capital of these undertakings mounted from less than 200 thousand yen to more than 26 million.

Roads--

Prior to the establishment of the Government-General, 1910, there were not fifty miles of good road in the whole country, almost all travel and transportation being done on narrow, deep-rutted tracks. In the interest of cultural and economic progress the Government-General laid out a project for constructing a net-work of good roads throughout the length and breadth of the Peninsula. The first part of the programme provided for the construction, over a number of years, of about 8000 miles of first- and second-class roads, the cost to be borne by the general revenue of the country, and of about 7000 miles of third-class road, to be paid for out of local taxation. Of this programme there had been carried to completion by the end of 1923 between 60 and 70 per cent of the proposed road-mileage —more than 5000 miles of first-and second-class roads and a little under 5000 miles of the third class.

The classification of the roads is made according to the width—24 feet or more for the first class, not less than 18 feet for the second, and not less

た。これは、1918年には7パーセントまで、1919年には8パーセントにまで上げられた。この政策は、私鉄建設に著しい影響を及ぼした。1923年には私鉄の営業距離は、333マイルに増加し、更に建設中または計画中の路線は合計で1340マイルに上ったのである。

　1912年から1922年の10年間で、私鉄が運んだ旅客数は15万6523人から199万5259人に増加し、貨物総重量は手荷物を含め4161トンから53万6650トンに増加した。同期間にこれらの事業への払込済資本金は、20万円未満から、2600万円にまで上った。

道路

　1910年の總督府の設置以前は、道路と呼べるほどの道路は50マイルもなく、殆どの旅行や輸送は、細く、轍の深く刻まれた道を使って行われていた。總督府は、文化や経済の発展のために、半島を縦横に網羅する良質の道路の建設計画を立てた。当初の計画としては、数カ年計画で8000マイルの一級道路と二級道路の建設を国の一般歳入から負担し、7000マイルの三級道路を地方税から支払うこととした。

　この計画の内、1923年の終わりまでに、予定された道路距離の60から70パーセント― 一級道路および二級道路の5000マイル以上、三級道路の5000マイル弱が完成された。

　道路はその幅によって分類され、一級道路は24フィート以上、二級道路は18フィート以上24フィート未満、三級道路は12フィー

than 12 feet for the third. Of the total mileage now open to traffic, about 4000 miles can be used by automobiles.

Streets--

The most recent issue of the Annual Report on Administration of Chosen is that covering the year ending on March 31, 1923. It deals as follows with the question of street improvements.

Towns in Chosen for the most part contain narrow, dirty, and crooked streets, causing great inconvenience to communications and to sanitary and fire-brigade arrangements, and naturally hindering their development, so of late years much has been done for their improvement by straightening, grading, and widening existing streets, and by constructing new ones as circumstances required.

Keijo (Seoul) is the capital of Chosen and quite different in scale and plan from other towns, so it was decided to conduct street improvements in it at national expense. Forty-three of its streets were selected for improvement, of which thirteen were completed at a cost of three million yen in the eight years from 1911 to 1918. The most important of these were made from 72 to 90 feet in width and provided with sidewalks. Where the traffic is heaviest the macadamised surface is tarred. Other roads were made not less than 48 feet in width, thus bringing about an extraordinary change in both the appearance and traffic-efficiency of the city.

The second programme takes in nine streets, the budget estimate for

ト以上 18 フィート未満であった。現在、開通している道路の総距離のうち、約 4000 マイルは自動車が通行可能である。

街路

『朝鮮總督府施政年報』の最新版は、1923 年 3 月末日で終了する年度を扱っているものだ。街路の改良についての問題について次のように扱っている。

朝鮮の市街の大部分は、狭くて汚く、曲がった街路であり、交通や、衛生や消防隊の手はずなどに非常に不便であり、また発展の妨げとなっていた。そこで、近年ではこの改良のために、現在の通りを真っ直ぐにしたり、勾配をゆるくしたり、道幅を広げ、また必要に応じ新たな街路を作るなど、多くのことが為されてきた。

京城（ソウル）は朝鮮の首都であり、他の都市とは、規模も計画もかなり異なっていた。そこで、その街路の改良は、国家予算で行うことが決まった。43 の街路が改良するものとして選定され、このうちの 13 は、1911 年から 1918 年の間に 300 万円の費用で完成した。これらの中で最も重要な街路は、幅を 72 フィートから 90 フィートに広げ、歩道が造られた。交通の最も激しいところは砕石を敷きタールで固められた。その他の道路は幅 48 フィート以上になり、市内は、見た目と、交通の効率の両面で、非常な変化がもたらされた。

2 つめの予定表は 9 の街路を含んだもので、予算は、1919 年

82 DESCRIPTIVE AND HISTORICAL

which is 3,400,000 yen spread over six years from the fiscal year 1919, and this is still in course of execution. Chosen being still in the first stages of modernization in many ways, it was highly necessary to lay down a permanent plan for street improvement in towns of importance and promise, so the Government-General incorporated in the budget for the fiscal years 1921 and onward an item for investigation regarding town-planning, and started work on it in four large cities—Keijo, Fusan, Taikyu, and Heijo.

There are now nine towns marked out for street improvement, including the principal seaports and provincial centers. The expenditure for this is to be defrayed out of local revenue with some assistance from the national treasury, and work in each is going on actively as a four to seven year enterprise.

A proper sewerage system is a very necessary aid to sanitation, so it was decided to carry on its establishment side by side with street improvement. On this work the city of Heijo was pledged to spend 580,000 yen in eleven years, Keijo 1,600,000 yen in seven years, and Taikyu 150,000 yen in five years. Part of the money thus allocated is provided by the national treasury and part by public bodies.

Maritime Transportation--

In order to insure regular maritime communication, both coastwise and foreign, the old Korean government found it necessary to subsidise local

度から6年に亘るもので340万円と見積もられている。これは
まだ遂行途中のものである。朝鮮は、まだ様々な面で近代化の
最初の段階にあるため、重要な都市や有望な都市について、恒
久的な街路の改良計画を立てることは非常に必要なことであっ
た。そこで、總督府は1921年度以降の予算に都市計画に関する
調査費を組み入れ、4大都市―京城、釜山、大邱、平壌―での作
業を開始した。

　今では、街路改良の対象として、主要な港や地方の中心都市
を含む9都市があげられている。このための歳出は、朝鮮での
収入に加えて、国庫からの支援で賄われることになっており、
この工事は、それぞれ4～7年の事業として、活発に行われて
いる。

　また、衛生のためには、適切な下水道システムが必要であっ
たため、街路の改良と並んで、その設置も進められることになっ
た。この工事に、平壌市は11年で58万円を、京城市は7年で
160万円を、大邱市は5年で15万円を、それぞれ費やすことが
約束された。このように振り当てられたお金の一部は国庫から、
一部は公的機関から供給された。

海運
　かつての朝鮮政府は、沿岸および海外との定期航路を維持するた
め国内の汽船会社に補助金を与える必要性があると考えていた。こ

84   DESCRIPTIVE AND HISTORICAL

steamship lines. This policy was adopted by the Government-General at the time of annexation, and has been continued down to the present time. At the beginning of 1923 it was granting an annual subsidy of 1,144,371 yen, distributed among 126 vessels of a total tonnage of about 20,000. The contracts under which these subsidies are granted prescribe the routes to be followed, the number of voyages to be made, and the time-schedule to be maintained. In 1923 there were eighteen routes, of which four connected Korea with Japan, North China, and Vladivostock, the remainder linking up the various Korean ports with each other.

Postal, Telegraph, and Telephone Communications--

Prior to 1876 there was nothing in Korea which could be dignified by the name of a postal service. In that year, however, the Japanese Government opened a post office at Fusan, when the port was opened to foreign trade, and later, as Japanese settlers became more numerous, the number of post offices was gradually increased. At first only ordinary mail business was done; but as early as 1880 money orders were made available and a postal savings system started. To these services a parcel post was added in 1900. In the meantime the Korean Government had, in 1896, engaged a Japanese adviser in the Communications Department and organized the post office on modern lines. An agreement was concluded in 1905 by which the postal service of Korea was placed under the charge of the Imperial Japanese Government; but in the following year the control was transferred to the newly-established Residency-General. When Korea was annexed to Japan in 1910 a Communications Bureau was created in the Government-General, and to it were assigned the control and

の航海補助政策は、併合時總督府に採用され、現在に到るまで継続されている。1923 年の初めには、年間 114 万 4371 円の補助金が与えられ、総重量約 2 万トンクラスの大型船 126 隻に分配された。補助金の契約内容には、航路、運行回数、時刻表まで記載されている。1923 年には、18 航路あり、そのうち 4 航路は朝鮮と日本、北部中国、ウラジオストックを結ぶもので、残りは朝鮮国内の港間を運行するものである。

郵便・電信・電話通信

1876 年までは、朝鮮には、郵便業務と偉そうに呼べるようなものは何もなかった。しかしながら、同年に、港が海外貿易のために開かれた時に、日本政府が釜山に郵便局を開設した。後に、日本からの移住者がもっと多数に上ると、郵便局の数も次第に増えた。

最初は、通常郵便業務のみが行われたが、早くも 1880 年には郵便為替が利用出来るようになり、郵便貯金業務も始まった。1900 年には、これらの業務に小包郵便も加わった。

その間大韓帝国政府は 1896 年日本の逓信省から顧問を招聘し、郵便業務を近代化した。1905 年に契約が締結され、これにより、朝鮮の郵便業務は日本帝国政府の管轄下に置かれたが、翌年新設された統監府に権限が移った。1910 年の併合の際、朝鮮總督府の中に通信局が新設され、全ての郵便、電信、電話業務の監督・管理を担うことになった。1923 年には、通信業務の正規職員は、1 万 1000 人

management of all postal, telegraph, and telephone business. In 1923 the permanent staff of the communication services numbered nearly 11,000 employees, with several thousand temporary workers engaged as occasion demanded.

As illustrating the rapidly increasing use made of the communication services it may be noted that between 1910 and 1923 the number of pieces of ordinary mail delivered in Korea advanced from 53 to 174 million, the number of parcels delivered from less than one million to more than two million and a half, the number of offices available for postal, telephone, or telegraph service from 395 to 739, and the number of telephone calls from less than 25 million to more than 82 million in the year.

There is a steadily growing resort to the Post Office Savings Banks. In 1910 the total amount deposited by Japanese was 3 million yen, and by Koreans 200 thousand yen; in 1922 these figures had grown to 17 million and 2,750,000 respectively.

Wireless apparatus was installed in 1910 on the Government signal-inspecting ship, and at three lighthouses; but the service has not yet been opened to the general public.

近くに上り、臨時に雇用する一時職員は数千人いた。

　急速に増えつつある通信業務の利用の例として特筆すべきことは、1910年から1923年の間に国内における年間の通常郵便の配達数が5300万通から1億7400万通に増加し、小包の配達数は100万個未満から250万個以上になったことである。さらに郵便・電話または電信業務を取り扱う局が395カ所から739カ所へと増え、電話の通話数が2500万通話未満から8200万通話へと上昇した。

　郵便貯金の利用は着実に増大していた。1910年には、日本人による貯金総額は300万円、朝鮮人のそれは20万円であった。1922年には、これらの数字はそれぞれ1700万円と275万円に増えた。

　無線電信は1910年に、政府の通信調査船と3基の灯台に導入されたが、一般にはまだそのサービスは開かれていなかった。

Historical--

A brief account of the relations between Korea and Japan in modern times will suffice to give the reader the broad facts pertinent to a consideration of the situation as it exists today.

In 1894 Japan declared war on China, largely for the purpose of settling once for all the international status of Korea, about which there had existed for centuries a dispute which constantly threatened the peace of the Far East. During more than two thousand years Korea had been alternately independent, and under the suze rainty of China, or of Japan. She had been repeatedly invaded from the north—by China, under both the Chinese and Manchu dynasties, by Mongols, and by nomadic tribes—and in 1592 the Regent of Japan, Hideyoshi, attacked Korea with an army of 300,000 men, as part of a project for the conquest of China. These various invasions and raids, together with the prevalence of piracy in Korean waters led the Korean authorities to adopt and to enforce with the utmost rigor a policy of absolute national seclusion, a policy which was followed for several centuries and was enforced with great rigor. It was from this circumstance that Korea became known throughout the world as the Hermit Kingdom. History has proved that this attitude of no-intercourse cannot be indefinitely maintained. In the case of Korea the matter was complicated by the question of the Chinese suzerainty. Was Korea a vassal state of China, or was she not? The answer made by Korea and China was at one time yes, at another time no. Thus, whenever it suited the purpose of the Koreans to claim the protection of China, the plea was made that the suzerain must defend the vassal; when, however, China sought to make its suzerainty effective for some purpose of her own, the Korean argument

朝鮮の歴史

近代における朝鮮と日本の関係を簡潔に説明すれば、読者は今日の状況に関する大まかな事実を充分理解出来るであろう。

1894年、日本は清に宣戦布告をしたが、これは何世紀にも亘り、極東の平和を脅かしてきた朝鮮の国際的立場をめぐる論争に終止符を打つためであった。2000年以上の間、朝鮮半島は独立と、中国または日本の属国としての歴史を繰り返してきたのである。

朝鮮半島は、北からは中国と満州の歴代王朝、モンゴル、そして遊牧民より繰り返し侵攻され、1592年には明朝支配の野望を持った日本の武将・豊臣秀吉の総勢30万名の遠征軍による襲撃を受けた。これらの様々な侵略と襲撃および朝鮮海域における海賊行為に対して、朝鮮は何世紀にも亘り徹底した鎖国政策を行ってきた。

このような状況から朝鮮半島は「隠遁した王国」として世界で知られるようになった。

しかし、交易拒否の姿勢を永久にとり続けることが不可能であることは歴史が証明している。朝鮮の場合、事態は中国の宗主権により複雑化していた。中国の隷属国なのか、否か、朝鮮と中国双方から出された答えは、時にはそれを肯定し、時には否定した。中国の保護を必要とした時は、宗主国が隷属国を守ることを懇願したが、中国が自国の目的のために宗主権を用いると、宗主権はもはや絵空事であり、毎年の朝貢の習慣は古来から続く儒教的儀礼であり、実質的な意味を持たないというのが朝鮮側の主張である。

was that the suzerainty was a mere figment, the annual tribute being paid solely on sentimental grounds in perpetuation of an ancient custom which had completely lost its practical significance.

Conversely, when Peking saw some advantage to be gained by insisting on the living force of the suzerainty the point was made very clear to the Koreans; but when, as occurred from time to time—as, for example, when French and American punitive expeditions attacked Korea in 1866 and 1871, respectively—foreign nations sought redress from Korea for wrongs done to their citizens, China disclaimed any kind of bond with Korea which made her responsible for the latter's acts.

No country had more reason to be irritated by the posture of Korean affairs than had Japan. In 1875 a Japanese war-ship was fired on by a Korean shore-battery without the slightest provocation. The Japanese at once captured the fort, and seized all the arms and ammunition in it. Tokyo decided that the occasion was favorable for bringing to an end the equivocal relationship between Korea and China. General Kiyotaka Kuroda was sent to Korea as Envoy Extraordinary and Plenipotentiary, charged with the task of concluding a treaty between Japan and Korea. This compact, known as the Treaty of Kwangha, was signed in 1876. It provided for the mutual opening of ports, for mutual permission to trade, and for the formal recognition by Japan of the independence of Korea. It is from this date that an account of Japanese-Korean relations, in modern times, may take its departure.

In 1880 a Japanese Legation was established at Seoul, and it was hoped by sober-minded Japanese statesmen that with direct representation at the Korean capital the relations between the two countries would assume a

逆に、北京側が宗主権の行使に利ありと判断すると、朝鮮に対して明確にそれを主張してきた。しかし諸外国から度重なる圧力を朝鮮が受けた時、例えば自国市民へ不当な行いをしたとして、1866年にはフランスが、1871年にはアメリカがそれぞれ征伐隊を送り朝鮮に賠償を求めたが、それに対し中国は朝鮮との結び付きを一切否定した。

こうした朝鮮の外交姿勢に最も苛立ちを覚えていたのが日本であり、それには正当な理由があったのである。1875年、日本の軍艦が朝鮮の沿岸砲兵隊によって発砲された。この時日本側に挑発行為は一切なかった。日本は直ちに要塞を占拠し、武器弾薬を押収した。この出来事を朝鮮と中国の曖昧な関係に終止符を打つ絶好の機会だと判断した日本政府は、日朝間の条約締結に向け、陸軍中将黒田清隆を全権特派大使として派遣した。

江華条約で知られるこの協定は1876年に結ばれた。この条約には、互いに開港すること、互いに貿易の許可をすること、日本が朝鮮の独立を公認することが盛り込まれていた。この日を境に、近代における新たな日朝関係が始まったのである。

1880年、日本公使館がソウルに設立され、冷静な日本の政治家たちは、首都に直接代表を置くことで二国間の関係が更に友好的になることを希望した。しかしこれらの希望は満たされることはなかっ

more friendly tone. These hopes were not destined to be fulfilled. There existed at the time a long-standing rivalry between a party headed by the King of Korea's uncle, the Tai Wen Kun, and the rich and powerful family of the Mins, of which the Queen of Korea was a member. In this domestic quarrel China intervened on the side of the Mins, sending troops into the Peninsula for the purpose of suppressing a revolt started by the Tai Wen Kun. For years Korea was the scene of coups d'état and of insurrections, in the course of which the Japanese Legation was twice attacked —once in 1882 by a Korean mob aided by Korean soldiers, and once in 1884 by Korean and Chinese troops acting in co-operation. On each occasion the Japanese Minister, with his wife and children, had to seek safety in flight.

The constant intrusion of China upon the field of Korean domestic affairs is what led up to the Chino-Japanese War of 1894-5. Japan had recognized the independence of Korea in 1876, by the Treaty of Kwangha; and there was, of course, a reciprocal obligation on the shoulders of Korea to repudiate the Chinese suzerainty. Notwithstanding this, the Korean Government, in 1894, asked China to send troops to Korea to put down a formidable rebellion. Early in June the Chinese force arrived, and the Japanese immediately countered by sending a military guard to her Minister in Seoul, and, a little later, by despatching to the Peninsula a force of some 5000 troops. The situation thus created was difficult in the extreme. The Japanese were not prepared to recognize the Chinese claim that Chinese troops were in the country as the defenders of a Chinese dependency; but they suggested that the Chinese and the Japanese should act together in restoring order and in initiating such reforms as should conduce to the future peace of the country. This proposal was rejected. In

た。その頃、朝鮮国王の大院君が率いる勢力と、大院君が高宗の妃に迎えた、裕福で力のある閔一族との間には長く続く対立があった。この国内の不和に関し、清は閔氏の肩を持ち、大院君の始めた反乱を鎮圧するために朝鮮半島に軍隊を送った。何年にも亘り朝鮮はクーデターと反乱の舞台となり、日本公使館も2回攻撃された。1度目は1882年、兵士をも巻き込んだ朝鮮人暴徒によるものであり、2度目は1884年朝鮮軍と清軍が共謀して起こしたものであった。いずれも日本公使は妻子とともに避難した。

　絶えず続く清による内政干渉が1894年〜1895年にかけての日清戦争をもたらしたのである。日本は1876年に江華条約によって朝鮮の独立を認めた。当然、その見返りとして朝鮮の側には、清の宗主権を断固拒否する義務があったのである。それにも拘らず李氏朝鮮政府は1894年、大きな反乱を鎮めるため、清の軍隊を要請した。清の軍隊は6月早々到着し、日本は即座にソウルにいる日本の公使に軍の護衛を送り、その直後、およそ5000の部隊を朝鮮半島に派遣した。一触即発の緊迫した事態であった。日本は、清の属国を守るために部隊を派遣したのだとする清の主張を認めるつもりはなかったが、両国が協力して秩序を回復し、朝鮮の将来的な平和をもたらす改革を始めるべきだと提案した。しかし、この提案は拒否された。

94 DESCRIPTIVE AND HISTORICAL

the meantime China had moved an army of about eight thousand troops to a point on the Yalu, near the Korean frontier. The Japanese Minister brought the matter to a head by delivering an ultimatum to the Korean Government in respect to its failure to live up to the terms of the Treaty of Kwangha. This was on July 20th; three days later the Japanese occupied the palace and, virtually, made the King prisoner.

Japan declared war on China on August 1st, actual fighting having taken place a few days earlier, both on land and at sea. The details of the fighting are of no interest in the present connection. Japan was completely victorious, the extent of her triumph being testified to by the terms of the Treaty of Shimonoseki. So far as Korea was concerned, Japan carried her point, the recognition of the absolute independence of the country.

Shortly after this the Queen of Korea was murdered under circumstances for which no terms of condemnation could be too strong. The facts are relevant to the relations of Korea and Japan at the time, for the murder had a very important influence upon the subsequent course of events. On October 8, 1895, a band of Korean and Japanese assassins, after long and careful preparation, entered the inner chambers of the Palace at Seoul and killed the Queen. Not only does the evidence establish it beyond doubt that one of the prime movers in this plot was the Japanese Minister at Seoul; but that evidence is supplied by the Japanese Judge of Preliminary Enquiry who investigated the murder. The findings of this judge make the most extraordinary reading. He describes the plot, names all the prisoners before him as having been concerned in it, states that its object was to murder the Queen, leads his conspirators to the outside of the palace, and continues:

第二章　朝鮮の描写と歴史　　95

同じ頃、清は国境近くの鴨緑江がある地点まで 8000 の部隊を移動
させていた。日本の公使は朝鮮が江華条約の条項を守らなかったこ
とに対し、同政府に最後通告を送り事態はさらに緊迫した。7 月 20
日のことである。3 日後日本は朝鮮の王宮を占領し、事実上、国王
を捕虜にした。

　日本は 8 月 1 日に清に宣戦布告したが、実際の戦闘は陸上と海上
両方で 2 ～ 3 日前から始まっていた。戦闘の詳細はここでは重要で
はない。日本の圧倒的勝利であったが、それは下関条約の条項によっ
ても証明されている。朝鮮に関しては日本の主張が通り、朝鮮の完
全独立が認められた。

　この直後、朝鮮の王妃が惨殺されたのであるが、その方法につい
てはどんなに強い言葉で非難されても仕方のないものであった。事
件は当時の日朝関係に関わるものであり、王妃殺害はその後の事態
に大きく影響した。1895 年 10 月 8 日、日本と朝鮮の暗殺者グルー
プが入念な計画の後、ソウルの王宮内部の部屋に侵入し王妃を殺害。
この陰謀の首謀者の 1 人が日本の公使である疑う余地のない証拠が
あった。その証拠がこの殺人を調査した予備審問の日本人裁判官に
よって提出されていたのである。この裁判官の発言は驚くべきもの
である。

　彼は陰謀について述べ、陰謀に関与したとして彼の前に並んだ全
ての被告の名前を挙げ、その目的は王妃殺害にあり、共犯者たちを
宮殿外へと導いたとし、こう続けた。

「夜明け頃、共謀者全員が光化門から王宮に入り、即座に王宮内部

"About dawn the whole party entered the palace through the Kwang-hwa Gate, and at once proceeded to the inner chambers. Notwithstanding these facts, there is no sufficient evidence to prove that any of the accused actually committed the crime originally meditated by them . . ."; and then immediately discharges all the prisoners!

This is certainly one of the most disgraceful episodes in the annals of colonial rule. It is relieved by only one mitigating circumstance, namely that there is no evidence to show that any of the Government officials in Tokyo were concerned in the matter.

The murder of the Queen improved the general aspect of affairs, from the Japanese standpoint, by removing a woman who had been their bitterest and most unscrupulous opponent, and by increasing the influence of the Tai Wen Kun, who was supple to the Japanese intentions.

The conception undoubtedly entertained in Tokyo at the conclusion of the war with China was that, with the question of the Chinese suzerainty definitely and finally disposed of, Korea, reformed and strengthened by Japanese aid and advice, would serve as an effective buffer state as against China or Asiatic Russia, should either of them attempt to use the Peninsula as a base for operations against Japan. It is very doubtful whether the real independence of Korea could have been preserved even under the most favorable circumstances; and as time passed the circumstances became, from the Japanese point of view, as unfavorable as could be imagined.

A Japanese statesman called upon to defend the Korean policy of his country in the years following the Chino-Japanese War would present his

第二章　朝鮮の描写と歴史　　97

の部屋へと向かったという事実はあるが、被告人全員に、この計画
の実行犯であることを裏付ける充分な証拠はない。」
そして、被告全員は直ちに釈放されたのだ！

　これは日本の統治時代に最大の汚点を残したことは確かである。
ただ、1つだけ救いがあるとすれば、東京の政府役人の関与を示す
証拠がないことである。
　王妃殺害により、最も辛辣で破廉恥な敵対者が取り除かれ、日本
の意に沿う大院君の影響力が強まったのであるから、日本の立場か
ら見れば状況が改善されたのである。

　日清戦争が終結した時、東京が間違いなく認識していたことは、
中国の宗主権問題に決着がついたことで、日本の支援と助言によっ
て改革を強めた朝鮮が中国やロシアに対し効果的な緩衝国となるだ
けでなく、中国あるいはロシアにとっては対日戦略基地にもなると
いうことである。最も有利な状況下でも朝鮮が真の独立を保てるか
どうかはとても疑わしく、時間が経つにつれ、状況は日本にとって、
どのように考えても、不利であることが分かった。

　日清戦争後の朝鮮政策を擁護するよう求められたとしたら、日本
の政治家は、以下のように状況を説明するであろう。

98   DESCRIPTIVE AND HISTORICAL

case somewhat as follows.

In going to war with China, Japan had thrown her own fate into the scales. If she should suffer defeat—and when you fight a people which outnumbers your own by ten to one, and whose territory and natural resources present an equal disproportion, defeat is certainly a very serious possibility—she was prepared to suffer the consequences. That among these would have been loss of territory and the payment of an indemnity cannot be doubted.

If Japan secured a complete victory—as, in the event, she did—she expected to gather such fruits as she could compel her adversary to deliver as the price of a treaty of peace. Among these fruits was the cession to Japan of the Chinese Peninsula of Liao-tung. Before the treaty was signed, however, France, Germany, and Russia intervened, and forbade the cession to Japan of any territory on the Chinese mainland. It was impossible for Japan to offer any resistance to an ultimatum with such formidable backing: her victorious troops were withdrawn; the Liao-tung Peninsula was restored to China.

Within three years of the date on which the principle of an inviolate Chinese mainland had been used as the pretext for forcing Japan out of Liao-tung, the three defenders of China against Japanese "aggression" were all in comfortable occupation of various parts of the "inviolate" Chinese mainland—Germany in Kiaochow, on a 99 years' lease; France in Kwangchouwan, on a 99 years' lease; and, as a crowning triumph of international cynicism, Russia, on a 25 years' lease of the very Lia-tung Peninsula from which she had been chiefly instrumental in ejecting Japan.

Although Great Britain had refused to take any part in the coercion

第二章　朝鮮の描写と歴史　　　99

　清と戦争を行うことにより、日本はその運命を秤にかけた。人口
で10倍も上回り、またその領土と自然資源においても同様の不均
衡さのある国と戦う時、敗北の可能性は充分にあったが、もし負け
る運命であるならば、日本は結果を甘んじて受ける覚悟があった。
その結果とは、領土の損失や損害賠償金の支払いなどを含むことは
疑う余地がない。

　もし日本が完全に勝利したならば―実際に勝利したのであるが、
平和条約の対価として対戦相手から戦利品を勝ち取ることが出来る
と期待した。その1つが清の半島である遼東半島の割譲であった。
しかし、条約が結ばれる前に、フランス、ドイツ、ロシアが干渉し、
清本土のいかなる領土も日本に割譲することを禁止した。このよう
に厄介な後ろ盾のある最後通牒に抵抗することは、日本にとって不
可能であった。勝利を収めたにも拘らず日本の部隊は撤退し、遼東
半島は清に返還されたのである。

　返還後3年も経たないうちに、仏独露の三国は日本の「侵略」か
ら守ったその代償として、「犯すべからず」と主張したその清の本
土に居心地良く居座ってしまったようだ。ドイツは99年の借地契
約で膠州湾を、フランスは99年の借地契約で広州湾を、そして、
遼東半島から日本を追い出すことに主な役割を果たしたロシアが、
その遼東半島を25年借地契約したのはまさに国際政治の高らかな
嘲笑を聞くようである。

　英国は日本に圧力をかけることはなかったが国益を優先させ、中

100 DESCRIPTIVE AND HISTORICAL

of Japan, her conception of her own national interest led her to adopt the policy of occupying Chinese territory on lease. In the south she secured a 99 years' lease of 370 square miles on the mainland opposite Hong Kong, as an offset to the French lease of Kwan-chouwan; in the north she leased the territory of Wei-hai-wei, 285 square miles, for so long a time as Russia should remain in possession of Port Arthur.

In what sense was Japan to interpret these manœuvres? Was it possible for her to see in them anything but a determination on the part of the great European powers to prescribe for and to enforce upon Japan a rule of conduct totally different from that by which they themselves would be bound; and which, if Japan should subscribe to it, would deprive her not only of every advantage attached to her geographical situation off the coast of Asia, but also of every further advantage which she might legitimately (according to the international code of ethics hitherto in force) expect to derive from her rapid development, from her strong and unifying sentiment of nationality, from her tireless industry, and from her heroic military qualities?

Was Japan, in brief, to accept the restrictions of a self-denying ordinance at the very moment when England had reached the climax of her territorial acquisitions in every quarter of the globe, when Russia and Germany were fortifying themselves on Chinese soil almost within sight of the Japanese coast, when France was reforming her administration, strengthening her garrison, and extending her control in Indo-China, when the United States had recently taken possession of the Philippine Islands?

To have yielded to such a preposterous demand would have constituted a betrayal of the Japanese nation in which no reputable statesman could

第二章　朝鮮の描写と歴史　　101

国清の領土の一部を租借した。南部においては香港の向かい側にある領土370平方マイルをフランスが広州湾を租借したことの埋め合わせとして借り、そして北部では、285平方マイルの威海衛をロシアが旅順に居座る間、ずっと租借したのである。

　これらの策略を日本はどのように解釈するべきだったのだろうか。行動規範とは本来自分たち自身が縛られるものだが、ヨーロッパ列強諸国は、全く異なった代物を日本に押し付けて来た。仮にその規範に日本が従ったなら、アジアの辺境に位置するという有利な地理的条件を活かせないばかりか、急速な発展、統制のとれた国民感情、精力的な産業、勇敢な軍隊の性質など日本が持つ美徳によって（従来の国際的倫理規定によれば）合法的に得られるはずのより有利な条件さえも奪われるのである。こうした列強諸国の意図に日本は一体何を見出せばよいというのか？

　大英帝国は世界中到るところで領土を獲得しその絶頂期にあり、ロシアとドイツは日本の沿岸から目と鼻の先の中国領土で自国の防備を強化している。フランスは行政改革をし、守備隊を強化しインドシナまでその支配を拡げており、アメリカといえば最近フィリピン諸島を占領したという。まさにそんな時に、端的に言えば、日本は自己否定的な制限を強いられるべきだったのだろうか？
　こんな不合理な要求に屈服することは、日本国に対する裏切りを意味し、信頼に値する政治家ならば同意しなかっただろう。である

conceivably have become an accomplice, since so to yield would have earned for the persons responsible the just execration of their own nationals and the just contempt of all men who esteem patriotism to be a virtue.

Thus, a hypothetical Japanese statesman. For my own part I am convinced that whatever chance there had ever been of Korea attaining independent nationhood, was destroyed when Germany, France, and Russia deprived Japan of the fruits of her victory over China, took those very fruits for themselves, and thus taught Japan the bitter lesson that if she wished to obtain a valid guaranty for her future security, to present to the world a valid sanction for her foreign policy, she must develop her own military strength.

This Japan proceeded to do. Prior to the Chino-Japanese War, Japan's expenditure on her army had, for a number of years, averaged less than seven million dollars; in 1903 the army estimates exceeded 25 million dollars. At the outbreak of the Chino-Japanese War Japan's navy consisted of about fifty vessels of a total tonnage of less than 75,000; at the outbreak of the Russo-Japanese War, 1904, the number of vessels had increased to 160, the tonnage to approximately 300,000.

I was in the Far East during the years 1902-4. Everyone with whom I discussed the matter, from Lahore to Wei-bai-wei, was confident that war between Japan and Russia was inevitable unless one or the other of two highly improbable contingencies should arise—one that Japan should decide to acquiesce in Russia's obvious intention of making herself the dominating power in Korea; the other that Russia should reverse her historic policy of thrusting southward from the Trans-Siberian Railway

から、要求に屈した責任者は自国民から罵られ、愛国心を美徳とする全ての人々からは軽蔑されただろう。

このように日本の政治家なら考えるだろう。

私の立場からはこう確信している。ドイツ、フランス、ロシアが日本から中国に対する勝利の報酬を奪い取って自分達のものにしたときに、朝鮮が独立国家になる可能性があったとしても、その可能性は失われた。こうして日本は、将来の安全を保障したければ、また外交政策の正当性を世界に示したければ、自国の軍事力を発展させなければならないという苦い教訓を得たのである。

日本の進んだ道はこうだ。日清戦争以前、日本の軍事費は何年にも亘り平均 700 万ドル以下であったが、1903 年には軍の見積もりは 2500 万ドル以上に上った。日清戦争が始まった頃、日本の海軍は総トン数 7 万 5 千以下で約 50 の軍艦を有していたが、1904 年の日露戦争勃発時には、軍艦数は 160、総トン数は約 30 万に増えていた。

私は 1902 年から 1904 年の間に極東にいた。ラホールから威海衛に至るまで、私がこのことについて話した全ての人は、可能性としてはほとんどあり得ないが、2 つのうちどちらかの事態が起こらない限り日本とロシアの戦争は避けられないと確信していた。その 1 つは、朝鮮進出へのロシアのあからさまな野望を日本が黙認すること。もう 1 つは、ロシアが南下政策、つまりいかなる人的、財政的

until she found herself, at whatever cost of men and money, mistress of an ice-free port in northeastern Asia.

The Russian advance toward the north Pacific had been carefully planned and effectively executed. At the beginning of the twentieth century Japan saw her great rival occupying the Liao-tung Peninsula, in virtual control of the Chinese Province of Manchuria, and in possession of two of the most formidable naval and military bases to be found anywhere in the world—Vladivostock, within a few hours' steaming of Korea's northeastern boundary; Port Arthur, within a few hours of her southwestern boundary. That these fortresses were separated by the Korean Peninsula, that the former was ice-bound for six months in the year, that the latter was too small to serve adequately the naval and commercial needs of Russia in that quarter were facts to be set side by side with Russia's diplomatic pressure on the Korean Court, her intimate relations with the anti-Japanese party in Korea, and her efforts to purchase land in or near Korea's southern ports. There were a number of attractive possibilities: the excellent ice-free port of Masampo might be leased, thus giving Russia a naval base within two hundred miles of the Japanese coast; it might be feasible to secure control of the proposed railroad from Wiju, on the Manchurian frontier, for the construction of which a French company had obtained a concession, thus assuring an all-rail connection from northern Manchuria into the heart of the Peninsula; and other, similar, opportunities presented themselves.

During the summer of 1903 Japan decided that the time was ripe to make a definite stand against Russia's steady advance through Manchuria to the Korean border, and to put an end to the ceaseless intrigues by which, within Korea itself, Russian agents were preparing for the day when the

犠牲を払ってもシベリア鉄道以南の不凍港の実権を握るという、歴史的悲願を手放すことである。

　ロシアの北太平洋への進出は入念に計画され、効果的に実施されたものであった。20世紀初め、ロシアは遼東半島を占領し、満州を実質的に支配し、世界で最も脅威となる軍事基地のうち2つを所有していた。1つは朝鮮半島北東の国境から蒸気機関車・汽船で数時間のウラジオストック、もう1つは朝鮮半島南西の国境から数時間の旅順である。またこれらの海軍基地の間に朝鮮半島があるということ、ウラジオストックが1年の内6カ月間氷で閉ざされてしまうこと、旅順は軍事的、商業的用途には小さすぎることは紛れもない事実である。これらの事実と並んで、ロシアの朝鮮宮廷への外交的圧力、反日勢力との親密な関係、そして朝鮮南部の港内もしくはその周辺の土地を買おうとしていること、これらも紛れもない事実である。そこにはいくつかの魅力的な可能性があった。不凍港である釜山港を租借することで日本沿岸から200マイルの所にロシアの海軍基地を作ることや、フランスが所有する満州国境の義州からの鉄道の権益を獲得し、北満州から朝鮮半島中心部までの鉄道網を確保すること、このほかにも同様の可能性が開けるかもしれないのだ。

　ロシアは満州から朝鮮の国境に向けて着々と南下を続けていた。1903年夏、日本は「機は熟せり」と判断し、ソウルの王宮の上にロシアの旗を掲げようと企てるロシアの陰謀に終止符を打つことを決断した。日露間の広範囲の問題にある程度の合意点を見出すために、

Russian flag would fly over the palace at Seoul. Negotiations were opened with St. Petersburg with a view to reaching some agreement on the broad question of Russian-Japanese relations in the Far East. Between August, 1903, and February, 1904, ten different drafts of a proposed treaty were discussed; but the evasive and otherwise unsatisfactory character of the Russian proposals and counter-proposals convinced the Japanese cabinet that it was hopeless to look for a peaceful solution of the problem. Japan having, in defence of her Korean policy, fought the most populous nation of Asia would now, in the same cause, fight the most populous nation of Europe. On February 5, 1904, the negotiations were broken off, and a few days later war was declared.

From this point onward Japanese policy toward Korea stiffened. The first evidence of the new attitude was the conclusion of a Protocol between the two countries on February 23, 1904. Although Japan reasserts her guaranty of the independence and territorial integrity of Korea, it is agreed that ". . . the Imperial Government of Korea shall place full confidence in the Imperial Government of Japan and adopt the advice of the latter in regard to improvements in administration"; and, further, that "in case the welfare of the Imperial House of Korea, or the territorial integrity of Korea, is endangered by the aggression of a third power, or by internal disturbances, the Imperial Government of Japan shall immediately take such necessary measures as the circumstances require, and in such cases, the Imperial Government of Korea shall give full facilities to promote the action of the Imperial Japanese Government. . . . Japan may, for the attainment of the above mentioned objects, occupy, when the circumstances require it, such places as may be necessary from strategical

サンクトペテルブルグに於いて日露交渉が始まった。1903 年 8 月から 1904 年 2 月の間に、10 もの内容の異なる条約案の下書きが作成された。しかし、のらりくらりとかわすロシア側の態度に、日本の内閣はもはや平和的な解決は望めないと確信した。対朝政策を守るため日本はアジアで最も人口の多い国と戦ったが、同じ目的で、今度はヨーロッパで最も人口の多い国と戦うことになった。1904 年 2 月 5 日、日露交渉は決裂し、数日後宣戦が布告された。

　この時点から、日本の対朝政策は硬化したのである。この新しい日本の姿勢は 1904 年 2 月 23 日に結ばれた二国間協定に見ることが出来る。日本は朝鮮の独立と領土の保全を確実に保証すると宣言したのであるが、それとともに以下のようなことも同意された。「大韓帝国政府は大日本帝国政府に完全なる信頼を置き、その施政の改善に関する日本の助言を受け入れること」、そして更に、「第三国の侵害や内乱によって大韓帝国皇室の安寧または領土の保全に危険ある場合は、大日本帝国政府は速やかに臨機必要な措置をとり、そしてその場合、大韓帝国政府は大日本帝国政府の行動を容易ならしめるため便宜を図ること。大日本帝国政府は前項の目的を果たす為、軍略上必要の地点を臨機収用することが出来る」ということである。

108 DESCRIPTIVE AND HISTORICAL

points of view."

Another agreement, signed on August 22, 1904, makes it mandatory on the Korean Government to engage a Japanese financial adviser, whose advice must be heard before any financial matter is acted upon; and a foreign diplomatic adviser, recommended by the Japanese Government, without whose previous counsel no important matter concerning foreign relations is to be dealt with. The final article of the agreement reads: "The Korean Government shall previously consult the Japanese Government in concluding treaties and conventions with foreign powers, and in dealing with other important diplomatic affairs, such as the grant of concessions to or contracts with foreigners."

It is obvious that one effect of this agreement was to make Korea a protectorate of Japan, whilst leaving public authority to be exercised in the name of the Emperor of Korea. The next step taken in the course which led, finally, to annexation, was an agreement dated November 17, 1905. The preamble contains the significant provision that "the following stipulations are to serve until the moment arrives when it is recognized that Korea has attained national strength." The agreement provided that the external relations of Korea should in future be conducted by the Department of Foreign Affairs in Tokyo; that Japanese diplomatic and consular officers should have charge of the subjects and interests of Korea in foreign countries; that Japan should assume responsibility for the execution of treaties already existing between Korea and other powers; that the Government of Korea should not in future enter into any act or engagement of an international character except through the medium of the Government of Japan; and that the Government of Japan undertakes to

第二章　朝鮮の描写と歴史　　　　109

　1904年8月22日に結ばれたもう1つの協定で、大韓帝国政府は日本人財務顧問1名を従事させ、いかなる財務決定をする前にも必ず顧問の忠告を聞くこと、そして、日本政府の推薦する外国人一名を外交顧問として従事させ、事前の勧告なしでは、外交に関する要務を行ってはならないと義務付けた。

　この協定の最終条項は以下のとおりである。「韓国政府は外国との条約締結、重要なる外交案件すなわち外国人に対する特権譲与または契約等の重要な外交事情に対処する際は、あらかじめ日本政府と協議すること」。

　この協定の目的とすることの1つは、国民の支配権は名目上大韓帝国皇帝に残しつつ、大韓帝国を大日本帝国の保護国にすることであった。最終的に併合に到る過程において、次にとられたステップは、1905年11月17日の協定であった。序文には次の重要な規定がある。「以下の条項は韓国が国力を獲得したと認められるまで効果を発揮するものである」。協定の内容には、大韓帝国の外交関係は将来において東京の外務省が実行する。大日本帝国の外交・領事の官吏が外国における大韓帝国の事務と利益を監理する。大韓帝国と他国との間に既に結ばれた条約を実行する責任は大日本帝国が持つ。大韓帝国政府は今後大日本帝国政府の仲介なしでは国際的性質を有する行為や約束をしてはならない。そして、大日本帝国政府は大韓帝国皇帝の安寧と尊厳を維持することを保証することなどが含まれている。

110 DESCRIPTIVE AND HISTORICAL

maintain the welfare and dignity of the Imperial House of Korea.

Article 3 completely changed the character of Japan's representation vis-à-vis the Korean Court. The envoy is replaced by a Resident-General, having the right of private and personal audience with the Emperor of Korea, and the Japanese consuls are replaced by Residents, to be stationed at the several open ports and at such other places in Korea as the Government of Japan may deem necessary.

It is to be observed that in this agreement no mention is made of Korean independence, the fact being, probably, that by this time Japan realized the impracticable quality of a policy which on the one hand made her responsible for Korea's national status, and on the other left her with no sufficient authority in the country to prevent the occurrence of events which might at any moment involve her in the most serious international difficulties.

On November 22, 1905, the Japanese Government issued a declaration to the powers in treaty-relation with Korea, in which is presented a clear and frank account of her new Korean policy. The document runs as follows:

The relations of propinquity have made it necessary for Japan to take and exercise, for reasons closely connected with her own safety and repose, a paramount interest and influence in the political and military affairs of Korea. The measures hitherto taken have been purely advisory, but the experience of recent years has demonstrated the insufficiency of measures of guidance alone. The unwise and improvident action of Korea, more especially in the domain of her international affairs, has in the past been the most fruitful source

第3条は朝鮮宮廷に対する日本の代表者の立場をすっかり変えた。特命全権大使は、大韓帝国皇帝と個人的・私的に内謁する権利を有する統監に代わり、また領事は理事官に置き換えられ、大韓帝国の各開港場および日本政府が必要とみなした場所に置いた。

　この協定では独立には触れられてはいないが、この頃には、現実性のない政策であることに日本も気づいていたからであろう。つまり、一方で国際社会での朝鮮の立場に対し責任を負いながら、日本が大韓帝国国内に対して充分な権限を持たない限り、いつ深刻な国際問題に巻き込まれるかもしれないという状況を生み出してしまうからである。

　1905年11月22日、日本政府は大韓帝国と条約関係にある列強諸国に、日本の新しい政策を明確、率直に説明した宣言を公布した。

　　日本の安全と平和に密接に関連した理由で、日本が、その近接な関係から、大韓帝国の政治的・軍事的事情に最重要な関心と影響を行使することが必要になった。

　　これまでにとられた手段は純粋に助言をするものであったが、近年の体験から助言だけでは不充分であることが証明された。大韓帝国の、特に国際事情分野においての、思慮の足りない軽率な行動は過去において最も複雑な状況を作り上げる元となった。現在の不満足な状況の抑制も規制もしない状態を許してお

of complications. To permit the present unsatisfactory condition of things to continue unrestrained and unregulated would be to invite fresh difficulties, and Japan believes that she owes it to herself and to her desire for the general pacification of the extreme East to take the steps necessary to put an end once for all to this dangerous situation. Accordingly, with that object in view and in order at the same time to safeguard its own position and to promote the well-being of the government and people of Korea, the Imperial Government has resolved to assume a more intimate and direct influence and responsibility than heretofore in the external relations of the Peninsula. The Government of His Majesty the Emperor of Korea is in accord with the Imperial Government as to the absolute necessity of the measure, and the two Governments, in order to provide for the peaceful and amicable establishment of the new order of things, have concluded the accompanying compact. In bringing this agreement to the notice of the powers having treaties with Korea, the Imperial Government declares that in assuming charge of the foreign relations of Korea and in undertaking the duty of watching over the execution of the existing treaties of that country, they will see that those treaties are maintained and respected, and also engages not to prejudice in any way the legitimate commercial and industrial interests of those powers in Korea.

Both in respect of foreign and of internal affairs the new arrangement proved to be unsatisfactory. So far as reforming the Korean system of administration was concerned two circumstances combined to make the

くことは、更なる困難を引き起こし、日本は、日本のため、そして極東の全般的和平工作を望む理由から、この危険な状態を決定的に終わらせるのに必要な措置をとるのだと考えている。

　従って、この目的に鑑みて、また同時に、日本の立場を守り、韓国政府と人々の安寧を推進するため、日本帝国政府は朝鮮半島の対外関係において、従来よりもより親密で直接的な影響と責任を負う決意をした。

　朝鮮国王の政府は日本政府とこの政策の絶対的必要性について合意しており、両政府は新しい秩序を平和的、友好的に確立するため、添付の協定を結んだ。韓国と条約を結んでいる諸勢力にこの協定について通知することで、日本政府は、外交を管理し既存条約の実施を監督する義務を遂行するにあたり、諸勢力がそれらの条約が維持・順守されていることを見届けることを宣言し、諸勢力の合法な商業・産業権を害することはしない。

　この新しい取り決めは、内政、外交の両面で不満足なものであることがわかった。大韓帝国の行政改革は２つの状況が絡み合ってその施行を絶望的なものにしていた。まず、大韓帝国の官吏は各局で

114   DESCRIPTIVE AND HISTORICAL

task hopeless; the Korean officials were bound to listen to the advice of their Japanese advisers in the various departments, but they were not bound to follow it; and most of these officials were dishonest and grossly incompetent. The situation might have prolonged itself had it not been for a highly injudicious step taken by the Korean Emperor, in 1907, in direct violation of that article of the agreement of 1905 under which Korea pledged herself not to enter into any act of an international character, except through the medium of Japan. In July, 1907, there appeared at The Hague three Koreans who sought recognition as delegates to the Peace Conference, offering as their credentials a document bearing the seal of the Korean Emperor. When this news reached Japan it created a good deal of excitement, since it appeared to contain the threat that the whole Korean problem was about to be opened up again. Public opinion was seriously disturbed, and the press was almost unanimous in demanding a strong course of action. Such a course the Government decided to adopt.

At the time, Marquis Ito (a sincere friend and well-wisher of Korea) was Resident-General in Seoul. To him was sent Viscount Hayashi, the Japanese Minister of Foreign Affairs, with authority to act in the circumstances, after consultation with the Resident-General. He arrived in Seoul on July 18. During his service as Resident-General, Marquis Ito had reached the firm conviction that Korean affairs could never be put in any decent state of order as long as the throne was occupied by the Emperor, who had shown himself to be wholly untrustworthy, and who, moreover, had done everything possible to hinder the progress of internal reform. Fortunately there had recently been appointed a new Korean Cabinet, composed of men who saw clearly that unless the Emperor and his Court

日本人顧問の忠告を聞く義務があったが、それに従う義務はなかった。そして、これら官吏の殆どが不誠実で極めて無能であったのだ。そして、大韓帝国皇帝は1907年、日本政府の仲介なしでは国際的性質を有する行為や約束をしてはいけないと取り決めた第二次日韓協約に違反する行動に出た。しかし皇帝の極めて思慮のない行動がなければ、この状況は長引いていたかもしれない。1907年7月、ハーグ平和会議に特使と称する3人の朝鮮人が現れ、大韓帝国皇帝の印が押された文書を委任状として提出した。この知らせを聞いた大日本帝国は、朝鮮問題が再燃するのではないかと大いに動揺した。世論は多いに憤り、報道機関はほぼ一致して断固たる措置をとるべきだと主張した。そして日本政府は強硬措置に踏みきった。

　そのころ、伊藤博文公爵（朝鮮の友であり心からの支持者）がソウルにいた統監だった。日本の外務大臣の林子爵が、統監と協議の上、この状況に対処すべく、彼の下に送られた。林子爵がソウルに到着したのは7月18日であった。

　在任期間中、伊藤公爵は、国内改革の進展をありとあらゆる方法で妨害しようとする、全く信用の置けない韓国皇帝が王位に居座り続けるうちは朝鮮情勢は決して良い状況にはならないと確信していた。

　幸い、新しく任命された内閣は、皇帝と宮内府が政府に対し悪質な干渉をやめない限り、皇帝と王朝にも重大な結果が及ぶことはも

should cease their pernicious interference with the conduct of Government, it would be impossible to save the Imperial House from the most serious consequences. The present crisis put in the hands of the Cabinet a weapon which they were glad to employ in the general interest of the country. Even before the arrival of Viscount Hayashi the Cabinet had urged upon the Emperor the advisability of abdicating in favor of his son. The day after the Viscount's arrival their arguments prevailed; and on July 17, the Korean Minister of Justice carried to the Resident-General the Emperor's announcement of his abdication. Shortly after the matter became generally known there was serious rioting in Seoul, precipitated by a mutinous regiment of Korean troops.

After a series of conferences between the Japanese Representatives and the Korean Cabinet, and between the latter and the new Emperor, an agreement was signed between Japan and Korea on July 24, 1907.

This agreement left the Imperial Korean House still on the throne; but it placed Japan in practical control of the administration of the country, by making the appointment and dismissal of all high officials in Korea dependent upon the concurrence of the Resident-General, by providing for his previous assent to the enactment by the Korean Government of all laws, ordinances, and regulations, and by binding the Government to appoint as Korean officials any, Japanese subjects recommended by the Resident-General.

Having in view the general conditions of the country in the period after the new agreement, it is difficult to see how Japan could long postpone an act of annexation, unless she was prepared to face indefinitely the risks and inconveniences of an anomalous administrative system. A Treaty of

はや避けられないと理解していた。

　目下の危機に対し国益を守るため、内閣は進んで皇帝に引導を渡したのである。林子爵が到着する以前にすでに、内閣は皇帝に退位のやむなきを説き、皇帝の子息に譲位するよう迫った。子爵が到着した次の日、その主張が通り、7月17日、法務大臣は統監に皇帝退位の声明を届けた。皇帝退位の報が民衆の間に広まると、ソウルでは大暴動が発生し、それは暴動に加わった大韓帝国軍の隊によって拡大していった。

　日本政府代表と大韓帝国内閣、そして大韓帝国内閣と新帝との間で何度も協議した後、1907年7月24日、大日本帝国と大韓帝国の間に協定が結ばれた。

　この協定は李王室を残したが、主要な要職の任命と解雇は統監の同意によりなすこと、大韓帝国政府の全ての法律、法令、規則の制定は統監の前もった承認がいること、統監に推薦された日本の臣下を官吏として任命することなどにより日本を大韓帝国統治の実質的支配者の立場に置いた。

　新しい協定が結ばれた後の朝鮮の一般的状況を見ると、日本が特異な統治制度の抱える危険性と不都合な状況にずっと向き合う覚悟がない限り、併合を長く先送りすることは難しかったことが分かる。併合条約は両政府の間で交渉され、1910年8月22日に、子爵寺内

118   DESCRIPTIVE AND HISTORICAL

Annexation was negotiated between the two governments, and was signed
on August 22, 1910, by Viscount Masakata Terauchi, Resident-General,
and by Yi Wan Yong, Minister President of State.

In the first Annual Report compiled by the Government-General,
which succeeded the Residency-General, the subject of the annexation is
thus dealt with:

The Governments of both Japan and Korea, exerting for more
than four years, their utmost efforts in the way of administrative
reform, and looking forward to the consummation of the desired end,
the improvements and progress made were by no means small. But
they failed to find in the Protectorate régime sufficient guarantees
of the permanent welfare of the Imperial Family of Korea and of the
prosperity of the people.

In spite of the fact that a number of pacificatory measures with
regard to insurgents were put into effect, insurgents and brigands
continued to appear in certain localities, and could not be put down.
Escorts of police or gendarmes were often needed for officials,
individuals, and letter-carriers, travelling in the remote interior or
mountainous regions. Even a certain class of peaceful people, instigated
by reckless agitators, were led to believe that Japanese revenue
officers would carry away to Japan the money collected as taxes; and
thus, frequently, they attempted to do injury to these officials. In the
blindness of fury and inspired by shortsighted superstition and mistaken
patriotism, a band of Koreans assassinated Mr. Durham White Stevens,
a citizen of the United States, Councillor to the Korean Government, in

正毅統監と李完用首相によって調印された。

　統監府を引き継いだ總督府がまとめた最初の年次報告の中で、併合について以下のように書かれている。

　　日本と韓国の両政府は４年以上にもおよび統治改革に最大の努力を続け、希望する目的の成就を心待ちにし、そこで得られた改善と進歩は決して小さくはなかった。しかし、保護国政権の下では、韓国王家の永久的な繁栄と人々の幸福を充分に保障することは出来なかった。

　　暴徒に対しては数多くの融和的な措置が取られた事実にも拘らず、暴徒と盗賊はある地域に出没し続け、鎮圧することは出来なかった。人里離れた内部や山の多い地域を移動する官吏、個人、郵便配達人はよく警察や憲兵の護衛を必要とした。平和な人々の階級でさえも、無謀な扇動者に煽られて、日本の司税局の官吏が税金として集めたお金を日本に持ち去ると信じ込まされ、しばしばこれらの官吏に怪我を負わせようとした。激怒で物事が見えなくなり、短絡的な迷信と誤った愛国心に刺激された朝鮮人の一団が、1908年３月サンフランシスコで、休暇でワシントンへ向かっていた、大韓帝国外交顧問であるアメリカ人ダーラム・ホワイト・スティーブンス氏を暗殺した。

　　翌年10月には、6月まで統監を務めていた伊藤公爵が、北部

March, 1908, in San Francisco, on his way to Washington on furlough. In October of the following year, Prince Ito, who had filled the office of Resident-General in Korea till June, was also assassinated by a Korean in Harbin Station, when he was on a visit to North China. In the following December, a Korean further attempted to kill Mr. Yi Wan-Yong, the Prime Minister of the Korean Government. Thus distressing conditions still existed in Korea, and uneasiness and anxiety often kept the Imperial Family of that country in a state of misery, while the Ministers of State had to be constantly escorted by armed policemen.

In these conditions the Imperial Government failed to find in the régime of a Protectorate in Korea sufficient hope of realising the improvements which they had had in view, despite the fact that many reform measures had been introduced for the benefit of the Korean people. Stability of public peace and order not being firmly established yet, a spirit of suspicion and misunderstanding still dominated the whole Peninsula, and the mass of people were burdened with anxiety. Most of the Japanese and foreigners in Korea had to confine their residence to cities, ports, or towns along the railway lines and could not enter the interior to engage permanently in business.

In order to sweep away evils rooted during the course of many years as well as to secure the wel-being of the Korean Imperial Family, to promote the prosperity of the country, and at the same time to insure the safety and repose of Japanese and foreign residents, it had been made abundantly clear that, the Protectorate system being unable to achieve these aims, Korea must be annexed to the Empire and brought under the direct administration of the Imperial Government. There

中国へ訪問中にハルビン駅で朝鮮人によって暗殺された。同年
12月には、朝鮮人が首相の李完用の暗殺を試みた。それ故、大
韓帝国では苦悩に満ちた状態はまだ続いており、不安と心配が
頻繁に朝鮮王家を苦難の状態に陥れ、大臣はいつも武装した警
察官に護衛されなければならなかった。

　このような状態で、大日本帝国政府は、人々の利益の為に多
くの改革政策が導入されたにも拘らず、保護国政権の下では期
待していた改善を実現する充分な希望を持てなった。治安と秩
序の安定がまだしっかりと確立しない中、疑いの精神と誤解が
朝鮮半島全体を包んでおり、多くの人々が不安に苛まれていた。
国内にいる日本人と外国人のほとんどが住居を都市、港、鉄道
沿いの町に制限し、商売を永久的に行うため内部に移ることは
出来なかった。
　何年にも亘って根付いてしまった悪を取り除き朝鮮王家の幸
福を守る為、韓国の繁栄を守る為、そして同時に日本人と外国
人居住者の安全と安心を確実にする為、保護国体制ではこれら
の目的を果たすことが出来ないので、韓国は帝国に併合され帝
国政府の直接統治に置かれなくてはならないということが非常
に明確になった。
　この目的を達成する他の道筋がないので、日本は早くも1909

122   DESCRIPTIVE AND HISTORICAL

being no other way to attain the object in view, the Japanese conceived the policy of annexation as early as July, 1909. Even afterward the actual condition of affairs in Korea had continued to grow worse and worse, with no apparent hope of improvement. The assassinations of Mr. Stevens and Prince Ito, and the attempt to assassinate Premier Yi, mentioned already, induced certain classes of Koreans to tender to their Sovereign and the Resident-General a petition for annexation, so that the question became a matter of public agitation among officials as well as among the people of Japan. In fine the necessity of annexation grew day by day, and the measure was finally carried into effect on August 29, 1910.

That the aims set forth in the foregoing quotation have been pursued during the past sixteen years with a great, and in some directions with an astonishing measure of success is made evident in the body of the present volume. For the first nine years of the Government-General's existence Korea was administered under a system which, though it yielded many benefits for the Korean people, was applied with far too much military harshness and inflexibility. It was most unfortunate for everybody concerned that a rule of this character should have existed at the time when the extremely difficult and arduous work of organizing a new government was in progress. In such an undertaking the authorities could have found no more powerful ally than a spirit of friendliness among the people.

The measures taken to stamp out the Independence Movement of 1919, stupid, cruel, and unjustifiable as some of them undoubtedly were, accomplished their purpose. From that time onward Korea has enjoyed

年 7 月には併合政策を考えていた。その後も、韓国の実状態は悪くなる一方で、明らかな改善な見込みはなかった。前述のスティーブンス氏と伊藤公爵の暗殺、李首相の暗殺未遂に誘発されて、ある階級の朝鮮人達は国王と統監府に併合の嘆願書を提出したので、事態は日本の官吏と人々の間に同じ動揺をもたらしていった。結局併合の必要性は日に日に増し、ついに 1910 年 8 月 29 日に実行に移された。

　前述の引用で示された目標が、過去 16 年間で大きな、そして分野によっては、驚くべき成功をもたらしたことが本書で明らかにされている。總督府設立後の最初の 9 年間は、多くの利益を朝鮮民衆にもたらしたものの、軍の過度に厳しい統制下で統治されていた。新しい政府を組織するために非常に困難で努力を要する取組みがなされている時に、このような性質の統治がなされたことは関係者にとり最も残念なことであった。このような事業をなす時には、権力者にとって民衆の友好的な精神よりも力強い味方はなかったはずだ。

　1919 年の独立運動に対する強硬措置の中には、残酷で、道理に合わないものもあったが、その目的を果たしていた。その時から朝鮮は、過去の歴史にはなかった平和と発展を満喫しているのである。

a period of internal tranquillity and of general progress for which the previous history of the country affords no remotest parallel.

Of the Independence Movement itself I have little to say in the present connection. The Independence Party contained many Koreans of excellent intelligence and education, inspired by a deep nationalist feeling. Whether or not the Japanese administration of the country had been so conducted as to justify an attempt to subvert it has no bearing upon the "right" of the Koreans to make the attempt. The "right" of revolt is inherent wherever Government exists, whether that government is of native origin or has been imposed from without.

Whenever such revolts occur those who take part in them fall into three groups—one is made up of men and women profoundly convinced that success will result in benefit to the general welfare, and who have no aim other than this; one contains those who, from selfish motives of personal advantage, wish to substitute themselves for those then in power; one is a nondescript rabble which welcomes the opportunity of fishing in troubled waters. Those who belong to the first group deserve and usually receive the respect which mankind pays to those who offer their lives and their property in support of an honestly held conviction; and of these sincere patriots the Korean Independence Movement contained an unusually large proportion.

It seems to me that there is absolutely no possibility of Korean Independence being reached by the road of revolt. The Koreans cannot drive the Japanese out of the country; and if the cause of Korean Independence were espoused by any nation powerful enough to create a serious threat to the Japanese occupancy, the first move made to carry out

第二章　朝鮮の描写と歴史　　125

　独立運動自体に関してはここで言うことはあまりない。独立派に
は深い民族感情に衝き動かされた、優れた知性と教養のある多くの
朝鮮人が参加していた。日本の朝鮮統治が国家転覆の試みを正当化
するほどのものであろうがなかろうが、朝鮮人の「権利」とは何も
関係がない。体制への反乱の「権利」は、その政府が自国のものであっ
ても、外部から押し付けられたものであっても、政府が存在すると
ころではどこにでも本質的にあるものだからだ。

　このような反乱が起こる時、これに参加する者は３つのグループ
に分けることが出来る。まずは反乱の成功が人々に福利をもたらす
と深く信じて疑わず、その目的遂行のために参加する男女のグルー
プ。次に、権力者に替わり自分自身が権威の座に就きたいという、
個人の利益を追求する自己中心的な動機で参加するグループ。残り
は、単に漁夫の利を得たいという暴徒の群れである。最初のグルー
プに属する者は、誠実なる信念を守るために自己の生命財産を差し
出す者に対して人々が抱く尊敬の念に値し、また普通その尊敬を受
けるのであるが、朝鮮独立運動参加者の多くがこうした誠実な愛国
者であった。

　反抗の道を突き進んだとしても、朝鮮独立へと到達する可能性は
絶対にないように私には見える。朝鮮人は日本人を追い出すことは
出来ない。そして、もし朝鮮独立の大義が、日本の占領を深刻に脅
かすほどの力を持った国によって支持されたなら、一触即発の状況
を生み出し、必ずや一夜にしてアジアを戦争の渦に巻き込むだろう。
さらには世界のパワーバランスが崩れ、１カ月以内には世界大戦が

that threat would, without question, plunge Asia into war overnight, and would bring most of the balance of the world into the struggle within a month. There is one possibility, and one only, of an independent Korea. If at some future time the League of Nations, or some similar Association of Powers, should prescribe a universal surrender of all colonial dependencies to their native inhabitants, Korea would be one of Japan's contributions to the general settlement. Such a possibility is, of course, too remote to call for present discussion.

I found informed opinion both in Korea and in Japan divided on the question of what, short of independence, would be the ultimate status of the Peninsula. Two theories held the field—one that it will become an integral part of the Japanese political system, sending elected representatives to the Imperial Diet; the other that it will eventually be given Dominion home-rule within the Japanese Empire.

Speaking as a person in whom the idea of Korean Independence incites neither mental nor moral resistance I may express my belief that those Koreans will be doing their country the greatest service who co-operate with the Japanese in building up the cultural and economic conditions favorable on the one hand to the granting, and on the other to the successful use, of local self-government.

During the past year the news from Korea justifies the hope that a trend in this direction has already set in. To whatever extent it exists the credit is due chiefly to the humane and conciliatory attitude of Governor-General Saito toward the Korean people, and to the wise measures which, for more than six years, have been the fruit of an unstinting employment of his unusual energy and of his still more unusual administrative talents.

勃発するだろう。朝鮮独立の可能性は１つ、いや、ただ１つだけある。もし、将来において、国際連盟や、それに類似した連合が、世界中の植民地属国をその原住民に引き渡すことを命じたならば、朝鮮は日本が紛争解決に貢献した１つの証となるだろう。もちろん今この様な可能性を論じてもあまりにも現実味がないだろう。

　私は消息通の間で意見が二分していることに気付いた。朝鮮に於いても日本に於いても、朝鮮半島の最終的な立場—完全な独立はなくても—はどうなるのかという質問に対して、２つの意見が幅を利かせているようだ。１つは、選ばれた代表を大日本帝国議会に送り、日本国に同化するという意見。もう１つは、大日本帝国の枠組みの中で朝鮮は、自治領という形で統治権を与えられるであろうという意見である。

　朝鮮独立に心理的に、また道徳的にも抵抗を感じない者として意見を述べると、自治の獲得に向け、また自治体として成功するためにも、日本人と協力して文化的、経済的にも有利な状況を築き上げる朝鮮人たちは、自国のために大きな貢献をしていると私は信じている。

　昨年朝鮮から伝わって来た情報によれば、この国が既にこの方向に動いているのではないかという希望的観測は、どうやら正しいようである。それがどの程度であっても、それは齋藤總督の、朝鮮の人々に対する思いやりのある融和的な姿勢と、また６年以上に亘り並はずれた気力と、かつ極めて優れた行政手腕を惜しみなく発揮した賢明なる政策の賜物であると言える。

CHAPTER III

第三章

CHAPTER III

SUMMARY

The internal administration of Korea has, for many years, been a matter of earnest solicitude to the Japanese. The dangers and annoyances associated with corrupt and grossly inefficient rule in a country whose southern coast-line is within a few hours' steaming from Japan will be obvious to those who have had occasion to study the causes of the Spanish-American War, and to those who, today, are hoping to see Mexico develop in such a way as to encourage the most cordial relations with the United States.

There exists, indeed, a certain type of mind to which the contagion of misrule conveys no threat to domestic tranquillity on the other side of a frontier, to which the circumstances of American territorial expansion, and of the extension of British rule in India, teach no lesson. Intelligent observers, however, are aware that bad government can be as poor a neighbor as bad health, that social unrest can cross a boundary line as readily as small-pox or yellow fever, that the "land-grabbing" of the English-speaking races, which followed the original conquest or settlement was due in large measure to the necessity of bringing within the national sovereignty a neighbor who, for one reason or another, was a menace to the national welfare.

In the case of Korea the menace to Japan arose from two main causes—first, that centuries of misrule had reduced the Korean people to a condition from which it was hopeless to expect that, through a popular

第三章

概論

　朝鮮半島の国内政治は、日本人にとって、長年に亘り極めて憂慮すべき問題であった。日本から汽船に乗って数時間あまりで行ける国。そこでの汚職や、低迷する政治がはらんでいる危険性と問題点については、米西戦争の原因を調査してきた研究者達や、メキシコがアメリカと友好的な方向へと発展出来るよう望んでいる者達にとっては明白に理解出来ることであろう。

　ある国での失政の悪影響が国境を挟んだ隣国の平穏に何の脅威にもならないと考えている者、つまりアメリカの領土拡大やイギリスのインド統治から何も学ぼうとしない者もいることは確かである。しかし聡明な者なら次のことを観て取るだろう。悪政が伝染病のように劣悪な隣人となり得ること。社会不安は天然痘や黄熱病のように簡単に国境を越えて伝染する可能性があること。また英語圏の人種によって行われてきた征服・植民そして「土地の略奪」は、多くは必要性から始まったものであるということ。つまり自分達の国益を脅かす隣人を自国の統治権内に置く必要があったということだ。

　朝鮮の場合、日本にとって脅威となった原因は2つある。第1には過去数世紀に亘る失政である。内政改革を通して独立を維持するに足る富と力を持ち国家としての体裁を整えようとする希望など断

demand for internal reform, Korea might lift itself into the rank of a State having sufficient wealth and sufficient power to maintain its independence; second, and as a consequence of the first, that, either by force or by guile, Russia or China might take possession of the Peninsula, thus creating a strategic situation which could not be tolerated by any person or party responsible for the national defence of Japan.

All available evidence tends to prove that for many years Japanese policy toward Korea was concerned chiefly with securing for that country the position of an independent sovereign State, and for herself the acceptance by the great powers of the principle that Japan's interest in Korean affairs was to be considered predominant, in the sense that England's special interest in Egypt, and that of the United States in Latin America, had received tacit recognition in the world's chancelleries.

In support of the first conception Japan declared war on China in 1894 and, in the Treaty of Shimoneseki, exacted the renunciation of China's suzerainty over Korea and the acknowledgment of that country's independence. In defence of the second conception Japan, having in view the Russian occupation of Vladivostok and of Port Arthur, the conversion of these places into two of the most formidable fortresses in existence, the extension of the Trans-Siberian Railway to the Korean frontier, and the persistent Russian intrigues in Manchuria and in Korea itself, fought the Russo-Japanese War, 1904-1905.

At the conclusion of the War Japan decided that in the interest of Korea, in her own interest, and in the general interest of peace and progress in the Far East, her power to influence the Government of Korea in respect of administrative reform, which had hitherto depended upon diplomatic

念するほど追い詰められた状況だった。第2の原因は、第1の原因の結果として生じたものだが、ロシアや清が力や策略によって朝鮮半島を占領し、日本の国家防衛にとって許しがたい戦略的状況を作り出してしまう可能性があったことであった。

　あらゆる状況が証明しているように、日本の長年に亘る対朝鮮政策は、まず第1に朝鮮の独立国家としての地位を保証することを主眼としていた。そして第2に、他の列強に対して、朝鮮の問題に関しては原則的に日本の権益が優先されることを認めさせようとしていた。すなわち、イギリスやアメリカが自国の国益のためにエジプトやラテンアメリカで特別な権益を持つことを世界から暗黙のうちに承認されていたようにである。

　第1の点は、日本は1894年に清に宣戦布告し、下関条約で清に対し、朝鮮の宗主権を放棄し独立を認めるよう強要していることで証明された。第2の点は、満州と朝鮮への執拗な陰謀を企てていたロシアに対して、1904年から1905年まで日露戦争を戦ったことで証明された。当時ロシアはウラジオストクと旅順を占領して、この2つを現存する最も恐るべき要塞に変えていた。またシベリア横断鉄道は朝鮮国境まで延長されていたのである。

　戦争の結果日本が導き出した結論とは、朝鮮の国益、自国の国益、並びに極東の平和と繁栄という普遍的利益においては、統監府を設置することによってのみ朝鮮政府に対し影響力を行使することが出来るということだ。朝鮮政府は行政改革において、これまで外交手

procedure and upon the activities of several Japanese advisers in various departments, could be made effective only by establishing a Residency-General somewhat after the pattern of that set up by the British in the Federated Malay States, a system which had yielded the most beneficial results. This was done in 1905, and had the practical effect of making Korea a Japanese Protectorate. Under the original arrangement the results of the new policy were unsatisfactory, because it was not mandatory upon the Korean officials to follow the advice of the Resident-General. This situation was remedied in 1907 by the conclusion of a Convention between Korea and Japan, under the terms of which the Government of Korea "shall follow the direction of the Resident-General in connection with the reform of the administration" and "shall not enact any law or ordinance, or carry out any important administrative measure, except with the previous approval of the Resident-General."

Three years' experience under the new system showed that it could not be operated successfully in face of the hostility, of the indifference, incompetence, or dishonesty of the Korean officials. In Korea, as elsewhere, divided authority and responsibility—the method of diarchy—led to little but social unrest and administrative impotence. Accordingly, under the terms of a Treaty signed on August 22, 1910, by the plenipotentiaries of the two countries, the Emperor of Korea made complete and permanent cession to the Emperor of Japan of all rights of sovereignty over the whole of Korea. A week later the Emperor of Japan issued an Imperial Rescript announcing the annexation and ordering the establishment of the office of Governor-General of Korea. From August 29, 1910 Japan has had full responsibility for, and full power in, the

続きと、様々な分野での日本人顧問の活動などを頼みにしてきたが、朝鮮に及ぼす日本の影響力は、マレー連合州にイギリスが設けたような統監府、つまり最も有益な結果をもたらしてきたシステムに倣うことで行使されうると決断したのだった。こうして統監府が1905年に設立され、朝鮮は実際に日本の保護国になったのである。当初の取り決めの下では新しい政策の結果は満足のいくものではなかった。なぜならば、朝鮮の官吏に対する統監の勧告には強制力がなかったからである。この状況は1907年に日韓協定が締結されたことで改善された。朝鮮政府は条項に基づき、行政改革に関し統監の指導を受けること、統監の事前の承認がなければ、いかなる法律や法令も制定してはならず、いかなる重要な行政処分も実施してはならないとされたからである。

　新システムでの3年間に亘る経験で分かったことは、朝鮮人官吏の反感、無関心さ、無能さ、不正に直面しては、改革は上手くいかないということである。朝鮮では、他の国と同様に、権威者と責任者が分裂していた。そのような両頭政治体制で社会不安や行政の無力さを導いたのだった。そこで1910年8月22日、二国間の全権大使によって調印された条約の下、大韓帝国皇帝は日本の天皇に、朝鮮全土の統治権の完全かつ恒久的な譲渡を行った。1週間後に、日本の天皇は日韓併合と朝鮮總督府の設立を命ずる勅令を発表した。1910年8月29日から日本は朝鮮の行政に全責任と全権を担ったのである。

administration of Korea.

The Japanese proclamations issued at the time of the annexation were couched in conciliatory language, and the measures adopted when the transfer of authority was effected were well calculated to mollify public sentiment. The imperial house of Korea was liberally provided for, its dignity was preserved by granting to the ex-emperor and to other members of the imperial family the same privileges and honors enjoyed by princes of the imperial blood in Japan, peerages were conferred upon a number of Korean nobles.

An imperial donation of thirty million yen (fifteen million dollars U.S.) was made by the Emperor of Japan, of which about one third was bestowed upon Korean noblemen, meritorious public servants, scholars, indigent widows, widowers, orphans, and others, the balance, of something over seventeen million yen, being set aside as a permanent fund of which the annual interest was to be devoted to giving various forms of aid to Koreans. If the imperial donation to Korea was only equal to three-quarters of that which the United States had paid in respect of the cession of the Philippine Islands, it should not be overlooked that the American money went to the Spanish Government, whereas the Japanese Donation went to the Korean people.

The problems confronting the Government-General of Korea were neither few nor simple. The purpose of the Japanese was to set up a thoroughly modern administrative system, to develop the natural resources of the country, and to foster trade and industry. The road to success was encumbered with every imaginable obstacle. The whole machinery of administration had to be planned, a complete civil service had to be

併合の際に発表された日本の声明文は宥和的な表現で書かれており、国家権力の譲渡が行われたときに採択された政策は朝鮮国民の感情を和らげられるようによく考えられていた。朝鮮王室の維持のため充分な歳費が与えられ、元王とその一族には日本の皇族が享受したのと同じ特権と名誉を認めることによってその威信も維持された。また、貴族の称号が多くの朝鮮の上流層の人々に与えられた。

日本の天皇からは3000万円（1500万ドル）の恩賜金が贈られたが、そのうちの約3分の1は朝鮮の貴族、功績のある官吏、学者、経済的に恵まれない未亡人や孤児などに贈与された。残りの1700万円余りはその利子によって朝鮮の人々を様々な形で援助出来るような恒久的な資金として蓄えられた。

日本の皇室から朝鮮への寄付が、米国がフィリピン諸島の購入の際に支払った金額の4分の3にしか相当しないとしても、米国の資金がスペイン政府に支払われたのに対して、日本の寄付は朝鮮の国民に贈られたものであることを看過すべきでない。

朝鮮總督府が直面している問題は、数が少ないわけでも、問題の質が単純なわけでもない。日本人の目的は、あくまでも近代的な行政システムを作り、朝鮮の天然資源を開発し、貿易と産業を促進させることであった。しかし、その成功への道は、まさに苦難の道のりであった。行政機構の立案、完全なる官制の設立、多数の技術専

created, a large staff of technical experts had to be engaged, a financial system had to be devised capable of yielding the revenue essential for the carrying out of the government's policy.

The situation presented but one favorable circumstance, the docile character of the mass of the Korean people. There was not, at the time of annexation, nor has there since arisen, any ground for serious anxiety on the part of the Japanese military authorities. It is, therefore, difficult for a foreign observer to understand why the Japanese Government should have made the rule that the Governor-General of Korea could only be appointed from the roster of officers of the army or navy. Experience proved that in this matter a serious mistake in policy had been made, and in 1919 the restriction was removed, the appointment being thrown open to civilians.

The selection of military officers for colonial governorships has been a common practice both of the Dutch and the British; but it is an objectionable procedure. History furnishes, indeed, instances in which the talent for conducting military enterprises has been combined with the talent for civil administration; but such instances are extremely rare. The task of administering the affairs of a colonial dependency is one which calls for a temperament totally different from that which goes to the making of a good military man. The success of a military commander, sound technical knowledge being assumed, will depend upon the extent to which he enforces discipline and exacts compliance with thousands of precise and inflexible regulations; his duties are to issue orders and to see that they are obeyed without argument or protest; he need give no thought to the feelings engendered by his administration.

A civil administrator, on the other hand, can only succeed if he adopts

門家の雇用、そして財政システムは政府の政策を実行していくのに不可欠な歳入をもたらすことが出来るように工夫されなければならなかった。

　唯一好ましいと思える状況は、大多数の朝鮮人が従順であったことだ。日韓併合時も、その後も、日本の軍部指導者の側には何の不安材料もなかったのである。であるから、外国人の目には、日本政府が朝鮮總督を軍幹部からのみ任命することは不可解なことのように見えた。しかし、経験を重ねるとその方針の間違いが明らかとなり、1919年にはその制約が取り除かれて文民からも広く登用されるようになった。

　軍幹部が植民地の長官に選ばれるのは、オランダや英国にもよくある慣習であったが、問題もあった。歴史の中に、軍事的な任務遂行能力と民政を行う能力を併せ持った人物の例を見つけることは出来る。しかしそれは極めて稀である。植民地統治には、優秀な軍人に必要な気質とは全く異なるものが要求される。軍人は適切な専門知識を備えるのは当然として、どこまで軍の規律を励行しうるか、どこまで厳格に軍規を遵守させられるかが、軍司令官として成功する鍵になる。彼の職務は、命令を発し、異議や抗議の余地を生むことなく従わせることである。つまり彼は自分の統治によってどんな感情が発生するかを考慮する必要はないのである。

　一方、文民行政者はギブ アンド テイクの方針をとり、歩み寄り

a policy of give and take, and carries it out in a spirit of compromise. A large proportion of his work is constructive in its nature, and needs, for its fruition, the goodwill of the people. What is necessary above all things is that the administrator's rule should bear the impress of urbanity and conciliation—the two qualities least to be expected in a military man.

From 1910 to 1919 Japanese rule in Korea, though it accomplished much good for the people, bore the stamp of a military stiffness which aroused a great deal of resentment, hampered the progress of reform, and was largely responsible for the discontent which culminated in the proclamation of Korean Independence by the leaders of the Korean nationalists on March 1, 1919.

The merciless severity with which the revolt was repressed shocked the public sentiment of the world. In Japan itself the indignation reached such a height that the government was compelled to find means of appeasing it. The Governor-General of Korea was recalled, the rule excluding civilians from eligibility for that post was canceled, the new Governor-General, Admiral Baron Saito (now Viscount), though not a civilian, was recognized throughout the Far East as a man of high administrative ability, of generous and humane disposition, and of great personal charm.

The New Korea of which I write is the Korea which has developed under the wise and sympathetic guidance of Governor-General Saito. I may quote here a few paragraphs of an article by Bishop Herbert Welch, Resident Bishop, in the Korean capital, of the Methodist Episcopal Church. The article appeared in *The Christian Advocate of May 13, 1920,* and the

第三章　概論　　　141

の精神で実行した場合にのみ、成功出来るのである。その仕事は性質上、建設的な部分が多くを占めており、その実現のためには人々の善意を必要とする。とりわけ必要なのは、その統治に優雅さと調停能力を併せ持つことである。この2つの性質は軍人には最も期待出来ないものだ。

　1910年から1919年までの日本統治は、人々の数多くの善政を施してきたにも拘わらず、軍事面での頑なさが滲み出ており、その行動が人々の間に敵意を生じさせ、改革の進展の妨げとなった。そして、1919年3月1日、朝鮮の民族主義者たちの指導者による独立宣言で頂点に達した不満の大きな原因となったのである。

　軍部の無慈悲なまでの厳格さによってこの反乱が鎮圧されたことは世界にショックを与えた。日本国民の怒りも激しく、政府はそれを鎮める方法を見つけることを余儀なくされた。朝鮮總督は召還され、その地位に就く資格から文民を排除するという決まりは無効となった。新しく總督になった齋藤 實男爵（現 子爵）は、元海軍大将で文民ではないが、極東中で、行政能力に優れ、寛大で慈悲深い気質を持ち、人柄も大変魅力的な人物として知られていた。

　本書は、齋藤朝鮮總督の賢明で思いやりのある指揮の下に発展してきた新しい朝鮮について語っている。私はここに、メソジスト監督教会で全ソウル駐在監督であるハーバート・ウェルチ監督の記事から2、3の文章を引用しよう。この記事は、1920年5月13日の

142   SUMMARY

quotation derives particular significance from the circumstance that Bishop Welch has always been an outspoken critic of everything he has deemed to be blameworthy in the Japanese administration of Korea.

Referring to Baron Saito's assumption of the Governor-Generalship, Bishop Welch says:

A sharp contrast at once became evident with the methods and spirit of the preceding administration. The Governor-General himself was simple and unaffected in manner, genial, approachable, evidently anxious to know and to propitiate foreign opinion in the country. His advent was marked by the speedy disappearance of countless swords and uniforms. . . . His chief associate, Dr. R. Midzuno, the Administrative Superintendent, an official of high standing and wide executive experience, seemed to share with the Governor to a large degree the ideals of simplicity, directness and the permeation of the government activities by the civilian as contrasted with the military spirit. . . .

Meanwhile, on the Korean side the past year has unquestionably brought a further crystallization of opinion which is hostile to any Japanese government. The minds of many are fixed on complete national independence as the only goal, and they declare that they have no interest whatever in the question of reforms by the present or any Japanese administration. On the other hand many, including some of the most intelligent and far-seeing, are persuaded that there is no hope of speedy independence, and that they must settle down for

"The Christian Advocate" に掲載された。ウェルチ監督は、日本の朝鮮統治に関し非難するべきことがあれば、その都度、率直に批評してきた人物であるから、以下に紹介する内容は注目に値する。

　齋藤男爵の總督就任に言及して、ウェルチ監督は以下のように述べている。

　　就任早々、齋藤總督の統治方法と精神は、前政権と際立った対照を見せていた。總督自身は気さくでその物腰には気どりがなく、愛想が良くて親しみやすかったし、国内における外国世論の動向に注意を払い和解しようとしていたのが明らかだった。彼の着任とともに、總督府から軍事色が素早く消えて行った。彼の側近である政務総監の水野錬太郎博士は幅広い行政経験を持つ高官であった。また軍人魂とは対照的に、文民政治の理想は「素朴さ」「率直さ」「浸透性の良さ」であるとする總督と、その姿勢を大いに共有しているようだ。

　　一方朝鮮世論は、明らかに前年の事件で日本統治への敵意を更にむき出しにしている。多くの者が完全な国家独立が唯一の理想であると信じ込み、現政権を含め、日本主導のいかなる行政改革にも全く興味はないと彼らは言明するのである。その一方で、現時点での独立は望むべくもなく、長期に亘り腰を据えて、朝鮮国民の健康状態、知識、道徳性および行政能力を育て上げるべきであると確信する者も、一部の最も知的で先見の明

a long period to build up the Korean people, in physical conditions, in knowledge, in morality, and in the ability to handle government concerns. . . .

It must be fully recognized that the Japanese government has by no means as yet won the hearts of the Korean people; rather they are further off from that today than fifteen months ago. . . . On the other hand, there are elements of decided encouragement. One of these I find in the character of the Governor-General, Admiral Baron Saito himself. He came to Korea last September with the possibility in his thought of declaring a general political amnesty — wiping the political slate clean and making a new start on the basis of a liberal and humane policy. He was met at the railway station in Seoul by a bomb thrown by the hand of a fanatic, an action which was promptly disavowed by representative Koreans, yet which could not but affect somewhat one's view of the situation.

Baron Saito, however, instead of taking a strong hand, as some would have justified him in doing under those circumstances, has continued of mild and friendly temper. I have implicit trust in his sincerity, and I believe that with time enough he will show the strength, even in spite of the difficulties which confront him in Korea, and of the backfire of criticism and opposition from the militaristic and bureaucratic groups in Tokyo, to bring to pass large things for the welfare of the Korean people. . . .

The foregoing paragraphs were written in 1920, when Governor-General

がある人たちを含め多数いたのである。

　日本政府はまだ決して朝鮮国民の気持ちをつかんだわけではなく、むしろ15カ月前よりも現在の方が、人々の気持ちが離れてしまっていることを肝に銘じるべきである。その一方で好材料も確実にあるのである。そのうちの1つを、私は海軍大将、齋藤男爵自身の性格の中に見出している。9月に赴任してきた時点で、彼は全面的な政治的な恩赦を宣言しようと考えていた。つまり過去の政治を水に流して自由で慈悲深い政策を基礎に新しいスタートを切ろうとしていたのである。齋藤男爵はソウル駅で狂信者の手により爆弾を投げつけられた。朝鮮の代表者たちは即座に関与を否定したが、そのような目に遭えば多少なりとも影響されないわけはなかった。

　そのような状況であれば強硬な態度をとっても正当化されると主張する人々もいるだろうが、齋藤男爵は高圧的な態度をとる代わりに、寛大で友好的な姿勢をとり続けた。私は彼の誠実さに絶対的信頼を寄せている。朝鮮で多くの難問に直面しようが、東京の軍や官僚からの非難と反対の集中砲火を浴びようとも、彼は持ち前の強靭さで、時間をかけ、朝鮮の人々の幸福のために大きな事を成し遂げるだろうと私は信じている。

以上のウェルチ監督の文章は1920年、齋藤總督が朝鮮に着任し

Saito had only been a few months in the country. At the time of my own visit to Korea, in 1922, the Governor-General had nearly completed three years of his tenure of office. He had latterly had the advantage of having as Vice-Governor-General, or Administrative Superintendent (the two titles appear to be used indiscriminately in the official documents) Mr. T. Ariyoshi, one of Japan's most expert and highly regarded civil administrators— a man whom, from my own observation, I know to be a tireless worker and sympathetic toward the Korean people.

The general consensus of opinion in Korea in 1922, except in so far as it reflected the feelings of the anti-Japanese extremists, was that Governor-General Saito had been animated by a sincere desire to rule Korea through a just and tolerant administration, that he had accomplished notable reforms, that in the matter of education he had ministered very generously to the cultural ambitions of the people, and that in regard to their political ambitions he had, whilst setting his face sternly against anything which could encourage the vain hope of independence, shown himself eager to foster local self-government, and to infuse into the personal relations of the Japanese and Koreans a spirit of friendliness and cooperation.

Discussing Korean affairs with a good many people — Korean, Japanese, and foreign, official and non-official — I found almost unanimous agreement on two points: one, that native sentiment had, in recent years, shown a continuing tendency to become less anti-Japanese; the other, that the remarkable increase in the country's prosperity had been accompanied by a striking improvement in the living conditions of the Korean people at large.

Writing now, four years after the date of my visit, and having in mind

てまだ数カ月の頃に書かれたものである。私が朝鮮を訪れたのは1922年で、彼は3年間の任期をほとんど終えようとしていた。總督が後に副總督あるいは政務総監（この2つの官位は公文書では区別されず使われるようだ）として有吉忠一氏を迎えたのは好都合なことであった。有吉氏は日本で最も専門的知識があり評判の高い文官の一人で、私個人の見解では、仕事熱心で、朝鮮の人々に対して思いやりのある人物である。

　1922年の朝鮮においては、反日の過激論者を除けば、斉藤總督に対する世間一般の評価は次のようであった。總督は、公明正大で寛容な施政により朝鮮を統治しようという真摯な思いで生き生きしていた。そして、彼は卓越した改革を成し遂げた。教育の問題においては、実に惜しみなく人々の教養に対する意欲に力を貸し、政治的野心については、無益に独立を望む気持ちを助長するものは如何なるものにも断固反対する一方、熱心に地方自治を促進し、日本人と朝鮮人の関係に友好と協力の精神をしみ込ませようとしていたのである。

　私は朝鮮事情について多くの人と話し合ってきた。朝鮮人、日本人、外国人、官民の両サイドの人々であったが、2つの点については、ほとんど同意見であった。1つには、朝鮮の国民感情としては、近年、反日感情は収まっていく傾向が続くということ。もう1つの点は、国家が著しく繁栄したことは朝鮮人全般の生活状況に著しい改善を伴ったということであった。

　朝鮮に来て4年経った今、こうして書いていて、最近の朝鮮事情

148   SUMMARY

the most recent accounts of the state of Korea, I can express my conviction that there has occurred a steady and accelerating improvement in the general conditions of the country, in the administrative organization and personnel, and in the temper of the intercourse between the Koreans and the Japanese.

In the following pages I present a brief summary, under specific heads, of the salient features of Korean progress from the time of annexation down to the date of the latest available information. With reference to statistics it is to be noted that the official fiscal year begins on April 1 and ends on March 31 of the year following. The unit of money is the yen, which has a par value of fifty cents, U. S., fluctuating, however, with the movement of the foreign exchange market.

を考慮に入れても、国全体の状況や、行政組織とその人事を見ても、朝鮮人と日本人の関係性は、着実にそして加速度的に改善されてきていると私は確信を持っている。

　以下に私は、特定の項目について、併合時から最新の情報に至るまで、朝鮮の発展の目覚ましい特徴についての短い要約を示すこととする。なお統計に関しては、正式な会計年度は4月1日から翌年の3月31日であることに注意して欲しい。また通貨の単位は1円であり、為替平価は米ドルの50セントと価値が同じではあるが、外国為替市場の動きで変動する。

150   SUMMARY

Material Progress

Production--

About eighty-two per cent of the total population of Korea depend directly upon agriculture for their livelihood. The area under cultivation increased from about 10,600,000 acres in 1912 to nearly 15,000,000 in 1923.* During the same period the estimated value of agricultural produce rose from 435,000,000 yen to 1,169,000,000 yen. A considerable proportion of the increases noted above was due to measures taken by the Government for improving the condition of the farmers. Among these may be named organization of various forms of agricultural credit, the reclamation of waste lands, the construction of irrigation works, the improvement of farming methods, and the introduction of new agricultural industries.

In respect of the first of these measures it may be noted that in 1912 the amount of outstanding agricultural loans was less than five million yen, and in 1923 was more than 134 million yen, a large part of the increase representing investment in agricultural improvements of one sort and another. As an instance of the introduction of new industries silk culture is an example. In 1910 the total value of Korean sericultural products was only 400,000 yen; in 1923 it had risen to nearly 26 million yen.

Closely associated with agriculture is forestry. Under native rule there had been an almost complete neglect of forest conservation, so that at the time of annexation there was a serious shortage of fire-wood and of

---

* When two or more crops are raised in one year on the same land the area is counted for each crop.

物質的発展

生産

　朝鮮の人口の約82パーセントは生計を農業に直接的に依存している。耕作面積は、1912年では約1060万エーカー（約4万2900平方キロ）であったものが、1923年には1500万エーカー（約6万平方キロ）近くにまで増加した。* 同時期、農産物の推定原価は4億3500万円から11億6900万円に上がった。上記に記された増加の大部分は、農家の状態を改善するために政府がとった対策に負うものである。これらの対策とは、農業金融の組織化、荒地の開拓、灌漑の工事、農法の改善、新しい農産業の導入が挙げられるだろう。

　1番目の対策については、1912年の時点で未償還の農業の貸し付け金額は500万円未満であったが、1923年には1億3400万円以上となり、増加の大部分が農業の様々な改良のための投資であった。新しい産業の導入例としては養蚕が挙げられる。1910年、朝鮮の養蚕の生産物の合計額は40万円にすぎなかったが、1923年は約2600万円まで増加した。

　農業と密接に関わっているのが林業である。従来の統治では森林の保護はほとんど無視されてきたので、併合時には薪や建築用材の

---

* 2種以上の作物が同じ年に同じ土地で栽培される場合、その面積はそれぞれの作物のものとして加算される。

building lumber. What was even worse was that the denuded mountain sides could no longer absorb the heavy rainfall of the wet season. This resulted in serious annual floods and in the loss of the land's natural supply of moisture. As early as 1907 the Japanese Residency-General had induced the Korean Government to undertake afforestation work; and in 1911 the Government-General issued its new forestry regulations. In the same year the Governor-General established an Arbor Day. Since annexation more than a thousand million seedlings have been planted for the purpose of re-establishing the Korean forests. The Government, further, encouraged the formation of Forestry Associations, and of these there were in 1925 three hundred and fifty, with a total membership of nearly a million.

The Government also interested itself in the development of the Korean fisheries. Measures were taken to improve the methods of fishing and of curing and packing aquatic products. Between 1912 and 1921 the value of the catch increased from eight million to forty-five million yen; the value of the exports of fresh fish from 138 thousand to over seven million yen; the value of marine products manufactured, from four million to twenty-five million yen; and the value of manufactured marine products exported, from less than two million yen to more than eleven million.

In the mining industry the total output was valued in 1912 at nearly seven million yen and in 1921 at over fifteen million yen. In the main group of metals and minerals the gold production shows a decline in value, other production a marked increase. Coal mounted from something over 500,000 yen to a little over three million, iron ore from 156,000 to nearly two million, pig iron from nothing to nearly five million, concentrates from 275,000 to nearly five million.

深刻な不足があった。さらに悪いことには、はげ山の斜面がもはや雨季の大量の雨水を保水出来なくなってしまっていたということである。その結果、毎年深刻な洪水被害が起き、土壌の水分供給能力に不足が生じた。早くは1907年に於いて、日本の統監府は大韓帝国政府に対して植林に着手するよう勧めており、1911年に總督府は新しい造林規定を発表した。また、同年に總督は植樹祭を制定した。併合以来10億以上もの苗が、朝鮮の森林を再生させる目的で植えられてきた。政府はさらに森林組合の結成を促進して、1925年にはこれらのうちの350の組合で総会員数がほぼ100万人となった。

　總督府はまた漁業にも関心を示した。漁法の改良、水産物の保存および包装方法の改良が行われた。1912年と1921年の漁獲金額を比較すると800万円から4500万円へ増加、鮮魚の輸出金額は13万8000円から700万円以上に増加した。加工海産物の金額は400万円から2500万円に増加し、輸出された加工海産物の金額は200万円未満から1100万円以上に増加した。

　鉱業では総生産高の評価額は1912年にはほぼ700万円だったが、1921年には1500万円以上になった。主な金属と鉱物では金の生産量は減ったが、それ以外は著しい増加を示した。石炭は約50万円強から300万円強に、鉄鉱石は15万6000円から約200万円へ、銑鉄は0円から約500万円へ、精鉱は27万5000円から約500万円となった。

154   SUMMARY

In regard to manufactures, commerce and industry progress was
seriously hampered under native rule by the deplorable condition of the
native system of currency, by the insecurity of life and property, by the lax
or corrupt administration of law, and by the lack of governmental interest
in the general question of development and in the advantages to be derived
from scientific research in the various fields of industry. In each of these
matters the Government-General has introduced wide-reaching reforms, of
which the consequences can be observed in the following table:

TEN YEARS' GROWTH OF COMMERCE, MANUFACTURES, AND BANKING
(Values in thousands of yen)

	1912	1921
Exports by sea...........................	20,985	207,280
Exports by land..........................	356*	10,996
Imports by sea...........................	67,115	205,210
Imports by land..........................	467*	27,171
Total foreign trade......................	88,101	450,658
Paid-up capital of business corporations.....	103,720	1,083,551
Value of factory products..................	29,362	166,414
Number of Koreans employed in factories...	14,974	40,418
Number of Japanese employed in factories...	2,291	6,330
Government expenditure for advancement of commerce and industry................	2,932	8,797
Bank deposits...........................	27,837	171,891
Value of clearing house transactions........	98,488	852,053

* Figures for 1913.

第三章　概論　　　　　　　　　　　　　　　　　　155

　製造業に関しては、大韓帝国政府の下では商業や産業の進歩は深
刻に阻害されていた。これは旧来の貨幣システムの劣悪な状況、生
活と財産への不安、怠惰で腐敗した法治によるものであり、また発
展の可能性にも、産業の様々な分野の科学的研究から得られるであ
ろう恩恵に対しても、政府の関心が不足していたことが原因である。
これらの問題の1つ1つに總督府は大幅な改革を導入した。その結
果は次の表で見ることが出来る。

貿易、製造業、銀行業の年間成長

（金額は千円単位）

	1912	1921
海上輸出	20,985	207,280
陸上輸出	356*	10,996
海上輸入	67,115	205,210
陸上輸入	467*	27,171
総（対外）貿易量	88,101	450,658
会社法人の納入資本金	103,720	1,083,551
工場生産品の合計額	29,362	166,414
工場に雇用された朝鮮人数	14,974	40,418
工場に雇用された日本人数	2,291	6,330
貿易と産業発展の政府歳出	2,932	8,797
銀行預金	27,837	171,891
手形交換取引	98,488	852,053

＊数字は 1913 年度のもの

Government

On October 30, 1910, the Organic Regulations of the Government-General of Chosen (Korea) were promulgated by a Japanese Imperial Ordinance. The Regulations established a Secretariat, and five Departments, to which were assigned, respectively, General Affairs, Home Affairs, Finance, Justice, and Agriculture, Commerce and Industry. For the purpose of carrying on the government a large staff of Japanese officials was installed. As few of these officials had any close knowledge of local conditions or of the Korean language, the actual position was that although a complete administrative machine was set in motion, it was realised by the authorities that from the experience of its employment the necessity would become apparent of many changes designed to make the system increasingly suitable to the particular circumstances of the country.

From year to year various reforms were introduced; but it was not until 1919 that, following the outbreak and suppression of the Independence Movement, and the appointment of Admiral Baron Saito to the Governor-Generalship, a matured plan of general reorganization was undertaken under the authority of an Imperial Rescript.

The statement of the matters to be effected by the new plans shows that the authorities recognized clearly the character of the defects which had become apparent during the nine years which had elapsed since the original Organic Regulations had been put in force. The official list of the purposes to which the new measures were addressed was as follows:

(1) Non-discrimination between Japanese and Korean officials.

(2) Simplification of laws and regulations.

(3) Prompt transaction of state business.

政府

1910年10月30日、朝鮮（コリア）總督府の官制組織の規定が大日本帝国の天皇の勅令によって公布された。これによって總督官房と、総務、内務、財務、司法、農商工、の5つの部署が設立された。また行政のために多数の日本人の官吏が任命された。しかし、これらの官吏のうち朝鮮の国内事情や朝鮮語に精通している者がほとんどいなかったため、完璧な行政機構が始動されてはいたものの、国内の特殊な状況に合わせて組織を適宜修正していく必要性が明らかになってきたというのが実情であった。

年々様々な改革が導入されたが、独立運動の勃発と鎮圧、そして齋藤男爵が總督に任命されたことに従い、1919年になって初めて、天皇による勅令の下、熟慮を重ねた総合的な行政改革の計画が着手された。

新計画で改善される事項の報告書では、朝鮮總督府官制が施行されてからの9年間で明らかになった問題点について、当局がはっきりと認識していたことが示されている。新しく取り組まれる対策の目的の公式一覧は以下の通りであった。

(1) 日本人と朝鮮人の官吏を差別しないこと

(2) 法と規制を簡略化すること

(3) 国務の速やかなる処理

158   SUMMARY

(4)   Decentralization policy.

(5)   Improvement in local organization.

(6)   Respect for native culture and customs.

(7)   Freedom of speech, meeting, and press.

(8)   Spread of education and development of industry.

(9)   Re-organization of the police system.

(10) Enlargement of medical and sanitary agencies.

(11) Guidance of the people.

(12) Advancement of men of talent.

(13) Friendly feeling between Japanese and Koreans.

In a Proclamation to the People of Chosen, issued by Governor-General Saito on September 10, 1919, His Excellency made the following declaration:

I am determined to superintend officials under my control and encourage them to put forth greater efforts to act in a fairer and juster way, and promote the facilities of the people and the unhindered attainment of the people's desires by dispensing with all formalities. Full consideration will be given to the appointment and treatment of Koreans so as to secure the right men for the right places, and what in Korean institutions and old customs is worthy of adoption will be adopted as a means of government. I also hope to introduce reform in the different branches of administrative activity, and enforce local self-government at the proper opportunity, and thereby ensure stability for the people and enhance their general welfare. It is most desirable that

(4) 地方分権政策

(5) 地方組織の改善

(6) 朝鮮固有の文化と慣習の尊重

(7) 言論、集会、報道の自由

(8) 教育の普及と産業の発展

(9) 警察組織の再編成

(10) 医療と衛生機関の拡大

(11) 国民指導

(12) 人材の育成

(13) 日本人と朝鮮人の間の友好的関係

1919年9月10日に発表された朝鮮民衆への訓示で、齋藤總督は次のように宣言をした。

　私の統制の下に部下である官吏たちを監督し、彼らがより公明正大な施政を行うよう最善の努力をするよう奨励し、形式を省いて民衆の便宜、民意の達成を図る。朝鮮人の任用と待遇には充分に熟慮して適材適所を確保し、朝鮮の制度および古い習慣の中でも取り入れる価値のあるものは取り入れ、統治の手段とする。私はまた行政の各部門に改革を導入し、機を見て地方自治を実施し、それによって国民の生活の安定、全体的な幸福と利益の増進を望んでいる。そして何よりも望んでいることは、官民ともに心を開き一致協力して朝鮮の文明を進歩させ開化政

the government and the governed throw open their hearts and minds to each other and combine their efforts to advance civilization in Chosen, solidify its foundations of enlightened government, and thus answer His Majesty's benevolent solicitude. If anybody is found guilty of unwarrantably refractory language or action, of misleading the popular mind, and of impeding the maintenance of public peace, he will meet with relentless justice. May it be that the people at large will place reliance on all this.

The reader of the administrative chapters in the present volume will see that Governor-General Saito has been as good as his word. He has kept his promise to rule with justice, firmness, and tolerance, and to keep in view the cultural and economic interests of the Korean people.

Among the more important of his administrative measures are to be noted the abolition of the gendarmerie, the abolition of the old Korean custom of flogging convicted offenders, the appointment of an increasing number of Koreans to high posts in the Government, the appointment or election of advisory councils, largely composed of Koreans, the delegation of a great deal of local administration to local authorities, thus contributing to the education of the people in local self-government, the expenditure of large funds in aid and in encouragement of agriculture, industry, and commerce, the notable increase in the expenditure on education, culminating in the founding of a University at which Koreans will be able to secure in Korea an education as thorough as they would be able to get in Japan proper.

治の土台をしっかりと固めることであり、それにより天皇陛下の慈悲深い御心に御応えすることである。もし不逞な言動を為し、民衆の心を惑わせ、治安の維持を妨げる者があれば、誰であろうと、容赦なく法の裁きに遭うことになろう。願わくば一般民衆はこれを頼みとするように。

　今この行政の章を読んでいる読者は、齋藤總督が有言実行の人であることを知るだろう。彼は正義と強い意志、そして寛容さをもって統治し、朝鮮人の文化と経済的利益を大切にするという自分の約束を守ってきたのである。

　彼の行政の中でより重要で注目しておくべきものとしては以下の通りである。

・憲兵を廃止したこと
・古い朝鮮の習慣であるむち打ちの刑を廃止したこと
・政府の要職に多くの朝鮮人を登用したこと
・審問委員会に多くの朝鮮人を任命あるいは選出したこと
・地方行政の大部分を地方当局に委託し、地方政府官吏の教育に寄与したこと
・農・工・商業の援助と奨励において多額の資金を支出したこと
・教育予算を大幅に増やして、国内に大学を設立し、日本本土と同水準の総合教育を朝鮮人に与えたこと

162   SUMMARY

Some of the foregoing points, and others bearing upon the general progress of the country, can be established statistically, as will be seen from the following table:

BUDGET ESTIMATES OF EXPENDITURES BY THE GOVERNMENT-GENERAL
ON VARIOUS SPECIFIED OBJECTS
(In thousands of yen. 1 yen = 50 cents U. S.)

	1918*	1921†	Increase
Local administration...........	4,440	10,133	128%
Medical and Sanitary..........	730	1,883	157
Education.....................	2,196	6,100	180
Encouragement of industry......	3,573	8,798	146
Public Works..................	7,341	15,329	108

BUDGET ESTIMATES FOR VARIOUS CLASSES OF EXPENDITURE
BY PROVINCIAL AND OTHER PUBLIC BODIES
(In thousands of yen)

	1918*	1921†	Increase
Medical and Sanitary..........	782	1,723	120%
Education.....................	4,897	19,382	287
Encouragement of industry......	2,139	5,411	153
Public Works..................	3,210	11,953	272
Social and Charitable..........	194	383	97

* The year before Governor-General Saito's arrival.
† The second year after his arrival.

The following explanations may be given of the terms used in the foregoing tables: "Local Administration" means in this connection the local administrative offices of the Government-General, situated in each province, county, and municipality; "Public Works" includes road-making, bridge-building, and the construction and repair of public buildings; "Encouragement of Industry" covers items such as subsidies and expert services to various agricultural and manufacturing enterprises. The term

第三章　概論　　163

　以下の表からわかるように、前述のいくつかの点、および国内の
一般的な発展に関し、統計上にその結果を見ることが出来る。

様々な行政目標に總督府が支出した推定予算額
（単位は千円　当時１円＝50セント）

	1918*	1921 †	増加
地方政府	4,440	10,133	128%
医療と衛生	730	1,883	157
教育	2,196	6,100	180
産業奨励	3,573	8,798	146
公共事業	7,341	15,329	108

「地方行政やその他の公共団体」による
様々な分野に対する支出推定予算額
（単位は千円　当時１円＝50セント）

	1918*	1921 †	増加
医療と衛生	782	1,723	120%
教育	4,897	19,382	287
産業奨励	2,139	5,411	153
公共事業	3,210	11,953	272
社会・慈善	194	383	97

*1918 年は齋藤總督着任の前年
† 1921 年は着任２年後

　なお、以下に、上の表に使われた用語について解説する。

　「地方政府」…總督府の地方官署を意味する。それぞれの道、府、
郡に置かれている。

　「公共事業」…道路建設、橋梁建設、公共建築物の建築と補修。

"Provincial and Other Public Bodies" refers to administrative units organized in provinces, districts, municipalities, and villages for dealing with education, sanitation, industrial encouragement, civil engineering, social and charitable undertakings in various localities, and with general administrative services in villages. The increases in expenditure on education and on public works register the practical character of Governor-General Saito's cultural policy; and it is to be noted that these increases were brought about within two years of Viscount Saito's assumption of office.

「産業奨励」…農業、製造業従事者たちへの助成金や専門的な技術の提供などの項目を含む。

「地方行政やその他の公共団体」…道、府、郡や面などに組織された行政単位。教育、衛生、産業奨励、土木、社会事業および慈善事業を取り扱い、また全般的な行政サービスを扱う。

教育と公共事業の支出の増加は、齋藤總督が実施した文化政策の実務的な性格をよく現している。そして齋藤總督の就任後2年以内に実施されたことは、注目すべき点である。

CHAPTER Ⅳ

第四章

CHAPTER IV

GOVERNMENT ORGANIZATION

I. THE GOVERNMENT-GENERAL

Prior to the annexation of Korea—effected by the Treaty of August, 1910—the influence exerted by Japan upon government in Korea passed through two phases. The first of these may be described as a period of diplomatic advice, during which the Japanese Minister at Seoul, aided by a number of Japanese advisers engaged by the Korean Government, attempted to improve the deplorable condition into which the internal administration of Korea had fallen under native control. This period came to an end in November, 1905, when the Japanese-Korean Convention formulated a new relationship between the two countries.

This Convention introduced the second phase of Japan's influence in Korean government. It may be described as a period of administrative control and participation. In accordance with the terms of the Convention, Japan established in Korea, in February, 1906, a Residency-General, with subordinate Residencies at various points. The functions of the Residency-General were defined in a Convention signed in July, 1907. It was then provided:

(1) That the Government of Korea shall follow the directions of the Resident-General in respect of administrative reforms;

(2) That the Government of Korea shall not enact any laws, ordinances, or regulations, or take any important administrative measures without the previous approval of the Resident-General;

第四章

政府組織

I 總督府

1910 年 8 月に締結された条約によって日韓併合は効力を発した。それ以前にも大日本帝国は大韓帝国の政府に影響力を行使していたのだが、その影響力は 2 つの時期に分けることが出来る。

1 つは、「顧問外交期」とも言えるもので、その間駐在日本公使は、大韓帝国政府より招聘された日本人官僚と共に、李王朝政権下の憂慮すべき内政問題の改善にあたっていた。この期間は 1905 年 11 月、日韓協約が締結され新しい日韓関係が築かれたことで終結する。

この協約により日本政府の影響力は次の段階を迎えた。これは、「行政関与期」と表現されるかもしれない。日本は協約の条項にしたがって、1906 年 2 月、大韓帝国に統監府を設立し、各地に所属官署を置いた。統監府の役割は 1907 年 7 月に調印された協約ではっきりと示された。以下がその規定であった。

(1) 大韓帝国政府は施政改善に関し統監府の指導を受けること。

(2) 大韓帝国政府は法律・法令あるいは条例の制定および重要な行政上の措置には予め統監府の承諾を得ること。

(3) That judicial administration in Korea shall be conducted independently of other branches of administration;

(4) That the appointment and dismissal of all high officials in Korea shall be made with the concurrence of the Resident-General;

(5) That the Government of Korea shall appoint, as Korean officials, Japanese subjects recommended by the Resident-General.

Under this arrangement considerable improvement occurred in the general administration of the country; but in two important matters the system failed of efficiency. These were finance, and the administration of justice.

In respect of the first of these Japan was confronted by the fact, almost universally overlooked, that whatever advantages may flow from administrative reform, and whatever economies such reform may eventually effect, these advantages and economies cannot be produced without increasing the initial cost of administration; in a word, that good government is cheap at the price, but that it cannot be had at a cheap price.

So far as justice was concerned the Korean system was such, both as to its procedure and its officials, that far-reaching reform appeared to be impossible unless its administration was placed in the hands of Japanese public servants.

In order to meet these difficulties Japan arranged for a loan, free of interest, estimated at ten million dollars, but actually reaching a total of thirteen million, for the purpose of stabilizing the Korean budget; and took over the administration of justice and of the prisons, whilst assuming the cost of these departments as a charge upon the Japanese Treasury.

(3) 大韓帝国の司法事務は普通行政事務と区別すること。

(4) 大韓帝国高官の任免は統監府の同意のもとで行うこと。

(5) 大韓帝国政府は統監の推薦する日本人を韓国官吏として任命すること。

　この協約のもとで施政の著しい改善が見られたが、2つの重要な分野においては効果を上げられなかった。金融と司法行政である。

　金融について日本は、どこの政府でもほぼ例外なく見逃されている、ある事実に直面していた。行政改革がどれほど好都合な結果を生み出す可能性があろうと、またその結果が景気にどう影響しようと、そのような可能性は行政への初期投資を増やさないと生まれないということである。良い政府というのは価格以上の価値があると思わせるものだが、それは安く手に入るという意味ではない。

　司法に関しては、朝鮮の制度は、法的手続きの問題と朝鮮人官僚の問題を抱えており、その為、法の執行を日本人官吏の手に委ねない限り、大きな改革は不可能のように思われた。

　このような困難に対応するため日本は1000万ドルの無利子の貸付けを準備したが、実際には大韓帝国の財政安定のために総額1300万ドルが費やされたのである。日本は法の執行と監獄業務も引き受け、それらの経費は大日本帝国の大蔵省が負担した。

172   GOVERNMENT ORGANIZATION

The period of administrative control and participation was brought to an end by the Japanese annexation of Korea in 1910. The circumstances which led to this step have been dealt with in the historical section of Chapter II.

Simultaneously with the annexation of the country the Government-General of Korea was established, on August 29, 1910. It was not, however, until September 30, 1910, that the Organic Regulations of the Government-General were promulgated by an Imperial Japanese Ordinance which made them effective as from the following day.

These Regulations provided for the appointment of a Governor-General, and of a Vice Governor-General; and for the erection of a Government-General to consist of the following six departments: Secretariat; General Affairs; Home Affairs; Finance; Agriculture, Commerce, and Industry; and Justice. Provision was made for the executive, administrative, technical, and clerical services; and an annual budget was prescribed as the basis of the financial system.

The Organic Regulations have been amended from time to time as experience indicated the necessity. Before describing the organization of the Government of Korea as it now exists a few paragraphs may be devoted to the form it assumed at the end of the first year after the creation of the Government-General.

At the head of the Government was the Governor-General, who conducted public affairs through the instrumentality of two groups of offices—one classified as the Government-General of Korea, the other as Affiliated Offices of the Government-General. The organization of these two groups at the end of 1911 is exhibited in the following table:

第四章　政府組織 I　　　　　173

　「行政関与期」は 1910 年に日本が大韓帝国を併合して終わりを迎
えた。この段階へと至った状況については第二章中の「朝鮮の歴史」
で取り扱っている。

　併合と時を同じくして、朝鮮總督府が 1910 年 8 月 29 日に設立さ
れた。しかしながら、効力を持ったのは 1910 年 9 月 30 日に大日本
帝国の勅令によって朝鮮總督府官制が公布されたその翌日からのこ
とであった。
　朝鮮總督府官制には、總督と副總監を任命し、官房、総務部、内
務部、度支部、農商工部、司法部の 6 つの部署によって總督府を構
成するよう規定された。管理、行政、技術そして事務業務などに対
する条項も作られ、年間予算が財政制度の基礎に基づいて定められ
た。

　朝鮮總督府官制は必要に応じてその都度修正されてきた。現在の
朝鮮政府の組織を説明する前に、總督府設置後の初年の末時点の朝
鮮政府の組織の形態について少し述べる必要があるかもしれない。

　政府の長は總督であり、總督は 2 つの官庁、すなわち朝鮮總督府
と總督府所属官署の機関を通じて公務を行った。1911 年末のこれら
2 つの官庁の構成は次の表に示してある。

174 GOVERNMENT ORGANIZATION

PERSONNEL OF THE GOVERNMENT-GENERAL, 1911

	High Officials	Subordinate Officials	Total
Government-General:			
Secretariat..................	5	5	10
Department of General Affairs	13	116	129
Department of Home Affairs..	26	140	166
Department of Finance.......	30	142	172
Department of Agriculture,...			
Commerce, and Industry...	23	66	89
Department of Justice.......	4	16	20
Total, Government-General.	101	485	586
Affiliated Offices:			
Courts, Police, Prisons.......	363	811	1,174
Local Government...........	404	2,321	2,725
Railway Bureau.............	55	405	460
Communications Bureau.....	39	1,005	1,044
Land Survey Bureau.........	29	1,069	1,098
Government Schools.........	24	91	115
Customs Service............	17	245	262
Hospital and Medical School..	15	28	43
Model Farm................	13	52	65
Monopoly Bureau...........	4	43	47
Printing Bureau.............	3	22	25
Bureau of Ancient Customs...	6	8	14
Government Lumber Station..	5	16	21
Government Coal Mine......	2	5	7
Central Council.............	....	2	2
Total, Affiliated Offices.....	979	6,123	7,102
Grand total...........	1,080	6,608	7,688

All the items in the foregoing table are, in a broad sense, self-explanatory, except "Central Council." This body was created at the time of the annexation, 1910, for the purpose of providing the Japanese Governor-General with a Korean advisory committee, which he could consult in regard to administrative measures. The Vice President and all members of the Council were chosen from the ranks of the Korean nobility, gentry, and officialdom. The president of the Council, the chief secretary, and the secretaries were chosen from the higher ranks of the Japanese officials

第四章　政府組織 I　　　175

1911 年總督府職員数

總督府	高級官吏	下級官吏	合計
總督官房	5	5	10
総務部	13	116	129
内務部	26	140	166
度支部	30	142	172
農商工部	23	66	89
司法部	4	16	20
合計	101	485	586
所属官署	高級官吏	下級官吏	合計
裁判所 警務 監獄	363	811	1,174
各道（地方政府）	404	2,321	2,725
鉄道局	55	405	460
通信局	39	1,005	1,044
臨時土地調査局	29	1,069	1,098
官立学校	24	91	115
税関	17	245	262
病院と付属講習所	15	28	43
勤業模範場	13	52	65
専売局	4	43	47
印刷局	3	22	25
取調局	6	8	14
営林廠	5	16	21
平壌鉱業所	2	5	7
中枢院	-	2	2
合計	979	6,123	7,102
総合計	1,080	6,608	7,688

　中枢院以外の機関については、おおよそ機関名から役割が分かる
だろう。中枢院は、1910 年の併合時に日本人總督の下に朝鮮人諮問
委員会を設置する目的で作られた。總督は行政措置に関連する事柄
を諮問委員会と協議出来た。中枢院の副議長と全ての委員は朝鮮の
貴族、上流層、官吏などの階級から選ばれた。中枢院の議長と書記

attached to the Government-General.

The members of the Council were given honorary official rank; but as they were not to be classed as Government servants, they were not included in the official figures from which the foregoing table was compiled. The actual number of Koreans in the Council at the end of 1911 was 71; and the Japanese staff of the Council consisted of one president, one chief secretary, one assistant secretary, and one interprete-secretary.

Provincial Government

By Imperial Ordinance No. 357, promulgated on September 10, 1910, provision was made for local government in Korea. The country was divided into thirteen provinces. The Organic Regulations for Provincial Government established a central authority in each province, headed by a Provincial Governor, and equipped with the administrative staff necessary to conduct the provincial business connected with Finance, Medical and Sanitary Service, Police, Education, Harbors, Forestry, Public Works, and so on.

Each province was subdivided into districts of three types—municipal prefectures, rural counties, and insular districts. The last-named group comprised two of the larger islands lying off the coast of Korea. As originally designed, the Government of Korea presented the following administrative pattern:

1 Government-General,

13 Provincial Governments,

12 Municipal Prefectures,

第四章　政府組織 I　　　　177

官長と書記官は、總督府に所属している日本人高官から選出された。

　中枢院の委員は名誉ある官位を与えられた。しかし彼らは政府官僚として見なされなかったので、前述の表の数字には含まれていない。1911年末の時点で、中枢院の朝鮮人員は71人で、中枢院の日本人は、議長1人、書記官長1人、副書記官1人、通訳官1人で構成されていた。

地方政府

　1910年9月10日に公布された大日本帝国の勅令第357番によって朝鮮の地方政府に対する条項が作られた。それにより国は13の「道」に区分された。朝鮮總督府地方官制法令に基づき、各道に道知事の率いる地方政府が設立され、財政、医療と衛生事業、警察、教育、港湾、山林、公共事業などに関連した地方業務を行う行政職員が配属された。

　各道はさらに、府、郡、島、の3種類の地区に分けられた。島には朝鮮沿岸に位置する島のうち大きな2つが含まれていた。最初の計画で朝鮮總督府が発表した行政体系は以下の通りである。

　　　總督府………1
　　　道政府………13
　　　府……………12

218 Rural Counties, and

2 Insular Districts.

The problem presented to Japan by its responsibility for the Government of Korea was one of extreme complexity. The task had neither that kind of simplicity which exists where a powerful and "superior" race assumes control of a people low in the scale of civilization, weak in physical resources, and devoid of the sentiment of nationalism, nor that kind of simplicity which exists when a mere transfer of political control occurs between two peoples of somewhat similar economic and social status.

In a word, the problem was neither that of England ruling the native tribes of New Guinea, nor that of Italy taking over the Austrian administration of Fiume.

The situation was, in fact, almost without precedent in modern times. Measured by the standards of Asiatic civilization the people of Korea constituted an advanced race; like the Japanese they owed much of their culture to China; unlike the Japanese they had been little affected by the political and economic progress of the Western world. Down to the middle of the nineteenth century the description "Hermit Kingdom" would have applied with equal force to Japan and to Korea. Each country possessed an ancient religion, an ancient philosophy, an ancient culture, an ancient aristocracy, and an ancient social organization. If the two countries had been compared at that time on the basis of their national evolution as Asiatic states it would have been impossible to attribute to the Koreans any inherent inferiority to their Japanese neighbors.

郡…………218

島……………2

　統治責任に伴い日本に与えられた問題は非常に複雑なものであった。力があって「優秀な」民族が、文明レベルが低く、物的資源にも乏しく、民族主義の心情がない人々を支配するという単純さ、あるいは似たような経済的・社会的水準の2つの民族間で統治権の移譲が起こる時のような単純さ―日本が抱えた課題はいずれの単純さとも無縁であった。

　つまり、その問題というのはニューギニアの原住民を支配するイギリスの問題や、オーストリアのフィウメの統治権を引き継いだイタリアの問題などとは違うものだったのである。実際その状況は現代においてほとんど前例がなかった。

　アジア文明の基準からしても朝鮮民族は進歩した民族で、日本民族と同じように中国から多くの文化的影響を受けてきた。しかし日本民族と違い西洋社会の政治的経済的な発展からはほとんど影響を受けなかった。19世紀中ごろまで「隠遁した王国」という表現は、日本と朝鮮に同じように当てはめられたであろう。両国は、それぞれ古来の宗教、哲学、文化、貴族政治そして社会構図を保有していた。もしこの2国が当時、アジアの国としての国家的進化の基準をもとに比較されたならば、朝鮮民族が隣の日本民族よりも元々劣等だとは言うことは出来ないであろう。

180   GOVERNMENT ORGANIZATION

At the present time a comparison of such a character would be wholly irrelevant to any practical issue. Since 1858 Japan has become westernized. If the process has conferred upon her many of the alleged advantages of Western progress, it has also infected her with the many evils which appear to be inseparable from the Western type of civilization. Her own problems are now those of the West; their solutions will be found, if at all, by adopting Western methods and by improving upon them, not by attempting to make Asiatic theories and Asiatic practices serve the necessities of a modern society of the Western type.

For my own part, having spent a number of years in various parts of Asia, I am unable to entertain the conviction, so commonly held in Europe and in the Americas, that Western civilization is superior to that of the East. But the question now before me is not one into which any speculations of this kind can enter. It is that of describing the Japanese administrative system in Korea, as an example of an attempt to govern an Asiatic dependency by Western methods.

For the purposes of such a discussion it is essential that two separate subjects should be kept separate—the right of Japan to govern Korea, and the way in which Japan is actually governing Korea. The former subject is one of great interest and importance, viewed from the standpoint of Imperialism as a phenomenon of statecraft; but it can receive no more than incidental treatment—as it does in the introductory chapter—in a volume devoted to a discussion of matters subsequent to the acquisition of a dependency.

第四章　政府組織 I　　　181

　現在の両国を同等に比較するのは、いかなる現実的な問題についても全く不適切である。1858年以来、日本は西洋化の道を歩んで来た。もしその過程が日本にいわゆる西洋の進歩の利点や恩恵を与えてきたとするならば、それはまた日本に西洋型の文明とは切り離すことが出来ない多くの邪悪なものを吹き込んで来たことでもある。日本の抱える問題は今や西洋国家の問題である。問題の解決策だが、それがあるとすれば西洋の方式を取り入れたり改善することで見つかるだろうし、アジア的な論理や実践をもって西洋型の現代社会が必要としているものを満たそうとしても無理だろう。

　アジアの様々な地域で何年も過ごした私の立場からすれば、ヨーロッパやアメリカで当たり前に受け入れられている「西洋文明は東洋文明よりも優れている」という確信を抱くことは出来ない。とは言え、今私の目の前にある問題には、そのような類の思索が入り込む余地はない。西洋の方式でアジア的植民地を統治しようと試みた1つの例として朝鮮内での日本の行政制度を記述しているのである。

　そのような目的のためには、2つの異なる主題—日本に朝鮮を統治する権利があるかどうかと、実際に日本がどのように朝鮮を統治しているか—を別々に議論することが大事である。1つ目の日本の権利というテーマは、国政の発露として帝国主義の観点から見ても大いに興味深く重要なものではあるが、植民地を獲得してからの出来事を論議するのに重点を置いた本書では副次的な問題である。それは序論の部分でも書いた通りだ。

182   GOVERNMENT ORGANIZATION

Any description of the Government of Korea, as it is now constituted, must start from the fact that Japan took over the responsibility in 1910, that she was confronted immediately by the condition of the country as it then was, and that in view of that condition she had to establish a Government, formulate a public policy, and construct an administrative machine.

Approaching these tasks from the base line of her own experience of half a century under a westernized Constitution, she found that the immediate situation was full of difficulty; but that, on a long view of her undertaking, the future held out the possibility of a success at least as great as that achieved by any other nation in the direction of governing dependencies.

The chief difficulty with which the newly-formed Government-General was faced was that in respect of modernizing the public administration of the country it could count upon little aid from the past. The existing body of Korean officials were for the most part indifferent, and in some part violently hostile, to reform along Western lines; the mal-administration which, by common consent, had for many years characterized the Government of the native Yi Dynasty, had affected adversely the whole of the Korean public service; the economic stability of the country had been wrecked by an unsound system of taxation and by a debased currency; means of communication were wretched; the country districts were overrun by bandits, banking facilities were inadequate for the development of commerce and industry, above all, the Korean people had been reduced by many years of stupid misgovernment and oppression to a state of pa-tient lethargy. Even if there be attributed to Japan no higher motive than

第四章　政府組織 I　　　183

　今の朝鮮總督府についていかなる記述をするにしても、日本が
1910 年に責任を引き継いだという事実、またその直後に日本は朝鮮
の現状に直面したということ、そしてその現状に鑑みて政府を設立
し、公の政策を制定し、行政機関を構築したという、これらの事実
から始めなくてはならない。

　日本は西洋化された憲法の下での半世紀に亘る独自の経験を基礎
にしてこうした課題に取り組むことで、今の状況が困難を極めるも
のであると気付いたのである。しかし長い目で見るならば、少なく
とも他の国が達成した属国支配と同程度には成功の可能性があるこ
とにも気付いた。

　新たに組織された總督府が直面させられた最大の問題は、国家行
政の近代化について、旧体制からの支援はほとんど当てに出来ない
ことであった。朝鮮官僚の多くは西洋的近代化路線には無関心であ
り、激しく敵対している面もあった。

　旧来の李王朝政府の悪政が、長年に亘り朝鮮社会に悪影響を与え
続けてきたことに異論を唱える者はない。

　不合理な課税システムと貨幣価値の下落によって国の経済は不安
定となり、通信手段は機能せず、地方は匪賊に荒らされ、金融機関
も商業や産業の発展に不適切であった。

　何よりの問題は、朝鮮の人々が長年の愚かな悪政と抑圧によって
持続的な無気力状態へと陥ってしまっていたことである。

　もし、日韓併合についての日本側の動機が投資目的でしかなかっ
たとしても、朝鮮国内の状況が改善されてこそ、その目的は達成さ

that of making a profitable investment out of the annexation of Korea, the pursuit of such an aim could only end in success if the general condition of the country was improved. The general policy through which this improvement was to be achieved was announced in a Proclamation issued on August 29, 1910, by Viscount Masakata Terauchi, the Japanese Resident-General. The Proclamation made official announcement of the annexation, and it was supplemented by a statement in the form of general instructions to the high Japanese officials who would be responsible for the administration of Korea until the Government-General had been organized. Divested of the rhetorical phrases which are to be found in all documents of this character, the Proclamation outlined a clear policy.

(1) To afford relief to the people by abandoning the Government's claim on unpaid'land taxes, by making a reduction of twenty per cent in the land tax about to fall due, by making a donation of seventeen million yen (about $8,500,000) from the Imperial Japanese Treasury for promoting education and for the relief of famine and other disasters.

(2) To establish law and order throughout the country, in order that life and property might be secure and the people supplied with an incentive to industry.

(3) To improve the means of communication and transportation, thus aiding material development whilst affording occupation to large numbers of Koreans.

(4) The creation of a Council of responsible and experienced Koreans to be consulted with reference to proposed administrative measures.

(5) The establishment of a charity hospital in each province to extend

れるのである。

　朝鮮を改善するための一般的政策は、1910 年 8 月 29 日に子爵寺内正毅統監によって公布された。

　その布告は併合の正式な宣言となり、そして總督府が組織されるまでずっと朝鮮施政の責任を担っていた大日本帝国の高官への訓示も併せて公布された。

　このような性質の文書に見られる修辞的な表現を除けば、布告は次のように明確な政策を示している。

(1) 国民の救済策として、政府は土地税の未払い請求を断念し、満期寸前の土地税を 20 パーセント減税する。大日本帝国大蔵省からの 1700 万円（約 850 万ドル）の寄付を教育の促進、飢饉やその他の災害支援に当てること。

(2) 国内の法秩序を確立し、生命と財産の確保および民衆の産業意欲の高揚を図ること。

(3) 通信および輸送手段を改善し、物的発展と朝鮮人雇用拡大を図ること。

(4) 行政の諮問機関として責任感があり、経験豊かな朝鮮人による委員会を設立すること。

(5) ソウルにある中央病院および 3 つの慈恵病院、および併合前に

186   GOVERNMENT ORGANIZATION

and supplement the work of the Central Hospital at Seoul, and of the three charity hospitals, institutions which had been put in operation by the Japanese before annexation.

(6) The extension of educational facilities and the adoption of an educational policy which should "instil into the minds of the young men the detestation of idleness and the love of real work, thrift and diligence."

(7) The guaranty of freedom of religious belief. The paragraph in the Proclamation of Annexation which deals with this matter was framed as follows:

The freedom of religious belief is recognized in all civilized countries. There is, indeed, nothing to be said against anybody trying to gain spiritual peace by believing in whatever religious faith he or she considers to be true. But those who engage in strife on account of sectarian differences or take part in politics or pursue political intrigues under the name of religious propaganda, will injure good customs and manners and disturb the public order, and, as such, will be dealt with by law. There is no doubt, however, that a good religion, be it Buddhism, or Confucianism, or Christianity, has as its aim the spiritual and material improvement of mankind, and in this not only does it not conflict with the administration of Government, but really helps it in attaining the purpose it has in view. Consequently all religions shall be treated equally and, further, due protection and facilities shall be accorded to their legitimate propagation.

日本人によって運営されていた各施設の業務の拡大と補完をするために、それぞれの地域に慈恵病院を設立すること。

(6) 教育施設の増設を図り、教育方針としては怠慢を憎み実務と倹約と勤勉を愛するよう青少年を導くこと。

(7) 信仰の自由を保障すること。この件を扱った布告文は以下のようなものである。

　　宗教信仰の自由は全ての文明国においては認められている。自分自身が真実だと考えているいかなる宗教的信念をも信じることで精神的安らぎを得ようと努力しているどのような人に対しても実際反論すべきではない。しかし、宗派が違うために争いを起こし、あるいは宗教の布教活動の名の下に政治に参加したり、政治的陰謀を画策したりするような人々は良き慣習や風習に害を及ぼし、公共秩序を乱し、それ自体が法で処理されでるあろう。しかしながら、良い宗教とは、それが仏教であろうと儒教であろうとキリスト教であろうと、人類の精神的物質的向上をその目的としており、この中には政府施政との対立がないだけでなく、政府が目指すところの目的を達成するのに役立つのである。その結果として全ての宗教は平等に扱われるべきであり、さらに適切な保護と便宜がそれら宗教の合法的な伝道には提供されるであろう。

The Instructions issued to Japanese officials at the time of annexation include a paragraph which is quoted in full here, because it discloses the fact that up to that time the relations between the Japanese and the Koreans had been marked by an attitude of contempt towards the natives, and that the Resident-General was fully aware of the obstacles which such an attitude would place in the way of his general policy of conciliation and development.

The aim and purpose of the annexation is to consolidate the bonds uniting the two countries, to remove all causes for territorial and national discriminations, necessarily existing between separate powers, in order that the mutual welfare and happiness of the two peoples may be promoted. Consequently, should the Japanese people regard the annexation as a result of the conquest of a weak country by a stronger one, and should speak and act under such an illusion in an overbearing and undignified manner they would act in a spirit contrary to that in which the present step has been taken.

Japanese settlers in Korea seem hitherto to have considered that they were living in a foreign land, and have often fallen into the mistake of adopting a superior attitude toward the people of the country. If, in connection with the inauguration of the new, order of things, they were to increase their self-conceit, and were to subject the people just incorporated into the Empire to any sort of insult, they would arouse ill-feeling, with the result that in everything they would be in collision with the natives, and the opportunity would be denied of establishing an intimate relation between the two peoples, which would be an

第四章　政府組織Ⅰ

　日韓併合時に日本の官吏たちに示された命令を、以下に一部引用
する。それはその時までの朝鮮と日本の関係で先住民に対する蔑視
の姿勢を見せていたという事実と、統監はそのような姿勢が友好と
発展の全般的な政策の遂行の邪魔になるということを充分認識して
いたという事実をこの文章は明らかにしている。

　　併合の目指すところは、両国の人々の相互の福利と幸福が促
　進されるように、両国を結び付ける絆を強固なものにし、別々
　の勢力に必然的に存在している領土内、国内の差別の全ての原
　因を取り除くことである。その結果として、万が一にも日本人
　がこの併合を、強大国による弱小国の征服であると見なし、そ
　のような間違った考えを持って、傲慢で品位のない言動をとる
　ようなことがあれば、今まさに進もうとしているところの精神
　に反することになってしまうであろう。朝鮮に移住した日本人
　は、これまで異国の地に暮らしているかのように考え、朝鮮の
　人々に対して優越感を抱いていた。新しい秩序の幕開けに際し、
　もし日本人がうぬぼれを強くし、今や帝国国民となった朝鮮の
　人々を辱めるようなことがあれば、敵意を生じさせて、全ての
　ことに於いて先住民と衝突することになるであろう。そうなれ
　ば両国民衆が親密な関係を築く機会は消え、将来において計り
　知れない災いとなるであろう。事態は今や新局面を迎えた好機
　である。この時を使って、日本人の移住民たちに朝鮮の人々に

190   GOVERNMENT ORGANIZATION

unmeasurable calamity for the future. It is opportune that things have now assumed a new aspect. Let the Japanese settlers take this occasion to change their ideas and their attitude toward the people of Korea. Let them always bear in mind that they are our brothers, and treat them with sympathy and friendship, thus, by mutual help and co-operation, enabling both peoples to contribute their share to the growth and progress of the whole Empire.

The Present Organization of the Government of Korea

Starting with the organization briefly described in the foregoing pages, the passage of time and the extension of governmental activities pointed to the necessity of effecting a number of changes in the routine of public business. Both as to methods and as to personnel experience served as a guide to a number of adjustments and reforms which, in the aggregate, have brought the administrative system to the highest state of efficiency attained since the annexation.

The actual development of administrative work in Korea, in the more important branches, is shown in the following table:

PUBLIC EXPENDITURES ON VARIOUS OBJECTS

(In yen.   One yen = 50 cents U. S.)

	Actual Outlay	Actual Outlay	Increase
	1911	1920	%
Central Administration.........	2,771,753	6,306,518	127
Local Administration..........	3,901,735	8,902,995	128
Courts and Prisons............	2,372,951	6,816,139	187
Schools......................	2,127,653	19,757,048	820
Public Health.................	893,684	2,793,942	212
Construction: buildings, roads, bridges, railroads......	14,401,000	35,620,104	147
Research: chiefly relrting to industry, and natural resources.	264,553	1,969,010	645

対する考えと態度を改めさせようではないか。朝鮮の人々は我が同胞であり、思いやりと友情をもって接することを日本人の心に留めさせ、そうして相互の助け合いと協力によって両国の人々が帝国全体の成長と進歩に共に貢献出来るようにしていこう。

朝鮮總督府組織

これまでに簡単に説明した組織が動き出してから、時間が経過し、政府活動も拡大した。それに伴い公共事業の日常的業務の多くに修正を加える必要性が出てきた。運営方法や人事に関し、これまでの経験を生かして修正改善を行ったので、行政制度は全体として併合以来最も高い効率性を誇っている。

次の表には、主だった行政部署における、行政業務の実質的な発展が示されている。

行政種別公共支出
（単位は円　当時1円＝50セント）

	実際の支出 1911年	実際の支出 1920年	増加 %
中央行政	2,771,753	6,306,518	127
地方行政	3,901,735	8,902,995	128
裁判所と監獄	2,372,951	6,816,139	187
学校	2,127,653	19,757,048	820
公衆衛生	893,684	2,793,942	212
建設（建物 道路 橋 鉄道）	14,401,000	35,620,104	147
研究（主に産業と天然資源）	264,553	1,969,010	645

192   GOVERNMENT ORGANIZATION

Allowing for certain minor changes in administrative organization effected between the years 1910 and 1919, Korea was, in effect, governed for the ten years following annexation under the provisions of the Organic Regulations of the Government-General, which were promulgated on September 30, 1910, and went into effect on the following day.

On August 19, 1919, an Imperial Ordinance was promulgated on the subject of the reorganization of the Government-General of Korea; and was put in force the same day. The general purpose of the reorganization is set forth in the following quotation from the Rescript:

We are persuaded that the state of development now reached in Korea calls for certain reforms in the administrative organization of the Government-General; and We hereby issue our Imperial command that such reforms be put into operation. The measures thus taken are solely designed to facilitate the working of administration and to secure enlightened and efficient government, in pursuance of Our settled policy, and for the purpose of meeting the altered needs of the country.

The instrument through which the Imperial Rescript was to be made effective was a revised "Organic Regulations of the Government-General" published at the same time as the Rescript. The revised Regulations embodied all amendments made from time to time since the issue of the original Regulations, and such additions of new matter as were needed to give effect to the Rescript.

The organization of Government in Korea, as fixed by the Regulations of 1919 is described in the following pages. The administration of

第四章　政府組織 I　　　193

　1910年から1919年の間、行政機構に多少の変化があったとはいえ、
朝鮮は事実上、1910年9月30日に公布され、その翌日から施行さ
れた朝鮮總督府官制の下で併合後の10年間統治されてきた。

　1919年8月19日、朝鮮總督府改編に関して勅令が公布され、同
日に施行された。再編成の全般的な目的は勅書から引用した以下に
述べられている。

　　　「朝鮮において達成された発展の状態は總督府の行政組織に
　　おいてある改革を求めていると確信し、よって改正を施行する
　　勅令を発表する。こうして取られた措置は、我々の確立した政
　　策の遂行によって行政の遂行を容易にし、開化され効果的な政
　　府を保障するためのものであり、朝鮮の変化への要求を満足さ
　　せるためのものである」。

　勅令は同時に発令された「官制の改革」を通して効力を発揮する。
この官制の改革法令は最初に公布されてから幾度となく改正を重ね
てきたが、新しく追加された内容は勅令が実行されるのに必要なも
のであった。

　1919年に改革された官制によって定着した朝鮮總督府の組織は次
ページ以下に記されている。政府の行政、つまり各政府組織によっ

government, that is to say the work performed by the organization, is described in the chapters following this.

At the head of the Government is the Governor-General, appointed by the Emperor of Japan, and directly responsible to him for the administration of government in Korea. Until 1919 it was obligatory that the Governor-General be selected from the Japanese military establishment. The new Regulations abolished this restriction, and made civil officials also eligible for the appointment.

Next in rank is the Vice Governor-General, sometimes described as Director of Civil Administration. His duties resemble those performed by the Secretary General in Java, and by the Colonial Secretary of a British Crown Colony. He is the Governor-General's right-hand man, and is responsible for all administrative decisions, unless or until they require the formal sanction of the Governor-General.

The Governor-General conducts the administration of Korea through the agency of two groups of administrative organs, one of which constitutes the Government-General, the other being designated as Affiliated Offices of the Government-General.

て行われる業務は、次の章で説明する。

　政府の首長は總督であるが、天皇によって任命され、朝鮮の政治
行政に直接の責任を負った。1919 年までは、總督は日本の軍幹部か
ら選出しなければならなかったが、新しい規定はこの制約を廃止し、
文民も總督に任命出来るようになった。

　それに次ぐ役職は、副總督であり、時に政務総監とも呼ばれた。
副總督の職務は、ジャワ島の事務総長、そしてイギリス王領植民地
の植民省長官が遂行していたものと似ている。副總督は總督の腹心
であり、正式に總督の許可が必要のないものや總督の許可がおりる
直前までの、全ての行政の決定に責任を負っている。

　總督は、２つの行政機関を通じて朝鮮の政務を行う。まず１つは
朝鮮總督府であり、もう１つは朝鮮總督府所属官署である。

196 GOVERNMENT ORGANIZATION

ORGANIZATION OF THE GOVERNMENT-GENERAL
(As of March, 1923)

Central Offices

GOVERNOR-GENERAL'S SECRETARIAT:
Private Secretaries Office, Councillors Office, Inspectors Office, Foreign Affairs Section, General Affairs Department, Public Works Department, Railways Department.

HOME AFFAIRS BUREAU:
Local Administration Section, Social Works Section, Officials Training Institute.

FINANCIAL BUREAU:
Internal Revenue Section, Customs Section, Budget Section, Financial Section.

INDUSTRIAL BUREAU:
Agricultural Section, Afforestation Section— Branches, Fishery Section, Commercial and Industrial Section, Mining Section—Branches, Land Investigation Section, Geological Investigation Office, Fuel Laboratory, Commercial Museum.

JUDICIAL BUREAU:
Civil Section, Criminal Section, Prison Section.

EDUCATIONAL BUREAU:
School Affairs Section, Compiling Section, Historic Remains Inquiry Office, Religious Section, Museum, Meteorological Observatory—Branches.

POLICE BUREAU:
Police Affairs Section, High Police Section, Peace Preservation Section, Sanitary Section, Export Cattle Inspecting Station.

第四章　政府組織Ⅰ

朝鮮總督府組織

―1923 年 3 月現在―

朝鮮總督府

總督官房：
秘書課、参事官室、監察官室、外事課、庶務部、土木部、
鉄道部

内務局：
地方課、社会課、行政講習所

財務局：
税務課、関税課、司計課、理財課

殖産局：
農務課、山林課、水産課、商工課、鉱務課、土地改良課、
燃料選鉱研究所

法務局：
民事課、刑事課、監獄課

学務局：
学務課、編集課、古蹟調査課、宗教課

警務局：
警務課、高等警察課、保安課、衛生課

Affiliated Offices

CENTRAL COUNCIL:
General Affairs Section, Investigation Section.

PROVINCIAL GOVERNMENT:
Governor's Secretariat, Internal Affairs Department, Financial Department, Police Department, Municipalities—Districts—Islands, Charity Hospitals, Police Stations.

POLICE TRAINING INSTITUTE.

COMMUNICATIONS BUREAU:
General Affairs Section, Supervising Section, Accounts Section, Engineering Section, Electric Works Section, Marine Affairs Section—Branches, Special Water-power Inquiry Section, Postal Money Order and Savings Supervising Office, Post Offices— Branches, Employees Training Institute, Sailors Training Institute.

MARINE COURT.

MONOPOLY BUREAU:
General Affairs Section, Management Section, Manufacturing Section, Branch Offices.

CUSTOMS:
General Affairs Section, Surveillance Section, Customs Duty Section, Inspecting Section, Branch Offices, Coastguard Stations.

LAW COURTS:
Supreme Court—Procurators Office, Appeal Courts —Procurators Offices, Local Courts—Procurators Offices, Local Branch Courts.

RRISONS—BRANCHES.

PUBLIC DEPOSITORIES.

朝鮮總督府所属官署

中枢院：
　　　庶務課、調査課

道：
　　　知事官房、内務部、財務部、警察部

警察官講習所

遞信局：
　　　庶務課、監理課、経理課、工務課、電気課、海事課、
　　　臨時水力調査課、遞信吏員養成所、海員養成所

海員審判所

専売局：
　　　庶務課、事業課、製造課

税関：
　　　庶務課、監視課、税務課、検査課

裁判所：
　　　高等法院－検事局、覆審法院－覆審法院検事局、地方
　　　法院－地方法院検事局、地方法院支庁

監獄※－支部

供託局

　　※原文で"RRISONS"と記載されているが、"PRISONS"の誤表記と解釈し
　　　て翻訳した。

LUMBER UNDERTAKING STATION:
General Affairs Section, Management Section, Saw Mill, Branch Offices.

GOVERNMENT-GENERAL HOSPITAL:
Medical Departments, Medicine Section, General Affairs Section, Nurses and Midwives Training Institute.

GOVERNMENT CHARITY ASYLUM:
Orphans Department, Blind and Deaf-Mutes Department, General Affairs Section.

MODEL FARM:
Branches, Sericultural Experimental Station, Sericultural School for Girls.

CENTRAL LABORATORY.

CATTLE-DISEASE SERUM LABORATORY.

FISHERIES EXPERIMENTAL STATION.

FORESTRY EXPERIMENTAL STATION.

営林廠：
　　　　庶務課、業務課、製作所

病院：
　　　　各分科、薬剤課、庶務課、看護婦助産婦養成所

済生院：
　　　　養育部、盲唖部、庶務課

勧業模範場：
　　　　勧業模範場支場、勧業模範出張所、蚕業試験場、女子
　　　　蚕業講習所

中央試験所

獣疫血清製造所

水産試験場

林業試験場

202 GOVERNMENT ORGANIZATION

PERSONNEL OF THE GOVERNMENT-GENERAL

The following table shows the number of officials of the Government-General engaged in each branch of administration. The figures refer to the fiscal year 1922–23.

	High Officials	Subordinate Officials	Total
The Government-General:			
General Secretariat	52	361	413
Bureau of Home Affairs	8	32	40
Bureau of Finance	11	51	62
Bureau of Industry	48	226	274
Bureau of Justice	5	20	25
Bureau of Education	11	35	46
Bureau of Police	24	49	73
Total	159	774	933
Offices Affiliated to the Government-General:			
Central Council	3	9	12
Higher Land Investigation Committee	....	1	1
Forest Investigation Committee	5	6	11
Bureau of Communications	51	1,502	1,553
Bureau of Monopoly	35	401	436
Customs	11	345	356
Supreme Court	12	5	17
Courts of 1st and 2nd Instance	258	650	908
Prisons	22	140	162
Government Higher Schools	84	266	350
Provincial Government and its Subordinate Agencies	487	4,853	5,340
Government Lumber Business	11	147	158
Government Hospitals and Asylums	22	47	69
Heijo Coal Mine Station	4	13	17
Model Farm	12	37	49
Experimental Stations	10	39	49
Police Training Institute	5	7	12
Total	1,032	8,468	9,500
Grand total	1,191	9,242	10,433

The terrible economic effects of the Japanese earthquake, 1923, made it necessary to adopt throughout the Empire a policy of drastic retrenchment in government expenditures. One of the measures carried out in Korea was the reduction by nearly twenty-five per cent of the number of government

第四章　政府組織 I

總督府職員数
表は各行政部署に従事する総督府職員の数
数字は 1922 - 1923 年の会計年度のもの

總督府	高級官吏	下級官吏	合計
総務官房	52	361	413
内務局	8	32	40
財務局	11	51	62
殖産局	48	226	274
法務局	5	20	25
学務局	11	35	46
警察局	24	49	73
合計	159	774	933
所属官署	高級官吏	下級官吏	合計
中枢院	3	9	12
高等土地調査委員会	-	1	1
林野調査委員会	5	6	11
通信局	51	1,502	1,553
専売局	35	401	436
税関	11	345	356
高等法院・検事局	12	5	17
覆審・地方法院	258	650	908
監獄	22	140	162
官立学校	84	266	350
道政府と付属機構	487	4,853	5,340
営林廠	11	147	158
病院と慈善機関	22	47	69
平壌石炭鉱山	4	13	17
勤業模範場	12	37	49
中央試験場	10	39	49
警察官講習所	5	7	12
合計	1,032	8,468	9,500
総合計	1,191	9,242	10,433

　1923 年に日本の地震で経済が大打撃を受けたため、大日本帝国中に徹底的な政府歳出の削減策の採択が必要となった。朝鮮で実行さ

204   GOVERNMENT ORGANIZATION

officials.

The Civil Service

Appointment and Salary--

Appointment to the government service in Korea is made in conformity with very elaborate rules and regulations, which, in the main, follow the lines of the Imperial Japanese services. Provision is made for a lower and for a higher examination of candidates, for salaries and allowances, for promotion, for pensions, for leave of absence, and for the appointment, resignation, and dismissal of officials.

Civil servants are classified by rank and by grade in the rank. The highest ranks are those of Shinnin and Chokunin; the next lower rank is Sonin; and the lowest rank attached to any official of the Government-General is Hannin. Promotion goes from grade to grade within the rank, and from rank to rank. For the appointment, resignation, or dismissal of civil servants of Sonin rank the Governor-General obtains the Imperial assent, through the Prime Minister of Japan; in respect of persons of Hannin rank the Governor-General decides.

The total salary of an official is made up of his regular salary, and his additional salary (for colonial service). In the Shinnin and Chokunin ranks the yearly total salaries range from that of the Governor-General, 12,000 yen, down to 6300 yen, which is paid to Chief Public Procurators of Local Courts and to Presidents of Professional Schools. In the Sonin rank the range is between 6300 yen and 1260 yen; and in the Hannin rank between

れた対策のうちの1つは、政府職員の25パーセント近くの人員削減であった。

官吏としての職務

任命と給与

官吏の任命は非常に詳細な規約に従って行われたが、そうした規約や規定は主に日本の業務方針に沿ったものである。高等および中等文官試験、給与と手当、昇進、年金、休暇そして官吏の任免に関する条項が記されている。

官吏は職位と等級によって分類される。最高職位は親任と勅任で、次は奏任、總督府所属官吏の職位で一番低いのが判任である。昇進は同一職位内で低い等級から高い等級へ、低い職位から高い職位へと行われる。奏任職位の官吏の任命、辞任あるいは解雇に対しては總督が、日本の総理大臣を通じて天皇の裁可を得ることになっていたが、判任に関しては總督の裁量で任免などが決定される。

官吏の給与は定期的な給与と手当（植民業務に対しての）で成り立っている。親任と勅任職の年間の総給与の範囲は、上は總督に支給される1万2000円から下は地方法院の検事長と専門学校の校長に支払われる6300円までである。奏任職では、総給料の幅は6300円から1260円、判任職では、雇用の性質に従って3840円から652円

3840 yen and 652 yen, according to grade and nature of employment.

In addition to the foregoing salaries there are three kinds of special allowances: residential allowance, where a residence is not provided; traveling allowances, approximately equal to out-of-pocket expenses; and bonuses. There is no fixed rate for the bonus, but it is usually between 80 per cent and 100 per cent of a month's pay. The general rule is that the lower the pay the higher the rate of the bonus.

Pensions--

The pension regulations are too elaborate to permit of detailed description in a volume of this size. The annual pension is based on the salary received at the time of retirement and on the number of years served. For one retiring after serving fifteen years and less than sixteen years the pension is one-third of his annual salary at the time of retirement. For each additional full year served, up to forty years, one-one hundred and fiftieth of the annual salary is added.

The pensions are paid from the public funds; but each civil servant above the Hannin rank must pay one per cent of his yearly salary to the pension fund.

Special provisions are made to cover the cases in which an official dies in office after fifteen years' service, or dies in execution of his duty with less than fifteen years' service, or dies after retirement on pension. These provisions exhibit a wise generosity, which other governments would do well to emulate. In any of the foregoing circumstances the pension is classed as an allowance-in-aid. The amount is fixed at one-half of the annual pension received by or due to the deceased at the time of his death;

の間で給料が決まる。

　前述の給与に加えて、3種類の特別手当がある。住居手当は住居が提供されない場合に支給され、また立て替えの経費とほぼ変わらない旅行手当と賞与金が支給される。賞与の支給率は決まっていないが、大抵1カ月の給料の80〜100パーセントの間である。一般的に給与が低ければ低いほど、賞与は高くなるということである。

年金

　年金の規定はあまりにも詳細すぎて、この本で詳しく説明したとしても足りないくらいである。年間の年金は退職当時に受け取った給与と勤務年数を基にして決める。15年間の勤務年数で、16年未満で退職をしたものにとっては、年金は退職当時の年棒の3分の1である。毎年勤務年数が加算されるにつれ最高40年まで、年棒の150分の1が加えられていく。

　年金は公共基金から支払われるが判任職以上の各官吏は、年棒の1パーセントを年金基金として支払わなければならない。

　官吏が15年間勤続後で亡くなった場合、または15年未満で職務中に亡くなった場合、退職後年金生活中に亡くなった場合など、それぞれに適応するように特別な規定が作られている。賢明な寛容さのある規定であり、他の国の政府もまねるのが良いと思われる。前述の状況の場合、年金は扶助金として分類されている。金額は故人死亡当時に受け取ったあるいは受け取る予定であった年間の年金金額の2分の1に定められている。しかし、もし公務遂行中あるいは

208 GOVERNMENT ORGANIZATION

but if death occurred while or through executing his official duty, the allowance is increased to four-fifths; and when death occurs through injury or disease caused by war or by a similar contingency the total amount of the pension is paid to the surviving beneficiary.

The allowance-in-aid is claimable by a relative of the deceased in the following order of precedence: (1) wife; (2) children under age, in the order of their rights as heirs; (3) husband, in case the deceased is a married woman; (4) father, but the father-in-law claims before the natural father if the deceased was an adopted son or daughter; (5) mother, with the same proviso; (6) children above age; (7) grandfather; (8) grandmother.

At the time of the annexation special regulations were framed for the treatment of Korean officials, placing them in a less favorable position than that of the Japanese officials. Governor-General Saito, shortly after his appointment, and in conformity with the policy of non-discrimination announced in an Imperial Rescript, annulled all the ordinances relating to the status and salaries of Korean officials, and applied in their stead the ordinances applicable to Japanese officials, thus removing a grievance which had been detrimental to the civil service. At the same time revision was made in the educational regulations which had the effect of making Korean teachers eligible for appointment as principals of public common schools—posts which up to that date, October, 1919, had been strictly reserved for Japanese. In the following year an ordinance was promulgated removing the restrictions which had hitherto existed on the authority exercised by. Korean judges and public procurators.

公務執行によって死亡した場合の受領金額は5分の4まで増える。そして戦争あるいは同じような不測の事態によって引き起こされ傷害や病気で死亡した時は、年金の総額は生存している受益者に支払われる。

　以下の優先順位で故人の親族は要求出来る。

(1) 妻

(2) 未成年の子供─相続人としての権利により

(3) 夫、故人が既婚女性の場合

(4) 父、故人が養子の場合、義理の父親の権利が実の父親より優先

(5) 母（4）に同じ

(6) 成年子女

(7) 祖父

(8) 祖母

　日韓併合時に朝鮮の官吏の待遇に特別な規定が作成され、これにより、朝鮮人官吏は日本人官吏よりも不利な立場に置かれていた。齋藤總督は着任後すぐに勅令に発表された非差別政策に従って朝鮮官吏の地位と給与に関する規定を全て無効にし、代わりに日本人官吏と同じ規定を適用することで、それまで行政業務の障害になっていた不平を取り除いたのである。同時に教育規定も改正し、朝鮮人教師たちにも公立学校の校長への道が開かれた。この職は1919年10月までは日本人が占めていた。その翌年、法令が公布され、朝鮮人判事と検事の権限を制限していた規定が取り除かれた。

CHAPTER V

第五章

CHAPTER V

GOVERNMENT ORGANIZATION

II. LOCAL ADMINISTRATION

One of the most important elements in the new policy inaugurated in 1919 on Viscount Saito's assumption of the Governor-Generalship was that of administrative decentralization. Indeed it may be said that the backbone of the new policy was that the Koreans should, in the largest possible measure consistent with the country's political status, learn to take part in the administration of their own public affairs.

I have had before me a great deal of material describing the extension of local self-government in Korea; but the whole subject is so fully and lucidly treated in the Annual Report on the Administration of Chosen, 1922-1923, that I have transcribed practically the whole of this chapter from that document.

Introductory--

The administrative divisions of the Peninsula were in a very confused state prior to the annexation of the country in 1910. In addition to provinces, urban prefectures, districts, and villages, there existed a number of other district organs, such as police and financial organs, local residencies for resident Japanese, Japanese municipalities, foreign settlements, Chinese exclusive settlements, and school associations for the education of Japanese children. The mixed relations of those

第五章

政府組織

Ⅱ 地方政府

　齋藤子爵が總督府に就任した 1919 年に新政策が開始されたが、その最も重要な要素の１つは、行政の地方分権化であった。新政策の中心となるのは、国の政治的立場と首尾一貫しながらも、可能な限り朝鮮人たちが自国の公務、行政に参加すべきであるということであったと言えるかもしれない。

　私は朝鮮の地方自治の広がりを描写したかなりの量の資料をそろえている。しかしそのテーマ全体は大変明快かつ充分に『朝鮮總督府施政年報　大正十一年度』で扱われているので、私はその文書からこの章全体を翻訳している。

概説

　1910 年の併合以前、地方制度は非常に複雑で混乱した状態にあった。道、府、郡、面、の他に、警察機関、財務機関がそれらと独立する形であった。また、日本人居留地やその行政事務のための理事庁、その他の外国人居留地、日本人子弟の教育のための学校組合もあった。さらには中国の専管居留地などもあり、それぞれ特殊な行政を執行していた。それぞれの関係は交錯しており、地方行政に統

214 GOVERNMENT ORGANIZATION

organs making it impossible to maintain uniformity and efficiency in matters of local administration, these differences all required to be adjusted simultaneously at the time of annexation. But during the time of transition, when everything else was necessarily unsettled, sudden radical changes were avoided as far as possible, and above all the question of the disposal of the settlement system was held over, as it required most careful negotiation with the powers interested. So, when the Government-General was established, the first step toward general reform in the local organization was to abolish all local residencies and financial bureaus, and to establish a financial department in each province, while giving prefectural and district magistracies part management of financial affairs. At the time of the enforcement of this readjustment the local administrative organs comprised 13 provincial governments, 12 municipal and 317 district magistracies, and 4,322 village offices, presided over by governors, prefects, sub-prefects, and headmen.

Although the administrative boundaries of municipalities, counties, and villages were left much the same as before the annexation, there were marked differences among them in area, population, and resources, and this was especially the case with villages, so that some villages bore much too disproportionate a burden of taxation, causing not a little difficulty in the execution of administrative duties. After careful study it was decided to amalgamate certain villages and alter the boundaries of others in order to secure greater uniformity and convenience in local administration. Accordingly, the area of each municipality was reduced to its natural limits by taking from it all attached villages, while the area of each district was

一と効率を期することは難しかった。これらは全て併合と同時に調整されるべきであった。しかし過渡草創の時期でもあり、諸般の秩序が未だに確立していなかったため、可能な限り急激な変化は避けられたのである。とりわけ居住システムの整理に関する問題は全て持ち越しとなった。これは関係各国などとの間で慎重な協議が必要だったためである。總督府が設立された時に、地方自治の改革全般のためにまず行われたのは、従来の理事庁と財務監督局および財務署を廃して、道に財務部を置き、さらに府・郡にも財務に関する権限を一部与えるということであった。地方行政機関としては、13の道の下に12の府を置き、さらに317の郡、さらに下に4322の面を置いて、道長官、府尹、郡守、面長、およびそれぞれの補助機関を配置して官庁事務が円滑に行われるようにした。

　府、郡、面の地図上の境界線は、ほぼ併合前の区分を踏襲したが、それぞれの地域は、面積、人口および豊かさなどにおいて著しい差があった。その結果として、特に面においては、実情からすると非常に不均衡な課税を負担することになった地域もあり、行政職務の執行に少なからず困難を来す原因となった。そのため慎重な調査検討の結果、地方行政におけるより大きな統一性と便宜を確保するために面を統廃合することが決定された。府については出来るだけ面積を縮小した。さらに府を面と同じように最小単位の行政区画とし、従来の府の下に置かれていた面は廃止された。郡については面積を

216   GOVERNMENT ORGANIZATION

restricted to about 40 square ri * containing about 10,000 people, and that

of each village to about 4 square ri containing about 800 families. This

readjustment of areas left the number of municipalities as before at 12, but

reduced districts from 317 to 220, and villages from 4,322 to 2,504. All

this was done to promote their administration, curtail local expenditure,

and secure a fair distribution of the burden of taxation on the people.

On the other hand, Saishu and Utsuryo are islands so distant from the

mainland that their administration could not be smoothly carried on owing

to difficulty of communication. So in May, 1915, they were made separate

districts, and the governor of each was empowered to issue all necessary

instructions for the good of the island, and was also made head of the is-

land police. Below are given the local administrative divisions as at pres-

ent constituted:

Province	Area	Percentage of Total Area	Divisions			Seat of Provincial Government
			Municipalities	Districts	Villages	
	Sq. ri					
Keiki.........	830.83	5.8	2	20	249	Keijo
North Chusei.	480.93	3.4	....	10	110	Seishu
South Chusei.	525.59	3.7	....	14	175	Koshu
North Zenra..	553.13	3.9	1	14	188	Zenshu
South Zenra..	900.41	6.3	1	22	269	Kwoshu
North Keisho.	1,231.16	8.6	1	23	272	Taikyu
South Keisho.	797.78	5.6	2	19	257	Shinshu
Kokai........	1,084.82	7.6	....	17	226	Kaishu
South Heian..	967.70	6.7	2	14	165	Heijo
North Heian..	1,844.24	12.8	1	19	193	Gishu
Kogen........	2,702.79	11.9	....	21	178	Shunsen
South Kankyo	2,073.36	14.5	1	16	141	Kanko
North Kankyo	1,319.19	9.2	1	11	81	Ranan
Total......	14,311.99	100.0	12	220	2,504	

* 1 square ri = 5.95 square miles.

約 40 平方里 *、人口約 1 万とした。面は、面積を約 4 平方里、人口およそ 800 戸を統廃合の標準とした。この再編成によって、府の数は以前と同じく 12、郡は以前の 317 から 220 に減り、面は 4322 から 2504 に減った。地方行政を推進し、地方支出を削減し、人々に課税負担の公平さを確保するため、これら全てはなされたのである。

　一方、済州島と鬱陵島は朝鮮本陸からかなり離れた島で、情報の伝達も困難であり、行政は円滑には実行されなかった。そのため 1915 年 5 月には、ここを島として特別区域とし、島司が島に対して必要な全ての指示を出せる権限を与えられた。島司は警察署長も兼ねることとなった。次に組織された地方自治体につきまとめる。

道	面積（平方里）	全面積に対する割合	行政区画			道庁所在地
			府	郡	面	
京畿道	831	5.8%	2	20	249	京城
忠清北道	481	3.4%	-	10	110	清州
忠清南道	526	3.7%	-	14	175	公州
全羅北道	553	3.9%	1	14	188	全州
全羅南道	900	6.3%	1	22	269	光州
慶尚北道	1,231	8.6%	1	23	272	大邱
慶尚南道	798	5.6%	2	19	257	晋州
黄海道	1,085	7.6%	-	17	226	海州
平安南道	968	6.7%	2	14	165	平壌
平安北道	1,844	12.8%	1	19	193	義州
江原道	1,703	11.9%	-	21	178	春川
咸鏡南道	2,073	14.5%	1	16	141	咸興
咸鏡北道	1,319	9.2%	1	11	81	羅南
合計	14,312	100%	12	220	2,504	

　* 1 平方里は約 5.95 平方マイル

　※江原道の面積は原文が誤記と思われるため上記表では修正

A Provincial Governor, while being held responsible to the Governor-General, executes laws and ordinances, supervises the administration of his province, controls all public corporations, and is also authorized to issue provincial ordinances. Formerly, the police organs existing in a province were entirely separate from all other local administrative organs, and the Governor had no power whatever over them, and in all police and sanitary affairs the head of the provincial police alone could set on foot measures deemed necessary, though he was required to obtain the approval of the Governor before issuing instructions. But with the progress of the times and the development of local administration it was recognized that a Provincial Governor ought to be in control of all police and sanitary affairs, so when the gendarme system was abolished in August, 1919, the police were transferred to the control of the Provincial Governors, and in each province a Third Department was instituted, composed of police, medical, and quarantine officers, and this was later renamed the Police Affairs Department. During the transition period special importance was placed on the unity and consistency of general administrative business, and a policy of centralization was adhered to, so that the powers of a Provincial Governor were somewhat circumscribed. As improvement in local administration was effected, and each year saw increase in official business, it was seen that this policy was losing in efficiency, so one of decentralization was gradually adopted, and following on the general revision in August, 1919, the powers entrusted to a Provincial Governor were by degrees widened.

After the annexation careful investigation was made concerning the revision of the existing system, and in March of 1914 it was found possible

第五章　政府組織Ⅱ　　　219

　地方長官たる道長官は總督府に従属し、責任をもって法と法令を執行し、自分の道を指揮し、全ての地方公共団体を監督管理し、道の条例を公布する権限も与えられた。

　以前は、地方の警察機関は一般の地方行政機関から分立していた関係上、道長官は警察に対していかなる権力も持ち得なかった。管内の警察・衛生事務については道警務部長が部令を発する場合に道長官の承認を要するという規定があっただけであった。実際には、警務部長は必要と思った措置を取ることが出来たのである。

　しかし時代の進歩と地方行政の発達に伴い、道知事が警察と衛生業務の全てを掌握するべきだと認められた。1919年8月に憲兵隊員制度が撤廃され、警察は道知事の管理下に移された。警察官・医官・検疫官からなる第三部が置かれ、後に警察部となった。

　権限が移行される期間は、一般行政事務の整理と統一に重きが置かれ、中央集権の方針が固守されたため、地方自治体の長である道長官の権限は幾分制限されてきた。しかし、地方行政が改善され、毎年役人の業務も増加してくると、中央集権の体制では効率的に対応することが難しくなった。そのため地方分権が進められるようになり、1919年8月の全般的な改正により、道知事に任された権限が徐々に広げられることとなった。

　日韓併合後、現存する制度の改正に関して慎重な調査がなされ、1914年3月には居留地制度も関係各国の領事館との協議を経て、撤

GOVERNMENT ORGANIZATION

to abolish the foreign settlement system by agreement with the nations interested. In the following month, new regulations relating to urban prefectures and school associations came into force, by which both were recognized as juridical persons, the jurisdictional district of the settlements being incorporated into that of their respective urban prefectures, while all business concerning the education of Japanese children was transferred to the hands of school associations formed within each prefectural jurisdiction. In this way the long pending question of the adjustment and unification of the local administrative system was brought to a satisfactory conclusion.

As a consequence of the revision of the system all business regarding the registration of perpetual leases, hitherto conducted by the consular representatives of the Powers concerned, was turned over to the law courts. Perpetual leases being particular real rights, the provision of ownership was applied correspondingly, and it was recognized that they could be made objects of other rights. Further, foreign lease-holders of land in perpetuity were given the option of converting their leases into actual ownership, while those preferring to make no alteration in their lands were required to bear as a rule taxes and other public charges on a par with actual landowners.

Since the enforcement of the local administrative readjustment, steady progress has been made in all lines of society, in industry, education, communications, and commerce, as well as in the various official functions. Especially note-worthy has been the recent development of local interests. So the reorganization of the Government-General being effected, it was decided to introduce greater reforms into the administration of

廃する準備が整った。

　同年翌月には、『府制及び改正学校組合令』が施行され、これによって府と学校組合が法人として認められ、外国人居留地は府の行政区域に編入された。また日本人子弟の教育に関する事務は、府の区域内に設置された学校組合に引き継がれることとなった。こうして、地方行政の長期に亘る調整と統一という懸案事項については満足のいく結果が得られたのである。

　制度改正の結果として、それまでは居留地の各国領事官によって行われていた外国人の永代租借権の登録に関する全ての業務は裁判所に引き継がれることになった。永代租借権は特別な物件として扱われ、永代租借権を実際の所有権に変える選択肢が与えられた。また所有権への変更を希望しない場合でも、土地所有者と同じように、税金やその他の公共料金を負担することが求められた。

　地方制度が整理統一されたことにより、公の業務だけでなく、社会秩序、産業、教育、情報伝達そして商業においても発展が成し遂げられた。

　特に注目に値するのは地方の重要性が増したことである。そのため、總督府の再編成によってより大きな改革を国の行政に導入し、特に地方分権化を目的とすることが決定された。そうすれば地方行政はよりしっかりと確立することになるだろう。

　この方向性の最初の段階として、1920 年 7 月に関連する諸法令の

the country, and in particular to aim at decentralization of power, so that a system of local self-government might be firmly established in the future. Accordingly, as the first step in this direction, in July, 1920, further amendment was made in the existing local system, providing for the creation of advisory councils for public corporations, the members to be either appointed or elected, in order to give advice about local finance and other important matters. By these organs it is hoped that popular sentiment will be reflected in the local administration, and that through them more complete organs of local self-government will gradually be evolved.

Formation of Local Councils--

After a year or so of careful inquiry into the subject the revised system of local administration was at last proclaimed on July 29, 1920, and advisory bodies were formed for the administration of provinces, municipalities, districts, and villages. Of course these organs were far from being real local self-governing bodies, since Chosen was still not in a condition to justify the immediate enforcement of a complete system of local self-government, and the people needed a course of training in the transaction of public affairs. Still, they marked an important step forward in the right direction.

In the local administrative system hitherto obtaining in Chosen there existed municipalities and villages as the lowest magistracies, the former in cities and towns and the latter in rural communities. Besides, there were organs called "the public common school expenditure" for the benefit of Korean children, school associations for the education of Japanese children, and water-utilization associations dealing with irrigation. Of

改廃がなされた。地方財政やそれ以外の重要な問題について助言を
与えることを目的として、諮問会議の創設のためにメンバーが任命
あるいは選出された。こうした機関によって一般の民意が地方行政
に反映され、より完璧な地方自治政府の機関へと発達することが期
待された。

地方議会の編成

　一年ほど慎重な調査と研究が行われた後、改訂された地方行政の
制度が1920年7月29日に布告されて、諮問機関が道、府、郡、面
の行政に対して組織された。

　もちろん、こうした組織は実際の地方自治とはかけ離れていた。
その理由として朝鮮は依然として地方自治の完全な制度を執行出来
るような状態ではなく、民衆は地方公共の事務に習熟するための教
育が必要だったからである。それでも、彼らは正しい方向性におけ
る重要な段階を進んでいた。

　朝鮮のそれまでの地方自治制度では、都市部に府を置き、農村部
には最も低い行政区分である面を置いていた。さらに、朝鮮の子供
たちのためには「公立普通学校費」があり、日本人の子供たちの教
育には「学校組合」があった。また灌漑の事務を扱う「水利組合」
があった。これらのうち最後の2つがかろうじて自治の様相を呈し

GOVERNMENT ORGANIZATION

these the two last only possessed anything of a self-governing aspect. Although the municipalities had their own advisory councils, and specially designated villages had advisers attached to them, they were composed of comparatively few members, and all were nominated by the Government, so it could not be said that they really represented popular desires and ideas. On the other hand, the prefects were always government officials, and even village headmen were appointed by the Government. Then, too, the public common school expenditure was under the management of prefects, sub-prefects, and island governors, whilst provincial expenditure was supervised exclusively by Provincial Governors. In addition, each province had three councillors and each city, district, and island two councillors, yet these men being appointed by the Government from among a few men of influence, and their posts being merely honorary, they too could hardly be considered representative of popular sentiment, so a revision of the local system was imperatively necessary that the way might be opened for expression of the popular will, and it was effected in the following manner:

In revising the organization of municipal advisory councils it was arranged that the members should be elected by popular vote instead of being appointed by the Government, and, at the same time, all villages were to be provided with advisory councils for discussion of village finances and other important affairs. Since, however, the elective system was quite new to the Koreans in general and, if enforced in all villages without exception, might become the source of endless disputes and confusion, it was arranged that only in specially selected villages should the members of the advisory council be elected by popular vote, and

ていた。

府は自身の諮問議会を持っており、特別に指定された面には付属の顧問がいたが、彼らは比較的少数のメンバーで構成されており、全員政府によって任命されていたので、民意を本当に代表していたとは言えないかもしれない。また、府における府尹は政府の官吏であり、面の面長さえ政府の任命によるものだった。

公立普通学費については官吏である府尹および郡守、島司の管理となっていたが、道の支出は道知事が独自に管理していた。道には3名、府、郡、島には2名の参事が置かれ、道知事、府尹、郡守、島司、それぞれの諮問に応じていた。しかし参事もまた政府の任命によるものであり、彼らの地位は単に肩書きだけで地方の名家などから選ばれる名誉職にすぎず、これもまた民意の代表者とはほとんど考えられなかった。民意を反映するという道が開かれるために地方制度の改正は否応なしに必要であった。それは次のように実行されることになった。

まず府の諮問機関である「府協議会」を改正し、従来のような政府の任命ではなく民衆の投票により構成員が選ばれるように準備された。また、全ての面にも財政やその他の重要事項を討議する諮問機関として「面協議会」が設置された。

しかしながら、一般民衆の投票による選挙制度は普通の朝鮮人にとっては全く新しいものであったため、もし全ての面で例外なく実行されれば、果てしない論争と混乱の種となるかもしれなかった。そのため、特別に選定された面だけで、国民の投票によって議員が

226   GOVERNMENT ORGANIZATION

that in all other villages the appointment of the councils should be left
to the discretion of the district or island magistrates who, in making
appointments, were to take into account the opinions of the principal
inhabitants in their districts.

Public common school expenditure, so-called, existed only for providing
an elementary education for Korean children. But new regulations were
framed to deal with all affairs relating to the general education of Koreans
throughout the country. To meet the expenditure the authorities were
empowered to levy school taxes, requisition labor and goods, collect rents,
raise public loans, and also form plans for consecutive expenditure. Then,
as advisory organs, school councils were created. In cities the members
are elected by popular vote, while in districts or islands they are appointed
from among candidates elected by village councils.

Further, as advisory organs to discuss provincial budgets, etc.,
provincial councils were created, the members of which are appointed
by Provincial Governors from among candidates elected by municipal or
village councils, as well as from among men of knowledge and repute.

The revised local system came into effect on October 1, 1920, and the
election of members of councils of municipalities and designated villages
took place on November 20 following. At first the Koreans seemed to
adopt a rather indifferent attitude, many of them evidently being duped
by the seditious talk of agitators. However, as the election day drew near,
inspired by the Japanese canvassing, they began to show great interest
and enthusiasm, and many offered themselves as candidates, and the
elections proceeded without a hitch. The following list gives the result in
12 municipalities and 24 specially designated villages:

選ばれるように準備され、他の全ての面では、議員の任命は郡や島の長の裁量に任されることなり、任命する時には、その区域の主たる住民の意見を考慮する形となった。

いわゆる公立普通学校費は朝鮮人の子供たちに初等教育を提供するためだけに存在した。しかし国中の朝鮮人の教育全般に関する事柄を扱うために、新しい規制の枠組みが求められた。教育のための支出に充てるため、政府は学校税を課し、また労働や物資の形で納めさせるようにし、また地代を徴収し、公共の貸し付けを工面し、さらに長期の予算計画をまとめるための権限を当局に与えた。

さらに諮問機関として「学校評議会」が置かれた。都市部では学校評議会の構成員は一般投票で選ばれ、郡や島では面協議会が選んだ候補者の中から任命された。また道の予算を討議する諮問機関として、「道評議会」が設置され、その構成員は経験と評判のある人々からだけでなく府協議会と面協議会によって選ばれた候補者の中からも任命された。

改訂された地方制度は1920年10月1日をもって実施された。続いて11月20日には、府と指定された面の協議会員の選出が行われた。最初、朝鮮人たちはむしろ無関心な態度を取っていたようだった。また彼らのうちの多くは政治運動家の扇動的な言葉にだまされていた。しかしながら、選挙日が近づくにつれ、日本人の応援演説に感化され、彼らは大いなる興味と熱意を示し始めた。多くの人が立候補し、選挙は順調に進んだのである。

次の表は12の府と24の面での選挙結果である。

MUNICIPALITIES

	Number of Voters	Votes Cast	Percentage	Number of members Elected
Japanese...........	6,251	5,486	88	134
Korean.............	4,713	3,122	66	56

VILLAGES

	Number of Voters	Votes Cast	Percentage	Number of members Elected
Japanese...........	1,399	1,224	88	130
Korean.............	1,623	1,198	73	126

The members elected were mostly leading persons in their localities. Especially creditable was it that the elected Koreans were all rising men with moderate ideas. Another very creditable thing was the fact that Japanese restricted the number of their own candidates by agreement among themselves, and that some elected Japanese resigned in favor of Koreans next to them at the polls, while not a few Koreans gave their votes for Japanese candidates.

A little later, the members of councils of villages other than those specially designated were appointed, and in this way the election and appointment of members of all the municipal and village councils were successfully completed. The election and appointment of members of school councils in cities, districts, and islands, as well as those of provincial councils, were all completed with equal success on December 20, 1920. The composition of these provincial councils is shown in the following list:

府

	有権者数	投票数	投票率	選出された議員
内地人（日本人）	6,251	5,486	88%	134
朝鮮人	4,713	3,122	66%	56

面

	有権者数	投票数	投票率	選出された議員
内地人（日本人）	1,399	1,224	88%	130
朝鮮人	1,623	1,198	73%	126

　選ばれた議員たちはほとんどが彼らの地方では指導者であった。特に賞賛に値することは、選ばれた朝鮮人たちは全て穏健な考えを持つ新進の人物たちであったということである。もう一つ大変賞賛に値することは、日本人たちは自分たちの間で合意して日本人の候補者を制限したことである。朝鮮人は少なからず日本人候補者に投票した。そして当選した日本人の中には、次点の朝鮮人に当選を譲る者が何人もいたのである。

　選挙を行うよう指定されなかった面の協議会員もやがて任命された。こうして全ての府と面で協議会員の選挙と任命は成功裏に終了した。また、道評議会、府、郡、島、における学校評議会員の選挙と任命も全て1920年12月20日に同様に成功裏に終了した。こうした議員任命と選出の結果は次の表に示している。

	Members Appointed	Members Elected	Total
Japanese................	63	24	87
Korean.................	56	219	275
Total..............	119	243	362

The first meetings of these councils after the reform initiated in the local administrative system were held between February and April of 1921, and each proved fairly successful and was well attended. The discussions were very smoothly conducted and were marked by great enthusiasm. Indeed, during the sessions all showed a co-operative attitude, and laid before the authorities questions and opinions reflecting the popular will, to which the latter responded with the utmost sincerity. On the whole, the meetings ended to the great satisfaction of all concerned.

Inspection of Local Administration--

In old Korea an institution existed for maintaining certain officials charged with the duty of going about incognito to inspect local administration and check official oppression. This was lauded as an excellent system under the Yi Dynasty, but these secret agents are said to have frequently abused their power by turning the misdeeds of local officials to their own profit. On the division between the judicature and executive being distinctly marked out, in 1907, officials were no longer able thus to abuse their power and oppress the people. However, in view of the fact that local public affairs had not only rapidly increased and become more complex in substance, and that the powers of Provincial Governors had been extended so as to carry on the administration in a manner more

	任命された議員	選出された議員	合計
内地人（日本人）	63	24	87
朝鮮人	56	219	275
合計	119	243	362

　地方行政制度で始まった改正後のこうした評議会の最初の会合が1921年の2月から4月の間に行われた。それぞれの会合はまずまずの成功をおさめ、出席率も良かった。討論は非常に円滑に行われ、大いなる熱意が目立っていた。実に、会期中は全員が協力的な姿勢を示し、当局の前に国民の意思を反映した質問と意見を提出し、それらに対し、政府は最大限の誠意をもって対応した。全体として会合は関係した全員の大いなる満足をもたらす結果となった。

地方行政の監察
　朝鮮には古来、お忍びで地方行政を調査し、地方役人の圧制を調べる義務を担った組織が存在していた。これは李王朝の最高の良政として賞賛されたが、こうした秘密任務の遂行者が、地方の役人たちの悪事を自分たちの利益になるように利用して権力を乱用することもよくあったと言われている。

　1907年に司法と行政が明確に分離されたことで、もはや役人はそのような権力を乱用して民衆を抑圧することは出来なくなった。しかしながら、地方公務の量が急激に増えて複雑になっただけでなく、より行き届いた地方行政のために道知事の権力が拡大されてきたと

232 GOVERNMENT ORGANIZATION

fitted to local conditions, it was found imperative to institute thorough superintendence of their doings in order to see that enterprises undertaken were really adapted to the situation, and that they contributed to the promotion of the popular welfare. At the same time, it was considered necessary to secure closer connection between the central and local governments in order to make the new administrative policy as effective as possible, and to probe fully popular sentiments. For these reasons a Local Administration Inspectorate was formed with a staff consisting of 2 chief inspectors, 5 special secretaries, and a number of clerks.

Local Finance--

At present the revenues of the provinces are mainly obtained by making additional levies on the land and urban land taxes, and by imposing household, market, abattoir and slaughtering, fishing, shipping, and vehicle taxes. To those sources of revenue must be added the subsidies from the national treasury and receipts derived from Government undertakings. The revenue thus obtained meets the outlays for education, sanitation, public works, industrial encouragement, etc., of a local nature. Besides, there is a certain amount of interest accruing from the Imperial donation funds which is spent on philanthropic undertakings. The incidence and management of local expenditure are much the same as those in Japan proper, but, unlike the mother country, from financial considerations the two items of local police and district office expenditure have been excluded from provincial budgets and are still borne by the national treasury.

The Budgets for Local Finance are shown in the table on page 234.

The local finance budget for 1925-26 makes a preliminary estimate of

いう事実も考え合わせると、地方行政が本当に状況に適合して行われているか、そして彼らが公共福利の促進に貢献しているかを見ていくために、地方行政に対して充分な監督制度を設けることが不可欠となった。同時に新行政制度が出来る限り効果的になり、国民感情に充分に深く応えることが出来るように、中央政府と地方政府の間に密接な関係を確保することが必要であると考えられた。こうした理由のため、地方行政監察団が専任監察官2人、特別書記官5人と多数の事務官で組織された。

地方財政

　現時点で道の歳入は、主として地税と市街地税付加税、戸税と家屋税、市場税、屠場税、屠畜税、漁業税、船税、車両税、などの地方税を主な財源としている。さらに、国庫補助金および政府事業から得られる収入などが加わる。こうして得られた歳入は道独自の教育、衛生、公共事業、産業奨励などのための支出に充てられた。さらに、臨時恩賜金から生じる利息も慈善活動に充てられた。地方歳出の負担と管理は日本本土のものと全く同じであるが、財政状況を考慮して地方警察と郡役所費の2項に該当するものの支出は地方予算ではなく、依然として国庫が担っていた。

　1925年度の地方財政予算は、歳入の予備推定を2256万7529円とし、提案された歳出は数字の上では帳尻が合っている。

　支出の最も著しい増加は教育に関するものであり約700万円まで増加している。衛生と病院に関しては約200万円まで増加した。

234 GOVERNMENT ORGANIZATION

22,567,529 yen for revenue, the proposed expenditures balancing at that figure. The most notable increases in expenditure are those for education, which rises to seven million yen, and for sanitation and hospitals, which rises to two million yen. The latter item is of special significance, since it discloses an advance in local expenditure in public health from 212,000 yen in 1922 to nearly ten times that amount in 1926.

LOCAL FINANCE BUDGETS

(In yen. 1 yen = 50 cents U. S.)

Description	1923	1922	1910
Revenue:			
Additional Levy on Land and Urban Land Tax	4,775,288	4,361,898	605,427
Household and House Tax	4,817,992	4,801,493	
Market Tax	593,924	581,388	137,535
Abattoir and Slaughtering Tax	664,622	684,630	241,347
Fishing Tax	158,181	151,089	......
Shipping Tax	1,142	3,119	......
Vehicle Tax	541,729	432,238	......
Receipts from Imperial Donation Funds	917,439	937,293	......
Subsidy from Central Government	2,804,691	3,618,778	235,427
Balance Transferred	1,714,847	1,360,725	56,390
Other Sources	2,445,735	2,361,005	33,644
Total	19,135,590	19,293,656	1,309,770
Expenditure:			
Civil Engineering	5,199,480	4,911,100	303,464
Industrial Encouragement	4,758,504	4,310,867	104,458
Affording Means of Livelihood	1,481,697	1,340,684	......
Education	5,581,195	6,698,395	164,238
Sanitation and Hospitals	296,273	211,922	35,281
Relief and Charity	31,304	33,880	3,600
Provincial Councils	81,820	83,671	......
Social Works	359,798	485,902	......
Transferred to Imperial Donation Funds	56,317	75,835	......
Miscellaneous	954,611	771,794	135,265
Reserves	334,591	369,606	......
Total	19,135,590	19,293,656	746,306

衛生と病院の項目は特に重要である、なぜなら 1922 年の約 21 万 2000 円から 1926 年はその金額のほぼ十倍まで増加したことを示しているからである。次の表は地方財政についてまとめたものである。

道財政予算（単位は円　当時１円＝５０セント）

歳入	１９２３	１９２２	１９１０
地税と市街地税付加税	4,475,288	4,361,898	605,427
戸税と家屋税	4,817,992	4,801,493	-
市場税	593,924	581,388	137,535
屠場税と屠畜税	664,622	684,630	241,347
漁業税	158,181	151,089	-
船税	1,142	3,119	-
車両税	541,729	432,238	-
臨時恩賜金からの収入	917,439	937,293	-
国庫補助金	2,804,691	3,618,778	235,427
譲渡の収支	1,714,847	1,360,725	56,390
他の財源	2,445,735	2,361,005	33,643
合　計	19,135,590	19,293,656	1,309,769

歳出	１９２３	１９２２	１９１０
土木費	5,199,480	4,911,100	303,464
勧業費（産業奨励）	4,758,504	4,310,867	104,458
授産費（生活手段負担）	1,481,697	1,340,684	-
教育費	5,581,195	6,698,395	164,238
衛生費（衛生と病院）	296,273	211,922	35,281
救恤費（慈善）	31,304	33,880	3,600
道評議会費	81,820	83,671	-
社会救済費	359,798	485,902	-
臨時恩賜金繰戻金	56,317	75,835	-
その他	954,611	771,794	135,265
予備費	334,591	369,606	-
合　計	19,135,590	19,293,656	746,306

※表の数字は『朝鮮總督府施政年報 大正十一年度』による

GOVERNMENT ORGANIZATION

On the revenue side one item alone calls for explanation—receipt from the Imperial Donation Funds. These, amounting in all to 30,000,000 yen were granted to Korea at the time of annexation, by the Imperial Japanese Treasury. Of the whole amount 17,398,000 yen were allotted to prefectures and districts as funds for such works as undertakings affording means of livelihood, educational works, and relief works. The funds are permanently in the care of the Provincial Governors, and the interest derived from them, aggregating 869,900 yen per annum, is devoted to the above-mentioned works in the proportion of sixty, thirty, and ten per cent respectively. These undertakings, carefully selected to accord with actual local conditions, have been established as widely as possible.

On the expenditure side it is to be noted that enterprises at provincial expense come under five heads, viz., (1) public works, (2) sanitation and hospitals, (3) relief and charity, (4) industrial encouragement, and (5) education. Public works are primarily concerned with road construction and repairs, rivers, harbors, water-utilization, irrigation, land-clearing, etc. Sanitation occupies itself chiefly with vaccination, inspection of carcasses, and also the building of isolation hospitals, public wells, street latrines, etc. Relief and charity works take care of the sick or dying on the road and other needy people. Industrial encouragement takes up the development of local industries such as agriculture, sericulture, forestry, fishery, weaving, paper manufacture, etc., and, for agricultural improvement, seedling stations are now maintained by all the provinces after the example of Japan proper. These stations conduct experiments with various species, and distribute among the farmers improved seeds, seedlings, and livestock, while they give the training needed in farming, carry on inspection of

第五章　政府組織Ⅱ　　237

　歳入については説明の必要な項目がある。「臨時恩賜金からの収入」である。臨時恩賜金は併合の際に大日本帝国の国庫から授与されたもので 3000 万円にも上る。総計のうち 1739 万 8000 円が、生活手段負担金、教育事業、慈善事業などを引き受けるような業務の基金として地方に割り当てられた。

　その基金は永久に道知事が管理するもので、そこから生じる利息は年間で総額 86 万 9900 円にもなり、生活手段負担金 60 パーセント、教育事業 30 パーセント、慈善事業 10 パーセントの割合で割り振られた。こうした事業は実際の地方の現状に合わせて慎重に選抜され、可能な限り広く設けられた。

　歳出面では地方政府支出の事業で上位 5 位に入るのが以下である。

(1)　土木費（公共事業）

(2)　衛生費（衛生と病院）

(3)　救恤費（救済と慈善）

(4)　勧業費（産業奨励）

(5)　教育費

　土木費は主に道路建設と補修、川、港、水利用、灌漑、土地整備などである。衛生費は主にワクチン注射、死体の検視また隔離病院、公共井戸、公衆トイレなどが占めている。救恤費は路地上での病気や瀕死の人やその他の貧しい人々を対象としている。勧業費は農業、養蚕業、林業、漁業と織物、紙工業などの地方産業の発達を担っている。農業の改善のためには、日本本土の例にならい、今や全ての道に種苗場が設置されている。種苗場では様々な種で実験を行い、

all rice and beans for export in order to secure uniform quality, and also send out itinerant technical experts for the practical guidance of the country people. Besides, as economic crops the planting of American cotton and the sugar-beet is extensively encouraged. In sericulture, the climatic conditions of Chosen being very favorable, remarkably good results have already rewarded this official encouragement, and to effect further improvement in it nurseries have been formed for the production of silkworm eggs of superior species, and stations for the combating of diseases attacking the silkworm and for controlling the sale of silkworm eggs and mulberry trees, and in addition, visiting experts are sent round to give the farmers proper suggestions for the betterment of their work. For forestry and fishery a number of experts have specially been appointed to instruct the people in these lines. Lastly, in education the establishment or maintenance of agricultural, industrial, and commercial schools of secondary grade is carried on, and by the aid of subsidies from the Imperial Donation Funds elementary educational works also.

Originally, enterprises with the Imperial monetary grant were of three kinds, but in view of the rapidly changing social conditions various social works have been added. Relief works are carried on in the time of calamities, giving succor to the sufferers by providing them with seed-grain, foodstuffs, huts, farming tools, etc. In educational works the aim is principally to subsidize elementary schools. Undertakings affording means of livelihood are chiefly for those having no fixed occupation or property, so as to enable them to obtain permanent employment. For instance, to those too poor to enter the sericultural school, boarding expenses are allowed, and to those successfully completing the training course capital is

第五章　政府組織Ⅱ

農家に改良した種、苗と家畜類を分配する一方、農場経営で必要とされる教育を施し、一定の質を確保するため輸出用の全てのコメや豆の検査を実行し、また田舎の人々の実務指導のために巡回する技術指導員を送る。さらに経済的作物として、アメリカ綿と甜菜の栽培が広範囲に亘って奨励された。養蚕業には朝鮮の気候の状況がとても好ましく、著しく良い結果を出している。そしてそこでさらなる改善をするために、高品質のカイコの卵を生産するための養蚕園が作られ、蚕を襲う病気を除去し、蚕の卵とクワの木の販売を管理するための養蚕所が作られ、加えて訪問指導者が農家を巡回して仕事の改善のために適切な助言を農民たちに与えるのである。林業と漁業に対しても、多くの指導者たちが人々に教えるために特別に任命されている。最後に教育においては中等レベルの農業、工業、商業学校の設立が進められ、臨時恩賜金からの補助金の援助で初等教育もまた機能している。

　元来、大日本帝国から財政交付がなされる分野は３つに限られていたが、急激に変化する社会情勢を考えあわせて、様々な社会事業が加えられてきた。災難時には援助事業が進められ、穀物の種、食料品、小屋、農機具などが被災者に援助として提供された。教育事業では、主にその目的は初等教育の補助であった。生活手段を与える事業は定職や定まった住居がない者に対して行われるが、彼らが終身雇用を獲得出来ることを目的としている。例えば、貧困のため養蚕学校に入学出来なかった者に対しては、寄宿費用が支給され、訓練課程を首尾よく終了した者に対しては自分で独立して事業を始

240   GOVERNMENT ORGANIZATION

furnished to enable them to start on their own account. As social works, the establishment of public markets, pawn-shops, bathhouses, lodging-houses, laundries, people's luncheon-rooms, agencies for laborers, free medical treatment of the sick poor, and the care of orphans are extensively carried on.

Municipalities--

At the time of annexation most of the urban prefectures were found in open ports, and in them Japanese municipalities, foreign settlements, and other local bodies existed side by side, each pursuing its own system, while for the management of public business relating to Koreans no organ was provided, so that many obstacles were encountered in conducting municipal administration. In April, 1914, therefore, new organic regulations for urban prefectures were enforced, and Koreans, Japanese and foreigners alike were brought under one uniform system.

Prefectural Municipalities were then created as legal bodies in the principal cities in Chosen, and their respective jurisdictional districts were made to coincide with those prefectures established as state administrative divisions. The Prefects, who are appointed by the State, represent ex officio the inhabitants and conduct all municipal business, and the municipal councils act as their advisory organs. Until recently the members were appointed by the Provincial Governor subject to approval by the Governor-General, but as a result of the reorganization of the Government-General, and in response to the demands of the times, the members are now elected by popular vote so that the councils may be really representatives of the general public.

められるように資本が与えられる。社会事業としては、公共市場、
質屋、浴場、宿泊所、洗濯場、人々の昼食休憩所、労働者のための
事務所、貧しい病人のための無料医療の確立、そして孤児の保護な
どが大規模に進められている。

府

　併合の頃には、都市部の行政地区である府のほとんどは開港場に
見い出されたが、その中には日本人自治区や外国人居留区、その他
の組織が一緒に存在してそれぞれが独自の制度で運営されていた一
方、朝鮮人に関する公共事業の管理にあたる組織は１つもなかった
ので、府が行政を行う上では多くの障害があった。1914年４月に府
についての新しい組織的な官制が施行されて、朝鮮人、日本人、外
国人が統一された制度の下にまとめられた。

　またその際に、朝鮮の主たる都市部には地方行政区としての府が
作られ、その府と合致するように、司法区域が定められた。

　府の長である府尹は国が任命した。府尹は住民を代表し、府に関
する全ての業務を行った。府協議会が、その諮問機関として機能す
る。府協議会の議員は、最近まで、總督府の承認を受けて道知事が
任命していたが、朝鮮總督府官制改正の結果として、時代の要求に
応じて、議会が真に一般大衆の代表となれるように、協議会の構成
員は民衆の投票によって選ばれている。

242   GOVERNMENT ORGANIZATION

The expenditure by municipalities was in principle to be defrayed with the income from rents, fees, and public properties, but these sources being inadequate the chief source of revenue is now found in municipal taxes, while receipts from rents and fees, municipal loans, and State and local subsidies follow in order. Municipal taxes consist of additional levies in the State taxes on urban land and the local taxes on buildings, and other special taxes of which the major are the business tax and the house tax. In imposing these taxes care is taken to avoid any pronounced increase in the burden on the residents, especially on the Koreans, so on the whole few complaints have been made; on the contrary, the income from municipal taxes improving year by year, the financial condition of the municipalities may safely be said to present a flourishing aspect.

The aggregate annual revenue of the twelve municipalities of Chosen has risen from about two million yen in 1918 to about eight million in 1922, the expenditure-estimates balancing at those figures. In practice the revenue shows a surplus over the expenditure, and this in 1923 reached the substantial sum of 1,714,847 yen.

The chief single source of municipal revenue is municipal taxation. The average per household in 1922 was 14.3 yen. The average does not, however, represent the actual incidence of municipal taxation, for the taxes are so framed that Japanese and foreigners pay a much higher sum per household than do the Koreans. In 1922 the per household figures were for foreigners 26.1 yen, for Japanese 32.4, and for Koreans 5.2.

Although there are many works that have to be undertaken and managed by municipalities, anything like sudden increase in the burden

府の経費は原則的には、使用料、手数料、そして公共財産から得られる収入で賄われることになっていたが、こうした財源は不充分で、現在では主な歳入源は府税となっている。さらには府債収入、国庫補助、道地方費補助となっている。府税は、国税である市街地税と、道の地方税である家屋税に付加税を課する特別税から成り立っている。他の特別税で主なものは、営業税、戸別税などがある。府税の課税にあたっては、府の居住者、中でも朝鮮人への負担が激増することがないように注意が払われたので、全体としてほとんど不満は聞かれなかった。府税としての歳入は年々増加し、府の財政状態は隆盛を極めていると言っても、あながち間違いではないかもしれない。

12ある府の予算の総額は、1918年度が約200万円だったが、1922年度には約800万円まで増加し、歳出推定額もその数字で決算されている。実際は、歳入は歳出を上回り、1923年度には171万4847円の歳入超過となった。

府の歳入の最も大きな財源は府税である。1922年度には1世帯当たりの府税の平均額は14.3円だった。しかしながら、その平均額というものは府税の実際の負担を表してはいない。というのも、税金は細かく規定され、日本人と外国人は朝鮮人よりも1世帯当たりかなりの額を支払うからである。1922年度には、1世帯当たりの額は外国人は26.1円、日本人は32.4円、朝鮮人は5.2円であった。

府が引き受けて処理すべき事業は多岐にわたったが、住民、特に朝鮮人への税負担が急激に増加するようなことは出来る限り避けら

on the inhabitants, especially on the Koreans, has been avoided as far as possible, and works most urgently needed and requiring big expenditure have been undertaken by raising public loans. The more important works undertaken by the municipalities are (1) waterworks, (2) sewerage, (3) general and isolation hospitals, (4) social works, and (5) street, road, and bridge construction and repair, scavengering, and maintenance of abattoirs, cemeteries, crematories, markets, parks, town halls, public libraries, and fire-brigades.

Villages--

In the days of the Korean Government village administration throughout the country was in a very confused state, no distinction being maintained between public and private affairs, yet it was concerned with hardly anything beyond the collecting of State taxes and census-taking. So, on the present régime being instituted in 1910, organic regulations for local government were promulgated, and contained a specific provision respecting village headmen. By it a headman was to act as assistant to the district magistrate in conducting the administrative business in a village, while he was required to have a public office, or, if conducted at his own house, to set apart a room for public business only, and at the same time permanent clerks were appointed to village offices. Later on every district held occasional conferences of village headmen and formed an institute for village clerks, so that the better management of their respective villages might be secured.

Formerly, villages were not authorized to make a levy for anything

れた。最も緊急に必要とされ巨額の費用を要するような事業については、府債の発行によって費用が賄われた。

府が行った最も重要な事業は（1）上水道、（2）下水道、（3）一般病院と伝染隔離病院、（4）社会救済事業、（5）市区整備、道路・橋梁の改修・清掃、屠場、墓地、火葬場、市場、公園、公会堂、公立図書館、消防などの施設の維持であった。

面

大韓帝国政府の時代、国中の面の行政は大変混乱した状態にあった。面の役人は公務と私事を混同し、税の徴収と人口の調査以上のことはほとんど為されていなかった。

現在では1910年に官制が整えられ、面行政の系統的な規定も公布されている。

面長に対する具体的な条項も定められている。

面での行政業務を行う際には、面長は群守の補佐を務めることとなり、また面長は、面事務所を新設するか、あるいは自宅で業務を行う場合は、公務専用の部屋を使用するように励行された。さらに常任の面書記を置き、組織と執務方法を定めた。あらゆる郡では、面長協議会と面書記協議会が開かれ、それぞれの村の改善が促されることとなった。

しかし当時は、給与と事務費以外の経費への権限が与えられてお

outside salaries and office expenses, so that being in reality without financial power to conduct any public enterprise, those most necessary for their development could only be carried out by various private associations or as joint undertakings, and great lack of uniformity was experienced. Accordingly, in 1914, the number of villages was reduced by one-half to give effect to financial readjustment, and, taking into account gradual improvement in popular conditions as well as in village affairs, a new village system was finally instituted in 1917. Indeed, the adoption of this new system might be called an epoch-making event in the history of local administration, for by this villages for the first time were distinctly recognized as public bodies of some importance.

According to this system, villages are the lowest of the administrative divisions, and are local bodies conducting all public business within their jurisdictions, with village headmen as sole managers. The expenses of village offices are met by the income from levies, fees, and rents, but, by those villages specially designated by the Government, loans can be floated for enterprises, and 4 to 8 honorary advisers were appointed to each as consultants.

After the reorganization of the Government-General in 1919 it was considered advisable to make further revision in the existing village system, and this was done in July, 1920. The most important revision was the creation of new village councils as advisory organs in all villages. Membership of these was made elective or nominative according to the standing of the village, and their function is principally to discuss village finances.

At present the number of villages is 2,504, including 41 designated

らず、いかなる公共事業も行うことが出来なかった。面の発展に最も必要とされる事業は、民間の組合あるいは共同組織によって実行された。これは行政として事務の統一性を欠く弊害を生じた。そのため1914年、財政再編成のために面の数が2分の1に減らされた。そして、面の状況だけでなく国民の状態における漸次の改善を綱領に入れて、1917年に新しい面の制度が制定された。実際この新しい制度の採択は地方行政の歴史において画期的な出来事と言っていいかもしれない、というのも、これによって面が初めて、重要な公共組織としてはっきりと認められたからである。

　新しい面の制度によると、面は行政区画の最小単位として、管轄内の公共業務全てを処理し、面長がその唯一の管理職である。面事務所の経費は、徴税、手数料、使用料などからの収入で支払われる。特に總督府から指定を受けた面については、公債を発行することが認められ、4人から8人の名誉職たる相談役を置いて面長の諮問機関とした。

　1919年の總督府官制改編の後で、当時の面制度において更なる改訂が適切であると考えられており、それは1920年に行われた。最も重要な改定は、全ての面に諮問機関として面協議会を創設することであった。協議会員は村の立場に応じて選挙または指名で選ばれ、主に村の財政について話し合うのが役割であった。

　現在、面の数は特別指定された41を含む2504である。それら

248 GOVERNMENT ORGANIZATION

ones. Their total expenditure figured in 1919 at some 6,093,000 yen and increased in the fiscal year 1922-23 to nearly 16,654,000 yen, largely due to the growing expansion of the various works with which they are charged. Public undertakings common to a majority of them are (1) the building of roads and bridges and the upkeep of ferry-boats and river-banks; (2) the holding of markets, and work in model forestry and farming; (3) the maintenance of cemeteries, crematories, abattoirs, isolation hospitals, water supply, drainage, cleansing, and disinfection; and (4) fire-brigades and defence against floods. Besides these, some villages maintain jetties, moorings, electric lighting and relief works.

School Associations for Japanese--

Formerly, in places other than cities or open ports in which Japanese municipalities were organized, the education of Japanese children was conducted by School Associations, and these were finally recognized as juridical persons by virtue of the regulations issued in 1909. On the abolition of Japanese municipalities and the adoption of the new municipal system, all public undertakings were transferred to the Prefectural Office. But educational measures for Japanese children could not be transferred to the local administration proper, since it bore on Koreans and Japanese alike, because the different conditions and language of the two peoples prevented their being brought under the same educational treatment for some time to come. On account of this, the regulations for school associations were revised, and a school association was required to be organized in each urban prefecture, and to it was transferred all educational matters affecting Japanese.

の歳出の合計は1919年度では609万3000円で1922年度ではほぼ1665万4000円にまで増加した。これは主に彼らに任された様々な事業が発展し続けていることによるものである。

多くの面で共通して行われる主たる公的事業は（1）道路や橋梁の建設・補修と渡船や護岸の維持管理、（2）市場の保有と森林と農業モデルの研究、（3）墓地、火葬場、屠場、隔離病院、水供給、下水道、清掃、防疫、（4）消防団と洪水に対する防災施設である。このほか、中には防波堤、係船停泊所、電燈、救済事業などを維持遂行している所もある。

日本の学校組合

以前は、日本人の自治区が組織されていた都市部や開港場以外の場所では、日本人子弟の教育は学校組合によって行われていた。これらは1909年に発表された規定のおかげで法人として完全に認められるようになった。

日本人自治区の廃止と新しい府の制度の採択により、全ての公的事業は府庁に移された。しかし日本人子弟に対する教育対策は地方府政に適切に移されなかった。朝鮮人と日本人の間には状況と言語において隔たりがあり、しばらくの間は同じ教育を施すのは難しかったからである。そのため、学校組合についての規定は修正された。学校組合が各都市の府に組織されることが求められ、日本人に関する教育についての全ての事柄は学校組合に移されたのである。

According to the revised regulations, a school association is formed by Japanese residents possessing a certain qualification. It being self-governing, in contrast to other government offices, it has a council composed of six to eighteen elected members. Prefects act ex officio as superintendents of school associations, provided the jurisdictional district of the association covers that of the urban prefecture, otherwise the superintendent is selected from among Japanese residents of good repute by the Provincial Governor, and, with few exceptions, the post is honorary.

School Associations maintain elementary schools in general, but those in cities maintain girls' high schools, commercial schools, and kindergartens in addition. Under the management of these school associations there were, at the end of March, 1922, 430 primary schools, thirteen girls' high schools, five commercial schools, and five elementary commercial schools.

As the school association system has been but a short time established its financial foundation is not yet sufficiently firm. Its chief source of revenue being found only in the levying of rates, its upkeep is not an easy matter in most cases, so the Government not only grants the associations special subsidies to aid in school building and equipment, but yearly subsidies also toward ordinary expenses. In the fiscal year 1920 the increase in salaries and expenses due to the extraordinary rise in prices, with the consequent increase in rates by about 80 per cent, caused considerable increase in the general accounts as well. The following table shows the aggregate budget of school associations and the average burden on each household for the last few years:

改訂された規定によると、学校組合は特定の資格を有する日本人居住者によって組織される。他の政府組織と対照的に、学校組合は自治的であり、選出された6〜18人の構成員からなる評議会を持っている。もし学校組合の担当する区域が府を含むならば、府の長は学校組合の監督者としての職務を行い、府を含むのでなければ、監督者は道知事によって信望のある日本人居住者の中から選ばれるが、ほとんど例外なくその職は名誉職である。

学校組合は通常、小学校の経営を行っていたが、都市部の学校組合では、女子高校、商業学校、さらに幼稚園も経営している。こうした学校組合の経営の下で、1922年3月末には430の小学校、13の女子高校、5つの商業学校、5つの初等商業学校が開校していた。

学校組合は短期間で設立されたので、その財政基盤は依然として充分に確固たるものではない。歳入の主な財源は賦課金であり、組合の維持は簡単な事柄ではなかった。そのため政府は組合に校舎や設備を援助する特別な補助金だけでなく通常の経費に対する毎年の補助金も供与している。1920年度では、急激な物価上昇が原因で人件費と経費が増加している。結果的に約80パーセントの増加であった。一般会計においても同様にかなりの額が増加することとなった。次の表は過去何年かの学校組合の予算総額と各世帯の平均負担額を示している。

	Number of Associations	Population forming Associations	Budget	Average Burden per Household
			Yen	*Yen*
1922.......	401	342,905	5,580,526	25.23
1921.......	394	322,437	4,418,749	24.38
1920.......	384	325,483	4,354,070	21.15
1919.......	363	312,541	2,391,245	11.79
1918.......	352	304,481	1,863,264	3.93

District Educational Bodies for Koreans--

What School Associations are to the education of Japanese children in Chosen, District Educational Bodies are to the education of Korean children.

In the fiscal year 1918 public schools for Korean children numbered 466 throughout the country, and the expenditure for them amounted to 1,835,000 yen, of which only 195,000 yen, namely about ten per cent of the whole, fell upon the Korean population, the average burden on each household being as low as six sen [*],while the rest was met by government assistance. However, in view of the ever growing need of common education among the people a programme was drawn up in 1919 to found 400 more schools within the next four years on the standard of "one school to every three villages at least," and this necessarily meant large increase in expenditure and consequent increase in the incidence of the school tax, as well as in the amount of government aid.

---

[*] 1 sen = ½ cent U. S.

	組合数	組合構成人員数	予算（円）	世帯平均負担額（円）
1922	401	342,905	5,580,526	25.23
1921	394	322,473	4,418,749	24.38
1920	384	325,483	4,354,070	21.15
1919	363	312,541	2,391,245	11.79
1918	352	304,481	1,863,264	3.93

朝鮮人の地方教育機関

日本人子弟の教育のために学校組合があったのと同様に、朝鮮人子弟の教育のためには地方教育機関があった。

1918年度で朝鮮人子弟のための公立校は466校となり、その歳出は183万5000円に上った。そのうちのたった19万5000円、つまり、全体の約10パーセントが朝鮮人の負担となった。一世帯の平均負担額は6銭＊ほどの低い額でしかなかった。不足分は、日本政府の補助で賄われたのである。

しかしながら、朝鮮人子弟の間に一般教育の必要性が引き続き高まっていることを考え「少なくとも3つの面につき1つの学校」を基準として、向こう4年以内に400を超える学校を設立するという計画が1919年に立てられた。このことは政府の援助額への支出が増えただけでなく、経費の大幅な増加や学校税の負担が増加したことも必然的に意味していた。

＊1銭は0.5セント

254 GOVERNMENT ORGANIZATION

The number of elementary schools for Koreans, and their financial condition is shown in the following table:

ELEMENTARY SCHOOLS FOR KOREANS

	1922	1921	1920	1919	1918
Schools.................	890	753	603	498	466
Expenditure (*Thousands of yen*).................	13,309	10,385	8,143	2,514	1,835
School Tax (*Thousands of yen*)	6,511	4,766	4,377	527	195
Average Burden per Household (*Yen*).............	2.03	1.49	1.39	0.16	0.06

It is to be noted that between 1918 and 1922 the expenditure on the elementary education of Koreans increased nearly eight-fold.

For information as to the Korean educational system above the primary grade the reader is referred to the chapter on Education.

Water-utilization Associations--

Agriculture leads all other productive industries in Chosen and, in especial, is the production of rice of great importance. In developing this industry therefore and thereby enhancing the wealth of the country nothing is more essential than irrigation works. Possessed with this idea, the Japanese Resident-General prevailed on the old Korean Government to promulgate Regulations for Water-utilization Associations so that they might conduct irrigation, drainage, reclamation of waste land, etc. But as these regulations were enacted simply to meet the needs of the times they soon fell out of date and could no longer cope with the situation, so new regulations were framed and put into force in October, 1917,

第五章　政府組織Ⅱ

朝鮮人の小学校数とその財政状態を示したのが次の表である。

朝鮮の小学校

	1922	1921	1920	1919	1918
学校数	890	753	603	498	466
経費 (千円)	13,309	10,385	8,143	2,514	1,835
学校税（千円）	6,511	4,766	4,377	527	195
世帯平均負（円）	2.03	1.49	1.39	0.16	0.06

1918 年から 1922 年の間に朝鮮人の初等教育への歳出がほぼ 8 倍に増加したことは注目すべきことである。朝鮮人の初等以上の教育制度に関する情報については、第九章を参照されたい。

水利組合

農業は朝鮮の他の全ての生産的産業の先頭に立っており、特にコメの生産は大変重要である。従って、この産業を発展させてそれにより国の福利を高める際に、灌漑事業よりも重要なものはないのである。この考えをもって、統監府は灌漑、下水、荒地の開墾などを行えるように大韓帝国政府に水利組合の規定を公布させた。しかし、こうした規定はその時代の必要性に見合うために制定されただけなので、すぐに時代遅れになってしまった。もはや状況に対応出来なくなったため、1917 年 10 月に新たに朝鮮水利組合令が制定施行された。こうして組合制度を確立するとともに、農業構想の発達に適

256   GOVERNMENT ORGANIZATION

thus consolidating the system of Water-utilization Associations as well as making them conform with the progress in agricultural ideas in the populace.

These associations are recognized by the new regulations as juridical persons with irrigation, draining, and flood prevention for their object, and the land served by any one association is regarded as its scene of operations, while the owners of the lands, houses, and other properties necessarily form its membership. The associations have each a president and secretaries, besides a council whose business it is to discuss financial and other important matters. The associations are also authorized to levy rates from their members for their maintenance, as well as to raise public loans for fresh enterprises, and in case of need they can co-operate by forming unions. In April, 1919, with the object of promoting their work the Government issued regulations for subsidizing these associations, and at the same time arranged to detail special engineers from the Government to assist them. Further, in December, 1920, new regulations for helping on land improvement work were published, and the amount of subsidy was increased.

At the end of the fiscal year 1922-3 existing associations numbered 50. Of these, four were organized previous to annexation, while of the 46 remaining 38 date from the year 1919 onward. For further particulars the reader is referred to the chapter on Agriculture.

合させるよう強化されたのである。

　こうして新しい法律によって、水利組合は、灌漑、下水、そして洪水防止を目的とした法人として認められた。組合の事業により利益を受ける土地の所有者、あるいは、水害予防事業の利益を受ける家屋や建物の所有者は組合員となった。水利組合にはそれぞれ組合長と組合員がおり、さらに評議会があって財政やその他の重要な問題を話し合うことになっている。また組合は組合員から維持費を徴収する権限が与えられ、新しい事業のために公債を発行することも認められた。必要ならば2つ以上の水利組合が水利組合連合会を設けることも出来た。1919年4月、こうした事業を促進する目的で政府はこれら組合に補助金を支給すると同時に、組合を援助するために政府から専門家を派遣する手配を行った。さらに1920年12月には土地改良事業を支援する新しい規定も公布されて、補助金も増額された。

　1922年度には、水利組合の数は50に上った。これらのうち併合前に組織されたのは4組合であり、併合後に出来た46組合のうち38組合は1919年以後に設立されている。さらに詳細については、農業に関する章を参照されたい。

CHAPTER VI

第六章

CHAPTER VI

THE LAWS AND COURTS OF KOREA

Prior to 1895 the laws in force in Korea were those of the native system which had been developed after the Chinese model, and which embodied rules of justice and methods of procedure wholly repugnant to the modern Western conception of such matters.

There was, before the introduction of the reforms, hereafter to be described, but one written code, the penal law; there was no independent judiciary, justice being administered by the Emperor's executive officers, who rarely had any legal training or any understanding of legal principles; torture was commonly employed not only to prisoners for the purpose of exacting confession, but also to witnesses for the purpose of securing the desired evidence.

In such circumstances it was inevitable that the administration of justice should be grossly corrupt, and that the power of the law was generally used for the enrichment or other gratification of those who could evoke it. As in China, so in Korea, foreign powers insisted on the right of consular jurisdiction over their nationals.

The first judicial reforms were undertaken shortly after the conclusion of the China-Japan war in 1895, at the instance of Japanese advisers. The Emperor of Korea promulgated an order for the constitution of law courts on March 25, 1895. It provided for the establishment of a special court to deal with crimes committed by members of the Imperial family, a court of appeals, circuit courts, local courts, and treaty-port courts for the purpose

第六章

司法制度と裁判所

1895年以前までの朝鮮王朝の司法制度は中国の法制度を手本とし体系化されてきたもので、近代西洋の法概念とは矛盾するものであった。

後述する司法制度の改革が行われる以前は、刑罰法が唯一の成文法であった。司法権の独立は確立されておらず、法の執行は皇帝の行政官が行っていた。彼らは法律教育を殆ど受けておらず、法律原理を全く理解していなかった。そして囚人の自白の強要はもちろんのこと、目撃者からも有利な証拠を確保するために拷問を常套手段としていた。

この様な状況下では司法行政の腐敗は避けがたく、法がもたらす「力」は、その執行者に富と満足を与える道具でしかなかった。それ故に中国と同様、朝鮮でも、諸外国は自国民の領事裁判権を要求したのである。

最初の司法改革は1895年の日清戦争終結直後、日本人顧問の要請により行われた。1895年3月25日、朝鮮の皇帝は裁判所令を公布した。朝鮮王族の犯罪に対処する特別法院、覆審法院、地方法院、巡回法院および国際的事件を処理する条約港法院の開設に向けてであった。

262   THE LAWS AND COURTS OF KOREA

of dealing with cases having an international aspect. The order was, however, more honored in the breach than in the observance, as only two of the courts were effectively established—the court of appeals and the local court at Seoul.

Referring to these paper reforms, the following comment is made in a volume entitled *Recent Progress in Korea*, published in 1910 by the Japanese Residency-General.

. . . the distinction between the judiciary and the executive existed only in form, and the administration of justice continued to be one of the principal means of satisfying covetous executive officials.

As if these evils were not enough, both the municipal and district magistrates, by special provisions of the law, were empowered to give decisions in any action whatever. These local officials discharged their judicial functions independently of the Law, for the Constitution of Law-Courts, thus largely defeating its object. The majority of the people, both governing and governed, had a very imperfect knowledge of judicial proceedings, and in spite of Regulations clearly providing for appeals from judgments pronounced by municipal and district magistrates, litigants who had adverse judgments given against them by a district magistrate often went to a second district magistrate instead of going to the appellate tribunal fixed by law. Nor was it rare for the magistrate to whom such appeal was made to give hearing to it.

The police stations also frequently usurped some of the functions of a law-court, while the Military and the Household Departments not only sometimes caused people to be arrested in an arbitrary manner,

しかしながら、遵守するより違反する方が名誉であるかの如くこの勅令は遵守されず、実際にはソウルの覆審法院、地方法院のみが開設されただけであった。

　日本統監府が 1910 年に出版した "*Recent Progress in Korea*" の中で、この実態のない改革について以下のように述べている。

　　…司法府と行政府の分離は形式上存在しているのみで、今なお、司法行政は強欲な政府高官の私腹を肥やす温床になっていた。それでも足りないのか、地方法院は特例を設け、どのような訴訟でも判決を下す権限を持っている。彼ら地方官吏は司法の役割を担っていたが、裁判所令を無視して独自に行っており、これはこの法の趣旨を大いに傷つけるものである。国民の大多数、統治する者もされる者も司法手続きについての知識がないため、地方判事が下した判決に対する上訴請求について法規に明記されているにも関わらず、訴訟当事者たちは地方法院によって自分たちに不利な判決が下された時、法に定められた覆審法院に上訴をせず、他の地方法院に第二審請求をするのである。またそのように上訴を受けた裁判所が審理を開催してしまうことも珍しくなかった。

　　警察署もしばしば、裁判所の司法権を侵害し、一方では軍部や内務府も時として法を無視して人民を逮捕するだけでなく、囚人に判決を下すこともあるのである。要するに全ての行政部

but actually pronounced judgment on their prisoners. In short it is not too much to say that nearly all offices of the executive departments meted out justice and always abused this power at the expense of the helpless masses. Amidst all this complicated judicial system, the Seoul Court, and the Supreme (Appellate) Court stood somewhat prominent on account of their comparatively regular constitution.

In 1906 the whole governmental situation in Korea was changed by the establishment of the Japanese Residency-General, in conformity with the terms of an agreement signed on November 17, 1905. Although the Japanese immediately introduced certain reforms in the judicial system, and insured their execution by placing a Japanese legal councillor in the Korean Department of Justice and in each court of trial, it was not until 1907 that a thorough overhauling of the whole system was undertaken. The power to do this was conferred on Japan by an agreement, signed on July 24, 1907, which had the practical effect of making Korea a Japanese protectorate. In this compact it was specifically provided that the judiciary should be separated from the other branches of administration, and that the Government of Korea should not enact any law, ordinance, or regulation without the previous assent of the Resident-General.

Acting upon this agreement, law courts were opened in August, 1908, competent Japanese being appointed judges, public prosecutors, and clerks, in association with selected Korean judicial officers. But the financial resources of Korea proved to be insufficient for an adequate reconstruction of the judicial system, which would have involved large expenditures for court houses, and for modern jails to replace the unsanitary and otherwise

署が人民を裁き、己が権力を乱用し、無力な一般大衆を犠牲に
していると言っても過言ではない。このような複雑怪奇な司法
制度の中、高等法院および覆審法院は比較的正規の組織であり、
多少なりとも優れた組織であると言える。

1905年11月17日、第二次日韓協約の調印を受け、1906年に統
監府が設置されたが、これにより大韓帝国内の政府組織が全面的に
変わったのである。日本は直ちに司法制度改革に取り組み、大韓帝
国法部および各公判廷に日本人司法官を送り込み改革の地固めをし
た。にもかかわらず、司法制度全体が整備されたのは1907年のこ
とであった。1907年7月24日に調印された協定によって、その権
限は日本に与えられ、実質的に朝鮮は日本の保護国となった。具体
的にはこの協定により、司法は他の行政機関から独立し、大韓帝国
政府は統監府の事前承認無しにはいかなる法律、条例、あるいは法
規をも制定することは出来ないと規定された。

この協定に基づき1908年8月裁判所が開設され、選りすぐりの
朝鮮人司法官吏と共に、有能な日本人判事、検事、書記官が任命さ
れた。司法制度の立て直しとしては、裁判所や、不衛生極まりない
古い監獄を近代設備の整ったものにするなど、膨大な予算が必要で
あったが、大韓帝国政府は充分な財源を持ち合わせていなかった。
1907年、当時懸案であった行政司法改革を推し進めるため、日本

266   THE LAWS AND COURTS OF KOREA

unsatisfactory prisons of the old type. In 1907 the Japanese Government, in order to advance the cause of the administrative and judicial reforms which were then contemplated, had arranged for the Government of Korea to borrow approximately twenty million yen, in six annual instalments, the loan to bear no interest and to have no fixed date of redemption. When it became clear that this sum would not suffice to finance the judicial as well as general administrative reforms, an agreement was concluded on July 12, 1909, under which the whole of the judicial and prison administration of Korea was transferred to the Japanese, who undertook to defray all the expenses of reforming and of administering these services.

Accordingly, in October, 1909, all the law courts which had been established by the Korean Government under the reforms of 1908 were converted into Residency-General Courts, and in addition twenty-six new district courts were established. As the administrative organ of justice and prisons a Judicial Bureau of the Residency-General was created by an Imperial Japanese Ordinance. At the end of 1909 there were in Korea one Supreme Court, three Courts of Appeal, eight Local Courts, nine Branch Local Courts, and eighty District Courts.

The transfer of the Korean Law Courts to Japanese administration did not make Japanese law applicable to Koreans, for the Residency-General Courts were required to administer justice in conformity with Korean law. Japanese residents in Korea continued to be subject to the jurisdiction of their own Consular Courts, as were all other foreigners whose governments had concluded treaties with Korea providing for extraterritorial rights. These were, of course, extinguished in 1910 when the constitutional status of Korea was completely changed through the annexation of the country

政府は大韓帝国政府に対し約2000万円の借款を準備した。これは6年分割、無利子、返済期限を設けないというものだった。しかしこの金額では、行政のみならず司法改革には充分でないことが明らかになり、1909年7月12日新たな協約が締結され、大韓帝国の司法・監獄行政を大日本帝国に委任することになり、日本は改革と施行に要する費用を負担することになった。

　これに伴い1909年10月、1908年の改正で大韓帝国政府によって設置された全ての裁判所は統監府裁判所に改められ、新たに26の区裁判所が設置された。司法業務機関として統監府法務局が勅令によって新設された1909年末には大韓帝国国内の裁判所は、高等法院1カ所、覆審法院3カ所、地方法院8カ所、地方法院支庁9カ所、地方法院出張所80カ所で構成されていた。

　大韓帝国裁判所行政が、大日本帝国に委譲されたからといっても、日本の法律がそのまま朝鮮人に適用されたわけではない。統監府裁判所は、大韓帝国の法律に基づいて司法業務を行うよう求められた。日本人居住者は引き続き日本の領事裁判所の管轄下にあり、これは大韓帝国政府と治外法権の条約を締結している外国政府の国民も同様である。しかし1910年の日韓併合により朝鮮の憲法上の立場が完全に変わり、日本および諸外国の領事裁判権は消滅した。それ以来、一般的な原則として日本の法律を朝鮮にそのまま適用すべきだ

by Japan. The general judicial principle then adopted was that Japanese law should be held applicable to Korea; but in view of the wide differences between the social conditions of the two countries, the courts were authorized to apply Korean laws and ordinances in so far as Japanese law was not specifically provided as applicable, when both parties to a civil suit are Koreans. In civil suits between Koreans and non-Koreans it was provided that Japanese laws and ordinances should be applied, with such modifications as local customs and usage showed to be equitable.

In the matter of the criminal law the Japanese Code was to be applied, except in regard to murder or armed robbery committed by Koreans. This exception was made on the ground that these forms of crime were at that time of too common occurrence, and were of such brutal cruelty in their commission, that the more severe punishments provided by Korean law were better calculated to check them than the milder penalties of the Japanese law.

In respect of minor offences the Japanese retained, so far as Koreans were concerned, the usual Korean punishment of flogging; but an exemption was made in the case of women, of boys under sixteen, of men over sixty, and of persons who were sick or insane at the time of sentence. Flogging as a penalty was finally abolished in 1920.

との考え方がとられていた。しかし両者の社会状況があまりにも違いすぎることから、民事訴訟の当事者双方が朝鮮人である場合、明らかに日本の法律の方が適切でない限りは、裁判所は大韓帝国の法律および法令を適用する権限を与えられるようになった。また、民事訴訟の一方の当事者が朝鮮人でない場合は、その土地に合った慣習法や慣例を公平に取り入れつつ、日本の法律を適用すべきであるとしている。

　刑法に関しては日本の法体系を適用すべきだとするも、朝鮮人による殺人、強奪に関してはこれに該当しないとしている。この様な例外措置が設けられたのは、この種の犯罪があまりにも頻繁に起こっており、なおかつ極めて残忍な犯行手口であったことから、日本に比べより厳しい刑罰を科す大韓帝国の法律の方が、犯罪の抑止力として適切だと考えられていたからである。

　軽犯罪に関しては、朝鮮總督府は朝鮮人が対象の場合に限り伝統的なむち打ちの刑をそのまま残した。ただし違反者が女性の場合や、16歳未満の男子や60歳以上の男性の場合、または判決時に病気であったり、精神を患っているとみなされた者は免除された。むち打ち刑は1920年には廃止された。

270   THE LAWS AND COURTS OF KOREA

At the time the new system was inaugurated a distinction was made between Japanese and Korean judges, the latter being authorized to sit only in cases in which Koreans alone were concerned; and the same distinction applied to public prosecutors. This distinction was abolished in 1920.

The Sources of Law in Korea--

Civil and criminal law in Korea, substantive and adjective, is derived from several sources; from the Imperial Constitution of Japan, from Treaties between Japan and other Powers, from such laws of the old Korean Government as were made valid at the time of annexation, from Residency-General Ordinances made valid at the same time, from Imperial Japanese Laws, passed by the Diet and sanctioned by the Emperor, having specific application to Korea as originally passed, or made applicable later, from Imperial Edicts (Chokrei), and from Decrees (Seirei) of the Governor-General.

The power of the Governor-General in respect of issuing Decrees is clearly defined and limited in an Imperial Ordinance, promulgated at the time of annexation. When local circumstances call for the enactment of a law, he may draft such a law, but it cannot be put in force until the Imperial sanction has been received through the Prime Minister of Japan. In case of emergency, the Governor-General may issue a Decree and make it immediately effective; but he must at once forward it to Tokyo for the Imperial sanction, and if this is withheld, he must withdraw it from operation. No Decree may be in conflict with any part of Japanese law which has been extended to Korea, or with any Imperial Laws or Ordinances which have been promulgated for special application to Korea.

第六章　司法制度と裁判所　　　271

　新しい法制度が始動したころ、朝鮮人判事は朝鮮人に関する事件のみ担当し、日本人判事と朝鮮人判事の間で役割分担がされていた。検事にも同様の措置がとられていたが、この役割分担も1920年には廃止された。

法源について

　朝鮮における民法および刑法の法源は実質的にも形式的にも複数ある。大日本帝国憲法、日本が諸外国と結んだ条約、併合後も効力を有する大韓帝国政府政令および日本の統監府の命令、そして天皇の裁可を受けた大日本帝国議会制定法であるが、これは朝鮮統治のために特別に作られた法律もしくは後に国内に適用されたものを含んでいる。天皇の命令（勅令）および總督の法令（政令）が法源である。

　總督の政令発令権は併合時に公布された天皇勅令により明記され、また制限も加えられている。国内情勢により新たな政令が必要になった場合には、草案は總督が作成するのだが、公布するには、日本の内閣総理大臣を通して天皇の裁可を受けなくてはならない。緊急時において總督は政令を発令し、直ちに施行出来るのだが、直ちにその旨を本国に通達し天皇の裁可を受けなければならない。そして裁可が下りなかった場合は公布を取り下げなくてはならないのである。總督によるいかなる政令も、朝鮮に適用された日本の法律、あるいは朝鮮統治のために公布された帝国法律・勅令と相反するものであってはならない。

Japanese laws, in part, or in their entirety, are often adopted as the contents of a Governor-General's Decree. In respect of Decrees formulated in Korea by the Governor-General the procedure is as follows:

A draft is prepared either by the Council or by the department immediately concerned with the particular subject; this is then referred to other departments for consultation; if the draft was originally made by a department, it is at this stage referred to the Council for discussion; it then goes to the Chief of the Archives Section, for reading; from him to the Vice Governor-General, for examination, then to the Governor-General, for his final approval; as approved it returns to the Chief of the Archives Section for transmission to Tokyo for Imperial sanction; in Tokyo it is received by the Colonial Bureau, which transmits it to the Secretary of the Cabinet, who, in turn refers it to the Bureau of Legislation, for discussion; it is then returned to the Secretary of the Cabinet, and by him submitted to the Prime Minister for deliberation at a Cabinet meeting; the Prime Minister reports it to the throne, and, Imperial sanction having been given, the document is returned to the Secretary of the Cabinet for transmission back to Korea; the Decree then becomes effective on publication in the Korean official gazette.

Local rules and regulations are issued by the Governor-General in the form of administrative ordinances (Furei) and by the Governors of the thirteen provinces of Korea. These latter do not require the previous sanction of the Governor-General before going into effect. Municipal by-laws are drawn up after consultation with the Municipal Council, and require the sanction of the Governor-General before they are applied.

第六章　司法制度と裁判所　　　273

　總督の政令は部分的にせよ全体的にせよ、日本国内の法律がその
内容に取り入れられており、政令は以下のような手順で作られてい
る。

　草案は朝鮮總督府中枢院、もしくは事案が直接関連する部署に
よって作成され、その後他の部署に回され審議される。總督府内部
署で草案が作成された場合、その時点で中枢院に諮問し協議される。
その後文書課課長のもとに回される。課長から副總督のもとに回さ
れ精査を受けた後、總督に届けられ最終認可が下される。その後再
び文書課課長のもとに戻され天皇の裁可を受けるために東京へ通達
される。東京では外地局がこれを受け取り、書記官長に回される。
書記官長は内閣法制局に持ち込み、審議後に書記官長に戻される。
その後、書記官長から総理大臣に提出され、閣議にかけられ協議さ
れる。総理大臣より上奏され、裁可が下されると文書は書記官長に
戻され總督府に送られる。政令は朝鮮官報を通じて通達されその時
点で効力を発揮する。

　地方における法律・法令は行政条例（府令）という形で總督そし
て各道知事によって公布される。知事たちはその発令においては事
前に總督の認可を受けずとも良い。地方自治体の規約は道評議会に
審議を受けた後作成され、總督の認可を受けた後に施行される。

274 THE LAWS AND COURTS OF KOREA

Civil Procedure--

A plaintiff institutes a civil suit by a written application to a local court or its branch, which sits with a collegiate bench, and is a court of first instance. Judgments of such courts may be carried to appeal to a court of second instance; and from the second decision an appeal lies to the Supreme Court, such appeals to be lodged within thirty days of the notification of a judgment to the parties concerned. In the court of second instance, as in that of first instance, the facts of the case are examined. In the Supreme Court questions of law alone are generally dealt with in appealed cases, though the Court may, at its discretion, enter into the facts.

The work of the courts in civil suits shows a steady increase in recent years. This is due in part to the growing complexity of civil relations, which has been the natural accompaniment of the economic development of the country, and in part to the gradual spread among the people of confidence in the administration of justice.

The following table shows the number of civil suits instituted in courts of first instance, for several years, classified according to the subject. matter.

CIVIL CASES INSTITUTED IN THE COURTS OF FIRST INSTANCE
IN KOREA

Cases Referring to	1912	1921	1922	1923	1924
Land..............	6,827	5,587	5,532	5,750	7,493
Buildings..........	695	1,228	1,379	1,640	2,106
Money.............	21,515	35,997	31,501	36,064	38,322
Rice..............	2,080	1,893	2,284	2,262	2,843
Other goods........	531	911	838	896	888
All other matters....	3,089	3,431	3,774	4,994	5,340
Total..........	34,737	49,047	45,308	51,606	56,991

第六章　司法制度と裁判所　　275

民事訴訟の手続き

　民事訴訟を起こす際、原告は地方法院もしくはその支所に訴状を提出し、複数の判事による一審を受ける。控訴の場合は覆審法院が担当するが、二審以降の上告は高等法院が担当する。この場合控訴状は訴訟当事者への判決の通達から30日以内に提出しなくてはならない。第二審は第一審同様、事件の事実認定が行われる事実審である。高等法院での控訴審は通常法律審であるが、事実誤認があったとされる場合は事実審をする裁量権を有する。

　近年裁判所が民事訴訟を扱う件数が年々増加しているが、国内の経済発展に伴い自然と民事の問題が複雑化していることにも原因があるだろう。また国民の間に司法行政への信頼感が広がったからでもあろう。

　次の表はここ数年の第一審における民事訴訟の件数を事案別にまとめたものだ。

第一審裁判所による民事事件の判決数

訴訟内容	1912	1921	1922	1923	1924
土地	6,827	5,587	5,532	5,750	7,493
建物	695	1,228	1,379	1,640	2,106
金銭	21,515	35,997	31,501	36,064	38,322
米	2,080	1,893	2,284	2,262	2,843
他の物品	531	911	838	896	888
その他	3,089	3,431	3,774	4,994	5,340
合　計	34,737	49,047	45,308	51,606	56,991

　※1924年の欄の合計が合っていないが数値は原文のままとした

276   THE LAWS AND COURTS OF KOREA

About seven per cent of the decisions of the courts of first instance are carried to appeal in the courts of second instance; and of these appeals about half are dismissed. About sixteen per cent of the decisions of the courts of second instance go to appeal in the courts of third instance; and of these appeals about two-thirds are dismissed.

Criminal Procedure--

All criminal cases are brought into court by the public procurators, whose position corresponds, roughly, with that of district-attorney in the United States. The procurator acts either upon his own information, or upon the complaint of a victim, or upon the statement of a witness, or upon evidence gathered by the judicial police, a body of men assigned to the duty of criminal investigation. They are specially selected, and rank above the assistant police inspectors of the ordinary police.

A person caught in the actual commission of crime may be arrested by an ordinary policeman; otherwise he must produce a warrant issued by a procurator or by one of the judicial police, as auxiliary to a procurator. The police may hold a suspect under detention for not more than ten days, to prevent him from absconding, or from destroying or concealing evidence.

The following table shows the number and nature of the sentences imposed in criminal cases by the courts of first instance. Penal servitude involves hard labor; imprisonment does not. A major fine is one which exceeds twenty yen; a minor fine is below twenty yen. Detention, as used in the table, means imprisonment for less than thirty days. Flogging was abolished as a penalty in 1920.

第一審判決の約7パーセントが第二審に控訴されているが、そのうち約半数は棄却されている。また第二審の16パーセントほどが上告され、その約3分の2が棄却されている。

刑事訴訟の手続き

　刑事事件裁判は検事官が公判請求をして裁判となるが、この国の検事官の立場は米国の地方検事に近い。検事官は、自ら捜査して得た情報や被害者からの事情聴取、目撃証言、もしくは犯罪捜査を担当する司法警察が集めた証拠を基に起訴するかを決める。検事官は特別に選ばれた官僚であり、地位としては警部補より上である。

　現行犯の場合一般警察はその場で犯人を逮捕することが出来るが、そうでない場合は、警察官は検事官もしくは検察を補佐する司法警察官が発行した逮捕令状を提示しなくてはならない。警察は被疑者に逃亡もしくは証拠隠滅の可能性がある場合は、10日を超えない範囲で勾留することが出来る。

　次の表は一審裁判での刑事事件の件数と刑罰の内容である。懲役には労役が含まれるが禁錮刑の場合労役はない。20円を超えるものは罰金刑であり、科料は20円未満となっている。表に記された拘留とは30日未満の収監である。むち打ち刑は1920年に廃止された。

278   THE LAWS AND COURTS OF KOREA

SENTENCES IMPOSED IN CRIMINAL CASES BY COURTS
OF FIRST INSTANCE

Nature of Sentence	1912	1921	1922	1923
Death	81	69	17	30
Penal Servitude:				
For Life	44	47	16	26
For a term	9,533	16,744	12,892	9,585
Imprisonment:				
For Life	0	0	1	0
For a Term	19	60	62	66
Major Fine	846	8,657	12,155	11,576
Minor Fine	309	1,162	1,022	1,074
Detention	42	53	61	50
Flogging	4,321	0	0	0
Total	15,195	26,792	26,209	22,377

In a population of nearly eighteen million, of which less than four hundred thousand are Japanese and foreigners, the figures given above refer, naturally, for the most part to Koreans. The racial distribution of serious crime, that is to say of crimes which involved penalties of death, penal servitude or imprisonment, was as follows in 1923: Japanese 638; foreigners 147; Koreans 8,922.

The total number of convicts entering the prisons of Korea in 1923 was 8,978, and of these, 5,299 had sentences to serve of less than one year. This leaves a balance of 3,679 persons—21 per 100,000 of the total population—who may be assumed to have committed more or less serious crimes. Of the penalties, twenty-seven were death, twenty-three penal servitude for life, twenty-seven penal servitude for fifteen years or more,

第一審裁判所による刑事事件の判決数

判決	1912	1921	1922	1923
死刑	81	69	17	30
終身刑	44	47	16	26
有期懲役	9,533	16,744	12,892	9,585
終身禁固	0	0	1	0
有期禁固	19	60	62	66
罰金	846	8,657	12,155	11,576
科料	309	1,162	1,022	1,074
拘留	42	53	61	50
むち打ち	4,321	0	0	0
合計	15,195	26,792	26,209	22,377

　朝鮮半島の人口は 1800 万近くあるが、うち日本人を含む外国人居住者の数は 40 万人に満たない。従って表内の数字は当然のことながら、殆どが朝鮮人であるとみてよい。1923 年中の重犯罪件数、つまり刑罰に死刑、懲役または禁錮が含まれる犯罪を民族ごとに分けた数字は次のとおりである。

　日本人……………… 638 人

　朝鮮人…………… 8922 人

　その他外国人……… 147 人

　1923 年に収監された受刑者総数は 8978 人で、うち 5299 人は 1 年未満の刑期である。残りの受刑者数は 3679 人で、人口 10 万あたり 21 人となる。これら受刑者は多かれ少なかれ重犯罪を犯した受刑者であろう。刑罰のうち、死刑は 27 件、終身刑 23 件、15 年以上の懲

and seventy-one penal servitude for terms from ten years to less than fifteen years.

From the foregoing figures one may deduce that the Koreans are a law-abiding people, and that the Japanese are giving them a mild administration of criminal justice so far as the character of the sentences is concerned. At the present time, when the prevalence of serious crime in the United States is being investigated by a number of states and cities, by private organizations, by university faculties, by the Federal Government, and by a National Crime Commission, one feature of the administration of criminal justice in Korea is of particular interest—the extremely high percentage of convictions.

During the twelve years ending with 1923 there was no year in which less than 95.1 per cent of the cases tried in the criminal courts ended in the conviction of the accused; and the average for the period was 96.8 per cent of convictions. The circumstance that less than five persons charged with crime in each hundred, so charged, escaped conviction contributed no doubt to the excellent record of Korea in respect of the incidence of crime.

A convicted criminal in a court of first instance may take an appeal to a court of second instance, and from the decision there rendered he may appeal to a court of third instance. In 1923 there were 2,292 cases of criminal appeal before the courts of second instance; of these, 939 were withdrawn, 607 were dismissed. In 565 cases the decision of the court of first instance was reversed in whole; and in thirty-six cases in part. Of appeals to the courts of third instance there were 196, of which 164 were dismissed, and seven withdrawn. The decision of the lower court of appeal was reversed in whole in seven cases, and in part in one case.

役は 27 件、10 年以上 15 年未満の懲役刑は 71 件となっている。

　前述の数字をみると、朝鮮人は法律をよく守る国民で、刑事事件に関し日本は緩い刑罰を課しているように思えるかもしれない。昨今米国では重犯罪の発生率に関する調査が多くの州や都市で行われており、民間の調査会社、大学、連邦政府、国家犯罪委員会などの組織が実施している。朝鮮の刑事司法の状況で特筆すべきは高い有罪判決率だろう。

　1923 年までの 12 年間で、有罪判決率が 95.1 パーセントを下回る年は無かった。また平均すると 96.8 パーセントの有罪判決率であった。刑事裁判では被告 100 人に対し有罪判決を受けなかった者が 5 人に満たないという状況で、これが朝鮮の犯罪発生を抑止したことは疑いない。これは輝かしい記録である。

　一審で有罪判決を受けた被告は二審に控訴することが出来、二審での控訴判決に対して三審に上告出来る。1923 年には刑事裁判の一審判決に対する控訴は 2292 件。うち 939 件が取り下げ、607 件が棄却された。一審判決が覆ったケースが 565 件、一部棄却判決は 36 件となっている。三審への上告は 196 件。内 164 件が棄却、7 件が取り下げであった。

　下級審での控訴判決が全面的に覆ったケースは 7 件、一部棄却は 1 件であった。

THE LAWS AND COURTS OF KOREA

The Judiciary--

The judicial staff of Korea consisted at the beginning of 1923 of 162 Japanese and 37 Korean judges, of 67 Japanese and 10 Korean public prosecutors, of 4 Japanese chief clerks, of 4 Japanese interpreters, and of 432 Japanese and 232 Korean clerks and assistant interpreters.

The judges are appointed directly by the Emperor of Japan, and their tenure is for life, up to the legal age of retirement, which for the president of the Supreme Court is fixed at sixty-three, and for other judges at sixty. An extension of not more than five years can be granted by the Governor-General after the passage of a resolution by the General Council of the Supreme Court in favor of it.

The regulations governing the eligibility of persons to be appointed as judges in Korea are strict and precise; and they are in the main identical with those in force in Japan proper. The independence of the judiciary is protected by the rule that a judge can be dismissed only if he has been sentenced to imprisonment by a Court of Law, or if a special commission of his colleagues on the bench have sentenced him to disciplinary punishment. Both Koreans and Japanese are eligible for admission to the bar, under the regulations for barristers.

The standing of the judiciary has been greatly improved in recent years by raising the salaries of all judicial officers. This has had the effect of attracting to the service a higher type of men than could be secured for the pittances paid during the period of native Korean rule. Thus, the salaries of judges and of public procurators have gradually been raised from a minimum of 500 yen a year to one of 1,200, and from a maximum of 2,200 yen a year to one of 6,500. At the other end of the scale the salaries

裁判官

　1923年初頭における朝鮮の裁判所職員は、日本人判事162名、朝鮮人判事37名、日本人検事官67名、朝鮮人検事官10名、4名の日本人主任書記官、4名の日本人通訳、加えて432名の日本人書記官および232名の朝鮮人書記官と補助通訳官で構成されていた。

　裁判官は天皇の勅命により任命され終身任期である。定年は高等法院長は63歳、その他判事は60歳となっている。高等法院協議会で任期延長決議が通過し、總督の許可が下りれば5年まで定年を延長することが出来る。

　朝鮮では裁判官の任命資格は厳正かつ緻密に規定されており、日本本土とおおむね同様の基準が適用されている。裁判官の独立性を保証する意味から、罷免は司法裁判所において懲役の判決を受けた場合と特別委員会で同輩判事より懲戒処分を受けた場合に限られる。日本人朝鮮人とも法廷弁護人への道は開かれている。

　近年司法官僚の給与が上がったことにより裁判官の地位は著しく改善され、その結果、薄給であった大韓帝国政府時代に比べ優秀な人材を集めることが出来るようになった。裁判官、検事ともにその給与は徐々に上がり、年収の最低額は500円から1200円に、最高額は2200円から6500円に引き揚げられた。末端にいる秘書や学生通訳官の給与も、最低額120円から480円に、最高額は600円から

of secretaries and student-interpreters have been raised from a minimum of 120 yen a year to one of 480, and from a maximum of 600 yen a year to one of 1,920. Similar advances have been made in the salaries of the intermediate grades of the judicial service.

Courts of Law--

In 1925 there were in Korea one Supreme Court, three Courts of Appeal, eleven Local Courts, forty-six Branches of Local Courts, and 160 Detached Offices of Local Courts, the last named dealing only with business under the law of registration, and with notarial matters.

Both civil and criminal cases are first heard in Local Courts or their Branches. The first appeal goes to one of the Courts of Appeal; the next, and final, appeal is heard by the Supreme Court. Decisions of the Korean Courts cannot be carried for appeal to the Courts of Japan proper.

As a general rule a single judge presides at a Local Court; but in civil suits involving a sum of money greater than a thousand yen, and in criminal cases when the penalty attached to the offence is death, or penal servitude, or imprisonment for more than one year, a collegiate bench of three judges sits. In the Appeal Courts cases are heard by three judges, and in the Supreme Court by five, sitting as a collegiate bench. Trial by jury does not exist in Korea.

Petty cases are seldom taken to the Law-Courts; but are summarily disposed of by the chief of a police station, first offenders being generally dismissed with a warning. The matter of summary jurisdiction is dealt with

1920 円に上がっている。中間官吏職の給与も同様に引き揚げられている。

裁判所

1925 年の時点で朝鮮内の裁判所は、次のようになっている。

高等法院………………………　　1 カ所

覆審法院………………………　　3 カ所

地方法院………………………　　11 カ所

地方法院支庁……………　　46 カ所

地方法院出張所………　　160 カ所

出張所は登記と公証業務のみ担当する。

　民事も刑事も共に、まずは地方法院もしくは支庁で審議される。控訴はいずれかの覆審法院に持ち込まれ、二審以降は高等法院で審議される。朝鮮裁判所での判決に対し日本本土の裁判所に控訴提起をすることは出来ない。地方法院では、一般的には 1 人の判事が裁判を構成する単独制をとっているが、1000 円以上の訴訟を扱う民事裁判や、死刑・懲役・1 年以上の禁錮の刑罰が予想される刑事裁判に限り 3 人の判事が裁判を担当する合議制をとっている。控訴審では 3 人の判事が裁判を担当し、高等法院では 5 人の判事による審議となる。陪審員制度は取り入れられていない。

　軽犯罪事件の場合、裁判所に持ち込まれることは殆どなく、警察署長による略式裁判の処置がとられ、初犯は訓戒のみで釈放される。

286 THE LAWS AND COURTS OF KOREA

in the chapter on Police and Prisons.

Suspended Sentences--

A considerable proportion of the sentences passed upon criminals are converted into suspended sentences, known locally as a stay of execution of sentence. Persons sentenced to penal servitude or imprisonment for two years or less are eligible to have their sentences suspended, provided such persons have not been sentenced to imprisonment during the seven years immediately preceding the new sentence. Suspension of sentence is granted by the sentencing court either on the application of the public prosecutor, or of the judge's own motion. That the public prosecutors are favorable to the grant of this form of relief is proved by the fact that of the 6,709 suspensions of sentence granted during the five years ending with 1921, more than 30% were at the instance of public prosecutors.

In this connection it may be mentioned that, in the case of a first offender, and particularly in that of a juvenile first offender, it is the policy of the public prosecutors to admonish instead of to prosecute him, where the individual circumstances of the offender indicate that this leniency is advisable.

この問題については第七章でも取り扱う。

執行猶予

　被告に下された判決の相当数に刑の執行延期措置、つまり執行猶予が付く。2年以下の労役や懲役の判決が下された受刑者がその対象となるが、あくまでも、その受刑者が過去7年間禁錮刑に処されていない場合である。執行猶予はその裁判が行われた裁判所の検事もしくは担当判事の要請により付与される。1921年までの5年間の執行猶予件数は6709件であり、そのうちの30パーセント以上が検事からの要請であった。この数字から検事がこの救済策を好んで用いていたことが分かる。

　このような点から初犯、特に未成年者の初犯は、犯罪者の個人的な環境を考慮し、寛大な処置をとる方が望ましいと判断された場合は、検事は起訴処分にせず訓戒のみで釈放していた。

CHAPTER VII

第七章

CHAPTER VII

POLICE AND PRISONS

I. Police Administration

Historical--

Prior to the year 1894 police administration in Korea was under the full control of the Korean Government. Police work was regarded as a branch of military affairs; and throughout the various provinces the local garrisons acted as the local police forces. In Seoul, the capital city, there was a separate police organization known as the Potochong (Burglar Capturing Office); but the Chief and other officials of this metropolitan police force were all soldiers.

Observers are generally agreed that under the old Korean police system the people at large had more to fear than to hope for from the activities of the police. Little protection was afforded to life and property, and the police force was, in practice, rather the corrupt instrument of a few influential people than an impartial agent for the preservation of law and order.

Under the terms of an Agreement concluded between Japan and Korea in 1894, the Korean Government engaged the services of a number of Japanese officials for the purpose of removing the gross abuses which had long existed in the police administration of the country. Acting in conformity with Japanese advice the Government separated police affairs from the military administration, and created a Bureau of Police Affairs

第七章

警察と監獄

Ⅰ 警察行政

歴史的背景

1894年以前の警察行政は、李氏朝鮮政府の全面的な指揮下にあった。警察業務は軍事業務の一部と見なされ、各道ではその地区の守備隊が警察の役割を果たしていた。首都ソウルには独立した機構である捕盗庁（泥棒を捕まえる部署）が置かれていたが、最高責任者、警察官僚は全員武官であった。

旧警察機構に対し、朝鮮人民が全体としては期待よりも恐怖を感じていたと観ることには異論の余地はないだろう。生命財産への保護は殆どなされず、警察力とは実際のところ、法と秩序の公平な護衛官というより、一握りの特権階級の為の腐りきった道具でしかなかった。

1894年に締結された日本と朝鮮の間の協約のもと、李朝政府は長い間はびこっていた警察行政の腐敗を一掃するため、数人の日本人役人を顧問として招聘した。日本側の助言に従い警察業務を軍事行政から切り離し内部に警務部を新設した。地方の警察業務はそれぞれの道観察使がその任を担い、従って地方の警察業務指揮権は武官から文官に委譲されたのである。

in the Home Office. Provincial Governors were made responsible for the police affairs of their provinces, thus transferring the local control and execution of police work from the military to the civil authorities.

In Seoul the office of the Potochong was renamed Kyongmu Chong (Police Affairs Office); its functions were extended; and a school was established for the training of Korean police officials. It was hoped that the various changes introduced at this time would reduce, and finally eliminate the abuses of the old system. Ten years' experience of these early reform measures showed, however, that changes in administrative technique were powerless to offset the defects of an inferior police personnel.

Accordingly, in 1904, the Korean Government engaged the services of Mr. Maruyama, an experienced Japanese police official, with a view to placing the police administration upon a sound basis. Mr. Maruyama brought over from Japan twenty-one police inspectors, eighteen sergeants, and 1,205 policemen, and distributed them among the Metropolitan and Provincial Police Offices. He also enlarged the curriculum of the Training School for Police Officials.

In 1905 the police situation was altered by the appointment in Korea of a Japanese Resident-General, who replaced the Japanese Minister to the Court of Korea. The creation of a Residency-General called for corresponding adjustments in the administrative regulations of Korea; and amongst these not the least important were those which affected the police force.

Hitherto the Japanese officials, and their subordinates, doing police work in Korea had been known as the Advisory Police, since they held no rank in the Korean service. This arrangement having proved unsatisfactory

第七章　警察と監獄

ソウルの捕盗庁は警務庁（警察業務を行う部署）という名称にかわり、その機能も拡大し、朝鮮人警察官僚を訓練する警察学校も設けられた。様々な改善策の導入により、古い機構の弊害が軽減され、更には一掃されることが期待された。しかし10年に亘って改善策を打ち出してきたにもかかわらず、警察官僚の無能さの前では運営方法の改善など焼け石に水でしかなかった。

1904年、大韓帝国政府は警察行政をしっかりした基盤に置きたいとの見地から、経験豊かな日本人官僚の丸山氏を顧問として招聘した。丸山氏は日本から警部21名、巡査部長18名、1205名の警察官を率い、首都および地方警察署に配属させた。また、警察官僚訓練学校のカリキュラムも増設した。

1905年に、朝鮮王室に派遣された日本公使に代わって統監が任命され、これにより警察を取り巻く状況が一変した。統監府設置により、大韓帝国の行政法令見直しが要請されたが、中でも警察力に関係する法令は無用の長物になっていたのである。

それまで大韓帝国内で警務に取り組んでいた日本の官僚、およびその部下たちには、政府の公的な地位を与えられてはおらず、警務顧問として知られてはいたが、このような処遇は行政の効率化を推

from the standpoint of administrative efficiency, the Korean Government, in October, 1907, abolished the Police Advisorship, and made Korean officials of all members of the Japanese police force in Korea.

The Director of Police Affairs in the Central Government was left with the power to issue instructions to the Chiefs of the Police Departments in the Provinces, and to the Captains of local police stations in respect of any agitation among the people, of any movements of insurgents, and of any other matters of national importance.

The extent to which the Japanese interested themselves in the reform of the Korean police system may be measured roughly by the fact that the expenditure on the police force was increased from $196,453 in 1906 to $1,349,599 in 1909. In the latter year the ordinary police force was made up of 36 Japanese and 11 Korean inspectors, 156 Japanese and 102 Korean sergeants, 1,924 Japanese and 57 Korean interpreters, and 63 Japanese physicians — a total of 5,554.

In addition to the ordinary police force the Japanese maintained for a number of years in Korea a force of gendarmes. This gendarmerie was originally established after the China-Japan War of 1894, for the purpose of guarding telegraph lines. Later, its functions were extended to include protection of the railroads and the performance of ordinary police work.

The necessity of having such a force available was emphasized by the outbreak of insurgency in various parts of the country after the establishment of the Residency-General in 1905. Apart from the special problems created for the authorities by the insurrection, the general question of maintaining law and order in the country districts was one of great complexity.

進する上では不充分であることが判明した。よって 1907 年 10 月、大韓帝国政府は顧問制度を廃止し、国内にいる日本人警察関係者全員を官吏として登用したのである。

中央政府警務局指揮官に残された権限としては、扇動、反乱の類、国家の治安を脅かすあらゆる動きに対し、各地方警務局および警察署の責任者への指示を出すことであった。

警察部隊に充てられた予算が、1906 年の 19 万 6453 ドルから、1909 年には 134 万 9599 ドルに増加したことからも、日本政府が大韓帝国内の警察機構の改革にどれほどの関心を払っていたかが伺われる。1909 年には普通警察部隊の人事構成は、警部 36 名が日本人、11 名が朝鮮人であり、巡査部長は日本人 156 名、朝鮮人 102 名、通訳官は日本人 1924 名、朝鮮人 57 名、それに加え、63 名の日本人医者からなる、総勢 5554 名であった。

普通警察部隊に加え、日本政府は数年間憲兵隊を大韓帝国内にも置いた。憲兵隊はもともと 1894 年の日清戦争後、通信機能保持のために設置されたものだが、その後は鉄道保護および普通警察業務の執行にまでその権限は拡大されていた。

1905 年の統監府設置後、各地で反乱が勃発したため、こうした警察力を地方にまで行き渡らせる必要性が高まった。警察当局にとって、反乱によって作り出された特殊な問題とは別に、国内各地域の法と秩序を維持するという一般的な問題も複雑であった。

朝鮮奥地では人々が長年に亘り匪賊にひどく苦しめられていた

296   POLICE AND PRISONS

For many years the people of the interior had suffered greatly from the activities of outlaws. Without the co-operation of the Koreans the Japanese gendarmerie would have made little headway in suppressing these marauding bands. The task was one of extreme difficulty, owing to the reluctance, through fear of reprisals, of the local population to give information to the authorities, or to appear as witnesses at trials.

In order to overcome these obstacles, as far as possible, a force of native Korean gendarmes was enrolled and placed under the command of the Commandant of the Japanese Garrison Gendarmerie.

At the end of 1909 there were 2,369 Japanese and 4,392 Korean gendarmes, stationed at 499 points.

After the Annexation--

In 1910 Korea was annexed to Japan and made an integral part of the Empire. The Annexation was proclaimed in Korea on August 29, 1910, but the complete control of police affairs had been transferred to the Japanese two months before this date.

During the next ten years the Government-General carried out many changes in police organization. These led, finally, in 1919 to the disbandment of the gendarmerie, to the establishment of a Bureau of Police Affairs in the Government-General, and to the transfer to the Provincial Governments of control over the local police. This last step placed the police administration in Korea upon the same basis as that of Japan proper. In each of the thirteen provinces a police Department was set up, with a Provincial Secretary as its official head; and to the ordinary duties of preserving law and order there were added those of a sanitary police. In

が、朝鮮人の協力なしには日本の憲兵隊もこうした略奪行為を鎮圧することは出来なかっただろう。人々は報復を恐れ、当局への情報提供や裁判に証人として出廷することを躊躇したため鎮圧は困難を極めていた。こうした障壁を出来る限り克服するために朝鮮人憲兵隊を採用し、朝鮮駐箚憲兵隊司令部の指揮下に置いた。1909年末には2369名の日本人憲兵、4392名の朝鮮人憲兵が499カ所の憲兵分遣地を担当していた。

併合後

　1910年、大韓帝国は日本に併合され、大日本帝国の不可欠な一部になった。1910年8月29日「併合の宣言」が公布されたが、その2カ月前に警察業務は完全に統監府に移譲されていた。

　併合後10年に亘り、朝鮮總督府は数々の警察機構改革を推し進めた。その結果ついに1919年には憲兵制度が廃止され、總督府内に警務局を設置し、各道政府に地方の警察権を委譲した。最終的には、朝鮮内の警察行政は日本本土の警察行政の基盤の上に行われることになった。13の道には警察部が設置されて道長官がその長の役割を担い、また治安維持に加え公衆衛生業務が普通警察の管轄となった。警察に課せられた責務は重くなる一方であり、その業務は複雑さを増した。警察力の合理化を図るため警察官練習所（訓練学校）の規模は大幅に拡大され總督府直轄の独立した機構となった。

298   POLICE AND PRISONS

order to increase the efficiency of the force, whose work was constantly
becoming heavier and more comprehensive, the police training school was
greatly enlarged, and was given the status of an independent institution
under the direct supervision of the Government-General.

In the following table the composition of the Korean Police Force in
October, 1922, is given. Under the head "Officers" are included 13 Chiefs
of Police, all Japanese; 41 Japanese and 14 Korean Police Superintendents;
377 Japanese and 140 Korean Police Inspectors; and 730 Japanese and 268
Korean Assistant Police Inspectors.

PERSONNEL OF KOREAN POLICE FORCE, 1922

Province	Officers		Policemen		Total	Grand total
	Jap.	Korean	Jap.	Korean		
Keiki..........	161	60	1,456	1,161	2,617	2,838
North Chusei.....	50	18	391	329	720	788
South Chusei.....	65	25	607	465	1,072	1,162
North Zenra......	67	25	659	501	1,160	1,252
South Zenra......	91	36	981	697	1,678	1,805
North Keisho.....	94	37	1,002	768	1,770	1,901
South Keisho.	101	36	996	658	1,654	1,791
Kokai..........	77	30	799	642	1,441	1,548
South Heinan.....	78	26	762	538	1,300	1,404
North Heinan	113	38	1,113	691	1,804	1,955
Kogen..........	87	36	731	628	1,359	1,482
South Kankyo....	93	29	819	568	1,387	1,509
North Kankyo....	83	27	713	514	1,227	1,337
Total........	1,161	422	11,028	8,160	19,188	20,771

次の表は 1922 年 10 月時点の朝鮮總督府警察の構成を示したものである。警察官僚には 13 名の道警察部長が含まれるが全員日本人である。警視は日本人 41 名、朝鮮人 14 名であり、日本人 377 名、朝鮮人 140 名からなる警部、および日本人 730 名、朝鮮人 268 名からなる警部補となっている。

朝鮮の警察の構成　1922 年

地域	警察官僚		警察官			総計
	日本人	朝鮮人	日本人	朝鮮人	合計	
京畿道	161	60	1,456	1,161	2,617	2,838
忠清北道	50	18	391	329	720	788
忠清南道	65	25	607	465	1,072	1,162
全羅北道	67	25	659	501	1,160	1,252
全羅南道	91	36	981	697	1,678	1,805
慶尚北道	94	37	1,002	768	1,770	1,901
慶尚南道	101	36	996	658	1,654	1,791
黄海道	77	30	799	642	1,441	1,548
平安南道	78	26	762	538	1,300	1,404
平安北道	113	38	1,113	691	1,804	1,955
江原道	87	36	731	628	1,359	1,482
咸鏡南道	93	29	819	568	1,387	1,509
咸鏡北道	83	27	713	514	1,227	1,337
合計	1,161	422	11,028	8,160	19,188	20,771

※表では合計が合っていない項目があるが数値は原文のままとした。

In addition to the above, there were attached to the police staff thirteen civil engineers, two harbor doctors, two veterinary surgeons, four harbor officers, six assistant harbor officers, three assistant veterinary surgeons, thirty-six assistant engineers, and four student-interpreters.

Taking the population in 1922 as approximately 17 million, there was one policeman to 818 inhabitants. The total area of Korea being 85,156 square miles, the police force if evenly distributed would have averaged about one policeman to four square miles.

Summary Police Jurisdiction--

Chiefs of police stations in Korea may exercise summary jurisdiction in cases where persons are charged with trivial offences. Such cases are, for the most part, connected with gambling, simple assault, violation of the traffic regulations, and so on. No offender can be tried by summary jurisdiction unless he assents to that process; and if he assents to it and is then dissatisfied with the result he can appeal the decision in one of the ordinary law courts. The right is seldom exercised, as first offenders in petty cases are usually let off with a warning. Although the chief of a police station may inflict a penalty as severe as three months' penal servitude, he usually imposes a fine of not more than 100 yen, or simple detention for not more than three months.

In the year 1921 there were 73,262 cases decided by summary police jurisdiction. Of these, 71,802 ended in a conviction of the defendant; and against these decisions there were only 54 appeals, of which 42 resulted in confirmation of the sentence, and 12 in reversal.

第七章　警察と監獄 301

　前述の警察職に加え、13 名の土木技師、2 名の港湾医、2 名の獣医、
4 名の港湾官吏、6 名の港湾官吏補助、3 名の獣医補助、36 名の技
師補助、4 名の通訳生が含まれる。

　1922 年の朝鮮の人口が約 1700 万であることから、住民 818 人に
1 人の警察官がいることになる。また朝鮮の総面積は 8 万 5156 平方
マイルであり、平均すれば 4 平方マイルに 1 人の警察官が配置され
ていることになる。

簡易司法警察権
　朝鮮の警察署長は、賭博行為、軽い暴力行為、交通違反など、軽
微な法律違反を犯した者に対しての簡易裁判権（その場で裁く権利）
を行使することが出来る。しかしいかなる違反者も本人の同意なし
に簡易裁判で裁かれることはなく、また同意の上の裁判であっても
その判決に不服の場合は通常の裁判所のいずれかに控訴することが
出来る。実際には瑣末な事件は通常、説諭のみで釈放されるのでこ
うした権利も実際に用いられることは殆どなかった。警察署長は最
高 3 カ月の懲役刑を課す権限を有するが、多くの場合 100 円を超え
ない範囲での罰金刑、もしくは最高 3 カ月の拘留に止めている。
　1921 年で現在 7 万 3262 の事件が簡易司法警察によって処理され
ており、うち 7 万 1802 の事件で被告に有罪判決が下され、そのう
ち不服申し立ては 54 件のみ、42 件の有罪確定、12 件の判決取消し
という結果である。

302   POLICE AND PRISONS

Cost of the Police Force--

The following table shows the total cost of the Korean Police System.
The figures refer to the ordinary police. The Judicial Police is made up
of officials who have the authority, ex officio, to investigate crimes. The
officials having this power are Provincial Governors, Chiefs of Police
departments of Provincial Governments, Police Superintendents, Police
Inspectors, and Assistant Police Inspectors, whose salaries are carried in
the budgets of their several offices.

COST OF THE KOREAN POLICE SYSTEM

(In thousands of yen. 1 yen = 50 cents U. S.)

1915	4,217	1920	16,702
1916	4,173	1921	22,754
1917	4,183	1922	22,265
1918	4,212	1923	21,924
1919	4,840	1924	22,402

The marked increase after 1919 was due to the abolition of the
gendarmerie, and the absorption of that force into the ordinary police force.
It will be noted that in the fiscal year 1924-5 the cost of the Korean police
system averaged less than sixty-five cents per head of the population of the
country.

警察の経費

次の表は朝鮮の警察機構にかかった諸経費の総額である。

なお、数字は普通警察の経費である。司法警察は職権として犯罪への捜査権を有する役人で構成されている。司法権を有する者は各道知事、各道警察部長、警視、警部および警部補であるが、彼らの給与は所属する部署の予算で賄われている。

朝鮮普通警察の経費
（単位は千円　1円＝50セント）

	経費			経費
1915	4,217		1920	16,702
1916	4,173		1921	22,754
1917	4,183		1922	22,265
1918	4,212		1923	21,924
1919	4,840		1924	22,402

1919年以降に著しい増加がみられるが、これは憲兵警察制度が廃止されて普通警察に吸収されたことに伴うものである。1924年度における警察機構の経費は、人口1人あたり65セント以下になることがみてとれる。

304 POLICE AND PRISONS

II. Prison Administration

Under native Korean rule the prisons, like those of almost all Oriental countries, were horrible beyond description. Sanitary conveniences were lacking, gross ill-treatment of the prisoners was common; and overcrowding was carried to an almost incredible point. When the Japanese took over the prison administration they found that the average floor-space per prisoner was less than five square feet.

From year to year since annexation the number of prisons has been increased, and their condition improved, so that today, the larger prisons, at least, will bear comparison with those of any country, and are greatly superior to most of the prisons in the United States.

Under the old system the prisons were under the control of the Home Department of the Korean Government, and were usually attached to police stations. At present all prisons in Korea are under the direct control of the Governor-General, and their administration is supervised by the Judicial Bureau of the Government-General. On the spot the responsibility for prison administration lies with the chief public procurator of a Court of Appeal. As a rule the staff of a prison consists of a Governor, a physician, a chaplain, with a complement of warders, technical experts, and interpreters. In the larger prisons there are in addition teachers and pharmacists.

Each year a certain proportion of the warders —about ten per cent—are sent to a training institute to receive a course of instruction in matters connected with their duties. In addition to this, a special course of training

Ⅱ 監獄行政

　李朝政府時代の監獄は、殆どの東洋諸国が同じ様な状況であった
と思うが、その実情の酷さは到底書きつくせるものではなかった。
衛生設備などというものはなく、囚人に対する扱いの酷さは当たり
前になっており、獄中は信じがたいほどの過密さであった。大日本
帝国が監獄行政を引き継いだ時点では、囚人１人あたりに対し獄中
で与えられた床面積は５平方フィートであったとのことだ。併合後
は年々監獄の数が増加し、状況も改善されており、今日少なくとも
大きな監獄の環境は他国に引けをとらないであろうし、米国の殆ど
の監獄より格段良いとさえ言える。

　併合前の旧体制では監獄は政府の内部の管轄であり、警察署に付
随していた。現在では、全ての監獄は總督府の指揮下にあり、その
運営管理は總督府法務局の指揮下にある。現場では控訴裁判所の検
事長がその任を負っている。
　原則として監獄の職員は各道知事、医師、聖職者、看守、技術専
門家および通訳であるが、大きな監獄では教師や薬剤師も加わる。

　毎年一定の割合―約10パーセント―で、看守は訓練所に送られ
職務に関連する指示・教育を受けているが、それに加え、監獄の改

is given to a number of picked men each year, in order to fit them for promotion in the prison service. Forty men were given this special course in 1922, the subjects of study and the hours devoted to them being as follows:

Criminal law, 50; penology, 25; factory administration, 25; accountancy, 30; drill, gymnastics, etc., 45; prison laws and regulations, and their application — indoor business, 65, outdoor business, 60; sanitation, 12; education, 10.

Chief warders and the more efficient warders are occasionally sent to Japan to attend higher technical courses.

The following table gives the number of new convicts for each of the ten fiscal years ending with 1921-22.

NUMBER OF PERSONS ENTERING PRISON UNDER SENTENCE
IN KOREA

	Japanese		Koreans		Foreigners		Total
	Male	Female	Male	Female	Male	Female	
1915...	1,073	66	13,544	867	366	5	15,921
1916...	1,059	52	16,587	990	376	7	19,071
1917...	980	49	18,840	1,124	300	4	21,297
1918...	890	53	17,863	1,164	344	3	20,317
1919...	672	31	20,383	802	159	2	22,049
1920...	661	32	13,075	568	125	3	14,464
1921...	645	23	13,601	675	150	4	15,098
1922...	527	14	10,447	579	122	6	11,695
1923...	517	20	7,835	462	140	4	8,978
1924...	362	14	8,255	313	99	3	9,046

善を推し進める上で相応しい人材を育てるための特別講座が設けられており、選ばれた者が受講出来る。1922年には40名の看守がこの特別講座を受講した。講座内容および授業時間は以下のとおりである。

刑法50時間、刑罰学25時間、作業場管理25時間、会計学30時間、訓練体育など45時間、監獄法およびその適用―監獄内部65時間、監獄外部60時間、公衆衛生12時間、教育学10時間。

看守長および優秀な看守には折々に日本本土で上級専門講座も受けさせている。

以下の表は、1921年度までの10年ごとの新規受刑者の数を表している。

朝鮮における新規受刑者数

	日本人		朝鮮人		その他		総計
	男	女	男	女	男	女	
1915	1,073	66	13,544	867	366	5	15,921
1916	1,059	52	16,587	990	376	7	19,071
1917	980	49	18,840	1,124	300	4	21,297
1918	890	53	17,863	1,164	344	3	20,317
1919	672	31	20,383	802	159	2	22,049
1920	661	32	13,075	568	125	3	14,464
1921	645	23	13,601	675	150	4	15,098
1922	527	14	10,447	579	122	6	11,695
1923	517	20	7,835	462	140	4	8,978
1924	362	14	8,255	313	99	3	9,046

308   POLICE AND PRISONS

The foregoing figures include, up to the end of 1920, Korean male convicts whose penalty was flogging, but who were not held in prison after the punishment had been inflicted. Flogging was abolished in 1920. The average number of floggings administered annually between 1915 and 1920, both included, was 7,210.

Having regard to the early age at which Koreans reach maturity, there is very little juvenile crime in the country. Of the 8,978 persons convicted of crime in 1923, only 546 were under twenty years of age, and of these only eighty were females. Between the ages of 20 and 30 there were 3,786; between 30 and 40 there were 3,029; between 40 and 50 there were 1,191; and over 50 there were 426. Perhaps the most striking single feature of the prison statistics is that of a total population of Korea, nearly 18,000,000 persons, only 486 females were convicted of crime in the year 1924.

First Offenders--
Under the present prison law and regulations first offenders are kept apart from other convicts, both in the cells and in the prison work-shops, and are given special treatment. They are better paid than old offenders for the work they do in prison; are afforded more chances of writing to and of meeting their relatives; particular care is taken with their schooling and admonition, and upon their release they are either returned to their near relatives or are placed in the care of one of the Prisoners' Protection Associations.

前述の数字のうち、1920年末までは朝鮮人男性に対するむち打ち刑による受刑者も含まれるが、むち打ち刑は刑の実施のみで収監はされない。この刑は1920年に廃止されたが、1915年から20年までの間で実施された件数は年平均7210件となっている。

　成人に達するのが早い朝鮮の実情を考慮に入れたとしても、国内の青少年犯罪は非常に少ない。1923年の受刑者8978名中、546名のみが20歳未満であり、うち女性受刑者は80名のみである。20代の受刑者は3786名、30代は3029名、40代は1191名、50歳以上は426名である。統計上見られた最も顕著な特徴を1つ挙げるとしたら、朝鮮の人口が1800万人であることに対し、1924年の女性受刑者はわずか486名であるということだろう。

初犯の受刑者
　現行の監獄法令の下での初犯の受刑者たちは、監房でも、また監獄での作業場でも他の受刑者と隔離され特別待遇を受けている。獄中での労働に対し支払われる給与も今までの受刑者より高く、手紙を書いたり親族と面会する機会も多く与えられている。また彼らの教育や訓戒に対しても特別な配慮が払われ、釈放の際にも近くの親族の元に戻すか、もしくは囚人保護協会に預けられる。

310   POLICE AND PRISONS

Recidivism--

It will be seen from the following table that about eighty per cent of the
yearly batch of prisoners are first offenders. In the table male and female
prisoners are combined into a single total. The detailed figures show,
however, that almost all the female prisoners are first offenders. During the
four years ending with the fiscal year 1921-22 the total number of female
prisoners was 3,360, of whom all but 128 were first offenders.

PRISONERS CLASSIFIED ACCORDING TO RECIDIVISM

	1st Offence	2nd Offence	3rd Offence and over	Total
1918.......	16,289	2,633	1,395	20,317
1919.......	19,038	1,854	1,157	22,049
1920.......	11,743	1,756	965	14,464
1921.......	12,545	1,689	864	15,098

Pardons--

In accordance with Japanese custom pardons are granted to prisoners
or their sentences are reduced on occasions of national importance. Since
the annexation of Korea in 1910 five such occasions have occurred. The
first was at the time of annexation, when 1,711 prisoners benefited by the
Imperial grace; the second was at the time of the demise of the Emperor
Meiji in 1912, when 4,767 prisoners were affected; the third followed the
death of the Dowager Empress Shoken in 1914, when 8,872 prisoners
were shown clemency; the fourth was the occasion of the coronation of
the Emperor Yoshihito in 1915, affecting 10,208 prisoners; the fifth was

常習的犯行

次の表から読み取れることは、毎年の囚人の約80パーセントが初犯であるということだ。男女の囚人の合計数が表示されているが、詳細に数字を追っていくと女囚の殆ど全員が初犯であることが分かる。1921年度までの4年間の女囚の合計数は3360名であったが、そのうち128名以外は全て初犯であった。

囚人の再犯区分

	初犯	再犯	3回以上	合計
1918	16,289	2,633	1,395	20,317
1919	19,038	1,854	1,157	22,049
1920	11,743	1,756	965	14,464
1921	12,545	1,689	864	15,098

恩赦

日本本土の慣習に従い、国家の重大事の機会に囚人に対し赦免、もしくはその量刑の軽減が図られる恩赦が行われるようになった。1910年の併合以降、5回の恩赦が実施された。最初の恩赦は併合の際に行われた大赦で、1711名の囚人がその恩恵をこうむった。2回目の恩赦は1912年の明治天皇の崩御に伴って行われ、4767名の囚人がその対象となった。3回目は1914年の昭憲皇太后の崩御によるもので対象者は8872名。4回目は1915年の嘉仁天皇の即位に伴うもので1万208名の囚人に対し行われた。5回目は1920年の李王世

in 1920 when, on the marriage of the Korean Prince Yi to the Japanese Princess Nashimoto-no-Miya, the sentences of 3,546 prisoners were reduced. Among these was a large number of political prisoners who had been convicted and sentenced for taking part in the disturbances connected with the independence movement of 1919.

Prisoners' Labor--

Under the old Korean Government little was done to provide work for the prisoners. It was not until after annexation that this matter was taken up seriously with a view as well to making an offset against the increasing expenditure on prisons as to counteracting the evils which invariably result from the enforced idleness of persons in confinement. At the present time about ninety-six per cent of healthy and able-bodied prisoners are kept at work. From time to time the scope of prison work has been extended, the principal occupations now being weaving, papermaking, tailoring, straw-work, brick-making, cabinet-work, and farming.

According to the Japanese system of Government accountancy, the wages of prisoners, whether coming from the proceeds of the sale of their work, or actual payments by employers of prison labor, are incorporated in the State revenue account, the actual wage paid to, and becoming the personal property of prisoners is charged against prison expenditures. In recent years the average daily wage paid to prisoners has been between six and eight cents.

子李垠と梨本宮方子女王との成婚に伴うもので、3546名の囚人が減刑の恩恵を受けた。これらの囚人の多くは1919年の独立運動の騒乱に加わったとして有罪判決を受けた政治犯たちであった。

獄中労働

李朝政府の時代には囚人を労働につかせることは殆どなく、この問題については併合後に初めて真剣に検討されるようになった。これは増大する監獄の運営費を埋め合わせるためだけでなく、監禁中に強いられる無為が生み出す悪事を緩和させるという観点から検討された。現在、監獄では約96パーセントの健常者が労働に従事している。労働の範囲はその時々で拡がっているが、主だった作業としては、機織り、製紙、洋服の仕立て、藁細工、煉瓦製造、家具作り、そして農作業である。

日本の政府会計のシステムでは、囚人の作った製品の販売による収入であっても、雇用者から刑務作業に対して支払われる給与であっても、それは国家の歳入に組み込まれた。また労働報酬として実際に囚人に支払われ本人の個人資産となった額は監獄の支出として計上された。近年、囚人の平均日給は6～8セントである。

314   POLICE AND PRISONS

Morbidity and Mortality of Prisoners--

Both the sick rate and the death rate among prisoners in the jails of Korea are very low when compared with those of countries of similar situation in respect of the general public health.

In the five years ending with 1923 the average daily population of the prisons was 15,220; the annual average of deaths in prison was 288; and the daily average number of patients under treatment in the prison hospitals and sick bays was 1,083. These figures show an average annual death rate of 18.9 per thousand; and a morbidity rate of 71.1 per thousand.

囚人の罹患率および死亡率

　朝鮮の監獄内の囚人の罹患率および死亡率は、公衆衛生の面で同じような状況下にある他国と比較した場合、非常に低いと言える。

　1923年までの5年間で、囚人数は、平均すると1日当たり1万5220名である。そして獄中の囚人の死亡者数は年平均288名である。監獄の病院もしくは監獄内の病室で治療を受けている囚人は1日当たり平均1083名となる。よって、死亡率は年平均で、千人に対し18.9名、罹患率は千人に対し71.1名である。

CHAPTER Ⅷ

第八章

CHAPTER VIII

GOVERNMENT FINANCE

Historical--

Under the old Korean régime the finances of the country were administered by two organizations, the Finance Department of the Korean State, and the Financial Department of the Imperial Korean Household. Although, in theory, these departments were independent of each other, each collecting its revenue from different sources, in practice the distinction was often disregarded, the latter encroaching from time to time on the revenues payable to the former, and occasionally exacting appropriations from it.

The principal sources of revenue upon which the Imperial Korean Household depended were the mining tax, the courier service tax, the house tax, the income derived from the sale of official appointments; and later the profit on the ginseng monopoly, which the Imperial Household took away from the State Financial Department in 1899.

Another source of Imperial Household revenue was the profit made on the minting of coins.

A curious sidelight is thrown upon the Korean conception of economic law by the habit, which prevailed for many years, of selling to private individuals the right to mint coin and to put it in circulation as a competitor of the official coinage. An amusing abuse of this custom was the renting out of the official mint dies by corrupt officials to the highest bidder, for his private use.

第八章

政府の財政

財政の歴史

　旧朝鮮政府時代の国家財政は、朝鮮国家の財務部門と王家の財務部門という2つの組織に分かれて管理されていた。理論上は、それぞれの部門はお互いに独立しており、個々に異なる財源から収入を得るようになっていたが、実際にはその区別はしばしば無視された。王家の財務部は、朝鮮国家の財務部門に支払うべき収入を侵害することがあり、時にはそこから充当金を徴収することもあった。

　王家の主財源は、鉱業税、物流の手数料、戸税、公式任命を売って得られる収入であり、後には、1899年に政府から朝鮮人参の専売権による利益も奪い取った。
　李王家のもう1つの収入源は、貨幣の鋳造から得られる利益であった。

　朝鮮における経済概念の奇妙な一面として、通貨の鋳造とそれを公式硬貨と同様に流通させる権利を、長年に亘り私的個人に売って来たという習慣がある。この慣習の乱用が面白いのだが、退廃した官吏は、より多くの賄賂を出す人間に対して公的貨幣の打ち抜き型まで貸し出していたのである。

320   GOVERNMENT FINANCE

The principal tax collected by the Finance Department of the Korean State was the Land Tax, based upon a registry of occupancy, and upon an assessment made in respect of the situation, fertility, and irrigation facilities of the land. The standard of land taxation was called the kyel, which represented a figure arrived at by estimating the quantity of grain which could be produced from a given area of land.

The land tax was, until 1894, payable in kind, after which it had to be paid in money, and it was imposed upon the person using the land, not upon the owner. The actual collection of the tax was accompanied by many abuses. The desire of the officials to enrich themselves at the expense of the State, and of the people to evade payment of the tax, led to the falsification of the register, and to dishonest assessments.

In 1904 Korea agreed to engage a Japanese financial adviser and to accept his decisions in respect of financial reforms. In the years immediately following, many changes were effected in the Korean system of taxation, both in the direction of reforming the methods of collecting the old taxes, and in that of imposing new taxes. But it was not until after the establishment of the Residency-General, in 1906, that it was practicable to undertake a thorough overhauling of the Korean finances.

The financial reforms are thus described in the Report on Reforms and Progress in Chosen, 1918-1921:

To know the Financial condition of Chosen in its true aspect, it is necessary to have a general idea of what it was previous to annexation. From very early times the finance of the country lacked solid foundation, the taxation and the currency systems both being in the wildest confusion,

第八章　政府の財政

　朝鮮政府の財務部門による主要な税収は地税であり、土地占有の登記簿とその土地の立地条件、肥沃度、灌漑設備を考慮した評価額に応じて徴収された。土地に対する課税基準は「結」と呼ばれ、定められた面積の土地における穀物の推定収穫量から算出された。

　1894年まで地税は物品でも納税出来たが、その後は金銭で支払わなければならなくなった。さらに、課税対象は土地の所有者ではなく、その土地の使用者に対して課せられ、実際の税徴収時には多くの弊害を伴った。官吏は国の出費で如何にして自らの懐を肥やすかを考え、民衆は税の支払いから逃れることを考えていたので、土地登記の改竄や不正な土地査定が行われた。

　1904年、大韓帝国政府は日本人の財政顧問の雇用と、財政再建に関わる決定を容認することに同意した。翌年からただちに税の徴収方法を改善すると同時に新しい税を課するという両面において、従来の課税制度に多くの変革が行われた。しかし、実際には、1906年に統監府が置かれて、初めて財政の抜本的な改革が実行可能になった。

　この財政改革は『朝鮮施政年報　自大正7年度至大正9年度』に記述されている。

　朝鮮の財政状態を正しく見るためには、併合される前はどうだったかという全体像を知ることが必要である。ごく初期の段階から国家財政は確固たる基盤を欠いていた。税制と通貨制度は混乱の極みで、年間の支出は無目的に使われていた。

the annual expenditure wasted to no purpose, and the Court and Government having no definite distinction between themselves with regard to their revenues and expenditures. . . . With regard to expenditures each Government department spent as it pleased, being restrained by nothing save the lack of funds. The result of this mismanagement was that no reliable foundation existed on which to base accounts, and the compilation of the budget was a mere farce.

On the conclusion of the agreement between Japan and Chosen in August, 1904, resulting in the appointment of a financial adviser recommended by the Japanese Government and the establishment of the Residency-General in 1906, strenuous efforts were made to bring to an end the haphazard method of dealing with the finance of the country, by adopting the gold standard in order to secure a uniform currency, by establishing a central bank and making it the national treasurer, whilst giving it power to issue convertible notes, and by founding agricultural and industrial banks and people's banking associations in important centers, for the purpose of facilitating the development of industry.

The financial resources of the country were fully investigated, the financial law requiring the compilation of a yearly budget and the proper carrying of it into practice was strictly enforced, regulations relating to taxes for the purpose of ensuring an annual revenue, and its natural increment, and the equitable distribution of the tax burden were introduced, the system of tax collection was improved so as to combat and root out the vicious habit of extortion, and various taxes, as well as the income from the ginseng monopoly, etc., formerly collected by the Imperial Korean Household Department, were placed under the control of the Korean

第八章　政府の財政　　　323

　王家と政府の間でも、それぞれの収入と支出に関して、はっきり
とした区分がなかったほどである。政府の各行政組織も、支出に関
しては財源の不足以外には拘束もなく、好きなように使った。この
誤った管理の結果、会計の基礎となるべき信頼できる基盤も存在せ
ず、予算編成も単なる茶番であった。

　1904年8月、大日本帝国と大韓帝国との合意締結に基づき、日本
政府推薦の財政顧問が任命され、1906年には統監府が設置された。
精力的な努力が行われ、場当たり的国家財政の処理方法を終わらせ
るため、統一通貨を保証するための金本位制を導入し、中央銀行を
設立した。国庫金の取り扱い、兌換紙幣の発行権も与えられた。また、
産業化を促進する目的で、重要拠点には農工銀行と金融組合を設立
した。

　国の金融資産は完全に調べ上げられ、財政法は毎年の予算編成と
その適切な執行に必要とされるために厳密に遵守された。年間予算
の確保、自然増のための税に関する法規と、公平な課税の割当が導
入され、また、悪弊となっていた強奪と戦って根絶するために税金
の徴収制度が改善された。以前は王朝の財務部門が徴収していた朝
鮮人参の独占販売収入だけでなく、あらゆる税金を大韓帝国政府自
身の管理下に置き、王家と政府の資産に関しても明確な区別を行っ
て政府の財政領域を大幅に拡大させるという結果をもたらした。

324   GOVERNMENT FINANCE

Government itself, thus making a clear distinction between the properties belonging to the Imperial Household and to the State respectively, and a great expansion was effected in the financial sphere of the Korean Government.

The result produced by the above-mentioned measures was so great that the poor financial condition of the fiscal year 1905—plainly shown by the expenditure (9,550,000 yen) exceeding the revenue (7,480,000 yen) by over 27 per cent—improved so rapidly that in the fiscal year 1910 the revenue and expenditures, each amounting to over 23,960,000 yen, showed an even balance; and by the time the Government-General was established, as a consequence of the annexation in August, 1910, the finances of Chosen had been put on a firm basis, though only six years had elapsed since the work was first taken up.

Subsequent to the Annexation of 1910--

Korea having been annexed in August, 1910, the accounts for the first fiscal year, ending on March 31, 1911, covered only seven months. The first complete fiscal year was that of 1911-1912. From that year onward the Revenue and Expenditure Accounts of the Government-General are shown in the following table. The figures down to and including 1922-23 refer to actual revenue and expenditure, and for the following three years are those of the budget estimates.

In the budget estimates revenue and expenditure are made to balance, as is seen from the figures of the last three years. In practice the revenue has almost always exceeded the estimate, and the expenditure has always fallen below it. Referring to the first thirteen years in the table, in each

第八章　政府の財政　　　325

　上記の対策により生み出された結果は、多大なもので、1905 年
度の脆弱な財政状態—つまり、支出 955 万円が、収入 748 万円を 27
パーセントも超えるような財政が迅速に改善され、1910 年度では収
入と支出が均衡収支となり、それぞれ 2396 万円を超える額であった。
そして、併合により、1910 年 8 月に朝鮮總督府が設立された時、す
でに朝鮮の財政は強固な基盤に置かれていた。それも、財政改革が
最初に始められてから、たった 6 年しか経過していなかったのであ
る。

1910 年の併合に続いて

　大韓帝国は 1910 年 8 月に併合されたので、1911 年 3 月 31 日に終
わる会計年度初年の数字は、7 カ月間分だけのものであった。最初
の完全な会計年度である 1911 年度は 1911 年 4 月から 1912 年 3 月
であった。その年度以降の總督府の収入と支出の会計記録は以下の
表に示されている。表中の数字は 1922 年度分までが実際の収入と
支出であり、そして、それ以降の 3 年分は概算予算で示してある。

　概算予算での収入・支出は、最後 3 年間の数値に見られるように
収支の均衡がとられている。実際には、収入はほとんどいつも概算
を超えており、支出はいつも概算を下回っていた。

　表に示した最初の 13 年間では、それぞれの数値は最終的に確定

326   GOVERNMENT FINANCE

of which the figures are those of the finally settled accounts, it is to be
observed that there has been a substantial annual surplus of revenue over
expenditure. The surplus is always carried over to the following year and
is incorporated in the budget as an item of extraordinary revenue.

REVENUE AND EXPENDITURE OF THE GOVERNMENT-GENERAL
OF KOREA

(In thousands of yen. 1 yen = 50 cents U. S.)

	Revenue			Expenditure		
	Ordinary	Extraordinary	Total	Ordinary	Extraordinary	Total
1911.....	25,564	26,720	52,284	25,548	20,624	46,172
1912.....	28,765	33,362	62,127	28,000	23,781	51,781
1913.....	31,347	31,746	63,093	31,690	21,764	53,454
1914.....	35,692	26,355	62,047	32,278	22,822	55,100
1915.....	38,829	23,893	62,722	34,725	22,145	56,870
1916.....	44,764	23,438	68,202	36,188	21,374	57,562
1917.....	46,433	28,470	74,903	31,944	19,227	51,171
1918.....	59,371	40,740	100,111	34,811	29,251	64,062
1919.....	73,951	51,852	125,803	39,248	52,778	93,026
1920.....	71,343	75,000	146,343	64,213	58,008	122,221
1921.....	93,417	81,717	175,134	91,366	57,047	148,414
1922.....	100,248	69,112	169,360	96,089	59,023	155,113
1923.....	90,885	61,828	152,713	94,560	50,207	144,768
1924.....	102,384	38,440	140,824	106,209	34,615	140,824
1925.....	143,465	32,583	176,048	136,868	39,180	176,048
1926.....	149,454	38,553	188,006	140,339	47,667	188,006

The average revenue raised during the first three years covered by the
foregoing table was 59 million yen, the average for the three years 1921-23
(the latest for which settled account figures are available) was 166 million
yen. On this basis the revenue of the Government-General increased
by 181.3 per cent, as between 1911-13 and 1921-23. During the same
period the value of the import and export trade of Korea (upon which the
prosperity of the country depends) increased from an average of 88 million

第八章　政府の財政　　327

した収支であり、支出に対する収入の相当な年間黒字がみてとれる。余剰金は常に翌年度へ繰り越され、特別収入として予算に組み込まれている。

朝鮮總督府における収入と支出
（単位千円　当時１円＝ 50 セント）

	収　入			支　出		
	一般	特別	合計	一般	特別	合計
1911	25,564	26,720	52,284	25,548	20,624	46,172
1912	28,765	33,362	62,127	28,000	23,781	51,781
1913	31,347	31,746	63,093	31,690	21,764	53,454
1914	35,692	26,355	62,047	32,278	22,822	55,100
1915	38,829	23,893	62,722	34,725	22,145	56,870
1916	44,764	23,438	68,202	36,188	21,374	57,562
1917	46,433	28,470	74,903	31,944	19,227	51,171
1918	59,371	40,740	100,111	34,811	29,251	64,062
1919	73,951	51,852	125,803	39,248	52,778	93,026
1920	71,343	75,000	146,343	64,213	58,008	122,221
1921	93,417	81,717	175,134	91,366	57,047	148,414
1922	100,248	69,112	169,360	96,089	59,023	155,113
1923	90,885	61,828	152,713	94,560	50,207	144,768
1924	102,384	38,440	140,824	106,209	34,615	140,824
1925	143,465	32,583	176,048	136,868	39,180	176,048
1926	149,454	38,553	188,006	140,339	47,667	188,006

　収入の平均は、先の表でも示すように当初の３年間で 5900 万円で、1921 年から 1923 年（決算収支が得られた最後の年）の３年間では、１億 6600 万円であった。この数字に基づくと、1911 ～ 1913 年、および 1921 ～ 1923 年の間で、總督府の収入は 181.3 パーセント増加している。同じ時期の貿易収支（国の繁栄が左右される）は平均額

328   GOVERNMENT FINANCE

yen to an average of 456 million yen, or 418.1 per cent.

In round figures this means that the value of the principal element in the economic development of Korea has increased at two-and-a-half times the rate of the revenue raised by the Government-General. It is to be noted that in the system of accounting followed by the Government-General the proceeds of the flotation of public loans are merged in the revenue receipts. The revenue figures—classed as Ordinary and Extraordinary —include all receipts whether from taxation, loans, profits on Government enterprises, or any other source. The expenditure figures include all payments of interest on the public debt, and all repayments on account of loans.

Sources of Government Revenue--

The Ordinary Revenue of the Government-General falls under two general heads—Revenue from Taxation, and Revenue from Other Sources. Under the former head the total receipts during the ten years ending on March 31, 1921 were 218 million yen, of which 43.5 per cent was derived from the land tax, 32 per cent from customs duties, 8.5 per cent from the tobacco tax, 5.8 per cent from the liquor tax, 2.8 per cent from the rural household tax, 2.4 per cent from the mining tax; the remaining 5 per cent being distributed among small items, none of which reached a proportion as high as 2 per cent of the total.

Ordinary Revenue from sources other than taxation reached a total of 238 million yen in the ten fiscal years 1911-1920. To this total the Government Railways contributed 28.6 per cent, communications (postal, telegraphic, and telephonic) 18.2 per cent, revenue stamps 16.1 per cent, the rental of Government land 6.4 per cent, Government monopolies

が 8800 万円から 4 億 5600 万円と 418.1 パーセント増加している。

　概数で言うと、これは朝鮮の経済発展における主要な要素の価値が總督府の収入での比率で 2.5 倍に上げられたことを意味する。注目すべきは、總督府の会計制度で、国債発行による収益が歳入に組み込まれていることだ。

　歳入の数値は一般収入と特別収入に分類されているが、税収、国債、政府の事業利益などいかなる収入源からの収入も含めている。支出の方は公共債務の利子支払いや借款の返済も含めている。

政府歳入の収入源

　總督府の一般歳入は 2 つの一般的な項目に分けられる。すなわち、税収とその他の収入である。

　まず税収では、1921 年 3 月末までの 10 年間での総収入は 2 億 1800 万円であり、その内訳は 43.5 パーセントが地税、32 パーセントが関税、8.5 パーセントが煙草税、5.8 パーセントが酒税、2.8 パーセントが農村世帯課税、2.4 パーセントが鉱業税、残りの 5 パーセントは単独で 2 パーセントに達しない少額項目である。

　次に、税収以外の収入源からの一般収入は、1911 〜 1920 年度の10 会計年度で総額が 2 億 3800 万円に達している。その内訳は、国営鉄道が 28.6 パーセント、通信事業（郵便・電報・電話）から 18.2 パーセント、印紙収入が 16.1 パーセント、国有地の賃貸料が 6.4 パーセント、国営専売事業が 6 パーセント、国営の石炭産業が 5.9 パー

330   GOVERNMENT FINANCE

6 per cent, Government coal 5.9 per cent, Government lumber 5.3 per cent, revenue from salt, forests, opium, and water-works 4.1 per cent, printing, and the sale of weights and measures 3.2 per cent, Government undertakings other than those referred to above 2.3 per cent.

During the same ten-year period the Extraordinary Revenue amounted to 219 million yen. Of this total Government loans accounted for 59.9 per cent, subsidies from the Imperial Japanese Treasury for 34.7 per cent, the sale of Government property for 2.2 per cent, and various small items for the remainder.

Comparing the revenue figures given above with those for the five-year period immediately following, that is to say for the fiscal years 1921 to 1925, some changes are to be noted in the sources from which the revenue was derived. In the latter period the percentage of the revenue derived from the land tax fell to 38.9, and that from customs duties to 27.1, while that from the tobacco tax was reduced from 8.5 to 2.5, as a concession to tobacco-loving people. On the other hand the revenue from the liquor tax moved up from 5.8 per cent of the total to 20 per cent, and that from the sugar tax from 0.6 to 4.5 per cent.

In the category of Ordinary Revenue from sources other than taxation the only important change to be noted is the receipts from Government Monopolies, of which the proportion moved up from 6.0 per cent of the total to 31.9 per cent, owing to the establishment of the Tobacco Monopoly in 1921.

The sources of Extraordinary Revenue showed several important changes. Receipts from the sale of State properties rose from 2.2 per cent of the total to 8.8 per cent, surpluses from previous years rose from 1.9

セント、国営の木材伐採業が5.3パーセント、塩・森林・アヘン・水道事業からの収入が4.1パーセント、印刷業と度量衡販売から3.2パーセント、上記以外の国営事業からは2.3パーセントであった。

　同時期10年間の特別収入は2億1900万円であった。総額の内訳は、国債が59.9パーセント、大日本帝国国庫からの補助金が34.7パーセント、国有資産の売却益が2.2パーセント、種々の少額項目が残りを占める。

　上記の収入の数値と、この直後の5年間、すなわち1921 ～ 1925年度の会計年度とを比較して、収入が得られる源泉での若干の変化が見られる。後の5年間では、地税からの収入は38.9パーセントに下落し、関税からの収入も27.1パーセントに下落、同時に、煙草税からの収入は愛煙家に配慮して8.5パーセントから2.5パーセントに減らされた。一方で、酒税からの収入は総計の5.8パーセントから20パーセントに上がり、砂糖税からの収入も0.6パーセントから4.5パーセントに上がった。

　一般収入での税収以外の収入源において、記載すべき唯一の重要な変化は、政府の専売事業からの売上げで、その占める割合が総額の6.0パーセントから31.9パーセントに上がったことである。これは1921年に煙草専売公社が設立されたおかげである。

　特別収入の源泉もいくつかの重要な変化を示している。国有資産売却による売上金の割合が総額の2.2パーセントから8.8パーセントに上昇し、先の年度からの余剰金も1.9パーセントから22.1パー

332   GOVERNMENT FINANCE

to 22.1 per cent while the receipts from public loans declined from 57.4 to 37.1 per cent, and those from Imperial subsidies from 34.9 to 28.6 per cent.

During the five-year period 1921-25 the average total annual revenue was, in round figures, 161 million yen, the average annual revenue from taxation was 37 million yen, the average annual revenue from ordinary sources other than taxation was 71 million yen; and the annual average of the extraordinary revenue was 53 million yen.

Assuming that the average population of Korea during the period was 17 million it is seen that the total revenue of the Government-General was 9.5 yen ($4.75) per capita of the population; that the revenue from taxation was 2.2 yen ($1.10) per capita; that the revenue from ordinary sources other than taxation was 4.2 yen ($2.10) per capita; and that the extraordinary revenue—chiefly public loans, and subsidies from the Imperial Japanese Treasury—was 3.1 yen ($1.55) per capita.

Monopolies and Other Government Undertakings--

The Government-General maintains two monopolies—the manufacture and sale of tobacco and of ginseng.

Tobacco manufacture was started in Korea in 1903 by the Korean-Japanese Tobacco Company, and other companies soon entered the business. In 1921 the Government-General's Monopoly Bureau bought out the existing tobacco companies and started the manufacture of a variety of cigarettes and cut-tobacco. In 1923 tobacco manufacture afforded employment to 4,000 men and 1,000 women. In the fiscal year 1922-23 the production of cigarettes was something over three and a half billion

セントに上昇した一方で、国債の収益は 57.4 パーセントから 37.1 パーセントへと減少し、日本からの補助金も 34.9 パーセントから 28.6 パーセントになった。

1921 ～ 1925 年度の 5 年間における年間収入総額の平均は概算で 1 億 6100 万円、税金からの年間収入平均は 3700 万円、税収以外の一般源泉からの年間収入平均は 7100 万円、特別収入の年平均は 5300 万円であった。

その期間における朝鮮の平均人口を 1700 万人と仮定すると、總督府の総収入額は人口 1 人当たり、9.5 円（4.75 ドル）に相当し、税収からの収入は 1 人当たり 2.2 円（1.10 ドル）、税収以外の一般源泉からの収入は 1 人当たり 4.2 円（2.10 ドル）、特別収入—主に国債と大日本帝国国庫からの補助金—では、1 人当たり 3.1 円（1.55 ドル）であった。

専売事業とその他の政府事業

總督府は 2 つの専売事業を維持している。すなわち、煙草の生産・販売と朝鮮人参の生産・販売である。

大韓帝国での煙草の生産については、1903 年に日韓煙草商会により始められ、他の会社もすぐに事業に参入した。1921 年には、總督府の専売局が既存の煙草会社を買収し種々の紙巻煙草と刻み煙草の製造を開始した。1923 年には煙草生産により、男性 4000 人、女性 1000 人の雇用が与えられた。1922 年度における紙巻煙草の生産は 35 億本を少し超え、刻み煙草は 89 万 7500 ポンド、その販売により

334 GOVERNMENT FINANCE

pieces, and of cut-tobacco 897,500 pounds, of which the sale yielded about 18 million yen.

Ginseng is a perennial herb of the araliaceae family, highly esteemed in China as a stimulant and aphrodisiac. It was made a monopoly by the old Korean Government as early as 1899. After the annexation of Korea in 1910 the Government-General encouraged its cultivation by adopting scientific methods and by lending money, without interest, to associations of ginseng cultivators. In 1911 the amount of prepared ginseng sold was 2,120 pounds, which brought a price of 120 thousand yen. In the fiscal year 1922-23 the amount sold was 45,670 pounds, from which the receipts were 2,269,664 yen.

Salt manufacture is conducted by the Government-General by the process of natural evaporation; and salterns have been established at various places on the Korean coast. Up to the year 1921 crude salt only was produced, good table-salt being imported; but in that year a refinery was set up for the manufacture of superior qualities. In 1911 the production of salt was about six million pounds, yielding 80,000 yen; in the fiscal year 1922-23 the production of salt was 100 million pounds, from which the Government-General received a revenue of 860 thousand yen.

Lumber Undertaking Station--

The Lumber Undertaking Station is the special government office controlling the State forests covering about 5,500,000 acres in the basins of the Yalu and Tumen. It engages in various kinds of work tending not only to improve the forests themselves but to improve their indirect utilization.

The principal trees in the forests are mostly those found in the frigid

1800万円の利益を得た。

　朝鮮人参はウコギ科の多年生の薬用植物で、中国では興奮剤や精力剤として大いに尊重されている。朝鮮人参は既に1899年に大韓帝国政府により専売化されていた。

　1910年の併合以降、總督府は朝鮮人参生産者組合に対し、人参の栽培に科学的手法の導入を推奨し、無利子で資金の貸し付けを行った。1911年には加工された朝鮮人参の販売量は2120ポンドで、売上も12万円になった。1922年度には、販売量は4万5670ポンドで226万9664円の売上があった。

　塩の製造は總督府が自然蒸発製法により運営し、製塩所が朝鮮沿岸の各地に設置された。1921年までは粗塩だけが生産され、良質の食卓塩は輸入されていたが、その年のうちに高品質塩を生産するための精製所が設置された。1911年の塩の生産量は600万ポンド（約2722トン）で8万円の売上だったが、1922年度には、生産量は1億ポンド（約4万5360トン）に達し、總督府は86万円の収入を受け取った。

営林廠

　営林廠とはヤールー河と豆満江の流域にある約550万エーカーもの国有林を管理する政府の特別部局である。森林自体を改良するだけではなく、その間接的な活用方法を改善するような多様な種類の

336   GOVERNMENT FINANCE

zone, such as the larch, fir, birch, and aspen, all valuable for utilitarian purposes. As for afforestation, not only is the natural way utilized but plantation on a large scale is carried on, seedlings of the most suitable varieties for this region being raised in special nurseries.

For the proper protection of the forests the Station established sixty branches in 1919 to guard against wilful damage being done to them, and since the fiscal year 1915 protection unions have been organized in that region to the advantage of both officials and people, and such numbered 232 at the end of this fiscal year, guarding an area of over 1,245,000 acres. The result being very good it is proposed to encourage more such organizations in the future.

For further details as to the forests of Korea the reader is referred to Chapter XIII.

The preparation of timber was formerly carried on by private saw-mills under contract. As this proved unsatisfactory both to buyers and to the Station, it was decided that it should be done direct by the Station so that better adjustment between demand and supply might be maintained. A saw-mill at Shin-gishu was bought, enlarged, and equipped with modern machinery for this purpose, and in the fiscal year 1922-23 turned out 2,172,000 cubic feet of timber from logs measuring 3,852,000 cubic feet.

The timber prepared by the Station finds its market mostly in Chosen, though a small demand for piles and sleepers comes from Manchuria. Even in Chosen the output by the Station was at first taken solely by the Government, but of late years it has become recognized as excellent in

作業を任されている。森林内の主要な樹木は寒帯に見られるカラマツ、モミ、カバ、そしてポプラなどで、どれも実用的な理由で価値が高い。植林については自然な方法ばかりではなく、大規模な植林地を営み、その地域に最もふさわしい樹種の苗木を特別な養苗場で育てるのである。

　適切な森林保護のため、営林廠はまず1919年に60カ所の出張所を設置して故意による被害から守るようにした。官民両方にとって益をもたらすため、1915年度からは地域に保護組合が組織された。その年度末には組合員も232人に達し、124万5000エーカーを超える地域を保護するようになった。この結果が非常に良好だったため、将来このような組合をもっと増やすことが提案されている。

　朝鮮の森林についての更なる詳細は、十三章を参照されたい。

　材木の製材は、かつては政府が契約した民間の製材所で行われていた。これは買い手と営林廠の両方にとって不満があると判明したため、需要と供給のより良い調整がなされるように、製材作業も営林廠によって直接行われるべきとの決定がなされた。新義州の製材所は、この目的のために買い取られた後に拡張されて製材用の最新機械が設置された。1922年度には、217万2000立方フィートもの木材が385万2000立方フィートの丸太から製材された。

　営林廠により製材された木材は、殆どが朝鮮国内で売られた。満州からの杭や枕木の需要もわずかにあった。朝鮮国内でも営林廠に

338   GOVERNMENT FINANCE

quality and, the credit system being introduced, the general demand for it is increasing.

The total production in 1910 was 200,000 cubic feet, of which 121,000 was in lumber, 48,000 in logs, and 31,000 in standing trees. In the fiscal year 1922-23 the total sales amounted to 859,000 cubic feet, of which 176,000 was in lumber, 111,000 in logs, and 571,000 in standing trees. In 1910 the profit from this undertaking was 80,000 yen; in 1920 it rose to 850,000 yen; in 1922-23 it fell to 370,000 yen, owing to the universal depression in the business world.

Objects of Government Expenditure--

The budget estimates of the expenditure of the Government-General do not afford a clear view of the objects to which the expenditure was applied, for the items are in some instances given as the expenditure of the disbursing department or bureau, and this expenditure may be devoted to several different objects. For example, in the budget estimates for the fiscal year 1921-22 the expenditure of the local offices of the Government-General is given as 32,980,000 yen, and the expenditure on police is given as 378,000 yen. This latter sum represents, in fact, the cost of the central police administration; whilst the actual cost of the police force throughout the country accounted for about 23 million yen out of the 33 million yen set against the budget item "Local Offices of the Government-General." Again, the budget item, "Education," shows in 1921-22 an expenditure of about three million yen, whereas the actual expenditure on education under all items of the Government-General's budget exceeded six million yen.

よる生産品は当初、政府が単独で買い取ったが、後年になって品質が優れていると認識されるようになり、また掛売りが導入されると、一般需要も増大していった。

1910年の総生産量は20万立方フィートで、そのうち木材12万1000立方フィート、丸太4万8000立方フィート、立木3万1000立方フィートだった。1922年度の総売上量は、85万9000立方フィートで、木材17万6000立方フィート、丸太11万1000立方フィート、立木57万1000立方フィートであった。1910年にはこの事業からの収益は8万円で、1920年には85万円まで増加した。1922年度には37万円まで下落したが、これは経済界での世界恐慌が原因である。

政府支出の対象

總督府の支出における予算見積もりに関しては、支出がどの対象に割り当てられるのか、はっきりした見解が与えられていない。ある項目が場合によっては支払いをする支部あるいは部局の費用として組み込まれたり、あるいは、この費用がいくつかの異なる目的に割り当てられたりしているかもしれないからだ。

例を挙げると、1921年度には總督府の地方政府の支出への予算見積もりは3298万円で、警察の支出は37万8000円である。後者の金額は、実際には、中央の警察幹部の費用であり、一方、国全体での警察隊にかかる実際の費用は、予算項目の「總督府の地方政府」に割り当てられた約3300万円のうち2300万円を占める。さらに、予算項目である「教育費」は、1921年度の支出が約300万円である

340 GOVERNMENT FINANCE

The following table has been made up by analyzing the figures in the budgets according to the objects to which they were devoted, and recombining them under the several heads.

It will be observed that the largest single item of expenditure in each year is "Government Undertakings." These include the Government Railways, the Government Printing Office (abolished in 1923), the Tobacco Monopoly, the Ginseng Monopoly, Salt Manufacture, Sale of Opium (in charge of the Police Bureau, formerly in charge of the Monopoly Bureau), the Manufacture and Sale of Weights and Measures, Forests, Prison Work, the Lumber Station, Communications (Post, Telegraph, and Telephone), the Water-works (transferred to Municipal Bodies in 1922), and the Heijo Coal Mine Station (transferred to the Japanese Navy in 1922).

ESTIMATED EXPENDITURE BY THE GOVERNMENT-GENERAL OF KOREA, CLASSIFIED ACCORDING TO ITS OBJECTS

(In thousands of yen. 1 yen = 50 cents U. S.)

Objects	1920	1921	1922	1923	1924
Prince Yi Household........	1,500	1,800	1,800	1,800	1,800
Central Administration......	5,483	6,936	8,263	7,786	8,227
Local Administration.......	8,503	10,133	10,711	10,711	11,096
Law Courts and Prisons.....	6,034	7,117	6,962	7,295	7,561
Police....................	16,702	22,754	22,265	21,924	22,402
Medical and Sanitary.......	1,765	1,882	1,656	1,735	1,747
Education.................	4,595	6,099	7,279	5,995	6,017
Encouragement of Industry..	5,864	8,798	11,757	10,627	11,724
Government Undertakings...	33,570	68,742	57,653	51,241	45,352
Repairs and Construction....	8,897	8,582	6,298	4,703	4,312
Public Debt Charges........	7,441	9,485	11,700	12,797	13,568
Reserve Fund..............	2,500	2,500	2,500	2,500	3,250
Roads and other Public Works	7,108	6,743	7,914	6,182	4,621
Miscellaneous..............	4,351	900	2,142	1,083	1,018
Total................	114,317	162,474	158,993	146,007	142,700

のに対し、總督府予算の全項目の中の実際の教育関連支出は 600 万
円を上回っている。

　次に示す表は、予算が割り当てられた対象によって予算の合計を
分析し、それぞれの項目ごとに組み直したものである。いずれの年
でも単項目として最も高額な支出は「政府事業」である。

　この項目には、国有鉄道、国営印刷局（1923 年廃止）、煙草専売、
朝鮮人参専売、塩製造、アヘン販売（警務局が監督、以前は専売
局が監督）、度量衡製造・販売、森林、監獄業務、木材伐採事業所、
通信業務（郵便、電報、電話）、水道事業（1922 年に地方自治体に
移管された）、平壌石炭鉱山事業所（1922 年に大日本帝国海軍へ移
管された）などが含まれる。

朝鮮總督府による支出見積もり項目別分類
（単位 千円　1 円 =50 セント）

	1920	1921	1922	1923	1924
李王家維持費	1,500	1,800	1,800	1,800	1,800
中央行政	5,483	6,936	8,263	7,786	8,227
地方行政	8,503	10,133	10,711	10,711	11,096
裁判所と監獄	6,034	7,117	6,962	7,295	7,561
警察	16,702	22,754	22,265	21,924	22,402
医療と衛生	1,765	1,882	1,656	1,735	1,747
教育	4,595	6,099	7,279	5,995	6,017
産業促進	5,864	8,798	11,757	10,627	11,724
政府事業	33,570	68,742	57,653	51,241	45,352
補修と建設	8,897	8,582	6,298	4,703	4,312
公債負担金	7,441	9,485	11,700	12,797	13,568
予備金	2,500	2,500	2,500	2,500	3,250
道路他公共工事	7,108	6,743	7,914	6,182	4,621
雑費	4,351	900	2,142	1,083	1,018
合計	114,317	162,474	158,993	146,007	142,700

342   GOVERNMENT FINANCE

In respect of the items, "Local Administration" and "Education," it must be borne in mind that most of the expenditure on these objects is, in accordance with the decentralization policy of Governor-General Saito, carried on the budgets of Local Finance. These expenditures are given in Chapter V. It is sufficient here to remark that the total of the Local Finance Budget increased from less than a million yen in 1910 to more than 19 million yen in 1923-24.

The Korean National Debt--

The following account of the Korean National Debt is taken in the main from the Annual Report on Administration of Chosen, 1922-23, compiled by the Government-General.

Under the old Korean regime there existed no national debt lawfully raised by the Government. The credit of the national treasury was far too poor to admit of such being contracted, and plans laid for the welfare of the people were pigeon-holed almost as soon as conceived owing to the lack of means to carry them on to anything like fruition.

In 1904 the Korean Authorities, acting on the suggestion of the Japanese financial adviser, determined to make a fundamental reconstruction of the administrative system, and thereby rescue the country from its helpless condition and lay the foundation for national development.

But, to do this the Government realized there was no other way than to resort to a national loan for raising the funds necessary for that purpose, and Exchequer Bonds for 2,000,000 yen were, for the first time in the history of the country, floated in Tokyo in 1905 and the proceeds applied

項目として「地方行政」と「教育」があるが、心に留めておくべきことは、これらの項目の支出の多くが、總督府の齋藤總督の地方分権政策に従い、地方財政予算に組み込まれていることである。地方財政の支出については第五章で述べている。ここでは、地方財政予算の総計は、1910年には100万円に満たなかったが、1923年度には1900万円を超えるまでに増えたことを述べておけば充分であろう。

朝鮮国債

朝鮮国債についての以下の記述は、主に朝鮮總督府によりまとめられた、1922年度の年次報告書による。

過去の朝鮮政権時代には、政府により合法的に集められた国債は存在しなかった。国庫の信用があまりにも低すぎて、とても国債など発行出来るものではなく、人々の福利のための事業計画も、実現のための財源不足により、考えつく端から直ぐに棚上げにされた。

1904年、日本人の財務顧問から提言を受けて行動していた大韓帝国当局は、行政組織の根本的な再建を行い、それによって国を無力などうにもならない状態から救済し国家発展の基礎を築くことを決定した。

しかし、これを実行するには、目的のために必要な資金を集めるには国債に頼る以外に方法がないことを政府は認識した。そして、200万円相当の国債が、朝鮮史上初めて、1905年に東京で発行され、収入は年度収支の補正として計上された。それ以降、数回の国債が

344   GOVERNMENT FINANCE

to the adjustment of the Annual Account. From then on, several loans were made to get funds for the adjustment of the currency system, industrial undertakings, monetary circulation, and the various plans and enterprises taken in hand for the development of the Peninsula. The total of these loans amounted to 32,190,658 yen in all, of which 1,500,000 yen was loaned free of interest by the Imperial Government of Japan as a monetary circulation fund, and the rest at a yearly interest of 6 to 6.5 per cent was advanced by various Japanese banks and the Korean bank.

From 1908 onwards, loans amounting to 13,282,623 yen in all were advanced by the Imperial Government of Japan for unlimited periods and free of interest, to meet the increased expenditure necessary for the improvement of the administration. On the other hand, the Public Loan Special Account was established to make adjustment of all these loans, and by August 28, 1910, the eve of annexation, the exchequer bonds of 2,000,000 yen had been redeemed, and the net balance of the national debt on the same day stood at 45,590,106 yen.

As a result of the annexation, the redemption of the bonds for the monetary circulation fund (1,500,000 yen) and the loans contracted for administrative purposes (13,282,623 yen), all advanced by the Tokyo Government, became unnecessary, and the debt incurred by the currency adjustment was transferred, by a law issued in March, 1911, to the Special Account of the Currency Adjustment Fund of the Imperial Government. At the same time the Government-General borrowed 2,094,677 yen from the Bank of Chosen for the construction of roads, subsidies for local engineering works, and enlargement of Heijo Coal Mine Station. The total debt to be borne by the Government-General at the end of the fiscal year

資金を得るために発行され、通貨制度の調整、産業事業、貨幣流通、そして半島の開発のために進行中の様々な計画と事業などに充てられた。これら国債の総額は3219万658円となり、そのうち150万円は無利子で大日本帝国政府から貨幣流通基金として貸し付けられた。残りは年利6～6.5パーセントで日本の諸銀行と朝鮮の銀行から前払いされた。

1908年以降は、融資総額1328万2623円の全額が無期限に無利子で日本政府から貸し出され、増え続ける行政の改善に必要な支出に充てられた。一方、これら総ての融資を調整するために国債特別会計が創設され、1910年8月28日、すなわち併合直前までに200万円相当の国債が返済され、同日の国債収支残高は4559万106円であった。

併合の結果、貨幣流通基金（150万円）のための国債と行政に充てるための融資（1328万2623円）は全て東京の政府から融資されたものの、償還不要となり、通貨調整により負った債務は1911年3月に公布された法律により、帝国政府の通貨調整基金の特別会計に移された。

同時に、總督府は道路建設、地方の土木建築工事に対する助成金、そして平壌炭坑鉱山事業所の拡張のため朝鮮銀行から209万4677円を借りた。總督府が負った借金の総額は、1910年度末には、たった2117万5422円までに減少した。

346   GOVERNMENT FINANCE

1910 was thus reduced to 21,175,422 yen only.

After 1911 the annual revenue of Chosen was not sufficient to meet the expenditure on continuous undertakings found necessary for the development of the Peninsula. It was decided, therefore, to resort to public loans for the raising of funds required for harbor-works, construction and repair of roads and railways, etc.

The maximum amount of national bonds to be issued by the Government-General was fixed in 1911 at 56,000,000 yen by the Industrial Bond Special Account Law. But the enlargement of Heijo Coal Mine Station and the progress of other Government undertakings made it necessary to raise the maximum issue to 96,000,000 yen. The amount, however, being still considered insufficient, it was again raised to 168,000,000 yen in March, 1918, and to 178,000,000 yen in March, 1919.

In the past few years the pressing need of providing for cultural plans has necessitated increase in the amount practically each year; thus in August. 1920, it was raised to 206,500,000 yen to admit of the enlargement of Government hospitals, police offices, prisons, and salt fields; in March, 1921, to 230,600,000 yen to allow for the flotation of a public loan to pay the compensation called for by the establishment of the tobacco monopoly; and in March, 1922-23, to 393,700,000 yen.

Later statistics than those given in the Annual Report for 1922-23 show that the total amount of loans contracted since the annexation of 1910 down to March 31, 1925, was, in round figures, 443 million yen, of which 108 million was for conversion transactions. During the same period 189 million was repaid, leaving the outstanding amount of debt on March 31, 1925, at 254 million yen. This is equal to approximately 14.5 yen ($7.25)

第八章　政府の財政

　1911 年以降、朝鮮の年間収入は朝鮮半島の開発のために必要とされた継続的事業への支出を満たすには不充分であった。そこで、港湾事業、道路と鉄道の建設と補修などに必要な資金を調達するため公債に頼ることにした。

　総督府によって発行される国債の上限額は一般事業債に関する特別会計法により 1911 年に 5600 万円に固定されたが、平壤炭坑鉱山事業所の拡張と他の政府事業の進展により国債の発行上限を 9600 万円まで上げる必要が生じた。しかしながら、発行額は未だ不足と考えられ、再び発行上限は上げられて、1918 年 3 月には 1 億 6800 万円、1919 年 3 月には 1 億 7800 万円となった。

　この数年間、文化的な計画を提供するのが急務となり、ほとんど毎年増額を余儀なくされた。こうして、1920 年 8 月には官立病院、警察署、監獄、塩田の拡張のために、発行上限が 2 億 650 万円まで認められた。1921 年 3 月には煙草専売公社の設立により生じた補償金支払いに必要な公共債の公募のため上限が 2 億 3060 万円まで許され、1922 年の 3 月には 3 億 9370 万円まで認められた。

　1922 年度の年次報告書以降の統計では、1910 年の併合から 1925 年 3 月 31 日までの公債の総額は、概算で 4 億 4300 万円で、そのうち 1 億 800 万円は両替取引によるものであった。同時期に 1 億 8900 万円が返済され、残りの未払い債務額は 1925 年 3 月 31 日時点で、2 億 5400 万円となった。この金額は人口 1 人当たりで換算すると

per head of the population. The rate of interest on the various loans has varied with the condition of the money market from year to year. The average has been between 5 and 5 1/2 per cent. Most of the borrowing has been done for short terms, of three to five years.

14.5円（7.25ドル）に相当する。種々の融資における利率は年ごとに為替市場の状況によって変動した。利率の平均は5〜5.5パーセントであった。借入れのほとんどは3〜5年の短期間であった。

CHAPTER IX

第九章

CHAPTER IX

EDUCATION

The principles in conformity with which the present educational system of Korea is operated are derived from certain general precepts set forth in an Imperial Rescript promulgated on October 30, 1890, by the late Emperor Meiji of Japan. The Rescript was originally issued for the guidance of the Japanese people; but in 1911, the year following the annexation of Korea, an Imperial Message extended its application to the new dependency. The essential educational principles are laid down in the following paragraph:

Be filial to your parents, affectionate to your brothers and sisters; as husbands and wives be harmonious, as friends true; bear yourselves in modesty and moderation; extend your benevolence to all; pursue learning and cultivate the arts, and thus develop your intellectual faculties and perfect your morality; furthermore, be solicitous of the common-weal and of the public interest; should emergency arise, offer yourselves courageously to the State.

An educational system having as its aim the creation of a citizenry after the ideal model erected in the Rescript is charged with a task far transcending in scope that undertaken, in practice, by the public schools of the United States. The Rescript, in fact, contains only six words which

第九章

教育

今日の朝鮮の教育制度の基盤となる理念は 1890 年 10 月 30 日に明治天皇によって公布された教育勅語の教えに由来するものである。勅語はもともと日本国民への指針として公布されたが、日韓併合の翌年の 1911 年に天皇の「御言葉」として新しい属領にも適用された。次の文面は教育勅語の一部であるが、この教育の根本理念が示されている。

父母に孝行をつくし、兄弟姉妹仲よくし、夫婦互に睦むつび合い、朋友互に信義を以って交り、へりくだって気随気儘の振舞いをせず、人々に対して慈愛を及すやうにし、学問を修め業務を習つて知識才能を養ひ、善良有為の人物となり、進んで公共の利益を広め世のためになる仕事をおこし、常に皇室典範並びに憲法を始め諸々の法令を尊重遵守し、万一危急の大事が起つたならば、大義に基づいて勇気をふるひ一身を捧げて皇室国家の為につくせ。

勅語に示された理想的模範に基づく国民教育を目的としたこの教育制度は、米国の公立学校に実際に課せられている教育の使命をはるかに超えるものである。米国の公立学校の教育指導綱領―教育の

354   EDUCATION

we can identify with the main purpose, or at any rate with the main actual function of the American public school — scholastic instruction.In a Notification issued by the Government-General to the teachers of Korea on January 4, 1916, the three controlling motives of educational policy are declared:

(1) The fostering of loyalty and of filial piety are to be made the radical principles of education, and special attention is to be given to the cultivation of moral sentiments.

(2) Practical utility shall always be held in view when imparting instruction.

(3) Robust physical development is to be striven for.

In enlarging upon these principles, the Notification explains that by adhering to the first principle men will be made good subjects of their Emperor, and good sons to their parents, and will acquire those habits of diligence and thrift which lead to social and business success, and to the enhancement of the prosperity of the nation.

Referring to the necessity of making education the handmaiden of practical, as well as of patriotic and of moral, purposes, the Notification says:

目的・効用を述べている—に該当する言葉は勅語の中には6つしか見当たらない。1916年1月4日寺内正毅・朝鮮總督から朝鮮の教師に対し通牒が出され、その中で教育方針の大綱となる3つの方針が伝えられた。

(1) 忠と孝の徳性を育てることが教育の根本であり、道徳心を育むことに心を砕きなさい。

(2) 実用を旨として教育指導にあたりなさい。

(3) 頑強なる身体の育成に励みなさい。

　通牒でこれらの方針をさらに詳しく説明している。
　第一の方針を忠実に実行すると、その結果は付いてくるのである。つまり人は天皇に対しては良き臣民となり、両親に対しては良き子となる。また勤勉と倹約の習慣を身につけ、それは社会的成功をもたらし、国運の発展を導くのである。

　そして、教育を愛国的、道徳的な目的と並んで、実用的な目的に沿うものにする必要があるとして、次のように言及している。

The object of education is to raise up practical men able to meet the requirements of the State. How can it be expected that a man will establish himself and succeed in life, thus advancing the national interest, if he devotes himself to vain argument, and thus becomes of little use to the world, or if he is averse to industry and labor, and neglects the practice thereof?

It is therefore required of persons engaged in educational work that they pay earnest attention to the principle of the utilization of knowledge, to the promotion of the national welfare, and to the imparting of useful instruction, so that practical persons, able to meet the national requirements, will be found to be the rule and not the exception in the Empire.

The Notification proceeds to lay down nine rules for the guidance of teachers. These are reprinted in the Appendices. Their gist is that the individuality of each pupil must be carefully studied, and the tuition adjusted to the individual character and circumstances; that education must also adjust itself to the needs of the times and to the general condition of the people; that adhesion to conventional forms is harmful, and that teachers should, therefore, devise varied methods of imparting physical, moral, and intellectual instruction; that every occasion must be availed of so to guide pupils that they will become by habit lenient towards others but strict towards themselves, industrious, thrifty, honest, and trustworthy; that the various studies must be co-ordinated, so that each will supplement and not conflict with others; that the general aim must be to give a mastery of a narrower, rather than a superficial acquaintance with a broader field

教育の目的は、国家の必要とするものに応えられる実用的な人材を育て上げることだ。もし国民が無益な議論に時間を費やし、世間で無用な者となり、勤労を厭い実践を無視したら、どうやって自己を確立し、人生で成功することが出来ようか。ひいては国益を増進することなど出来ようか。

それゆえ、教育に携わる者は、国家の必要事に応えられる実用的な人材が国民の多数を占めるよう、知識の実務的利用、国の福利厚生の促進、有用なる教授に真摯に心を砕くべし。

この通牒の中で教師への指針として９項の規則を設けている。これらは巻末附録に掲載されており、要点は以下のとおりである。

「生徒一人一人の個性を注意深く観察し、授業は個人の性格と状況に合うように調整しなくてはならない。教育自体も時勢と民度に適合しなければならない。従来型を固守することは害になり、教師は体育、徳育、知育の教授方法を工夫すべきである。生徒が常日頃から人に対しては寛容であり、自己に対して厳しくあること、勤勉で節約に励み、誠実で信頼に値する人物になるように、あらゆる機会を使って指導しなくてはならない。各種科目が矛盾し合わず補完するように統合させなければならない。授業の目的は広範囲に亘る知識を表面的に身に着けさせるのではなく、狭い知識分野に精通さ

of knowledge; that everything must be done to engage the interest of the pupils and to establish sound methods of study, so that the pupils may desire to supplement their school training by self-training; that physical robustness must be contributed to by gymnastics and games; that the attitude of the teacher should combine affection with dignity, and example with precept; teachers must realize that far-reaching as well as immediate results are to be held in view; that the beneficent results of education cannot be expected to flow from scholastic instruction alone, and that teachers must, therefore, aim to advance the objects of education by taking frequent counsel among themselves, and by keeping on friendly terms with the elders of the local communities.

Historical Development of the System--

The educational system of Korea as it exists today represents the results of a slow process of evolution whose beginnings date back to the year A.D. 1398, in which year the Korean King Tai-cho, founder of the Yi Dynasty, established a university in Seoul, the capital city of Korea, and caused schools to be organized in the provincial districts.

During the reign of Tai-chong, the third ruler of the Yi Dynasty, four schools, preparatory for the university, were founded in Seoul. These institutions were all under Government control, and their up-keep was provided for by granting them endowments of farms and of the services of the slaves necessary to work them.

The education supplied in the university and in the schools was based on the Chinese model, that is to say the principal subject of study was the works of Confucius, and the principal reward held out to the students

せることである。生徒の自主学習の心を育てるべく、生徒の興味を
引き出し、適切な学習方法を確立するよう指導を惜しまないこと。
運動や遊戯を取り入れ強健な身体の育成を促すこと。教師は生徒に
対し威厳とともに愛情を以って接し、また生徒の模範となるべきで
ある。教師は目前の結果だけでなく、長期的な結果にも留意するこ
と。教育の恩恵は学問的指導からのみ得られるものではなく、それ
ゆえ、教師は同僚と意見交換を頻繁に行い、地域の年配者と友好的
な関係を築いて教育の目的達成に努めること」。

教育制度の歴史的発展

　今日の朝鮮の教育制度は、1398 年に李王朝の創始者である太祖国
王が朝鮮の首都ソウルに大学を設立し、その後各地に学校が出来る
ようになったのが始まりであるが、今日に至るまでその発展は遅々
としたものであった。

　李王朝の第３代国王である太宗が大学への予備校として４つの学
校を漢陽に設立した。これらの学校は全て政府の管轄下にある公立
の教育機関で、その維持は農家とそこで働く奴隷から得られた利益
で賄われていた。

　最高学府およびその予備校で行われていた教育は中国をモデルに
したもので、孔子の教えが勉強の主たる題材であった。教育がもた
らす最大の報酬は、科挙と呼ばれる文芸の試験に受かって役人の地

was the prospect of passing the final literary examination which would give them official rank and make them permanently eligible for official appointments.

Apart from the Government schools, there existed throughout the provinces a great number of private establishments, called *sohtang*, in which the sole subject of instruction was the reading and writing of the Chinese characters.

The system above described existed, without substantial change, for about five hundred years. If it did not produce any type of scholar other than the Confucian philosopher, it served well enough the needs of a predominantly agricultural population from which all avenues of change were cut off by an intense national conservatism, and by an almost complete isolation from the modern progress of the Western world.

At the time of the China-Japan war of 1894, the King of Korea renounced the historic suzerainty of China; and Japan became the natural heir to the influence which its great neighbor had for so many centuries exerted in the affairs of the Peninsula. In the Korean educational system there followed a period of ten years during which the Japanese, as part of their efforts to introduce a general reform of the native administration, turned their attention to the schools of Korea.

Acting on the advice of the Japanese Minister at Seoul, the King of Korea promised a thorough reorganization of the educational system. The undertaking met with little success, partly because the new regulations were framed almost exactly along the lines of those in force in Japan, without reference to the many differences presented by the general social conditions of the two countries; partly because there was practically no

位を得、生涯役職に就く資格を得る可能性を手にすることである。

官公立学校とは別に、道の至る所に、中国語の読み書きだけを目的とする「書堂」と呼ばれる私塾があった。

　上記に述べた制度は大きな変化もなく 500 年程続いた。もしこの制度が儒教の哲学者以外の学者を生み出さなかったとしても、人口の大多数を占める農民の要望には充分応えていたのである。なぜならば、国の強烈な保守主義に加え、鎖国により西洋の近代化の動きから孤立していたことからあらゆる変化の道筋を絶たれていたからである。

　1894 年の日清戦争によって、李氏朝鮮は自国の歴史に多大な影響を与えていた中国の宗主権を破棄し、その結果何世紀にもわたり隣国が行使してきた朝鮮半島への影響力は、必然的に日本が請け負うことになった。教育制度においても、日本はその後 10 年間、朝鮮政府の行政改革取り組みの一環として学校教育に目を向けることになった。

　ソウル在住の日本公使の助言により、朝鮮国王は教育制度の徹底的な再編成を約束した。しかしその試みはうまくいかなかった。新しい法令が両国の社会的要素の違いを考慮せずに、日本の法令をほとんどそのまま真似て作られたことや、その法令に沿って動ける朝鮮人教師が不足していたからである。

362   EDUCATION

supply of Korean teachers capable of making the regulations effective.

Matters assumed a new aspect with the establishment of the Japanese protectorate in 1905. In conformity with the terms of the agreements by which this arrangement was effected, a Japanese educational adviser, vested with administrative functions, was appointed by the Govern ment. In order to assist the carrying out of the changes which were now to be effected, a sum of 500,000 yen was placed at the disposal of the educational authorities by Prince Ito, the Japanese Resident-General, out of a total sum of five million, borrowed from the Industrial Bank of Japan in 1906, for the purpose of facilitating various public undertakings. Omitting the numerous changes effected in school management, and in school curricula, the broad features of the educational reforms carried out at this time may be summarized as follows:

(1) The Education of Girls. Hitherto the Government of Korea had made little provision for female education; and Korean girls had been chiefly dependent in this respect upon the schools founded by the various Christian missionary bodies. In 1908, however, a girls' high school was established at Seoul by the Korean Government.

(2) Commercial Education. A Commercial, Agricultural, and Technical School had been founded in 1904, and a private Commercial School in 1906. The latter owed its existence to the generosity of Baron Okura, who expended 200,000 yen on the project.

In conformity with the new policy three separate Government schools were built, for Commerce, Agriculture, and Technology, respectively. From this small beginning there developed, in the course of about six years, ten public schools devoted to agriculture or forestry, and two devoted to

第九章　教育　　363

　1905 年朝鮮が日本の保護国となると、状況は新しい局面を迎えた。合意書の条件に基づき、行政責任を与えられた日本人教育顧問が、政府によって任命されたのである。

　また改革を進めるべく、1906 年に公共事業のために日本興業銀行から借りた 500 万円のうち 50 万円が統監である伊藤博文卿により教育機関に充てられた。学校運営と教科課程に関し様々な改革がなされたが、この時期に行われた教育改革の大まかな特徴は以下のようにまとめられる。

（1）女子教育。それまでの朝鮮政府は女子教育に関しほとんど何の政策も施さなかった。女子教育は主にキリスト教の伝道グループの設立した学校に限られていた。しかし 1908 年、朝鮮政府によりソウルに官立漢城高等女学校が設立された。

（2）商業教育。1904 年に農商工学校が、1906 年に私立商業学校が設立された。後者は大倉喜八郎卿が 20 万円もの寄付をし、設立に至ったのである。新政策に従い、農商工学校は商業、農業、工業の 3 つの公立学校に分離された。小さな変化ではあったが、その後およそ 6 年かけて、10 校の農業または林業の公立学校、2 校の商業の公立学校が設立された。

commerce.

(3) Supervision of Private Schools. During the first few years of the Protectorate there arose a strong popular demand for increased educational facilities. The demand ran far ahead of anything that the Government, with reference to financial considerations, could do to satisfy it. The result was that hundreds of private schools sprang up all over the country, province vying with province to take the lead in this direction.

This rapid development was accompanied by certain abuses to which the Government could not remain indifferent. In the effort to finance these schools questionable methods were resorted to by many of the interested parties; in not a few cases the schools were schools in name rather than in fact, and became centers of amusement rather than of study; in others the text-books supplied to the children were found to be quite unsuitable to the purposes of a sound education.

It was, therefore, decided to bring all private schools under the direct supervision of the Government. This was accomplished in 1908 by the promulgation of the Private School Regulations. According to official statistics compiled in 1910 the number of private schools recognized by the Department of Education was 2,220, of which mission schools numbered 823.

Owing to events which are described in another chapter, Korea was annexed to the Japanese Empire in August, 1910. With the concurrent lapse of all Korean official authority the educational system passed under the full control of the newly created Government-General.

In the first Annual Report issued by the new administration, considerable space is devoted to education. The official point of view is expressed, as to general educational policy, in the following quotation:

（3）私立学校の監督。日本の保護国となった最初の数年間は教育
　　施設の増設に対し国民からの強い要望があったが、その要望は
　　政府の財政能力をはるかに超えていた。結果、各地域が競い合
　　うような風潮になり何百もの私立学校が国中に建てられた。

　この急速な進展に伴い、学校運営に関わる不正が持ち上がり政府
としても無視出来ない状況になった。学校の資金調達をするために
多くの関係者がいかがわしい方法を使った。いくつかのケースでは、
学校とは名前だけで、学問よりは娯楽の施設となっていたり、また、
生徒に配られた教科書が健全な教育の目的には全く不向きなもので
あったりもした。

　その結果、全ての私立学校が政府の直接監督下に置かれた。これ
は1908年の私立学校令の公布により実施された。1910年に編纂さ
れた公式統計によると、總督府学務局が認可した私立学校は2220校、
うちミッションスクールは823校であった。

　他の章で述べられている理由により、1910年8月、大韓帝国は大
日本帝国に併合された。大韓帝国の公的支配権の全てが同時に失効
したことにより、教育制度は新しい朝鮮總督府の完全支配下に置か
れた。

　朝鮮總督府発行の最初の年次報告書にはかなりのページが教育に
割かれている。教育政策全般についての公的見解が以下の引用に記
されている。

EDUCATION

The educational administration in the Peninsula had hitherto been carried out by two different offices. Education for native Koreans was conducted by the Educational Department of the late Korean Government, under the guidance of the Resident-General, while education for Japanese children in Korea was supervised by the Local Affairs Department of the Residency-General. When the Government-General came into existence after annexation, all educational administration, both for Japanese and Koreans alike, was brought under the uniform supervision of the Educational Bureau created in the Home Department of the Government-General.

It was decided, however, that the dual system of education—Korean schools for Korean children and Japanese schools for Japanese children—which had hitherto existed in the Peninsula, should be continued hereafter, since different standards of living did not allow amalgamation. The education for Japanese children being practically on the same system as that prevailing in Japan proper, did not need modification in the near future; whereas the educational system for native Koreans, though certain improvements had been made during the Protectorate régime, required further reforms so as to meet existing conditions. At the same time, readjustment of the educational system required much careful consideration, since any hasty reforms at the period of annexation were not likely to secure good results.

第九章　教育

　これまでの朝鮮半島における教育行政は2つの異なった行政機関により遂行されていた。朝鮮人への教育は統監府の下で大韓帝国の教育機関によりなされ、朝鮮に住む日本人への教育は統監府の地方政府によって管理された。併合後に、朝鮮總督府が設立されると、日本人と朝鮮人両方の教育管理は、總督府内務部の学務局が一括して監督した。

　しかし、朝鮮半島にこれまであった、「朝鮮の子供は朝鮮人学校へ、日本の子供は日本人学校へ」という二本立ての教育制度は、生活基準の違いによって融合の余地がないため続けることが決められた。

　日本人子弟の教育は本土で行われている教育と実質的に同じなので、とりあえず変更する必要はなかった。

　一方、朝鮮人に対する教育制度は、保護統治時代に改善はなされたものの、現在の状況に見合う更なる改革が必要であった。同時に、併合時の急激な改革は良い結果を生みにくいので、教育制度の見直しには注意深い配慮が必要であった。

368   EDUCATION

A year later the new educational system for Koreans was put into effect by an Imperial Ordinance, issued in August, 1911, and in October of the same year the Governor-General promulgated an Ordinance, setting forth the complete rules and regulations applicable to schools in which Koreans were to be taught.

The progress made in providing educational facilities for Koreans between the first fiscal year before annexation and the first complete fiscal year after annexation may be judged by the following figures. In 1909 there were 139 public schools for Koreans, in 1911 there were 280; in 1909 there were 16,506 Korean students in the schools, in 1911 there were 30,201; in 1909 there were 731 teachers in these schools, in 1911 there were 1,295.

Present State of the Educational System--

The present state of the Educational System of Korea reflects the combined influences of several factors. Of these the more important have been the constantly increasing expenditure on education, the carrying out during the past five years of the progressive cultural policy inaugurated by the present Governor-General, Viscount Saito, the work of the Extraordinary Educational Investigation Committee of 1920, the promulgation of the new Chosen Educational Ordinance of 1922, and the marked improvement which has occurred in the general social conditions of the Koreans, due to the rapid economic development of the country since annexation.

The gradual rise in the standard of living of the Koreans, especially of those who live in or near the larger towns, and the growing enthusiasm amongst them for educational opportunities, have led on the one hand to

１年後の1911年８月、朝鮮人への新しい教育制度が天皇の勅令により施行、同年10月には總督が法令を公布し、朝鮮人学校に対する規制が公にされた。

併合前後２年間の年度中の朝鮮人への教育施設提供の進捗状況は次の数値から判断出来る。朝鮮人向けの公立学校は、1909年には139校、1911年には280校。朝鮮人学生の数は1909年には１万6506人、1911年には３万201人。これらの学校で働く教師の数は1909年には731人、1911年には1295人であった。

現在の教育制度の状況

現在の朝鮮の教育制度においては、いくつかの要因が複合的に影響していることが見てとれる。

その中でも特に重要な要因としては、教育予算の増大、現總督、齋藤子爵が打ち出した過去５年に亘る進歩的な文化政策、1920年の臨時教育調査委員会の取り組み、1922年の「朝鮮教育令ニ関スル論告」の公布、併合後の急速な経済発展によりもたらされた朝鮮人の一般的な社会状況の著しい改善が挙げられる。

特に大きな町やその周辺では、朝鮮人の生活水準が徐々に向上し、教育熱も高まった。その結果朝鮮人学校の数が大幅に増え、また、朝鮮人学校と日本人学校の分離政策が見直されることになった。

a large increase in the number of schools for Koreans, and on the other to the modification of the principle of separate schools for Koreans and for Japanese.

The co-education of the two races is spreading to such an extent that the authorities realize that it is no longer possible to retain the classification of the schools into those for Japanese and those for Koreans. In Colleges, Normal Schools, and Industrial and Commercial Schools, racial co-education only is the rule. So far as primary and secondary education are concerned the schools are now classified as being for "those habitually using the Korean language," and for "those habitually using the Japanese language." Thus, Koreans may attend the schools primarily for Japanese, and vice versa.

In respect of their management the schools in Korea are divided into three classes. A Government School is one conducted directly by the Government-General; a Public School is one maintained either by a provincial body, or by a Korean District Educational body, or by a Japanese School Association; a Private School is one, either secular or religious, maintained by a private body or by an individual.

Private Schools are divided officially into two main groups. Of these, one comprises schools which comply in full with the requirements of the Government school system; and these are granted the same privileges as a Government School. In Government documents they are described simply as Regular Schools; whereas in unofficial literature they are usually referred to as Recognized Schools. The other group of Private Schools comprises what are known officially as Various, or Non-Standardized Schools, and unofficially as Non-recognized Schools. They fall into two

２つの民族の共学は広範囲に広がりつつあり、總督府は、学校を日本人用と朝鮮人用に分けることは不可能であると気付いている。専門学校、師範学校、工業・商業学校では民族共学のみである。初等・中等教育では、「習慣的に朝鮮語を使っている人」のための学校と、「習慣的に日本語を使っている人」のための学校に分かれている。それ故、朝鮮人も日本人の通う学校に出席することが出来、その逆も然りだ。

　学校運営に関し、国内の学校は３つに分類される。官立学校は總督府の直接運営であり、公立学校は地方政府、朝鮮地域教育機関、または日本学校組合が維持し、私立学校は、宗教関係、非宗教関係どちらでも、民間団体もしくは個人が維持する。

　私立学校は公式には主に２つのグループに分けられる。１つは官立学校制度の必要条件を全て満たす学校で、官立学校と同じ特権が与えられる。
　政府の公文書にはこれらの学校は正規学校と表現されているが、非公式の文書にはよく公認学校と言及されている。
　もう１つのグループは、公式に各種普通学校または非標準学校、非公式には非公認学校として知られる。このグループの学校はさら

classes—Designated Schools, and Non-designated Schools—the former being those which though not fully conforming to the requirements of the regular school system are possessed of equipment and efficiency approved by the Government as equal to that of Government Schools of the same grade. They are granted the same privileges as Government Schools in regard to the admission of their graduates to the higher educational institutions in Korea. A Non-designated School is one which has failed to secure the approval referred to above.

Before presenting some figures relating to the schools in Korea it is necessary to refer to the serious discrepancies which exist between the statistics given in the official publications of the Government-General and those printed in the annual volume *The Christian Movement in Japan, Korea, and Formosa*, published by the Federation of Christian Missions, Japan. The explanation is that in the official statistics *sohtang*, private establishments somewhat similar to the ancient dame-schools, are not included, since they are not considered worthy to be classed as schools. The missionary statistics, on the other hand, include establishments of this rudimentary character. This is quite natural, for the missionary reports offer to their readers an account of the total activities undertaken. Furthermore, with reference to such expressions as "Common School," and "Higher Common School," the official statistics count under them only such schools as have a definite, recognized official standing based on the Government Regulations, whereas the missionary publications include under those heads schools which do approximately the same grade of work as the Government schools so designated. The matter has been taken up between the Government-General and the Federal Council of Missions;

に２つに分類される－指定学校と非指定学校だ。

前者は、正規の学校制度の必要条件を充分に満たしてはいないが、相当する官立学校と同じ設備と効率性を備えていると政府から認められている学校である。指定学校の卒業者は朝鮮の高等教育機関への入学に関して、官立学校卒業と同じ特権を持つことが許される。非指定学校には上記の特権はない。

　朝鮮の学校に関する統計を紹介する前に、總督府の公式出版物と日本ミッション同盟出版の年刊『日本、朝鮮、台湾におけるキリスト教の動き』との著しいデータの相違について触れておく必要がある。それは、公式統計には「書堂」は含まれていない。これは個人が自宅を開放して運営している塾のようなもので、学校と分類するには相応しくないと考えられていたからである。一方、宣教会の統計には書堂が含まれている。

　宣教会の報告が読者にその全ての事業の説明をするのは極めて自然なことである。更に、公式統計では「普通学校」や「高等普通学校」の項目には總督府に公認された学校のみ含まれているが、宣教会の出版物には官立学校とほぼ同等レベルの教育を施している学校も含んでいる。この問題については總督府とキリスト教連合会の間で取り上げられ、教育統計の一致した用語が審議されている。

　この章で使われている統計数値は全て公式資料からのものである。

374   EDUCATION

and an agreed terminology for educational data is under consideration. All the statistics given in this Chapter are taken from official sources.

In respect of the entry "Common Schools" maintained by District Educational Bodies in 1914 it is to be remarked that such bodies were not in existence at that time, and that the expense of maintaining them was provided for from the Imperial Donation Fund, fees, contributions, State and Provincial subsidies, and an assessment levied upon Koreans (these schools being at that time exclusively for the use of Korean children) on a basis similar to that now followed by the District Educational Bodies, which were founded in 1920.

The management of Government Middle Schools, Higher Common Schools, and Girls' Higher Common Schools was transferred to Provincial Bodies in 1925. In addition to the free concession of all the premises and other properties belonging to those schools, the Government-General grants the various Provincial Bodies subsidies equal to 80 per cent of the annual expenditure incurred by the Government in recent years in their management, viz., in round figures, 530 thousand yen to Provincial Bodies for the nine Middle Schools, 656 thousand yen for the fourteen Higher Common Schools, and 108 thousand yen for the two Girls' Higher Common Schools.

「普通学校」のうち、地域教育機関によって運営されているものについては、1914 年にはそうした機関は存在しなかったので、学校の維持費は帝国寄付基金、授業料、寄付金、国や地方の交付金、朝鮮人に課された賦課金（当時普通学校には朝鮮人生徒のみ通っていた）によって賄われていた。この賦課金は 1920 年に設立された地域教育機関により現在課されているものと同様のものである。

1925 年には中等学校、高等普通学校、女子普通高等学校の運営は地方政府に移管された。これらの学校の敷地および所有物の無料使用権に加え、總督府は様々な地方政府に補助金を交付しているが、この数年は總督府運営予算の 80 パーセントに匹敵する額になっている。つまり概算で、9 校の中等学校の運営費として地方に 53 万円、14 校の高等普通学校に 65 万 6000 円、2 校の女子普通高等学校には 10 万 8000 円を、それぞれ運営費として地方に交付している。

376   EDUCATION

Number of Schools and of Teachers in Korea

Schools maintained by	Schools		Teachers				
	1914	1924	1914		1924		
			J.*	K.†	J.*	K.†	F.‡
The Government-General:							
Elementary.............	0	1	0	0	20	0	0
Common..............	2	3	0	0	18	10	0
Middle................	2	9	37	0	217	0	4
Higher Common........	2	14	55	19	261	36	1
Girls Higher Common....	1	2	17	6	35	10	0
Agricultural...........	0	1	0	0	14	1	0
Industrial.............	0	1	0	0	27	2	0
Senmon Gakko (Colleges).	1	5	16	1	169	8	2
Normal...............	0	1	0	0	37	2	1
University Prep........	0	1	0	0	16	0	0
Provincial Bodies:							
Agricultural...........	15	20	65	24	128	34	0
Commercial............	2	13	12	3	111	13	3
Industrial.............	0	1	0	0	18	1	0
Fishery...............	0	4	0	0	19	6	0
Elementary Agriculture..	53	6	96	84	13	7	0
Elementary Commercial..	4	7	10	5	39	9	0
Elementary Industrial....	1	7	3	2	33	7	0
Normal...............	0	13	0	0	113	22	0
District Educational Bodies:							
Common..............	381	1,087	487	1,280	1,904	4,588	0
Non-Standarized.......	0	159	0	0	124	348	0
School Associations:							
Elementary............	264	442	722	0	1,757	0	0
Middle................	0	1	0	0	8	0	0
Girls High.............	6	21	63	0	251	0	4
Commercial...........	4	2	39	0	32	2	0
Non-standardized.......	1	0	11	0	0	0	0
Private Bodies or Individuals:							
Elementary............	0	1	0	0	1	0	0
Common..............	20	51	28	74	26	258	4
Higher Common........	2	8	7	11	42	141	11
Girls' Higher Common...	2	5	15	12	30	36	8
Commercial............	1	3	12	2	32	9	4
Senmon Gakko (Colleges).	1	3	14	0	18	36	21
Non-Standardized:							
Secular..............	776	374	147	2,571	230	1,223	3
Religious.............	473	271	32	2,052	61	1,163	115

* Japanese.   † Korean.   ‡ Foreign.

朝鮮における学校の数と教師の人数

学校を管理している機関	学校数		教師数				
	1914	1924	1914		1924		
			日本人	朝鮮人	日本人	朝鮮人	他
總督府：　小学校	0	1	0	0	20	0	0
普通学校	2	3	0	0	18	10	0
中等学校	2	9	37	0	217	0	4
高等普通	2	14	55	19	261	36	1
女子高等	1	2	17	6	35	10	0
農業学校	0	1	0	0	14	1	0
工業学校	0	1	0	0	27	2	0
専門学校	1	5	16	1	169	8	2
師範学校	0	1	0	0	37	2	1
大学予備課程	0	1	0	0	16	0	0
地方政府：農業学校	15	20	65	24	128	34	0
商業学校	2	13	12	3	111	13	3
工業学校	0	1	0	0	18	1	0
林業学校	0	4	0	0	19	6	0
初等農業	53	6	96	84	13	7	0
初等商業	4	7	10	5	39	9	0
初等工業	1	7	3	2	33	7	0
師範学校	0	13	0	0	113	22	0
地域教育機関：普通学校	381	1,087	487	1,280	1,904	4,588	0
各種学校	0	159	0	0	124	348	0
学校組合：　小学校	264	442	722	0	1,757	0	0
中等学校	0	1	0	0	8	0	0
女子高等	6	21	63	0	251	0	4
商業学校	4	2	39	0	32	2	0
各種学校	1	0	11	0	0	0	0
民間・個人：小学校	0	1	0	0	1	0	0
普通学校	20	51	28	74	26	258	4
高等学校	2	8	7	11	42	141	11
女子高等	2	5	15	12	30	36	8
商業学校	1	3	12	2	32	9	4
専門学校	1	3	14	0	18	36	21
各種学校：一般	776	374	147	2,571	230	1,223	3
宗教	473	271	32	2,052	61	1,163	115

378   EDUCATION

The number of students in the schools enumerated in the foregoing table has increased between 1911 and 1924 from 110,789 to 542,679, the greatest increase being in the number attending the Common Schools, which rose from 20,121 to 361,710 (almost entirely Korean children), and the Elementary Schools, which rose from 15,509 to 56,049 (almost entirely Japanese children).

The above figures do not include the pupils in two classes of institutions—Kindergartens, and *Sohtang*. The number of children in the former increased from 606 in 1911 to 4,510 in 1924; in the latter from 141,604 to 256,851. The *Sohtang* are elementary private schools conducted by Koreans, in which little is taught except the Chinese classics and brush writing.

At the time this volume goes to press no details are available as to the courses of instruction established in the newly-founded University, or of the number of students who have entered it.

The School Curriculum--

The curricula of the schools vary, of course, according to the kind of school—Common, Industrial, Commercial, Higher Common, and so on. I select for description the standard curriculum of a Common School having a six-year course.

Morals. 1 hour a week for the whole course, on the essential points of morals.

National Language. 10 hours a week for the first year, 12 for the second and third, and fourth, 9 for the fifth and sixth.

Korean Language. 4 hours a week for the first and second year, 3 for the

第九章　教育　　　379

　前ページの表が示す生徒数は、1911 年から 1924 年にかけて 11 万
789 人から 54 万 2679 人に増えている。最大の増加は、普通学校の
2 万 121 人から 36 万 1710 人（ほぼ全員朝鮮人）、小学校では 1 万
5509 人から 5 万 6049 人に増加している（ほぼ全員日本人）。

　上記の数字には幼稚園と書堂の児童は含まれていない。幼稚園の
児童数は 1911 年の 606 人から 1924 年の 4510 人へと増加、書堂で
は 14 万 1604 人から 25 万 6851 人へ増加している。書堂は朝鮮人に
よって経営されている初等私立学校で中国の古典と書道以外はほと
んど何も教えていなかった。
　本書が出版される時点では、新しく設立された大学の課程や生徒
数の詳細なデータはない。

学校教科課程
　勿論、教科課程は、普通、工業、商業、高等普通学校など学校の
種類によって異なる。以下に 6 年制の公立小学校の標準教科課程を
述べる。

道徳……全過程で週に 1 時間。正しい品行の要旨を教育する
国語……1 年生は週に 10 時間、2、3、4 年生は 12 時間、
　　　　5、6 年生は 9 時間。
朝鮮語…1、2 年生は週に 4 時間、その他は 3 時間。

rest of the course.

Arithmetic. A progressive course leading up to vulgar fractions, percentage, and the use of the abacus. 5 hours a week during the first two years, 6 in the third and fourth, 4 in the fifth and sixth.

Japanese History. 2 hours a week in the fifth and sixth years.

Geography. 2 hours a week in the last two years.

Natural Science. 2 hours a week in the last three years.

Drawing. 1 hour a week in the fourth year, and 2, hours for boys and 3 for girls in the fifth and sixth years.

Singing. 1 hour a week throughout the course.

Gymnastics, Drill, and Sports. Varies for boys and for girls, averages about 2 hours a week throughout the course.

Sewing. 2 hours in the fourth year, and 3 hours in the fifth and sixth.

Manual Work. In the first, second, and third year manual work may be taught 1 hour per week, and in the fourth and fifth year 2 hours.

In the first, second, and third years drawing may be taught one hour per week. With regard to practical exercises, they may be given outside the stated number of hours for instruction.

Salaries of Teachers--

Presidents of colleges and universities receive salaries varying from 4,500 yen to 5,200 yen per annum, and if they are Japanese they receive in addition a Colonial allowance of 40 per cent of the salary, and, if official residence is not provided, a rent allowance of from 600 to 700 yen.

Professors in colleges and universities, and Principals of Normal, Industrial, and Secondary (High) schools fall into 12 salary grades,

算数……分数、比率、算盤に至るまでの段階的な課程。

　　　　1・2年生は週5時間、3・4年生は6時間、5・6年生は4時間。

日本史…5・6年生は週に2時間。

地理学…5・6年生は週に2時間。

自然科学…4・5・6年生は週に2時間。

図画……4年生は週に1時間、5・6年生男子は2時間、女子は3時間。

唱歌……全課程で週1時間。

体育、訓練、運動…男子と女子で異なる。全課程で週に約2時間。

裁縫……4年生は週に2時間、5・6年生は3時間。

手工……1・2・3年生は週1時間、

　　　　4・5年生は2時間教えることがある。

1・2・3年生にも週1時間の図画が教えられることがある。実践については決められた教育時間以外で教えられることがある。

教師の給料

専門学校と大学の学長の年給は4500円から5200円で、日本人教師の場合、外地手当として給料の40パーセントが更に支払われ、官舎が与えられない場合は住宅手当として600円から700円が支払われる。専門学校と大学の教授と普通・工業・中等（高等）学校の校長は12級俸に値し、年に1200円から4500円、日本人なら40パー

382   EDUCATION

receiving from 1,200 to 4,500 yen per annum with, for Japanese, 40 per
cent as Colonial allowance, and rent allowance of from 312 to 396 yen.

Other teachers, in all kinds of schools, are classified in one of eleven
grades of Sonin rank, or are of Hannin rank. Those of Sonin rank receive
an annual salary of from 1,100 to 3,800 yen, with, for Japanese, 40 per
cent Colonial allowance, and a rent allowance of from 312 to 396 yen.
Those of Hannin rank receive from 480 to 1,920 yen per annum, with 60
per cent Colonial allowance, and rent allowance of from 156 to 264 yen
for Japanese.

Religion in the Schools--

The question of religious instruction in the schools of Korea has been
the subject of a great deal of heated and ill-informed discussion. The facts
are quite simple and are accessible to anyone who desires to get at the
truth of the matter. The Chosen Educational Ordinance was put into effect
in 1911. New Regulations were issued under this Ordinance in 1915, by
which the teaching of the Bible and the holding of religious exercises
were prohibited as a part of the regular curriculum in private schools that
wished to be recognized by the Government-General as grading with the
Government schools of equal curriculum, and to claim for their graduates
privileges similar to those granted to graduates of the Government schools.
As a matter of public policy such a rule was essential to the organization of
a sound educational system, and for a plain reason. To all schools, whether
public or private, which fall within the regular school system, a definite
grade is assigned—Common, Higher Common, and so on—and for each
grade a fixed curriculum is prescribed, assigning a definite number of

セントの外地手当と賃貸住宅手当が312円から396円支払われる。

　他の教師は、全ての学校において、11段階に分かれる中で「奏任」か「判任」の等級に分類される。奏任は年給1100円から3800円で、日本人なら40パーセントの外地手当と賃貸住宅手当が312円から396円支払われる。

　判任は年給480円から1920円、日本人なら60パーセントの外地手当と156円から264円の賃貸住宅手当が支払われる。

学校における宗教

　学校での宗教教育については充分な情報がないまま、議論されてきた。事実は極めて簡単で、この問題の真相を知りたいと思う者はここで理解することが出来る。1911年に朝鮮教育令が施行され、これにより新しい規制法が1915年に発令された。この規制法では、私立学校で、正規の科目として聖書を教えることや宗教儀式は出来なくなった。この規制に従わない場合、私立学校は官立学校と同格の学校として総督府から認定されず、また官立学校卒業生に与えられている特典も認められなかった。公共政策上、健全な教育制度を作るにはこのような規則は必要であり、また明らかな理由もあった。学校制度においては、公立私立を問わず全ての学校に対し、普通学校や高等普通学校などの明白な等級が与えられ、それぞれの等級には決まった教科課程が規定され、科目に対して週ごとに指定した時間が決められている。

EDUCATION

hours per week to the study of the different subjects.

It is obvious, therefore, that if a private school were allowed to vary the prescribed curriculum, the description "Common School Graduate" would mean as many different things as there were different curricula. Any private school which teaches the prescribed curriculum for its grade and meets the requirements of the Government in respect of the quality of its teachers, the school equipment, and so on, is free to read the Bible, give religious instruction, and conduct religious exercises within the school premises, provided it carries on these activities outside the hours for the official curriculum; and it can receive Government recognition of its grade, with the right to the attendant privileges.

New Regulations issued in 1923 go further than this. On this point the Rev. Alfred W. Wasson, Treasurer of the Korea Mission of the Methodist Episcopal Church, South, writes explicitly in the *Korea Mission Field*, July, 1923, in an article on the "Significance of the New Educational Ruling of the Governor-General."

The new ruling [he says] provides a way for church schools to obtain a different kind of recognition which will leave them with unrestricted liberty of religious instruction and at the same time permits them to enjoy some of the privileges of schools having full government recognition. In order not to be misleading, it is necessary to add that, as a matter of fact, mission schools which have obtained full government recognition do give regular and systematic religious instruction. This is not done clandestinely nor in violation of the law. It is done with the full knowledge and consent of the authorities, and it is not contrary to

それ故、もし私立学校が規定の教科課程から逸脱することを許されたら、「普通学校卒業生」は多様な教科課程の数と同様に多様な解釈が出来ることを意味してしまう。規定の教科課程を教え、教師の質や学校設備などに関して政府の必要条件を満たしている私立学校は、規定教科の時間外であれば、聖書を読み、宗教教育を施し、学校の敷地内で宗教的儀式などを行うことが出来る。そして政府公認の等級と、それに付随する特権をも得られるのである。

　1923年に発令した新しい法規はさらにこの事柄に踏み込んでいる。南メソジスト主教教会のアルフレッド・W・ワッソン牧師は、この点について1923年7月の"Korea Mission Field"の「總督府の新しい教育規定の重要性」という記事の中で明白に述べている。

　　　　新しい教育令は、宗教教育に制限なしの自由を与えると同時に、政府から完全公認されている学校と同じ特権のいくつかを享受出来るなど、ミッションスクールが別種類の認識を得られる道筋を与えている。誤解のないように付け加える必要があるが、事実、政府の完全公認を得ているミッションスクールは規則正しく体系立てられた宗教教育を施している。

　　　これは秘密裏に、または不法に行っているものではない。政府の充分な認識と同意の下で行われており、規定教科課程外で

the law, provided it is given outside of the prescribed curriculum.

Under the former régime only special and temporary permission was granted to conforming schools to use the school buildings as the places for holding chapel services and giving this extra-curriculum religious instruction. Under Baron Saito this permission has been made general and permanent.

Educational Finance--

The personnel and office expenses for educational administration are incorporated in the expenditure of the central and local offices of the Government-General, and are met by the State Treasury. Apart from the items referred to above, the educational expenditure is met by the Government-General, and by three classes of Public Corporations, viz., provincial bodies, District Educational bodies, and School Associations.

The Government-General supports its own institutions—ranging from the Imperial University to elementary schools. In addition it grants educational subsidies to local bodies, meets the expense of compiling textbooks, of sending students to Japan and to foreign countries, and of giving short courses of instruction for various special objects.

Provincial bodies support Normal Schools, Industrial Schools, and Secondary Schools. They subsidize the educational work of other local bodies, and meet the cost of various kinds of social and educational encouragement. Their sources of revenue are local taxes, subsidies from the Government-General, receipts from the Imperial Donation Fund, and from properties, fees, contributions, provincial loans, and some minor sources.

行われている限り法律に反するものではない。

　基準を満たしている学校が校内で礼拝を行ったり、教科課程以外の宗教教育を行うことに対し、前總督政権では、一時的な特例として許可が与えられるのみだった。齋藤男爵のもとで、この許可は一般的で永続的なものになった。

教育の財政

　教育関連の人件費および事務費用は總督府の中央と地方行政支出に含まれ、国庫から賄われる。上記以外の教育費は總督府と3つの政府団体、つまり地方政府、地域教育機関と学校組合で受け持つ。

　總督府は帝国大学から小学校に至るまで、官公立学校を補助する。加えて、地域団体に教育補助金を交付し、教科書の編修費用、学生を日本及び諸外国に送る費用、特別科目の短期コースの費用などを引き受ける。

　地方政府は普通学校、工業学校、中等学校を補助する。その他の地域団体の教育活動に補助金を払い、社会的・教育的な奨励事業の費用を受け持っている。地方政府の財源は地方税、總督府からの補助金、帝国寄付基金と不動産などからの収益、授業料、寄付、地方政府からの貸付、その他小さな財源である。

388   EDUCATION

District Educational bodies meet the expense of Common Schools, which are primarily for Koreans. Their sources of revenue are assessments on Koreans, subsidies from the Government-General and from provincial bodies, receipts from properties, fees, contributions, district loans, and some minor sources.

School Associations meet the expenses of Elementary, Secondary, and Industrial Schools established primarily for Japanese. Their revenue is derived from assessments on Japanese, and from other sources similar to those drawn on by the District Educational bodies.

The following table gives the total expenditure on education in Korea for the fiscal years 1919-20 to 1923-24 and for the year 1913-14, as a basis of comparison. The figures do not include the cost of the personnel and office management of the educational administration in the Central and Local Governments, which is met by the State Treasury out of general revenue. The figures are to the nearest thousand yen. The open figures represent the direct expenditure on education by the indicated agencies; the figures in brackets represent grants-in-aid (subsidies) made by the indicated agency to agencies subsidiary to it. All the subsidies become, of course, direct expenditures as they go down the line. The total expenditure of the year is, therefore, that of the open figures in the columns.

第九章　教育　　　389

　地域教育機関は主に朝鮮人向けである公立学校の費用を賄う。財
源は朝鮮人への賦課金、總督府と道からの補助金、不動産などから
の収益、授業料、寄付、地域からの貸付、その他小さな財源である。

　学校組合は主に日本人向けである小学、中等、工業学校の費用を
賄う。財源は日本人への税金と地域教育機関と同様の財源である。

　次ページの表は、朝鮮の教育費総支出額を、1913年度を基準と
して、1919から1923年度まで算出し比較したものである。数字は、
国庫の一般歳入から支払われている總督府と地方政府の教育行政の
人件費と事務費は含まない。数字は1000円単位で四捨五入されて
いる。括弧のない数字は各機関からの直接的な教育支出、括弧のあ
る数字はその機関から補助の対象機関に払われた補助金である。も
ちろん、全ての補助金は最後には直接支出となる。それ故、その年
の総支出は括弧に入っていない数字（直接出費）のみである。

390 EDUCATION

PUBLIC EXPENDITURE ON EDUCATION
(In thousands of yen. 1 yen = 50 cents U. S.)

Expenditure by	1913–14	1919–20	1920–21	1921–22	1922–23	1923–24*
The Government-General:						
Direct..............	550	1,536	2,493	4,155	4,172	5,033
Subsidies...........	(686)	(1,755)	(2,968)	(3,596)	(4,052)	(2,861)
Provincial Bodies:						
Direct..............	428	789	725	1,271	2,049	3,091
Subsidies...........	(269)	(1,737)	(3,458)	(3,873)	(3,953)	(2,489)
District Educational						
Bodies: Direct.......	1,157	3,214	8,157	10,245	13,306	13,903
School Associations:						
Direct..............	555	2,391	4,354	4,419	5,581	5,331
Total Expenditure...	2,691	7,920	15,729	20,089	25,108	27,360

* Budget estimates.

Both Japanese and Koreans pay school-fees, without exception. The average fee in a Common School is about 25 cents a month, in Elementary Schools, from 25 to 50 cents, in Higher Common Schools and in Middle Schools $1.25, in Girls' Higher Common Schools 75 cents, in Girls' High Schools from $1.50 to $2.25, in Industrial Schools $1.00, in Vocational Colleges $17.50 a year, and in the University Preparatory School $25.00 a year.

The educational assessment levied by District Educational bodies, paid by Koreans, averaged about 20 cents for the year 1923, per capita of the Korean population; that levied by School Associations, paid by Japanese, averaged about $3.30 *per capita* of the Japanese population comprised within all the School Associations in the country.

第九章　教育

教育の公共支出
（単位 千円　1 円＝ 50 セント）

支出	1913-14	1919-20	1920-21	1921-22	1922-23	1923-24*
總督府 　直接 　補助金	550 (686)	1,536 (1,755)	2,493 (2,968)	4,155 (3,596)	4,172 (4,052)	5,033 (2,861)
地方政府 　直接 　補助金	428 (269)	789 (1,737)	725 (3,458)	1,271 (3,873)	2,049 (3,953)	3,091 (2,489)
地方教育機関 　直接	1,157	3,214	8,157	10,245	13,306	13,903
地域教育組合 　直接	555	2,391	4,354	4,419	5,581	5,331
総支出	2,691	7,920	15,729	20,089	25,108	27,360

＊予算見積もり

　日本人も朝鮮人も例外なく授業料を払う。普通学校の平均授業料は 1 カ月 25 セント、小学校は 25 〜 50 セント、高等学校と中等学校では 1.25 ドル、女子高等普通学校では 0.75 ドル、女子高等学校では 1.50 から 2.25 ドル、工業学校は 1 ドル、専門学校では 1 年に 17.50 ドル、大学予備校では 1 年に 25 ドルである。

　地域教育機関から朝鮮人に課せられた税金は 1923 年には 1 人当たり平均約 0.2 ドルであった。朝鮮の全学校組合の管轄下に住む日本人に課された税金は、人口平均で約 3.3 ドルであった。

CHAPTER X

第十章

CHAPTER X

MEDICAL, SANITARY, AND SOCIAL SERVICE

Historical--

When, after the close of the Chino-Japanese War, Korea became virtually a Japanese Protectorate through the establishment of the Residency-General in 1906, one of the first matters to engage the attention of Japanese officials was the deplorable condition of everything connected with public health.

It is true that as early as 1897 the Home Department of the Korean Government had issued, on the advice of a Japanese expert, various regulations relating to vaccination, and for the prevention of cholera, typhoid, dysentery, and diphtheria, which from time to time had become epidemic in the Peninsula.

But these regulations, like so many others issued by the old Korean Government, were never effectively administered. Accordingly, one of the earliest acts of the Residency-General was to engage the services of about fifty Japanese physicians and to distribute them among the the police stations in the various provinces.

Their special duty was to supervise vaccination and sanitary measures in general.

Prior to 1906 the Korean Government maintained a hospital and a medical school; and a few other hospitals were supported by foreign missionary societies and by the municipal authorities of the various Japanese settlements in the country.

第十章

医療・公衆衛生・社会福祉

公衆衛生の歴史

　日清戦争が終わり 1906 年に統監府が設立されて、朝鮮が事実上日本の保護国になった時、日本の官吏が最初に注意を向けたことは、朝鮮の公衆衛生全般の嘆かわしい状態だった。

　大韓帝国政府の内務部は、日本人専門家の助言に基づきいち早く1897 年に、疫病に関する様々な法規を公布していた。これは朝鮮半島で時折流行していたコレラ、腸チフス、赤痢やジフテリアの予防ワクチンに関するものだった。

　しかしこれらの法規は、大韓帝国政府が発令した他の法規同様、効果的に実施されたことはなかった。それ故に、統監府が最初に行ったことは、約 50 人の日本人医師を様々な地方警察署に配置したことだった。

　この医師たちの特別任務はワクチンと衛生政策全般を監督することであった。

　1906 年以前は大韓帝国政府が病院 1 施設と医療学校 1 校を管理していた。そして外国の宣教会団体や国内の様々な日本人定住地の自治体が、その他少数の病院を援助していた。

The equipment and the accommodation of these hospitals were unsatisfactory and insufficient; and, on the advice of the Resident-General the three Government hospitals and the medical school were amalgamated into a single institution, called the Tai-han Hospital, situated at the capital city of Seoul. The Japanese Surgeon-General, Baron Sato, was appointed adviser as to buildings, equipment, staff, and so on, of the new hospital, and he became later its first president.

Korea is subject to outbreaks of epidemic diseases, of which the more important are cholera, typhoid fever, dysentery, and small-pox. Prior to the year 1910 very little had been done to prevent or to control these outbreaks. But in July of that year the police administration of Korea was transferred to the Japanese Residency-General, and Japanese Sanitary Police methods were gradually introduced throughout the country. In August, 1910, Korea was annexed to Japan. With the establishment of the Government-General a broad plan was formulated for giving the country a greatly improved system of medical and hygienic service.

Such matters cannot be carried forward very rapidly where the people are ignorant of or indifferent to the details of sanitary administration. The initial processes of improving the health of a people are costly, call for highly skilled technicians, and demand a degree of cooperation from the people themselves which can only be secured by the rigid enforcement of elaborate regulations.

In almost every instance in which a dominant power has undertaken to improve the health of people under its authority, discontent with the enterprise has been strong, and has not infrequently found its expression in violent resistance. The cost gives rise to the criticism that the people are

第十章　医療・公衆衛生・社会福祉　　397

　これらの病院の機器や収容設備は不充分であまり役に立つもので
はなかった。統監府の勧告により、3つの政府の病院と医療学校が、
ソウルに「大韓医院」という名で1つの施設として合併された。日
本の軍医総監であった佐藤進卿が大韓医院の顧問に任命され、建物、
機器、職員などに関する助言を行い、後に初代院長となった。

　朝鮮では疫病が発生しやすく、中でもコレラ、腸チフス、赤痢と
天然痘が大きな問題だった。1910年以前には、疫病の予防や対策は
滅多にされなかった。しかし、この年の7月から大韓帝国の警察は
統監府に移管され、日本の警察による衛生管理方式が徐々に国中に
導入されていった。1910年8月、大韓帝国は日本に併合された。朝
鮮総督府の設立とともに、国の医療衛生制度を大きく改善するため
の大規模な計画が組まれた。

　このような計画は、人々が衛生管理について詳しい事を知らな
かったり無関心であれば迅速には進まない。人々の健康を向上する
過程の初段階では費用がかかり、高度な技術を有する専門家が必要
である。また、人々からの協力が必要であるが、それは綿密な法規
とその厳格な実施によってのみ得られるのである。
　支配的勢力が、その権力を行使して人々の健康を改善するために
強権を発動すると、必ずと言っていいほど、計画に対する人々の不
満は強く、しばしば激しい抵抗となって現れる。費用面で人々が過
剰な税金を課せられると批判が膨らみ、法規を厳格に実施しようと

398   MEDICAL, SANITARY, AND SOCIAL SERVICE

being over-taxed; the strict enforcement of the regulations to the cry that the people are being dragooned by their rulers.

Fortunately the Koreans have, on the whole, shown an intelligent appreciation of the importance of the Japanese work in the field of medical service and sanitary regulation, so that although much remains to be done, further progress depends only upon the amount of money which can be made available.

Each year the *Report of Reforms and Progress in Chosen (Korea)*, compiled by the Government-General, devotes a chapter to medical and sanitary matters; and it is from these chapters that the following account is taken.

Certain measures for hygienic administration were put in force during the Protectorate régime, but their success was limited by the absence of co-ordinate regulations. Accordingly, in 1911 the Japanese Law for Supervising Food, Drink, and other Articles was extended to Korea, and the necessary administrative regulations were promulgated. In order to secure uniformity of method in sanitary administration, the whole of this work was concentrated in the Police Affairs Department of the Government-General, except the work of the Central Government Hospital in Seoul and of the Charity Hospitals in the Provinces; and the Police Affairs Department was provided with a chemical laboratory, its principal duties being to analyze samples of foodstuffs and of drugs and medicines sold in the Peninsula.

With its long coast-line on two oceans—the Sea of Japan on the east, and the Yellow Sea on the west—and with two river frontiers on the north, separating the country from Manchuria and from Asiatic Russia,

第十章　医療・公衆衛生・社会福祉　　　399

すると人々により支配者は威圧されていると叫ばれる。

　幸いにして朝鮮人は、全体として医療機関と衛生法規における日本の努力に対して理解と評価を示している。まだやるべき事は多く残っているが、更なる進展は財源がどのくらい確保出来るかに懸っている。

　毎年、總督府がまとめる『朝鮮總督府施政年報』には医療と衛生についての章があり、以下に述べることはこれを元とする。

　保護政治の時代においても、公衆衛生政策はいくらかは実施されていたが、それを調整する法規がなかったため成果は限られたものだった。そこで、1911年に日本の食品・飲料等管理の法律を朝鮮にも適用し、必要な行政上の法規が公布された。公衆衛生管理の方法を統一するため、ソウルの總督府医院と地方にある慈恵医院以外のすべて任務が總督府の警務總監部に集結された。警務部には化学分析室が与えられ、その任務は主に、朝鮮半島で販売される食品、医薬品のサンプルを分析することであった。

　朝鮮は東は日本海、西は黄海に挟まれた長い海岸線を持ち、北は満州と東北ロシアとの国境をなす2つの川に囲まれていたので、疫病とその他の流行性の病気を検疫することは非常に難しかった。

400 MEDICAL, SANITARY, AND SOCIAL SERVICE

respectively, the problem of quarantine against the introduction of plague and other epidemic diseases is a very difficult one.

This is well illustrated by the measures taken in the early days of the Government-General, 1911, to prevent the plague raging in Manchuria at that time from extending to Korea; and the illustration serves to show that from the very first the Government-General has realized its responsibilities in the matter of the public health.

When the prevalence of plagues was reported in October, 1910, from the Harbin district of Manchuria, instructions were issued to all Provincial Police Directors, and to the police Captains in the capital city of Keijo for adopting precautionary measures. Along the Yalu River and along the seacoast of Kokai Province, constantly visited by Chinese junks, a system of health-inspection was set up, and the people were encouraged to destroy rats. Chinese coming from the plague zone were subjected to ten days' quarantine, whilst quarantine stations were established for railway traffic at Shin-gishu on the Korean side of the mouth of the Yalu, and at Heijo, about 120 miles inside Korean territory.

By January, 1911, when the plague had advanced to within fifty miles of the Korean boundary still more stringent measures were called for. A Plague Prevention Committee was formed, consisting of high civil, and medical officials; a general quarantine was enforced against all vessels coming from infected regions; and a patrol of more than a thousand police and gendarmes was assigned to the south bank of the Yalu to shut off completely the passage of Chinese coolies across the frozen river. This guard was supplemented by police boats and a depot steamer, acting in concert with the Chinese authorities at the mouth of the Yalu. Similar

第十章　医療・公衆衛生・社会福祉　　401

　これは1911年、總督府が設立され間もない頃、満州で流行していた疫病が朝鮮に広がらないように取った措置によく表れている。そして、この事は、総督府がその設立当初より公衆衛生の実態に対し責任を実感していた事を示している。

　1910年10月、満州のハルビン地区から疫病の流行が報告された時、予防策をとるよう全ての地方警察部長と首都京城の警察局長に指示が出された。ヤールー河と黄海道(こうかいどう)の沿岸には絶えず中国の帆船が入ってきているので、健康検査のシステムが設置され、人々はネズミを殺すよう奨励された。疫病が流行する地区から来た中国人は10日間隔離され、検疫所は、鴨緑江河口の朝鮮側に位置する新義州(しんぎしゅう)の鉄道付近と、朝鮮領土の120マイル内陸にある平壌(へいじょう)に設置された。

　1911年1月には、既に疫病が朝鮮の国境から50マイル以内に迫ってきており、より厳しい政策が必要になった。上級官吏と医務官で構成される疫病予防委員会が設立され、疫病地帯からの全ての船舶に対し全面的な検疫が強制された。そして、凍った川を渡ってくる中国人の日雇い労働者を完全に遮断するため、1000人以上の警察官と憲兵が鴨緑江の南側の岸部に配備され巡察した。

　この巡察隊には、鴨緑江河口の中国当局と足並みをそろえて活動するため警察のボート数隻と母艦蒸気船一隻が与えられた。豆満江

measures were taken on the northeast frontier, along the Tumen river.

Thanks to these rigorous precautions the plague was stopped at the boundaries, and not a single case occurred among the Koreans.

In respect of cholera, its occurrence in epidemic form has been much reduced during the past fifteen years, the only serious outbreaks having taken place in 1919 and in 1920. In the former year cholera caused 12,000 deaths, and in the latter 13,000; whilst in 1921 only one death from this cause was reported, in 1922 twenty-three deaths, and in 1924 none.

第十章　医療・公衆衛生・社会福祉

に沿った北東地帯でも同じような手段がとられた。

　これらの厳しい予防策によって疫病は国境で止まり、朝鮮では疫病は 1 件も起こらなかった。

　コレラについては、過去 15 年間、流行は大きく減り、唯一の重大発生は 1919 年と 1920 年のみであった。1919 年にはコレラによる死亡者は 1 万 2000 人[1]で、1920 年は 1 万 3000 人であった。しかし、1921 年にはコレラによる死者は 1 人のみ、1922 年は 23 人、1924 年は 0 と報告された[2]。

※ 1 次ページ掲載の表と数値が異なっているが原文のままとした。
※ 2 次ページ掲載の表では 1923 年が 0 となっているが原文のままとした。

404   MEDICAL, SANITARY, AND SOCIAL SERVICE

Epidemic Diseases--

The occurrence of epidemic diseases during the twelve years ending with 1923 is shown in the following table. In respect of cholera, the most serious of them, it is to be noted that only forty-one cases and twenty-four deaths from this cause were reported in the three years 1921-23.

The statistics are official figures; but the medical reports warn the reader that, owing to failure to report, or to concealment of epidemic diseases on the part of the Koreans, the statistics cannot be regarded as accurate. All that can be said of them is that they are the best available.

EPIDEMIC DISEASES IN KOREA

Year	Cholera		Dysentery		Typhoid		Small-Pox		Scarlet Fever	
	Cases	Deaths	Cases	Deaths	Cases	Deaths	Cases	Deaths	Cases	Deaths
1912	122	78	1,945	400	1,593	252	1,142	164	40	7
1913	1	1	1,388	309	1,956	373	226	35	70	13
1914	.....	.....	1,396	343	2,402	425	140	12	336	121
1915	1	1	1,344	316	2,596	415	48	8	614	156
1916	2,066	1,253	1,189	306	2,365	437	48	6	223	48
1917	.....	.....	2,096	592	2,397	599	48	5	237	31
1918	.....	.....	1,126	267	3,750	703	330	111	125	12
1919	16,803	10,009	1,522	407	3,266	642	2,180	675	124	21
1920	24,229	13,568	974	253	2,140	422	11,532	3,614	371	106
1921	1	1	978	311	2,535	485	8,316	2,527	717	209
1922	40	23	1,932	529	3,801	768	3,673	1,160	585	139
1923	0	0	1,195	296	2,839	541	3,722	1,120	1,008	242

General Causes of Death--

During the five years ending with 1923 the average annual number of deaths in Korea was 369,000, which gives an annual average death-rate of approximately 21 per thousand of the population.

伝染病

1923 年以前の 12 年間に起こった伝染病を以下の表にまとめてある。最も恐ろしいコレラについて注目すべきは、1921 年から 1923 年の 3 年間で、41 件の発病と 24 件の死亡事例のみ報告されていることだ。

統計は公式なものではあるが、疫病を報告しないケースや、朝鮮人が疫病を隠したりすることがあるため正確なものではないと医療報告は読者に警告している。ただ言えることは、入手し得る統計の中では、これが最善だということだ。

朝鮮における流行病

年	コレラ		赤痢		腸チフス		天然痘		猩紅熱	
	発症	死亡	発症	死亡	発症	死亡	発症	死亡	発症	死亡
1912	122	78	1,945	400	1,593	252	1,142	164	40	7
1913	1	1	1,388	309	1,956	373	226	35	70	13
1914	–	–	1,396	343	2,402	425	140	12	336	121
1915	1	1	1,344	316	2,596	415	48	8	614	156
1916	2,066	1,253	1,189	306	2,365	437	48	6	223	48
1917	–	–	2,096	592	2,397	599	48	5	237	31
1918	–	–	1,126	267	3,750	703	330	111	125	12
1919	16,803	10,009	1,522	407	3,266	642	2,180	675	124	21
1920	24,229	13,568	974	253	2,140	422	11,532	3,614	371	106
1921	1	1	978	311	2,535	485	8,316	2,527	717	209
1922	40	23	1,932	529	3,801	768	3,673	1,160	585	139
1923	0	0	1,195	296	2,839	541	3,722	1,120	1,008	242

一般的な死因

1923 年以前の 5 年間で、朝鮮での平均年間死亡件数は 36 万 9000 人である。つまり 1000 人に対し約 21 人の平均年間死亡率だ。

406   MEDICAL, SANITARY, AND SOCIAL SERVICE

The causes of death, ranged in the order of their numerical importance, were in 1923 as follows: diseases of the nervous system 72,086, of the digestive tract 53,320, of the respiratory organs 46,691, infectious diseases 34,302, common colds 33,022, decrepitude 18,935, diseases of the circulatory system 14,899, constitutional diseases 10,789, insanity 9,820, diseases of the genito-urinary tract 9,576, diseases of the skin 8,128, diseases of the nose and throat 7,717. The foregoing accounted for about 89 per cent of all the deaths, the remaining 11 per cent being scattered among causes none of which accounted for as large a number as 2 per cent of the total.

The following sections are condensed from the *Annual Report on Administration of Chosen, 1922-23*, compiled by the Government-General.

Sanitary Equipment--

Formerly, sanitary conditions in Chosen were extremely bad, for there were very few native doctors possessed of modern knowledge and skill, whilst the sick were generally put into the hands of witches or exorcists, and refused to be medically treated. Public sanitary works were completely lacking, and even the drinking water was in many cases far from healthful. In consequence, various epidemics were constantly present, especially lung-distoma and dochmiasis. The only medical agencies worth mentioning were the few Japanese doctors and foreign medical missionaries practising in Keijo and a few other towns.

Early in the protectorate period, therefore, the first step toward putting an end to these insanitary conditions was taken by establishing in Keijo

数字的重要度の順番に見ると、1923年における死因は以下のとおりだ。神経系の病気7万2086件、消化器系5万3320件、呼吸器系4万6691件、感染症3万4302件、風邪3万3022件、老衰1万8935件、循環系1万4899件、体質性疾患1万789件、精神病9820件、生殖器・泌尿器系9576件、皮膚病8128件、鼻耳咽喉系7717件。

これらの病気は全死亡件数の89パーセントを占める。残りの11パーセントはそのどれにも当てはまらない死因であるが、いずれも死因率が2パーセントを超えるものはない。

次の内容は、總督府が編集した『朝鮮總督府施政年報　大正十一年度』を要約したものである。

衛生設備

以前は朝鮮の衛生状況は非常に悪かった。というのも、近代的知識と技術を持った現地の医者がほとんどおらず、病人は一般的に巫女や祈祷師に引き渡され、医学的に治療することを拒まれたからだ。公衆衛生事業は全くなく、飲料水も多くの場合、不衛生で良くなかった。その結果、様々な疫病、特に肺ジストマや十二指腸蟲症が絶えず発生した。医療を施していると言えるものは、京城とその他少数の町で診療している日本人医師か外国の医療使節団しかいなかった。

それ故、保護政治の初期に統監府がこの不衛生な状況を無くすためにしたことは、大韓医院と呼ばれる大きな病院を京城に、そして

a large hospital called the Taikan Iin (Korean General Hospital) and a few charity hospitals in other centers. At the same time, part of the public industrial funds were appropriated for the construction of water-works in the chief towns. On the present régime being instituted, further steps were taken to effect expansion in existing medical organs, and not only was the Government Hospital (the former Taikan Iin) in Keijo enlarged, but a charity hospital was erected in each province, and with the aid of the Imperial bounty granted at the time of annexation other charity hospitals were set up in remote districts, physicians were engaged on circuit work in parts difficult of access, and a segregating station for lepers was established on Shoroku Island off South Zenra Province, a place noted for its salubrious climate. All these humane undertakings, coupled with a good distribution throughout the country of police and other public doctors, have done much toward providing needy sick people with proper medical care. Nor did the good work of the new régime along this line stop here, for care was taken that even those Koreans living in out-of-the-way frontier regions and lacking medical facilities should be visited by itinerant physicians, or else charity hospitals were established where possible or doctors were specially appointed to the large centers.

Recognizing the pressing need for the introduction of many sanitary improvements, the Government first took in hand the matter of drinking water, and began by purchasing and enlarging the water-works in Keijo and constructing new ones at Jinsen, Heijo, and Chinnampo, while Fusan, Mokpo, Kunsan, Gensan, and a number of other towns were assisted in setting up their own systems by the grant of a half or more of the actual cost. Financial aid, too, was given for the digging of public wells

慈恵医院をいくつか他の場所に設立することであった。同時に、起業公債の一部が主要都市に水道施設を作るために充てられた。

　總督府設置後、現存の医療機関を拡大するための措置が取られ、京城にある總督府医院（前大韓医院）が増設されただけでなく、各道に慈恵医院が建てられた。そして、併合の際に大日本帝国より下賜された臨時恩賜金で、遠隔の地域には慈恵医院が建ち、なおかつ医師の巡回診療が行なわれた。患者の療養に適した、全羅南道沖の
小鹿島にはハンセン病患者の隔離施設が設立された。

　これら人道的な取組みは、国中にうまく配置された警察と公認医師の効果と相まって、貧しい病人に適切な医療を提供することに大きく貢献した。總督府の功績はこれに留まらず、医療施設を欠いた辺境地帯に住む朝鮮人にも巡回医師が訪問し、可能なら慈恵医院を設立、大きな都市には特別に医師を任命した。

　總督府は衛生面で多くの改善の必要性が差し迫っていることに応じて、まず飲料水の確保に着手した。京城の上水道を買収・拡張し、仁川、平壌、鎮南浦に新しい上水道を作った。そして、釜山、木浦、群山、元山とその他多数の町には、工費の半分以上の助成を受けて上水道敷設を補助し、国中で公共の井戸を掘るための助成金も支給した。同時に、財務局が疫病と牛疫の予防を素早く行えるよう相当な額の資金を毎年負担した。その結果、人々の間で予防接種が広まっ

410 MEDICAL, SANITARY, AND SOCIAL SERVICE

throughout the country. At the same time the Treasury yearly defrayed a considerable sum of money to permit of timely action being taken for the prevention of epidemics and cattle-plague, with the result that even small-pox, formerly most virulent in Chosen, is now far less the scourge it was, thanks to the greater enforcement of vaccination among the people. In addition, the authorities were not lax in arranging for the disposal of impurities and other insanitary matters, and their reward is seen in the much improved condition of the public health.

Under the old Korean Government nothing was done to further the public health, but since the establishment of the present régime various sanitary regulations have been drawn up and made effective as popular conditions called for them. Among the important regulations thus enacted were those relating to physicians, dentists, private hospitals, foods and drinks, drugs, slaughter-houses, house cleaning, scavengering, burial-grounds, crematories, plague prevention, disinfection, and quarantine.

Expansion of Medical Organs--

As already alluded to, charity hospitals were founded in important towns and public doctors stationed in various places. At the end of 1919 the number of hospitals was twenty and public doctors 216. These proving inadequate to serve the public efficiency, extension and increase was carried out as provided for in the supplementary budget of the fiscal year 1920, and the close of this year saw twenty-four charity hospitals in full working order.

Although popular confidence in the Government Hospital and Provincial Charity Hospitals steadily grew stronger, there still remained

たため、朝鮮で最も発病率の高かった天然痘さえも激減したのである。さらに、各当局は汚物、その他の非衛生的な物の処理にも手を抜かず、その恩恵は、飛躍的に向上した公衆衛生状態に見ることが出来る。

　以前の大韓帝国政府の下では公衆衛生の改善について何もなされなかったが、總督府の設立以来、人々の状況の必要性に応じて、様々な衛生に関する法規が立案され実施されてきた。このように実施された法規の中で重要なものは、医師、歯科医師、私立病院、飲食料、薬品、屠殺場、住居掃除、ゴミ処理、墓地、火葬場、疫病対策、消毒、検疫に関連するものである。

医療機関の拡張
　既に触れたように、慈恵医院は重要な都市に設立され、公認医師は様々な場所に配置された。1919 年の終わりには、病院は 20 施設、公認医師は 216 人であった。これでは充分な医療行為が実施できないということで、1920 年の事業年度補正予算で拡張・増設がなされ、同年度末には 24 の慈恵医院が稼働していた。

　總督府医院と地方の慈恵医院への人々の信頼は強くなっていったが、更にその信頼に答えるために多くのすべきことがあった。1919

412 MEDICAL, SANITARY, AND SOCIAL SERVICE

much to be done to make them more worthy of that confidence, and a scheme was elaborated for building more hospitals and making increase in the medical force, at the same time bettering its treatment, between the fiscal years 1919 and 1923 at the cost of 2,500,000 yen. Further consideration making it plain that the scheme was still too narrow a one, it was decided in 1920 to enlarge it at an additional cost of 4,590,000 yen, and to extend the period of its completion to 1926. A plan was also drawn up to establish thirteen more local charity hospitals.

As only a few sanitary experts were at first stationed in the country, the investigation and prevention of plague could not be conducted satisfactorily, so, in the fiscal year 1920, thirteen experts and twenty-six assistants were additionally appointed in the provinces, and thirty more public doctors sent to the remoter places.

The Central Health Society--

Along with the increase in factories, schools, and waterworks, undertakings connected with the public health have also increased, and the need for a sanitary advisory organ for the Government was not long in manifesting itself. Accordingly, on July 14, 1920, regulations were issued for a Central Health Society to be formed with the Administrative Superintendent as president, the members of it to be selected from officials and private individuals, and its first general meeting took place in October of 1921. At the same time a special committee was organized in much the same manner as the Society to deal with plague investigation and prevention.

第十章　医療・公衆衛生・社会福祉　　　413

年度から 1923 年度に 250 万円の予算でさらに多くの病院を建て、医療関係者を増やす綿密な計画が組まれた。しかし、この計画でもまだ足りないことが明白になり、1920 年には 459 万円の追加予算で拡大し、事業終了も 1926 年まで延長することになった。また、追加で 13 の地方慈恵医院を建設する計画も組まれた。

　当局は公衆衛生の専門家が朝鮮内に数人しか配置されておらず、疫病の調査と予防を満足に行えなかったことから、1920 年度には専門家 13 人と助手 26 人が地方に追加で配属され、さらに、公認医者 30 人が更なる僻地へ派遣された。

中央衛生會

　工場、学校、水道の増加に伴い、公衆衛生に関連する事業の数も増え、ただちに公衆衛生の諮問機関が必要になってきた。それ故、1920 年 7 月 14 日に、中央衛生會設立のための法規が発令され、政務総監を会長とし、会員は官・民より選ばれ、1921 年 10 月に最初の総会が開かれた。同時に、ほとんど同じ手順で、疫病の調査・予防に取り組む特別委員会が設置された。

414   MEDICAL, SANITARY, AND SOCIAL SERVICE

Hygienic Inspection--

Hygienic inspection is most indispensable in connection with the official control of foods, drinks, containers, and drugs, so from 1913 onward the provincial governments were gradually equipped with hygienic laboratories, and no province is now lacking such institution.

Important articles subjected to official inspection during this fiscal year totaled 65,005, of which 55,302 were found satisfactory, while 9,254 were declared injurious or unwholesome. Among the principal articles condemned were 2,294 samples of patent medicines, 156 of liquors, 4,046 of beverages, and 274 of containers.

Bacteriological Service--

Formerly, the country was troubled by the visitation of infectious diseases almost the whole year round, while no research work was ever carried on to ascertain the cause of them, but by 1920 each of the provinces had within it a bacteriological laboratory conducting tests, etc., with a view to cholera prevention. The manufacture of the various preventive vaccines and serums, however, is conducted by the one in Keijo only, and from this laboratory a large number of phials of the several vaccines and serums has yearly been dispatched to the provinces at a small charge or else free of cost, and the demand for them is ever growing.

Opium Control--

From of old opium-smoking has been somewhat prevalent in Chosen, especially in the frontier regions, and many were the victims of it throughout the country. So in the year 1905 the old Korean Government

衛生検査

衛生検査は、飲食料、飲食用器具、薬品の公的管理に最も必要不可欠であるので、1913年以降、地方政府は徐々に衛生検査所を備えるようになり、現在ではこの施設を欠いている道はない。

今年度、公式検査の対象となる項目は全部で6万5005項目で、そのうち、5万5302項目は条件を満たしているが、9254項目は有害もしくは健康に良くないことが明らかにされた。不良品とみなされた主な項目の中には薬品2294品、酒156品、飲料4046品、容器274個が含まれていた。

細菌研究

以前の朝鮮は一年中疫病の災難に悩まされていたが、原因解明のための研究が行われたことはなかった。しかし1920年までには、コレラ予防の目的で、検査などが行える細菌研究所が各地方に置かれるようになった。各種ワクチンと血清の製造は京城にある研究所でのみ行われた。この研究所から何種類かのワクチンと血清が大量の小瓶に入れられ、低料金または無料で各地方に送られ、需要は増える一方である。

アヘン取締

朝鮮、特に辺境地帯では、アヘン吸引の習慣が少なからず見られ、国中で多くの者が被害者となっている。それ故1905年に大韓帝国政府はアヘンとパイプの輸入・製造・販売を禁止し、刑法に特別条

416   MEDICAL, SANITARY, AND SOCIAL SERVICE

prohibited the importation, manufacture, and sale of opium and pipes, and inserted a special provision for it in the penal code then published, but found it impossible to enforce it effectively. After the annexation the Government-General took every measure to make the control of opium as strict as possible, and the new criminal law for Chosen issued in March, 1912, also contained a particular provision for it. Toward confirmed users of opium a rather moderate policy was taken at first, so that their cure might be effected by degrees, and their number gradually grew less. In September, 1914, the Government gave instructions to the police and other officials concerned to enforce in future the absolute prohibition of opium-smoking, and, taught by past experience, treated habitués in a semi-compulsory manner. This proved very effective, but it was still impossible to free the land of the evil as much opium was smuggled in from China, and in the frontier districts people secretly grew the poppy for making opium.

As a consequence of the stricter enforcement of the law against opium-smoking, the use of morphine and of cocaine increased, and it became necessary to issue new regulations to insure a stricter control of druggists and of the illicit sale of drugs. In 1920 the whole question of opium alkaloids and of other narcotics was reconsidered in view of Japan's adherence to the International Opium Treaty. Regulations were issued covering the import and export of all narcotic drugs, making them subject to Government sanction.

The production of opium reached about 17,000 pounds in 1919, fell in 1920 to 342 pounds, rose in 1921 to 5,900 pounds, fell in 1922 to 3,600 pounds, and in 1923 to 3,060 pounds.

項を盛り込み公表したが、効果的に取り締まるのは不可能であると
気づいた。

　併合後、總督府はアヘンの取り締まりを可能な限り厳重にするよ
うあらゆる手段を取り、1912年3月に発令した朝鮮の新しい刑法に
も特別条項を加えた。

　アヘン常用者に対しては、徐々に回復出来るよう最初はやや穏健
な対策が取られ、次第にその数も減っていった。

　1914年9月には、政府は警察と関係官吏に将来的にアヘン吸引の
完全禁止を実施するよう指示し、過去の経験に基づき、常用者を半
強制的に治療した。

　これはとても効果を奏したが、大量のアヘンが中国から密輸され、
辺境地帯で人々はアヘンを作るため秘密裡にケシを栽培していたの
で、朝鮮をアヘンの悪から自由にすることは依然不可能であった。

　アヘン吸引を厳重に取り締まる法律の実施の結果、モルヒネとコ
カインの使用が増え、薬物販売者と不法販売をより厳しく取り締ま
るための新しい法律が必要になった。1920年、日本は国際アヘン条
約（阿片条約および国際連盟の方針）の厳守に鑑み、アヘン・アル
カロイドとその他の麻薬について全般的な見直しがなされた。

　全ての麻薬の輸出・輸入に適用する法規が発令され、政府の制裁
措置の対象となった。

　アヘンの生産は、1919年には約1万7000ポンドに達し、1920年
には342ポンドに減り、また1921年には5900ポンドに増え、そし
て1922年には3600ポンド、1923年には3060ポンドに減った。

418   MEDICAL, SANITARY, AND SOCIAL SERVICE

Relief Work for Lepers--

There is a good deal of leprosy in Korea, a condition to which the first relief was contributed by medical missionaries, the matter never having engaged the serious attention of the old Korean Government.

After the establishment of the Government-General the prevalence of leprosy was the subject of a special inquiry which resulted, in 1916, in the selection of the island of Shoroku as a leper settlement where, in the course of time, all lepers in Korea were to be isolated for treatment.

In 1924 the Shorokuto Charity Hospital had a staff of three doctors, thirteen nurses, and sixteen other employees. The patients are treated with chaulmugra oil and its ethyl ester. The average number of patients treated per day has increased from 76 in 1918 to 192 in 1921.

Hospitals--

There was in Korea in 1923 a total of 101 hospitals. Of these, twenty-five were Government hospitals, of which twenty-three were Provincial Charity Hospitals; nine were maintained by public bodies; forty-one private hospitals were maintained as private institutions by Japanese, seven by Koreans, and nineteen by foreigners, the last named being conducted by the various missionary societies.

The largest hospitals are the Chosen Government Hospital and the Severance Union Hospital, both situated in Keijo.

The Government-General decided in 1920 to make a considerable addition to the hospital equipment of the country, allotting to that purpose about three million dollars. This work will be completed in 1927, thus adding thirteen Provincial Charity Hospitals, and two Branch Hospitals to

ハンセン病患者救済事業

朝鮮にはハンセン病患者が多くいるが、宣教会の医療使節団が最初に支援を施した。しかし以前の政府は特に注意を払わなかった。

總督府が設立されてからは、ハンセン病の流行が議題となり特別調査が行われ、その結果、1916年に、小鹿島がハンセン病患者の定住地として選ばれ、やがては朝鮮に住む全てのハンセン病患者が治療のためにこの島に隔離されることになった。

1924年には、小鹿島慈恵医院には医師3人、看護婦13人、その他職員16人がいた。患者は大風子油とそのエチルエステルで治療されていた。1日に治療される患者の平均数は1918年の76人から1921年には192人に増えた。

病院

1923年、朝鮮には全部で101の病院があった。これらのうち、官立病院は25、地方の慈恵医院は23、公的団体により運営される病院は9、日本人が運営する私立病院41、朝鮮人が運営する私立病院は7、様々な外国の宣教会団体が運営する病院が19であった。

一番大きな病院は朝鮮總督府医院とセブランス連合病院で両方とも京城にあった。總督府は1920年に病院の設備を大幅に増やす決定をし、そのために約300万ドルを充てた。この事業は1927年に終了予定で、さらに13の地方慈恵医院と、上述の病院の付属医院が二か所増設され、職員として52人医師が増員される。

420 MEDICAL, SANITARY, AND SOCIAL SERVICE

those mentioned above, and fifty-two physicians to the medical personnel.

In 1923 there were treated at the Chosen Government Hospital a total of 101,749 in-patient cases. The figures do not refer to the number of individuals treated, but to the case-day; that is to say, a patient is counted as a separate case on each day he is in the hospital. Of the total number of cases 95,168 were paying cases (68,245 Japanese, and 26,923 Koreans; and 6,581 were free cases (2,336 Japanese, and 4,245 Koreans).

The number of out-patients visiting the hospital in 1923 was 247,091, by case-day count. Of these 160,136 were paying cases (127,606 Japanese, and 32,530 Koreans); and 86,955 were free cases (2,866 Japanese, and 84,069 Koreans).

The Provincial Charity Hospitals treated 235,444 cases of in-patients in 1923, of which number 133,014 were paying cases, and 102,430 free. The case-day figures for out-patients in these hospitals was 1,755,093, of which 901,561 were paying cases, and 853,093 free. These figures refer to the number of dispensary treatments given, each treatment being counted as a case.

The Severance Union Medical College--

The following account is taken from the Severance Union Medical College Catalogue, 1925-6.

The College is the direct successor of the work established by Dr. H. N. Allen, the first Protestant missionary in Korea. He arrived in the country in 1884; and in gratitude for his having saved the life of Prince Min, the King established the Royal Korean Hospital, appointing Dr.

第十章　医療・公衆衛生・社会福祉　　　421

　1923 年、朝鮮總督府医院の入院患者治療件数は計 10 万 1749 件に
上った。この数字は個人の人数ではなく、治療数である。つまり、
1 人の患者が入院中に受ける治療は、1 日ごとに別のケースとして
数えられる。全件数のうち、9 万 5168 件は有料患者（日本人 6 万
8245 件、朝鮮人 2 万 6923 件）、6581 件は無料患者（日本人 2336 件、
朝鮮人 4245 件）である。

　同年に訪れた外来患者の治療件数は累積で 24 万 7091 件であった。
このうち、16 万 136 件は有料（日本人 12 万 7606 件、朝鮮人 3 万
2530 件）、8 万 6955 件は無料（日本人 2866 件、朝鮮人 8 万 4069 件）
である。

　同年、地方慈恵医院の入院患者件数は 23 万 5444 件で、そのう
ち 13 万 3014 件は有料、10 万 2430 件は無料であった。外来患者の
延べ治療件数は 175 万 5093 件で、うち 90 万 1561 件は有料、85 万
3093 件は無料であった。この数値は治療室での診察件数で、1 回の
診察で一件と数えられている。

セブランス連合医学専門学校

　以下は、セブランス連合医学専門学校案内 1925 ～ 6 年、から抜
粋している。

　　当学校は朝鮮最初のプロテスタント宣教師であるＨ . Ｎ . ア
　　レン博士のなした事業を直接受け継いでいる。アレン博士は
　　1884 年に朝鮮にやってきた。博士が閔王子の命を救ったこと

422 MEDICAL, SANITARY, AND SOCIAL SERVICE

Allen in charge. The work was successively carried on by Drs. Allen, J. W. Heron, C. C. Vinton, and O. R. Avison. In 1894 the work of the hospital was taken over from the Korean Government by the Northern Presbyterian Mission, and since then has been distinctly a missionary institution.

The first regular medical class was enrolled in 1900, and graduated in 1908. The continued existence of the College is due to the generosity of Mr. L. H. Severance, and of his son and daughter, Mr. John L. Severance, and Mrs. F. F. Prentiss, whose benefactions have exceeded $150,000.

Severance Union Medical College is incorporated under the laws of the Government-General of Korea, the Board of Managers consisting of representatives of the Missions and of the Churches and of the Alumni. The school was recognized by the Educational Department as a "Senmon Gakko' (which term corresponds to College) in May, 1917. And again in 1922 when the educational regulations were revised, the school was given recognition under the new ordinance, but graduates were still required to pass the government examination for license to practice medicine. However, in February, 1923, Governor-General Saito designated Severance Union Medical College as a school whose graduates from the regular course might be licensed without further examination, the government, through its Educational Department taking cognizance of all the examinations of the school. This gives the school full recognition under the government, and removes all handicaps.

At present six missions are actively co-operating in the work of the

に感謝の意を表して、国王は王立廣恵院を設立しアレン博士を責任者に任命した。この事業はアレン博士から、Ｊ．Ｗ．ヘロン、Ｃ．Ｃ．ビントン、Ｏ．Ｒ．アヴィソンへと引き継がれて運営されていった。1894 年には、病院の運営は李氏朝鮮政府から北プレスビタリアン宣教会へと引き渡され、それ以来宣教機関としての色合いが濃くなった。

医学校の第一期生は 1900 年に入学し、1908 年に卒業した。当学校が存続出来ているのは、15 万ドルもの寄付をしたＬ．Ｈ．セブランス氏、息子のジョン．Ｌ．セブランス氏と娘のＦ．Ｆ．プレンティス夫人の寛容さのお蔭である。

当学校は朝鮮總督府の法律の下に法人化され、管理委員会は宣教会、教会、卒業生の代表から構成されている。1917 年 5 月に学務局より「専門学校」（専門大学にあたる）と認定された。そしてまた 1922 年に教育令が改正され、当学校は新しい条例の中でも認可を受けたが、卒業生が医師開業免許を得るためには政府の試験に合格しなければならなかった。しかし、1923 年 2 月に齋藤總督は、学務局を通して總督府がこの学校の全ての試験を認知することで、セブランス連合医学専門学校の正規課程の卒業生は追加試験なしでも医師免許を得ることを可能とした。これは總督府の下で当学校が全面的に認証されたことを意味し、不利な条件は全てなくなった。

現在 6 つの宣教会が当学校と病院の運営に積極的に協力している：

424   MEDICAL, SANITARY, AND SOCIAL SERVICE

College and Hospital: Presbyterian Church in the U. S. A.; Methodist Episcopal Church; Presbyterian Church in the U. S.; Methodist Episcopal Church, South; Presbyterian Church in Canada; Presbyterian Church of Australia.

During the ten years ending with 1924 the number of out-patients treated during the year in the college dispensary has increased from twenty-seven thousand to seventy-one thousand, and the number of in-patients from 1,387 to 1,968. In the year 1924 the number of free cases in the hospital was 27.3 per cent of the total, or, counting days in hospital instead of number of patients, 43 per cent of the total case-day units. In the out-patient department 38.6 per cent of the treatments were free.

The College and Hospital are hampered in the highly useful work they perform by the lack of funds to extend equipment and increase the staff. Certainly no one who has visited these institutions can retain any other impression than that they deserve the most generous support from those who have the means to afford it.

Health Practitioners--

All persons in Korea who are in any way connected with the practice of medicine are under strict police supervision; and the regulations in regard to physicians and surgeons who follow the Western methods are practically the same as those which are in force in Japan proper, with the exception that in remote districts where there are very few thoroughly qualified medical men, a license to practice is issued to persons who have not the full legal qualifications.

The number of fully qualified doctors in Korea in 1923 was 1,202, of

U.S.A. プレスビタリアン教会、メソジスト監督教会、U.S. プレスビタリアン教会、南メソジスト監督教会、カナダ・プレスビタリアン教会、オーストラリア・プレスビタリアン教会。

1924 年までの 10 年間で、医学専門学校付属診療所で診察を受けた 1 年間の外来患者数は 2 万 7000 人から 7 万 1000 人に増え、入院患者数は 1387 人から 1968 人に増えた。

1924 年にはこの病院での入院患者の 27.3 パーセントが無料患者で、患者数ではなく入院期間で見ると 43 パーセントの治療事例が無料だった。外来患者の治療事例では 38.6 パーセントが無料だった。

セブランス連合医学専門学校と病院は、施設拡大と職員増員のための資金が足りず、このとても有益な業務に支障をきたしている。これらの施設を訪れる人は、ここが寄付と寛大な援助を受けるに値すると誰もが感じるであろう。

医療関係者

朝鮮で医療に関わる者は皆厳しい警察の統制に置かれる。西洋医学の内科医と外科医に関する法規は、ある例外を除けば、基本的に日本国内で施行されているものと同じである。その例外とは、充分な資格のある医師がほとんどいない僻地では、法的資格を満たしていなくても医療許可証が発給されるということだ。

1923 年に朝鮮で正式の医療資格を持つ医師は 1202 人、地方の許

426   MEDICAL, SANITARY, AND SOCIAL SERVICE

doctors with local licenses 86, of doctors of the old Chinese school 5,183, of vaccinators 1,581, of veterinary-surgeons 373, and of patent-medicine vendors 27,923. The last figure is of special interest because it shows an advance of 4,600 over the figure for 1918.

Vital Statistics--

The following table gives the official figures for five years on the matters named:

BIRTHS, DEATHS, MARRIAGES, DIVORCES PER THOUSAND
OF THE POPULATION

		1919	1920	1921	1922	1923
Live Births..	Japanese	23.37	23.25	24.25	24.72	22.89
	Koreans	27.78	27.71	29.85	34.02	40.69
Deaths......	Japanese	21.93	26.06	19.57	22.36	18.88
	Koreans	22.91	23.35	19.80	21.44	20.60
Marriages...	Japanese	1.91	1.85	2.03	2.26	2.30
	Koreans	8.53	8.34	9.12	11.27	14.80
Divorces....	Japanese	0.60	0.20	0.19	0.27	0.23
	Koreans	0.58	0.47	0.42	0.42	0.50

可証をもらった医師は 86 人、旧式中国学校出身の医師は 5183 人、種痘医師は 1581 人、獣医 373 人、特許医薬品販売業は 2 万 7923 人であった。最後の特許医薬品販売業の数は、1918 年から比べて 4600 人も増えているので、特に関心を引く。

人口動態統計
次の表は各項目の 5 年間に亘る公式統計を示したものである。

人口千人当たりの出生、死亡、結婚、離婚者の数

	1919	1920	1921	1922	1923
出生児数					
日本人	23.37	23.25	24.25	24.72	22.89
朝鮮人	27.78	27.71	29.85	34.02	40.69
死亡者数					
日本人	21.93	26.06	19.57	22.36	18.88
朝鮮人	22.91	23.35	19.80	21.44	20.60
結婚者数					
日本人	1.91	1.85	2.03	2.26	2.30
朝鮮人	8.53	8.34	9.12	11.27	14.80
離婚者数					
日本人	0.60	0.20	0.19	0.27	0.23
朝鮮人	0.58	0.47	0.42	0.42	0.50

428   MEDICAL, SANITARY, AND SOCIAL SERVICE

Social Service--

At the time of the annexation of Korea, his late Majesty the Emperor Meiji of Japan authorized the setting aside of 30 million yen from the Imperial treasury for the benefit of his new Korean subjects. Of this sum, 17,398,000 yen was invested as a permanent fund and distributed among various provinces. The interest, amounting to nearly 900,000 yen annually, is devoted to various forms of social service throughout the Peninsula.

The work supported by the interest on the Imperial Donation Funds is divided into three classes—affording a means of livelihood to the poor, education, and the relief of sufferers from flood and drought.

The first branch undertakes work of a fairly wide scope, including the employment of itinerant teachers who give instruction in sericulture, in the making of textiles, paper, and charcoal, and in fishery. Some portion of the revenue is used to supply implements needed in agriculture, sericulture, forest industries, stock-farming, and fishing, and to carry out other social services.

The second branch pays subsidies in the country districts for the encouragement of common-school education.

The third branch affords assistance to calamity-stricken people by supplying them with foodstuffs, seeds, agricultural implements, building materials, and so on. When this kind of relief is not required, the amount allotted to it in the local budgets is allowed to accumulate for future use.

A further Imperial donation was made in 1912 on the demise of the Emperor Meiji, to the amount of 200,000 yen; a third, of 115,000

社会福祉事業

　日韓併合に際して、明治天皇は新しく臣民になる朝鮮人のために、大日本帝国の国庫から3000万円を下賜した。このうち、1739万8000円は恒久的な基金として指定され各地域に配分された。年間90万円にも及ぶ利子は朝鮮の全域で様々な社会福祉事業に使われる。

　帝国寄付基金の利子によって支えられた事業は3つに分けられる。貧困者への生計手段提供、教育、洪水と干ばつの被災者支援である。

　1番目の、貧困者の救済事業はかなり広い範囲を含み、養蚕、織物・紙・木炭の製造、漁業などを教える巡回指導員の雇用なども含まれている。財源の一部は農業、養蚕業、林業、畜産業、漁業などで使われる道具を提供したり、その他の社会福祉事業を実施するのに使われる。

　2番目の教育事業は、普通学校教育推進のために地方に助成金を支給する。

　3番目の洪水と干ばつの被災者支援事業は、災害に襲われた被害者に食糧、種子、農業道具、建築材料などを提供して支援する。このような救済支援が必要でない時は、ここに割り当てられた地方予算は将来のために蓄積される。

　1912年に明治天皇が崩御された時、さらに20万円の帝国寄付金

430   MEDICAL, SANITARY, AND SOCIAL SERVICE

yen in the following year, on the occasion of the death of the Dowager Empress Shoken; and a fourth, of 200,000 yen at the time of the Imperial Coronation in 1915. These funds are in charge of the Government-General, and the annual interest is distributed from time to time for relief work in such districts as require it.

In addition to the foregoing, each public body engages in social relief work, drawing the necessary funds from its own treasury. The principal expenditure is incurred in respect of free medical treatment for the poor, the establishment of public markets under the management of prefectural or village authorities, the erection of lodging houses for laborers and for the unemployed, the maintenance of free public baths, advisory offices, and official pawnshops.

These arrangements are designed to meet the demands of what may be called ordinary public benevolences. Occasionally, however, the country is visited by some wide-spread calamity, when it becomes necessary for the Government to take special measures of relief.

A notable instance of this was the disastrous drought, of almost unprecedented severity, which occurred in 1919. On this occasion the prompt action of the Government prevented the loss of a single life from starvation. The relief measures involved a total expenditure by the Government of ten million yen, which was disbursed as follows: for the purchase and distribution of food, four million yen; for loans to sufferers, 3,600,000 yen; for public engineering works to absorb unemployed labor 2,400,000 yen.

The principal social service institutions under the direct management of the Government-General are:

が寄せられた。その翌年、昭憲皇太后が崩御された時、3度目の寄付金として11万5000円が、そして、1915年大正天皇が即位された時、4度目の寄付金として20万円が提供された。これらの寄付基金は總督府が管理し、年利は適宜、救済支援を必要とする地域に分配される。

　前述の事業に加え、公的機関は各々の財源から必要な資金を引出し社会福祉事業を行う。主な支出は、貧困者への無料医療、道当局などが管理する公設市場設立、労働者や失業者のための宿泊施設建設、無料公衆銭湯の維持、相談所管理と公認質屋の管理などである。

　こうした制度は、日常的公共慈善とでも呼ばれるような、民衆の必要性に応じるものだ。しかし、国が大規模災害に襲われた際は、總督府は特別救済支援をしなくてはならない。

　目立った事例としては1919年に発生した、ほとんど過去に前例のない程深刻で悲惨な干ばつであった。この時、總督府の迅速な対応のお蔭で1人の餓死者も出なかった。總督府が救済支援に掛けた費用は1000万円に上り、うち、400万円を食料の購入と配布に、360万円を被害者への貸付に、240万円を公共事業にあて、失業者の雇用の機会を作った。

　總督府の直接管理でなされる主な社会福祉機関は以下のものである。

432   MEDICAL, SANITARY, AND SOCIAL SERVICE

(1) A Charity Asylum in Seoul (Keijo) to which is attached land to the extent of about 325 acres. The Asylum is divided into two sections, one being concerned with the care and nurture of orphans, the other with the training of the blind and of deaf-mutes.

The orphans who complete the common-school course in the Asylum, and are of suitable physical condition, are as a rule trained as farmers at the Asylum farm. In order to encourage them to work and to provide them with a small fund to start life on when they leave the institution, the children are given an allowance based on the kind of work they have been doing, the time spent at it, the value of the product, and the record of general conduct. In 1921 the average per capita allowance was 37.63 yen.

The blind are usually trained as masseurs, and the deaf-mutes are taught needle-work.

(2) A Government Reformatory at Eiko, near Gensan on the east coast. This was opened in October 1923, with an annual budget of about 35,000 yen. It is called the Eiko School, in order to avoid the unfavorable impression produced by the word "reformatory." The school had sixty-five juvenile delinquents in 1925. Nothing is left undone for their moral, intellectual, and physical development, efforts being made to train them in some manual work, so that they may be capable of earning a livelihood when discharged

(3) The hospital for lepers, at Shorokuto. This is referred to on page 26 of this volume.

The expenditure incurred in 1925 in respect of these institutions was:

（1）ソウル（京城）にある慈善保護施設。ここには、約325エーカーの土地もある。この保護施設は2つの区域に分かれており、一方は孤児の保護と養育、もう一方は盲人と聾唖の訓練をしている。

　保護施設で普通学校課程を修了し健康状態も良い孤児は、原則として施設の農家で働く。働く意欲を持たせるため、また施設を離れる時に新しい生活を始めるための資金づくりのために、孤児たちには手当が支払われる。手当の基準は孤児院でやった仕事の内容、費やした時間、生産物の価値、日ごろの行い、である。1921年に与えられた1人当たりの平均手当は37.63円であった。盲人は普通按摩の訓練を、聾唖は裁縫を教えられる。

（2）東海岸の元山付近の永興にある總督府の感化院。これは約3万5千円の年間予算で1923年10月に開院した。「感化院」という好ましくない印象を与える言葉は避け、「永興学校」と呼ばれた。1925年に学校には65人の非行少年がいた。彼らの道徳的、知的、身体的育成を図るためにあらゆることがなされ、学校を去る時に生計が立てられるように、いくつかの手工作業が教えられる。

（3）小鹿島のハンセン病医院。これについてはこの章の「ハンセン病患者救済事業」で言及してある。

　1925年にこの3施設に掛かった費用は、済生院が8万8899円、

434   MEDICAL, SANITARY, AND SOCIAL SERVICE

for the Charity Asylum 88,899 yen, for the Reformatory 35,571 yen, for the Leper Hospital 54,489 yen. In addition to this direct outlay the Government-General granted subsidies from the State treasury, as follows: for general social service thirty-four thousand yen, for the protection of ex-convicts ten thousand yen; for private leper hospitals 36,400 yen.

A great deal of social service is being done (and has for many years been done) by various religious and philanthropic persons and institutions. Of these private undertakings, most of which receive grants-in-aid from the Government-General there were at the beginning of 1922 a total number of ninety-six. These institutions or associations were of the following classes: hospitals giving medical treatment free of charge 18, hospitals giving medical treatment at cost price 2, school for the blind and for deafmutes 1, for the relief of the families of dead soldiers 1, laborers' lodging house 1, association for social investigations 1, for the relief of orphans and indigent children 14, for the relief of calamity-stricken people 1, for the relief of wayfaring sick and dying 11, for encouraging social service 1, advisory office 1, general relief of the poor 17, for the care and treatment of lepers 3, for the protection and assistance of ex-convicts 23, mutual aid society 1.

Of the foregoing the majority are maintained by Christians of various nationalities—Japanese, American, Australian, English, French, and Canadian. It is estimated that the amount of money contributed yearly by the supporters of these various undertakings exceeds 250,000 U. S. dollars. This, however, is in addition to an immense amount of unpaid service rendered by missionaries and others.

感化院3万5571円、ハンセン病医院5万4489円であった。この直接経費に加え、總督府は以下のように国庫から補助金を支給した。一般福祉サービス3万4000円、前科者の保護1万円、私立ハンセン病医院3万6400円。

多くの福祉事業が（ここ何年にも亘って）、様々な宗教・慈善団体や個人によってなされている。これら民間の事業はほとんどが總督府から補助金を提供されているが、その数は1922年の始めには96あった。これらの機関・協会は以下のカテゴリーに分類された。無料医療を提供する病院18、有料医療を提供する病院2、盲人と聾唖の学校が1、死亡した軍人の家族への救済1、労働者の宿泊所1、社会調査1、孤児と貧困児童の救済14、災害被害者の救済1、旅行中の病気や事故の救護11、社会福祉事業促進1、相談所1、貧困者の一般救済17、ハンセン病患者の介護と治療3、前科者の保護と支援23、共済組合1。

前述のうち大多数は、日本、アメリカ、オーストラリア、イギリス、フランス、カナダなど様々な国のキリスト教者によって維持されていた。これらの事業の支援者から寄付された額は、年間で25万米ドルを超えていると推測される。しかしこれは、宣教師とその他の人々の莫大な無料奉仕に比べれば追加的な部分にしかならないであろう。

CHAPTER XI

第十一章

CHAPTER XI

THE ECONOMIC DEVELOPMENT OF KOREA

I. AGRICULTURE

Historical--

When, in 1910, the Japanese Government decided to annex Korea, it had no military problem to face. The Koreans had indeed an honorable military tradition; but it referred back to a period in the remote past, and under the Yi Dynasty Korea had followed the example of China and become profoundly pacifist.

Japan's immediate necessity at the time of annexation was to formulate a Korean policy of which the effect would be to insure a peaceful acceptance of their rule and to accustom the Korean people to the idea that a more happy and prosperous Korea was to be expected from a modernized Japanese administration than could have been hoped for from the continuance of the native system of self-government, which so far as the mass of the people was concerned was purely chimerical, and had in fact degenerated into a cruel and unscrupulous exploitation of the masses by the classes.

The period of the Japanese Residency-General, 1905-1910—the period of the Protectorate, as it is sometimes called—was an intermediate stage between purely native rule and purely Japanese rule. It was characterized by administrative confusion and by all the half-way measures which are inseparable from an attempt to govern by the method of condominium.

第十一章

経済発展

Ⅰ 農業

農業の歴史

1910年に日本政府が大韓帝国の併合を決定した際、軍事的な問題は何もなかった。確かに朝鮮には立派な軍隊の伝統があった。しかし、それははるか遠い過去の時代のものであり、李王朝時代は中国の例に倣って全くの無抵抗主義となっていた。

日本が併合の時に直ちに必要としたのは、朝鮮の政策を明確に打ち立てることだった。それは、彼らが統治を平和裏に受け入れることを保障するものであり、朝鮮の人々が自分達の自治制度を続けるよりも、近代的な日本の統治の方が、より朝鮮の幸福と繁栄が期待出来るのだと納得するためのものである。自分達による自治など、民衆にとっては全く得体の知れないものであった。実際の所、様々な階級によって民衆が残酷なまでに悪どく搾取されるまでに堕落していたのであった。

統監府の時期である1905〜1910―この期間は時に保護国時期と呼ばれる―は、自治と日本統治の中間的なものだった。それは、共同統治の試みとは切っても切れない行政の混乱と中途半端な手段が特徴として見られるものだった。

The natural tendency of the more powerful and advanced partner in such arrangements is to force the pace of reform; the equally natural tendency of the weaker and, administratively, backward partner is to retard it. The inevitable consequence is to frustrate the efforts of the reformers and to develop a spirit of mutual opposition injurious to every interest in the country.

The broad features of the policy adopted by Japan when, at the time of annexation, she assumed full control and responsibility in the Peninsula, were simple and, in my opinion, well conceived. What the country had suffered most from, what had reduced an intelligent and amiable people to a very low economic status and had made them apathetic toward their own plight, were administrative inefficiency and corruption, a debased currency, the insecurity of property rights, defective civil law, and a venal magistracy. Japan determined to change these conditions. Her efforts in the domains of law, order, and civil administration are described elsewhere in this volume. My present concern is with her economic policy.

Japanese statesmen were far too well informed to expect that their economic policy in Korea, whatever form it might take, would be immune from criticism either by Koreans or by foreign observers. If the Japanese settled in the Peninsula, invested capital there, stimulated commerce, industry, and agriculture, built schools, roads, hospitals, docks, and railroads, established law courts, banks and other credit agencies, agricultural, industrial, and other research institutions —thus adding enormously to the tangible assets of the country and contributing to the health, comfort, and prosperity of its inhabitants—criticism would address

第十一章　経済発展

　このような計画においては、力があり、進歩している方が改革の
ペースを押し付けるのが通例である。一方で、力のない、行政の遅
れている相手の方がその足を引っ張るのも通例であった。当然その
結果として改革者の努力は挫折し、その国にとっての利益を損なわ
せる互いの対立心が育っていくのだった。

　併合の際に、日本が朝鮮半島を全て支配下に置き、全責任を引き
受けることとして採用した政策の大きな特徴は簡潔であることであ
り、またよく練られたものであると私には思われた。朝鮮が最も苦
しんでいたことは、知識人たちや意欲のある人々が非常に低い経済
的地位に追いやられ、しかもその窮状に無感動となっていたことだ。
その原因は、行政の無能であり、汚職であり、通貨価値の下落であ
り、不安定な財産権であり、欠陥のある民法であり、また、金で動
く官吏であった。日本はそのような状況を変えようと決意した。法
や秩序、行政における日本の努力は本書の他の章に述べられている。
この章での私の関心は日本の経済的政策にある。

　日本の政治家たちは状況をよく理解していたので、朝鮮での経済
政策がどんなものであれ、それが朝鮮人や海外の専門家達からの批
判を免れるなどとは思っていなかった。日本人が朝鮮半島に定住し、
そこで資本を投下して、商業や工業、農業を奨励し、学校や道路、
病院、埠頭、鉄道を建設し、裁判所や銀行、その他の信用機関や農・
工業などの研究所を設立するなどして、莫大な有形資産を朝鮮に与
え、朝鮮人の健康や幸福、繁栄に多大な貢献をしたとしても、批評
家たちは、朝鮮の開発は日本人自身の利益のために行っているもの

442 THE ECONOMIC DEVELOPMENT OF KOREA

itself to charging the Japanese with exploiting the country for their own advantage.

If, on the other hand, the Japanese adopted another policy; if they refrained from an investment in its development, left things much as they were under native rule, and contented themselves with turning the Peninsula into an effective strategic frontier, the charge would be made that the Japanese interest in Korea went no further than carrying out the military plans of the General Staff, and that Japanese statesmen were utterly indifferent to the welfare of the Koreans.

Even a superficial knowledge of the history of British, American, French, and Dutch colonial dependencies would suffice to supply instances of the types of criticism to which I have alluded above.

Since the annexation of Korea was, from the standpoint of Japanese national policy, absolutely irrevocable, Japan determined to center its Korean policy around the development of the economic resources of the country. From the improvement in the general living conditions of the Koreans which such a course must inevitably produce it was to be expected, not indeed that opposition to the Japanese occupation would disappear, but certainly that the passage of time would provide convincing evidence of material advantages, of increased educational opportunities, of a broadening social horizon, which the Koreans would recognize as something to be set in the scales of judgment to weigh against the single fact of the loss of their political independence.

Of the total population of Korea about 82 per cent —in round numbers, 14,500,000—are dependent directly upon agriculture for their livelihood. The latest available figures, those for January, 1924, show the following

と非難するに違いなかった。

　一方、もし日本が別の政策をとって、朝鮮の発展のために投資することをせず、旧来の現地統制下の状態のままとし、軍事的な戦略上の前線とするだけだったならば、朝鮮に対する日本の関心は参謀たちの軍事計画を実行することだけで、日本の政治家たちは朝鮮人の福祉には全く関心がないと非難されたことだろう。

　イギリスやアメリカ、フランス、オランダの植民地支配についてのわずかな知識があれば、私が先に述べたような非難の具体例を挙げることが出来るだろう。
　日本の国策として、朝鮮の併合は決して中止することの出来ないものであった。そのため、日本は朝鮮政策の中心を朝鮮の経済的資源の開発と決定した。その結果、当然朝鮮人の生活全般の水準は良くなったのである。
　しかし、それによって日本の占領に対する反発が消えるだろうと期待していたわけではない。しかし時が経つにつれ、物質的な豊かさの向上や、教育の機会の増加、社会の展望の広がりを実感した朝鮮人が、そのことと政治的な独立を失うという唯一の対価と、どちらが良いかを考えるようになると期待したのは確かであろう。
　朝鮮人の全人口の82パーセント、おおよそ1450万人は専業農家である。1924年1月の調査では、出身別の農業人口は次の通りである。
　朝鮮人…………1432万9401人

444 THE ECONOMIC DEVELOPMENT OF KOREA

classification of the agricultural population: Koreans, 14,329,401; Japanese, 38,850; Chinese, 5,378; other foreigners, 17. The number of families engaged in agriculture was 2,702,838. Of these families 1,123,275 were tenant-farmers, 951,667 owned land and occupied other land as tenants; and 627,896 cultivated their own land without renting other land.

The average area of cultivated land per family increased from 2.59 acres in 1910 to 3.92 acres in 1923, whilst the total area under cultivation increased during the same period from 6,039,014 acres to 10,586,117.

The following table shows the area harvested in 1912 and in 1923. When two crops were raised in the same year on the same land the area of each crop is included. The figures are, therefore, considerably higher than those for the area under cultivation, since some areas produced two or more crops.

第十一章　経済発展

　　日本人……………… 3万8850人

　　中国人……………………… 5378人

　　その他の外国人…………… 17人

　農業に従事する世帯は270万2838戸、そのうち112万3275戸は
小作農、95万1667戸は自作農兼小作農、62万7896戸が自作農である。

　一世帯当たりの平均耕作面積は、1910年の2.59エーカーから
1923年の3.92エーカーに増加、同時期の耕作総面積は603万9014
エーカーから1058万6117エーカーに増加している。

　次のページの表は、1912年と1923年のそれぞれの収穫面積を示
している。

　2つの作物が同じ年に同じ土地で収穫された場合には、その地の
面積はそれぞれの作物の面積に加えられている。この表の数字は、
耕作地の実際の面積よりもかなり広くなっている。それは2つ以上
の作物を栽培している土地があるためである。

446 THE ECONOMIC DEVELOPMENT OF KOREA

AREA HARVESTED TO VARIOUS CROPS
(In cho. 1 cho = 2.45 acres)

	1912	1923
Rice	1,417,174	1,550,399
Barley	622,392	813,145
Wheat	267,422	356,269
Naked Barley	45,359	55,178
Beans	841,349	1,525,860
Italian Millet and Maize	634,954	874,517
Oats	53,817	117,312
Buckwheat	70,933*	102,640
True, and Great Millet	92,531	114,912
Deccan Grass	114,114	114,692
Cotton	64,565	158,879
Hemp	21,406	30,743
Sesame	12,726	22,943
Vegetables	87,238	199,035
Manure crops	1,682*	31,316
Paper Mulberry	....	4,992
Korean Rush	1,909	3,227
Total	4,349,571	6,076,099

* Figures for 1913.

The foregoing table omits reference to the area under the silk mulberry, which is dealt with in the section on sericulture, and to the areas under tobacco and ginseng, which are government monopolies and are dealt with under that head in the chapter on financial administration.

The table showing the area under cultivation calls for little comment. The large increase in the area under cotton indicates the success of the experiments conducted by the Government-General in the cultivation of that staple from American cotton seed. The twenty-fold increase in the cultivation of green manure crops reflects the educational work of the Government's agricultural experts.

第十一章　経済発展　　　　　447

様々な作物の収穫面積
（1 町は 2.45 エーカー）

	1912	1923
米	1,417,174	1,550,399
大麦	622,392	813,145
小麦	267,422	356,269
裸麦	45,359	55,178
豆類	841,349	1,525,860
粟とトウモロコシ	634,954	874,517
カラス麦	53,817	117,312
ソバ	70,933*	102,640
大あわ	92,531	114,912
稗	114,114	114,692
綿花	64,565	158,879
麻	21,406	30,743
胡麻	12,726	22,943
野菜類	87,238	199,035
肥料作物	1,682*	31,316
楮	-	4,992
いぐさ	1,909	3,227
合計	4,349,571	6,076,099

＊数字は 1913 年のもの

　この表には、養蚕用の桑についての面積が省略されているが、こ
れについては養蚕業の節で扱われている。また、煙草と朝鮮人参は
政府の専売品なので財政の章で扱われている。

　この耕作面積の表については説明の必要は殆どない。綿花の面積
の大幅な増加は、総督府の指導によるアメリカ綿の種からの繊維生
産実験が成功したことを示している。また、肥料作物の栽培が20
倍に増加しているのは、政府の農業専門員による教育指導の結果で
ある。

448   THE ECONOMIC DEVELOPMENT OF KOREA

Yield of Principal Crops--

Rice, barley, naked barley, beans, Italian millet, maize, and wheat, taken together, account for about 83 per cent of the total area cultivated each year. The yield of these staples during twelve years is given in the following table. The exact equivalent of the koku is 4.9629 bushels. As the table omits quantities less than a thousand bushels, the rate of five bushels to the koku gives a close approximation to the actual quantities.

Owing to the introduction of improved species of grain and to the adoption, under the guidance of Japanese experts, of improved methods of cultivation a steady increase is to be observed in the yield per acre of most of the crops.

YIELD OF PRINCIPAL CROPS
(In thousands of koku. 1 koku = 5 bushels)

Year	Rice	Barley	Beans	Italian Millet-Maize	Wheat	Naked Barley
1912	10,865	5,856	4,733	4,254	1,565	312
1913	12,109	6,717	4,824	5,056	1,809	348
1914	14,130	6,170	4,891	4,517	1,629	299
1915	12,846	6,793	5,224	4,878	1,690	344
1916	13,933	6,537	5,536	5,396	1,770	302
1917	13,687	6,931	5,690	5,766	1,788	389
1918	15,294	7,728	6,521	6,277	1,993	417
1919	12,708	7,270	3,891	4,207	1,670	361
1920	14,882	7,366	6,256	6,662	2,145	348
1921	14,324	7,615	5,979	6,483	2,170	394
1922	15,014	6,820	5,636	5,700	2,057	357
1923	15,175	6,031	5,855	5,841	1,680	346

主要作物の生産

　米や大麦、裸麦、豆類、粟とトウモロコシ、小麦は合わせて、毎年の全耕作面積の約83パーセントを占めている。これらの主要作物の12年間の生産量は以下の表に示している。

　単位の「石」は正確には4.9629ブッシェルである。表では1000石未満の量は切り捨てている。表の1石を5ブッシェルに換算した値は、実数に非常に近いと言える。穀類の改良種を導入し、日本人専門員による指導の下で、栽培の改良法を採用したお蔭で、殆どの作物で、1エーカー当たりの収量が着実に増加していることが認められる。

主要作物の生産量（単位は千石）

年	米	大麦	豆類	粟・トウモロコシ	小麦	裸麦
1912	10,865	5,856	4,733	4,254	1,565	312
1913	12,109	6,717	4,824	5,056	1,809	348
1914	14,130	6,170	4,891	4,517	1,629	299
1915	12,846	6,793	5,224	4,878	1,690	344
1916	13,933	6,537	5,536	5,396	1,770	302
1917	13,687	6,931	5,690	5,766	1,788	389
1918	15,294	7,728	6,521	6,277	1,993	417
1919	12,708	7,270	3,891	4,207	1,670	361
1920	14,882	7,366	6,256	6,662	2,145	348
1921	14,324	7,615	5,979	6,483	2,170	394
1922	15,014	6,820	5,636	5,700	2,057	357
1923	15,175	6,031	5,855	5,841	1,680	346

450   THE ECONOMIC DEVELOPMENT OF KOREA

Value of Agricultural Products--

As in other countries so in Korea the value of agricultural products
varies greatly from year to year in sympathy with the world-market. Thus,
in the absence of any important change in the quantity of production, the
total value of Korean agricultural crops increased by 100 per cent between
1917 and 1920, and decreased by 18 per cent between 1920 and 1923. The
estimated total value of Korean agricultural products during the fourteen
years following annexation is given in the following table:

ESTIMATED VALUE OF AGRICULTURAL PRODUCTS
(In thousands of yen. 1 yen = 50 cents U. S.)

1910	241,721	1917	702,913
1911	355,253	1918	1,103,971
1912	435,116	1919	1,389,219
1913	508,191	1920	1,433,714
1914	458,927	1921	1,097,364
1915	428,769	1922	1,184,934
1916	520,228	1923	1,168,703

In 1923 the total value of agricultural products was distributed as
follows, by percentage: rice 34.3; cattle and other stock 16.2; straw
products 10.0; Italian millet, and maize 8.0; beans 7.1; wheat, barley, and
naked barley 6.3; vegetables 5.9; all other products 12.2.

Sericulture--

The conditions of soil, climate, and labor combine to make Korea a
favorable field for sericulture. This industry has existed for many years
in the country; but prior to the establishment of the Government-General
little attention had been paid to the quality of the silk-worm eggs or to
the proper cultivation of the mulberry plantations. In recent years the

農産物の価格

他の国と同様に、朝鮮においても農産物の価格は、世界市場の傾向によって、その年その年で大きく変わる。そのため、生産量に大きな変化は見られないが、朝鮮の農業作物の価格は 1917 年から 1920 年の間に 100 パーセント増加し、1920 年から 1923 年の間に 18 パーセント減少している。併合後の 14 年間の朝鮮の農業作物の見積価格は次の表に示される。

農産物の生産高見積もり（単位 千円）

年	価格	年	価格
1910	241,721	1917	702,913
1911	355,253	1918	1,103,971
1912	435,116	1919	1,389,219
1913	508,191	1920	1,433,714
1914	458,927	1921	1,097,364
1915	428,769	1922	1,184,934
1916	520,228	1923	1,168,703

1923 年の農産物の合計価格のうちの、それぞれの作物が占める割合は以下の通り。米 34.3%、牛・その他の家畜 16.2%、藁製品 10%、粟とトウモロコシ 8%、豆類 7.1%、小麦・大麦・裸麦 6.3%、野菜類 5.9%、その他の産物 12.2%。

養蚕

土壌の状態や天候、労働力が朝鮮を養蚕に向いた地とした。この産業は既に朝鮮で長い間行なわれていた。しかし、總督府が設立される以前は、蚕の卵の質や桑の栽培法などに殆ど関心が払われていなかった。近年、政府の専門家達が優れた種の卵を持ち込み、桑の

452   THE ECONOMIC DEVELOPMENT OF KOREA

Government experts have done much to advance the interests of this industry, by introducing superior species of eggs, by distributing mulberry seedlings, by giving instruction in the care of silk-worms, the killing of pupae, the drying of cocoons, and so on.

The most recent steps taken in this direction were the establishment of sericultural control stations and of silk-worm egg-sheet preparation stations in each province, and the promulgation of regulations relating to the prevention of diseases, the inspection of egg-sheets, the attainment of uniformity of product, and other matters vital to the success of the silk industry.

In 1910 the number of families engaged in sericulture was about 76,000, producing approximately 70,000 bushels of cocoons; in 1921, 312,000 families were so engaged, and their product amounted to nearly 700,000 bushels of cocoons.

The area under silk mulberry trees has increased from 8,190 acres in 1910 to 78,226 acres in 1923. During this period the yield of cocoons increased from 69,650 bushels to 1,038,560 bushels, whilst the number of families engaged in the industry rose from 76,000 in 1910 to 312,000 in 1921, and to 401,563 in 1923.

苗木を配り、蚕の世話の仕方や、蛹の処理法、繭の乾燥法などの指
導をすることで、養蚕を主要産業とした。

つい先ごろは、養蚕取締所と原蚕種製造所が各道に設置され、病
害防止や蚕の卵が産み付けられた紙の検査、産品の均一性の確保な
どといった、絹産業の発展に欠かせない法令が公布されている。

1910 年には養蚕に従事する世帯は約 7 万 6000 戸で、7 万ブッシェ
ルの繭を生産していた。これが 1921 年になると、31 万 2000 戸の世
帯が従事し、繭の生産量は 70 万ブッシェル近くにもなっている。

桑が植えられた面積は 1910 年の 8190 エーカーが、1923 年には 7
万 8226 エーカーにまで増加している。同時期の、繭の生産量は 6
万 9650 ブッシェルから 103 万 8560 ブッシェルに増加している。一
方、養蚕業に従事する世帯は 1910 年の 7 万 6000 世帯が、1921 年に
は 31 万 2000 世帯、1923 年には 40 万 1563 世帯にまで増えている。

454   THE ECONOMIC DEVELOPMENT OF KOREA

The value of sericultural products has varied greatly from year to year with the ups and downs of the silk market, as disclosed in the following table:

VALUE OF SERICULTURAL PRODUCTS
(In thousands of yen. 1 yen = 50 cents U. S.)

1910	467	1917	8,717
1911	1,205	1918	13,052
1912	1,877	1919	15,605
1913	2,600	1920	11,274
1914	2,954	1921	10,653
1915	3,188	1922	17,008
1916	4,831	1923	24,633

Land Tenure--

In the official statistics the term "landlord" means a person who owns land and works it by the labor of others; the term "peasant-proprietor" a person who owns land and works it wholly or in part by his own labor; a "peasant-proprietor and tenant," a person who in addition to working the land he owns, works other land for which he pays rent to a landowner; and the term "tenant," a person who, having no land of his own, cultivates rented land only. But in this volume classes one and two are grouped together as "landowners," the third is called "landowner and tenant," the fourth "tenant-farmer."

At the beginning of 1924 there were in Korea 627,896 landowners, 951,667 landowners and tenants, and 1,123,275 tenant-farmers. The definitions refer to households, not to individuals. The figures show that of a total of 2,702,838 farming households, 1,579,563 owned the whole or part of the land they cultivated, and 1,123,275 owned no land. That is

第十一章　経済発展

生糸業の生産物の価格はその年その年の生糸市場の好不況に大きく影響されて変動している。その様子は次の表に示されている。

生糸生産額（単位は千円）

1910	467	1917	8,717
1911	1,205	1918	13,052
1912	1,877	1919	15,605
1913	2,600	1920	11,274
1914	2,954	1921	10,653
1915	3,188	1922	17,008
1916	4,831	1923	24,633

土地制度

　行政機関による統計の「地主」という用語は、土地を所有し他者の労働でその地を耕作する者を指す。また「自作農」という用語は土地を所有し、土地の全てまたは一部を自分で耕作する者を指す。「自作農兼小作人」とは自分の土地を耕作し、さらに他の地主の土地を小作料を払って耕作している者である。「小作人」とは自分の土地を持たず土地を借りて耕している者のことである。しかし本書においては地主と自作農を「土地所有者」としてまとめ、自作農兼小作人を「土地所有者兼小作人」、小作人を「小作農」としている。

　1924 年の初めの朝鮮には 62 万 7896 戸の土地所有者、95 万 1667 戸の土地所有者兼小作人、112 万 3275 戸の小作農があった。これは個人数ではなく世帯数である。合計で 270 万 2838 戸が農業に従事する世帯で、157 万 9563 戸が耕作地の全てもしくは一部を所有し、

456   THE ECONOMIC DEVELOPMENT OF KOREA

to say, more than 58 per cent of the families engaged in agriculture owned land, and most of these also rented land and cultivated it.

One of the early acts of the Government-General was to issue an order designed to prevent the formation of large landed estates by the amalgamation of small estates and the gradual squeezing out of the peasant proprietor.

This order worked on the principle of restraining the acquisitiveness of those above. It was supplemented later by two measures designed to assist those in humbler circumstances. One of these was to rent uncultivated State land on easy terms, and when their reclamation had been effected, to transfer them gratis to the cultivators. The other was to assist tenants occupying cultivated State lands to acquire ownership of them by allowing the purchase price to be paid in ten annual instalments.

The Government-General has, however, found it difficult to cultivate a sense of ownership among the tenants. They are inclined to regard the sum charged in addition to the rent of the State lands as a "squeeze," and cannot envisage it as an instalment method of paying for land which will ultimately become their own property, thus eventually extinguishing the annual rent charge.

The prevailing system of tenant-farming rests upon leases for limited periods, perpetual leases being of very rare occurrence. The leases fall into three classes: (1) those in which a fixed rent is agreed upon, regardless of the harvest obtained; (2) those in which the rent is fixed according to the estimate of the standing crop made by the landlord, or by his agent,

112万3275戸は土地を所有していなかった。つまり、農業に従事する世帯のうち58パーセント以上が土地を所有し、その内のほとんどが、さらに土地を借りて耕作していたことが分かる。

　總督府の初めの頃の法令では、小さな私有地を吸収合併して大きな私有地を形成することを抑止していた。これは自作農が圧迫されていくのを防ぐものだった。

　この法令は、土地所有者たちの強い所有願望を抑制するという原則に基づくもので、その後さらに、厳しい状況にいる小作農を援助するように2つの条例の施行によって補完されている。その条例の1つは、未耕作の国有地を負担の少ない条件で貸し出し、開墾が終了したら開拓者に無料で譲渡するものだった。もう1つは、開墾された国有地を借用している小作農が、十年分割で地代を払い、その土地の所有権を得ることが出来るようにしたものである。

　しかし、小作農たちに所有権の意識を持たせるのは容易ではなかった。彼らは国有地の賃貸料に加えて、土地の分割代金が請求されることを「ゆすり」だと思い込んでしまった。土地代を分割して支払って、その土地が最後は自分達のものになるとは思いもよらなかったのである。結局、この年割払いの方式は消えてしまった。

　小作農の制度の中で広く普及したのは、期限付きの借地契約だった。終身契約は殆ど行われなかった。借地契約の種類は次の3つに分けられる。（1）収穫量に関わらず、一定の小作料を払う。（2）小作人が立ち会って地主または代理人が現在育てている作物の収穫量を予測し、それに応じて小作料を決める（地主が自分で予測した

458 THE ECONOMIC DEVELOPMENT OF KOREA

in the presence of the tenant (this system favors the landlord, since his own estimate of the expected crop becomes the basis of the rental, and its adoption is increasing); (3) those in which the landlord and the tenant each take half of the crop.

The tenancy contracts are made each year between the completion of the harvest and the spring following. Landlords are free to change their tenants at any time other than that which lies between the planting of the crop and its harvesting. The usual practice is to allow the leases to run on unless slovenly farming or accumulated arrears of rent afford reasonable grounds for a change.

Korean landlords prefer for the most part to live in the towns, and as a rule they are represented on their rural properties by agents called *Sah-om*. As in other countries the difference between a contented and prosperous tenant and his opposite often depends on the character of the agent; and in Korea as elsewhere these rural agents often yield to those temptations which are presented by their position of authority and by the comparative helplessness of the tenants.

Farm rents are as a rule paid in kind. In cases where the landlord demands cash payments or where the tenant prefers that method, as he may well do if the delivery in kind involves too long a journey, the custom is for the produce to be valued at current market prices, and the amount thus determined represents the cash rental.

Rents vary greatly according to the kind of contract entered into and with reference to the quality of the land. Fixed rents vary between 35 and 50 per cent of the value of the average harvest, but they are lower than this in upland (dry) areas. Rent according to yield ranges between 30 and 70

収穫量が小作料の基準になり地主に有利なため、この方式が増えて
いった)。（３）地主と小作人とで作物を半分に分ける。

　借地権契約は、毎年収穫が終わってから次の春までに交わされた。
地主は作物の植え付けから収穫までの間を除いた期間なら小作人を
自由に変えることが出来た。しかし、いい加減な仕事ぶりや小作料
の度重なる滞納などがなく、通常通りに仕事を続けていくならば、
契約の更新は認められた。

　朝鮮人の地主は殆どの時間を都会で過ごすことを好み、田舎の自
分達の土地には「舎音」と呼ばれる管理人を置いた。他国でも同様
だが、小作人が利益を上げ生活に満足しているのか、その正反対で
あるかは、この舎音の性格によるところが大きかった。また、これ
も他国と同様であるが、大抵の舎音は自分たちを権威者として、小
作人たちに無力な立場を強いる誘惑には勝てなかった。
　一般的に、小作料は現物で支払われた。地主が現金での支払いを
要求するか、あるいは小作人が、現物の配達にかなりの距離を行か
なくてはならないなどで現金払いを望む場合は、作物の市場の時価
から値段を出して、小作料の金額を定めるのが通例だった。
　小作料は契約次第で、また、その土地の質によっても大きく変わっ
た。小作料が固定されたものの場合は、その金額は平均収穫量の相
場の35〜50パーセントであった。しかし、高地（乾燥地域）ではもっ
と低い金額だった。収穫量に応じた小作料の場合は、その作物の見

460   THE ECONOMIC DEVELOPMENT OF KOREA

per cent of the estimated value of the crop. Where the contract is on the basis of halving the crop, an actual division of the produce usually occurs; but this method is modified in practice by agreement between the landlord and the tenant as to who pays the land tax, who pays the cost of seed, and other matters.

Local Korean custom provides for a reduction in the contract rent—in cases where the rent is based on the yield of the harvest—when the harvest falls to 50 per cent or lower of the average yield. It is the common practice to reduce the rent *pari passu* with the reduction of the crop below the average; but if the crop goes below 30 per cent of the average the rent is entirely remitted.

Financing the Farmer--

Twenty years ago almost every phase of the agricultural industry was unsatisfactory. Cultivation was of the crudest, the application to the soil of manure or of chemical fertilizers was as to the former insufficient, as to the latter almost unknown. Farming implements were of a primitive kind, and were in many instances borrowed from the landlord.

In such circumstances the principal need felt by the farmer for credit was for ready money with which to purchase cattle and other stock. For such sums as the farmers were compelled to borrow a very high rate of interest was usually demanded.

During the period of the Japanese Protectorate, 1906-1910, the Korean Government was urged by its Japanese advisers to encourage agriculture by establishing People's Banking Associations, and by taking other steps to supply money at reasonable rates to agriculturalists. A beginning was

積価格の 30 〜 70 パーセントの間だった。収穫物を等分にするという原則の契約の場合は、実際にその収穫物を分け合うのが通例だった。しかし実際には、地主と小作人のどちらが地租や種の料金を支払うかなどといった契約の内容で、配分量は変わっていった。

地方では、小作料が収穫量に基づく契約の場合に、収穫が通年の 50 パーセント以下となった場合には小作料を軽減する慣習があった。収穫が平均をどれくらい下回ったかで、小作料もその割合に合わせて軽減されたのである。さらに、収穫が平均の 30 パーセントを下回った場合は、小作料は全て免除された。

農民への融資

20 年前は、農産業は全ての面で不充分だった。栽培方法は未熟で、肥料は不足しており、化学肥料のことを知っている者などほとんどいなかった。農機具は原始的なものばかりで、大抵の場合は地主から借りていた。

このような状況で、農民たちが最も必要と感じていたのは、牛やその他の家畜を買うための現金の信用貸しだった。農民たちがやむを得ず借りる金額には非常に高い利子が付けられていた。

1906 年から 1910 年の日本の保護国となっていた期間、大韓帝国政府は日本人顧問たちから農業を奨励するように勧められた。農民向けの信用組合を設立するなどして農家に適切な利子で資金を与えるなどの方法をとるようにと言われたのである。しかし農民向けの

462 THE ECONOMIC DEVELOPMENT OF KOREA

made, but it was not until after the annexation that any considerable extension of agricultural credit occurred.

The extent to which agricultural credit has been developed since the annexation is disclosed by the figures showing the volume of outstanding agricultural loans at the end of 1912 and at the end of 1923. In the former year the sum was under five million yen, in the latter it exceeded 134 million.

It is to be noted that this immense increase in agricultural loans does not represent merely a financing of the crops. A very large proportion of the money borrowed is spent on the construction of irrigation works, on the reclamation of waste lands, on the improvement of arable land, and so on. In fact the greater proportion of the loans has been devoted to such purposes, representing a revenue-producing investment.

Official Encouragement of Agriculture--

Since the whole economic structure of Korea rests upon the foundation of agriculture, the improvement of agricultural conditions became, naturally, a matter of earnest solicitude for the Government-General.

The Japanese administration in Korea, being well acquainted with the highly intensive agriculture of Japan, found very broad opportunities for betterment in the comparatively poor agricultural methods of the Koreans.

I am indebted to Mr. T. Hoshino's excellent *Economic History* of *Chosen* for the following summary of the steps taken by the Government-General to further the agricultural interests of the country.

The principal physical conditions of Korea are much the same as those of Japan, being both prominently mountainous, and having other

第十一章　経済発展　　463

融資が普及したのは日韓併合後のことだった。

　併合が表明されて以来、農業への融資は非常に拡大していった。それは、1912 年と 1923 年の農業への貸付金額の数字を見れば分かる。1912 年の合計が 500 万円未満だったのに対し、1923 年の合計は 1 億 3400 万円を超えていた。

　農業への貸付金の急激な増加は、単に作物に対する融資だけではなかった。借り入れられた金額のかなりの割合が灌漑施設や荒地の開拓、耕地の改良といったことに使われた。実際のところ、貸付金は収益を上げていくことに専ら使われていったのである。

公的機関による農業の奨励

　朝鮮の経済構造全体が農業を土台としていたので、当然、農業の改善は總督府の最も懸念する案件となった。

　日本の行政当局は、日本において非常に集約的な農業に精通していたので、朝鮮における比較的貧弱な農法には多様な改良が可能であることが分かっていた。

　以下に、總督府が朝鮮の農業の収益を上げるために採った政策をまとめているが、これには星野徳治氏の著作 "Economic History of Chosen" によるところが大きい。

　朝鮮の主な自然条件は日本にかなり近く、国土の大半を山地が占めていることや、その他の特徴が共通である。朝鮮は人口密度が日

464   THE ECONOMIC DEVELOPMENT OF KOREA

characteristics in common. Korea has a large population, though not half as dense as that of Japan; but it is rapidly increasing with the increasing security of life and property.

A striking feature of Korean agriculture was the extreme extent to which the system of local self-supply was carried. Thus the farmers in the north of the country used to produce sufficient cotton for their needs, although the south was much better suited to that crop. The difficulties of transportation may have furnished a good reason for this in the past; but the extension of roads and railways during recent years has removed every justification for this uneconomic cropping.

The first and most important step taken by the Japanese to improve the husbandry of the Koreans was the establishment of model farms. Of these the largest is that situated near Suwon, about twenty-five miles from Keijo, the capital city. It has branches in different parts of the country; and is officered by a competent staff of Japanese and Korean experts, who occupy themselves with agricultural experiments, with the study of plant biology, and with educational work in all matters relating to agriculture.

The Suwon Model Farm was established in 1906, under the Japanese Residency-General. At the time, an ineffective Korean school of agriculture, commerce, and industry existed in Keijo (Seoul). This was abolished, and an Agricultural and Forestry School was attached to the newly created Suwon Model Farm.

In order to help forward the work of the model farms, seedling stations were established in various parts of the country. The principal function of these stations is to make a local study of the soil, and to distribute seeds

本の半分以下とはいえ、その人口は多く、さらに、生命と財産の安全が高まるにつれて、急速に増加している。

　朝鮮農業の著しい特徴は、極端に一地域での自給自足となっていることである。例えば、綿の生産には朝鮮南部の方がずっと適しているが、北部においても、自分たちの地域で必要な分の綿を生産していた。過去においては、輸送が難しいからという言い訳が成り立っていたかもしれないが、近年の道路や鉄道の延長によって、この不経済な生産の仕方には正当性がなくなっている。

　朝鮮の農業の発展のために日本が行った最初で、しかも最も重要なことは、いくつもの勧業模範場を作ったことだった。農場の中で最も大きかったのが、首都から約25マイル離れた、水原に作られたものである。またこの農場の支場が朝鮮の各所に置かれ、日本人と朝鮮人の専門家たちが有能な職員として赴いた。彼らは、農業試験に従事して、植物生物学の研究を進め、また、農業に関するあらゆることの指導を行った。

　水原勧業模範場は1906年に統監府の下で設立された。当時、京城（ソウル）に農商工業の朝鮮人学校が一校あったが、全く貧弱なものであったため廃止され、新たに作られた水原勧業模範場の併設校として農林学校が設立された。

　また模範場の事業の補助として、種苗場が朝鮮の各所に設置された。その主な仕事は、地域の土壌の研究をし、種や苗を配布することだった。さらに、職員は農民たちに、改良された農機具の使い方

466 THE ECONOMIC DEVELOPMENT OF KOREA

and seedlings. In addition to this, members of the staffs instruct the farmers in the use of improved agricultural implements, in the introduction of new species of crops, in the utilization of waste lands, and in home industries such as the making of matting and other simple commodities for which local resources furnish the raw materials.

The work of the institutions mentioned above is supplemented by the employment of agricultural experts to travel about the country and deliver lectures.

The Government-General has done much to encourage the formation of agricultural associations throughout the country. There are at the present time nearly six hundred of such associations, with a total membership of about three million. In Keijo, the capital city, is the central one, called the Chosen Agricultural Association, which has a membership, including its suburban branches, of more than three thousand persons. Its principal functions are to publish books on agriculture, to answer questions submitted to it, to arrange public lectures and competitive exhibitions, and to grow and distribute seeds. It receives an annual subsidy from the Government-General.

Another important measure undertaken by the authorities was the investigation and regulation of the water supply for irrigation. In former times the Koreans had made considerable use of irrigation by drawing water from ponds and erecting dams across the streams and innumerable ponds and dams were made throughout the Peninsula. But under the blighting influence of the Yi Dynasty most of these works had been neglected to the point where they were almost useless.

を指導したり、作物の新たな品種を導入したり、荒地の利用法や、地元の産品を使ったゴザなどの単純な日用品を作る家内工業などの指導も行った。

上記施設の事業は、国内を移動して講義を行う農業専門家たちを雇うことで補完された。

總督府は、朝鮮全国の至る所で農業の組織化を奨励することに深く関わったのである。現時点で、それらの組織は600近くに達し、会員の総数は約300万人である。首都の京城には、それらの中心組織があり、朝鮮農会と呼ばれた。都市近郊の下級農会を含めると会員の数は3000人を超えた。この組織の主な役割は、農業に関する書籍の出版や、会員からの質問への回答、講演会や品評会の開催、育てた苗の分配であった。朝鮮農会は毎年總督府から補助金を受け取っていた。

政府当局が着手した、もう1つの重要な施策は、灌漑用の水量調査と調整だった。かつて朝鮮では、池や堰から水を引いて灌漑を盛んに行なっていた。池や堰は朝鮮半島の至る所に無数に存在していたが、李王朝における荒廃の影響で顧みられなくなり、殆ど役に立たない状態にまでなってしまっていた。

468   THE ECONOMIC DEVELOPMENT OF KOREA

An investigation made in 1908, at the instance of the Japanese Resident-General, showed that such ponds and dams numbered 6,300 and 20,700, respectively. It was found, however, that only 410 dams and 1,527 ponds were worth restoration. The Government, therefore, drew up a plan to encourage the people to repair these. It gave aid, in the form of subsidies; and by the end of 1918 all had been satisfactorily restored.

Irrigation--

For the purpose of establishing irrigation works on a large scale the authorities encourage the people to organize Water-Utilization Associations. In the *Annual Report on Reforms and Progress in Chosen* for the fiscal year 1921-22 the matter of irrigation is thus dealt with:

The regulations relating to water-utilization associations were promulgated during the protectorate régime, but their stipulations were too simple, and they were soon found to be quite unsuited to the progress of the times, so in July, 1917, new regulations were promulgated. It was found, however, that the farmers in general hesitated to shoulder the responsibility of engaging experts to make investigation, so regulations relating to subsidies to be granted to water-utilization associations were promulgated in 1919, whereby it was possible for any area of over 200 *cho* (about 500 acres) to be investigated by the Government-General on application being made by provincial governors, promoters of water-utilization associations, or by

日本の統監府の要請によって 1908 年に行われた調査によると、池と堰の総数はそれぞれ、貯水池 6300、堰 2 万 700 だった。その内の堰 410 と貯水池 1527 が修復するに足るということが分かったため、政府は修復を人々に奨励する計画を立ち上げた。補助金の形での援助を与えて、1918 年末には全ての貯水池と堰が使用に耐えうるまでに修復することが出来たのである。

灌漑

大規模な灌漑事業を立ち上げる目的で、当局は人々に水利組合を組織することを奨励した。1921 年度の『朝鮮總督府施政年報』の中で、灌漑については次のように述べられている。

水利組合に関する規定は以前の保護国体制でも公布されたが、その規定はあまりにも単純なもので、時代の流れに全くそぐわないものだということが分かった。そこで、1917 年 7 月に新たな規則が公布された。しかしながら、一般に農民たちは調査をするために専門家を雇うという責任を取りたがらないことが分かった。そこで、1919 年に水利組合に対して補助金が与えられるという規定が公布された。それによって、200 町歩（約 500 エーカー）以上であれば、道知事または水利組合の発起人、もしくは組合白体の申請を受けて總督府が調査を行うこ

470 THE ECONOMIC DEVELOPMENT OF KOREA

the associations themselves, and to grant a subsidy, not exceeding 15 per cent of the cost, to works covering (a minimum of) 200 *chobu** [註 1] and exceeding 40,000 yen in cost.

Later on, following on the framing of the scheme for effecting increase in the rice crop in December, 1920, regulations relating to subsidies for land improvement works were promulgated, by virtue of which even private undertakings were favored with subsidies varying from 25 to 30 per cent of the cost according to the kind of work to be done, and at the end of this fiscal year the number of associations actually in working order was 29, operating over an area of 40,600 chobu, while 21 other associations were actively engaged in preparatory or construction works designed to serve an area of over 26,100 chobu, the total expenditure on all these enterprises already amounting to over 31,000,000 yen. There still remain 80 tracts of land awaiting improvement, covering an area of 130,000 chobu.

In 1920 the Government-General drew up a programme to be executed in fifteen years from that year, and work on it is well under way. This aims at the improvement of at least one-half of the total area of uncultivated lands amounting to 800,000 chobu. Among other things the most important is the basic investigation relating to those lands to be improved or reclaimed, whereby the locality and area of the lands, method to be followed, and the estimated cost can be properly determined. In pursuance of this, special experts have been sent to the provinces since 1920, and the area actually explored by them up to the end of this fiscal year is over 3,534,000 chobu.

*A *Chobu* (sometimes written *cho*) is 2.45 acres.

第十一章　経済発展　　　471

と、さらに（少なくとも）200町歩 *[a] の地域で費用が4万円を
超えるものについては、費用の15パーセントを上限として補
助金が与えられることとなった。

　その後、1920年12月の稲作の増収のための事業計画案を受
けて、土地改良への補助金に関する規則が公布された。それに
よって、民間事業も奨励され、その事業内容によって25〜30
パーセントの補助金が与えられた。同年度末には土地改良を実
施している組合は29あり、その面積は4万600町歩、他の21
の組合は2万6100町歩以上の面積について改良工事の準備、
もしくは立案の段階であった。これら全ての事業の総支出額は
すでに3100万円を超えていた。さらに、80の地域が改良事業
を待っている状態で、その面積は13万町歩に及んでいた。

　1920年、總督府は15年計画を立ち上げ、その年から計画は
開始されて現在も進行中である。この計画は、80万町歩に及
ぶ未耕作地の少なくとも半分を改良することを目標としてい
る。それ以外に、この土地の改良・開墾に関して最も重要なこ
とは、この計画によってそれらの土地の所在や面積、開発の手
段、そして費用が正確に分かるということである。計画の遂行
のために、1920年より特別な専門家が各地方に送られ、同年
度末には353万4000町歩以上の土地が実際に調査された。

＊　町歩（町とも記す）は2.45エーカー ＝ 約0.01平方キロ

472   THE ECONOMIC DEVELOPMENT OF KOREA

Irrigation appeals to the common interest of agriculturists and visibly illustrates the facilities afforded by water-utilization associations, so the Government is encouraging their formation while recognizing private undertakings. Since these works affect people in various ways, however, it is provided that official permission for such must be obtained, and the number so far granted is 117, covering an area of over 9,600 chobu.

Agricultural Labor--

Agriculture in Korea is carried on chiefly by hand labor with the assistance of cattle, mechanical appliances being, as yet, little employed. Farm labor is usually self-supplied, that is to say it is provided by the farmer and his family. Unlike Japan, where women furnish much of the field work, the Korean custom has always been that the women do nothing but indoor work; although in recent years the women in some parts of the country are beginning to help their men in the fields.Daily-wage labor is little employed, except by Japanese farmers. The number of these is, however, small, amounting to about 140,000 families in the whole country. Apart from the labor of the farmer and his family, three sources of labor-supply are available:

(1) Farm hands are engaged for fixed periods, ranging usually between one and three years, though extending occasionally to five years. During the period agreed upon the farm hands are treated as members of the family, and are provided with food, lodging and clothing, and an annual

第十一章　経済発展　　　473

　　灌漑施設は農民たち共通の利益に訴え、また、水利組合によっ
てもたらされた設備ということを視覚的に納得させるものであ
る。そこで、政府は水利組合の設立を奨励し、また、私企業の
事業の認可も行っている。これらの事業は様々な形で人々に影
響を与えるので公的な認可を必ず受けなければいけないが、現
在までに117件の事業が認可され、それらの事業地域の総面積
は9600町歩である。

農業労働

　朝鮮における農業は専ら手作業によって行われる。牛の力は借り
るが、機械装置は今のところほとんど使われていない。農作業は通
常自給で賄われている。つまり農民とその家族ということである。
日本では、女性も外に出て農作業を行うが、朝鮮では、女性は屋内
の仕事のみを行うのが昔からの慣習である。それでも、近年では女
性が男たちの野良仕事を手伝う地域も出てきた。

　日給を支払って人を雇うことは日本人農家以外ではほとんど行わ
れておらず、全国でもその総数は14万世帯しかない。農民とその
家族を除けば、労働の供給源は3つの種類に分けられる。

(1) 決められた期間雇われる作男。通常は1〜3年の期間であるが、
時折、5年まで延長される場合もある。その期間中、作男は家族の
一員として扱われ、衣食住が提供され、また、条件によって異なる

474 THE ECONOMIC DEVELOPMENT OF KOREA

money allowance of from 50 to 100 yen, according to circumstances.

(2) Another system is that of *Koji*, or contract-labor. This is in the nature of a labor-tenancy. The tenants contract to supply the necessary farm labor for a certain fixed area. They live rent-free, and are paid, in advance, at rates varying between 10 and 15 yen per tan (about a quarter of an acre) for the area they have contracted to cultivate, though, both in respect of the amount and of the method of payment, the custom varies.

(3) In the southern part of Korea there are farmers' unions—called *Nosha* or *Tuh-re*, whose purpose is to render mutual joint aid in times of emergency, such as flood, when a large number of laborers is suddenly called for.

The usual terms on which the unions furnish labor in such circumstances are that the farmer benefiting by it shall supply the men with food, sake, and tobacco during the time they are working, and pay from ten to fifteen cents per man on each occasion on which the unions furnish such labor.

Broadly speaking the six months from June to November make up the hardest season for agricultural labor, the other six months being occupied with work of a lighter character. The distribution of work throughout the year is as follows:

January, gathering domestic fuel, manuring the autumn-sown wheat fields, straw-work; February, more or less a holiday month associated with the celebration of the Chinese New Year; March, gathering domestic fuel, transporting manure, sowing spring wheat; April, weeding wheat fields, transporting manure, preparing rice beds, sowing vegetable seeds; May,

が50〜100円の年間手当てがつく。

(2) 他に契約労働の形態もあった。小作人はある一定の面積の耕作地について必要な労働を請け負う。宿は無料で提供され、契約を結んだ耕作地の一反（約0.25エーカー）につき10から15円が前金で支払われる。但し、金額や支払い方法については様々な慣習があった。

(3) 朝鮮南部にはノウシャもしくはトゥレと呼ばれる農業組合がある。これは、洪水などの緊急事態で急に大人数の作業が必要になった時などの相互扶助を目的にしたものである。

　組合が労働力を提供する条件としては、助けられた者が働いている男たちに食べ物や酒、煙草を提供し、1人につき10〜15セントほどを支払う、というのが通例であった。

　大まかに言って、6月から11月までの半年は農業労働者にとって最も大変な季節で、残りの半年はより軽い作業に従事する時期である。一年を通じての仕事の配分は次の通りとなる。

　　1月……家庭の燃料用の薪集め、秋に種を播いた小麦畑への施肥、藁で日用品を作る。

　　2月……旧正月の祝いに合わせて大体が休みの季節となる。

　　3月……薪集め、肥やしの運搬、春小麦の種まき。

　　4月……小麦畑の雑草取り、肥やしの運搬、稲の苗床の準備、野

476   THE ECONOMIC DEVELOPMENT OF KOREA

sowing rice beds, tilling the paddy (young rice) fields, gathering grass and other green manure crops; June, transplanting rice shoots, harvesting the autumn-sown wheat, sowing beans and peas; July, transplanting rice shoots, weeding, gathering domestic fuel; August, weeding and other cultivation, gathering domestic fuel, sowing vegetable seeds for the autumn crop; September, gathering domestic fuel, and thinning out vegetables; October, sowing autumn wheat, harvesting rice; November, harvesting rice, gathering and pickling vegetables, delivery of rent in kind; December, manuring wheat fields, thatching, gathering domestic fuel.

The large amount of time devoted to gathering domestic fuel is explained by the circumstance that Korea, like China, has, through the total neglect in former times of every measure for forest conservation, been denuded of nearly the whole of its timber. This subject is dealt with, under the head Forestry, in the following chapter.

菜類の種まき。

5月……稲の苗床への種まき、田を耕し、牧草や他の緑肥の作物を集める。

6月……苗床で育った稲の田植え、秋播きの小麦の収穫、大豆やいんげん豆・えんどう豆の種まき。

7月……田植え、雑草取り、薪集め。

8月……雑草取りと他の作物の栽培、薪集め、秋に収穫する野菜の種まき。

9月……薪集め、野菜の間引き。

10月……秋まき麦の種まき、米の収穫。

11月…米の収穫、野菜の収穫と漬物作り、小作料の現物払い。

12月…小麦畑への施肥、屋根葺き、薪集め。

薪集めの時間がかなり多いのは、朝鮮は中国と同様にこれまでに森林を維持することを全く顧みることがなく、ほとんどの樹木を取り尽くしてしまっていたためである。この問題については、次の章の「林業」の節で取り上げる。

CHAPTER XII

第十二章

CHAPTER XII

ECONOMIC DEVELOPMENT OF KOREA

II. FORESTRY, FISHING AND MINING

Forestry

Historical--

Most of the following data are taken from the *Annual Report on Administration of Chosen, 1922-23*.

For many years the forests in the country were left untended and unprotected, consequently checking the progress of various kinds of industry, so the Government-General took the matter in hand by making investigation from 1911 onward of the State forests offering legal difficulties, by charging local offices with the investigation of forests possessed by private persons, by appointing forestry experts and stationing them in various places to give the people practical guidance in forestry, by leasing State forest lands denuded of trees to those making application under condition of afforesting them (which done, permanent possession is often granted gratis), by giving seedlings to those localities too poor to buy them, by putting a limit on the age, height, and spread of trees to be felled in order to protect immature forests, and by subsidizing the extermination of noxious insects. These measures have not only resulted in the condition of forests undergoing an entire transformation compared with that at the time of annexation, but have also induced in the people in general a

第十二章

経済発展

Ⅱ 林業，水産業，鉱業

林業

林業の歴史

　以下のデータのほとんどは『朝鮮總督府施政年報　大正十一年度』から抜粋要約したものである。

　朝鮮の山林は長年手入れされず、保護もされることなく放置されるままだった。それによって、様々な産業の発展に支障をきたしていたため、總督府はこの問題の解決に着手し様々な計画を実施した。1911 年以降に法的に問題となっている国有林についての調査を行い、私有地となっている山林については、地方政府に調査を命じ、山林の専門家を任命して各地に派遣し、植林の指導にあたらせた。荒れていた国有林は植林をするという条件で、申し出のあった者に造林貸し付けをし（植林を終えた地については山林の所有権の無償譲与もしばしば行われた）、近隣地域の貧しくて苗木の買えない者たちには苗木を提供した。また樹木の生育状態、繁茂状態によって伐採に制限を設けて未成熟な山林を保護し、害虫駆除の補助金の支給なども行った。

482   ECONOMIC DEVELOPMENT OF KOREA

love of arboriculture, thus contributing greatly to the rise of afforestation undertakings among them. For the purpose of providing models for afforestation and of cultivating the local resources, the Government-General has caused provinces and myen to lay out forests, granting them the necessary land, and also made provision for school forests by giving or leasing land gratis for the purpose. Officials and private persons are also encouraged to plant commemoration trees on the third of April, anniversary of Emperor Jimmu, every year, and every other opportunity is seized to encourage the people to effect improvement in forestry.

A close and exact examination being necessary for the drawing up of plans for the future, the forestry-investigating work was expanded, and more specialists were engaged in 1921 to conduct scientific investigation as to the planting, protection, and utilization of forests. In a suburb of Seoul an experimental forestry station was established this year to take charge of the work.

Before annexation there were no written laws worthy of the name relating to forestry administration, save that the felling of trees was prohibited, and even this was more honored in the breach than in the observance toward the latter years of the Yi dynasty, bringing in its train indiscriminate and secret felling, so that destruction of forests went to the extreme. Guided by the Resident-General, the Korean, Government promulgated a Forestry Law and regulations, and these were adopted as they stood by the Government-General, but revision being necessary on account of the lamentable condition of the forests and the progress of the times, new regulations were promulgated in June, 1911, and in 1912 regulations concerning State and private forests were drawn up, and

第十二章　経済発展　　483

　これらの措置により、併合当時に比べ、山林の状況は著しく改善
された。さらに、一般の人々の樹木栽培への関心を引き出し、その
ことが大衆の間に植林事業熱を高めることに大きく貢献していた。
總督府は、植林と地域資源の育成の模範モデルを提供する目的で、
各道や面の役所に対して山林計画を立てさせ、必要な土地を提供し
た。また造林教育のための学校林を準備し、そのための土地を無償
供与または貸与してきた。毎年4月3日の神武天皇祭には、官民と
もに記念植樹が奨励され、その他にも様々な機会を捉えて人々に山
林の改善に励むよう呼び掛けた。

　将来の計画立案のためには綿密で正確な調査が必要であることか
ら調査範囲は拡大され、1921年には専門家を増員し、植林と山林保
全およびその有効活用に関する科学的調査の指導にあたった。また、
この年に首都郊外に調査研究を担う林野試験場が設立されている。

　併合以前の李王朝には、伐採禁止令を除き、林野行政関連の法律
には成文法と呼べるものは存在しなかった。しかもこの法律も、李
王朝末期には伐採禁止の法律を遵守するよりも違反する方が名誉で
あるかの風潮で、見境のない盗伐が横行し、山林破壊は最悪の状態
にまで進んでいた。統監府の指導の下、朝鮮政府は森林令および規
制法をも公布し、それは總督府に引き継がれた。しかし、森林の
状態は悲惨なままで、また森林令は時代に合わせて改正が必要で
あった。そこで、1911年6月に新たな規制法が公布された。さらに
1912年には国有林と私有林に関する新法案が策定され、中央や地方
政府に専門家が配属された。

484   ECONOMIC DEVELOPMENT OF KOREA

experts attached to central and local offices.

State forest lands leased to the people covered an area of about 1,837,000 acres in the year 1921 and about 2,033,000 acres at the end of the fiscal year, 1922-23.

Condition of the Forests--

The total area of forest lands in Chosen amounts to about 39 million acres, or 71 per cent of the total area of the Peninsula, but, as they have long been neglected, the area of standing forests is estimated at about 13,500,000 acres only, and those are mostly found in the remote north and in the eastern highlands. Of the remaining area, about 18 million acres are covered with young trees and about 7,500,000 acres are entirely bare. Even the lands covered with trees show no signs of developing into good forests owing to lack of care and management, yet not only is the demand for material for building and fuel growing greater year by year, but the demand for railway sleepers, telegraph poles, bridge beams, piles used in mining, and wood-pulp is increasing, so the Government is doing its utmost to prevent too great and too indiscriminate a felling of trees, while at the same time pursuing measures to secure their protection and the planting of seedlings to replace the trees felled.

As the north and south of the Peninsula differ widely in climate, many varieties of trees are present. In the basins of the Oryoku and Tumen in the north, and on the higher mountains, the fir, larch, Korean pine, birch, etc., are found, and in the central and upper southern part the Japanese red and black pine, deciduous and evergreen oak, alder, etc., and in the lower southern part the oak, bamboo, etc. The fact that there are as many as 700

1921年に一般に貸与された国有林は約183万7000エーカーであったが、1922年度末には約203万3000エーカーになっていた。

山林の状態

朝鮮の山林総面積はおよそ3900万エーカーであり、朝鮮半島全体の71パーセントを占める。しかし、これらの山林は長い間、荒れるがままに放置されてきたため、成林地面積は1350万エーカーに過ぎないと見積もられ、多くは都市部から遠く離れた北部や東部の高地帯に残存するのみである。それ以外の地域のうち、およそ1800万エーカーは若木ばかりで、約750万エーカーは完全な禿山である。樹木で覆われた山林であっても、保護や管理がされておらず、将来的に上質な山林に育つ見込みはない。しかしながら、年々、建築資材や燃料の需要は増加する一方であり、さらに、鉄道の枕木、電柱、橋の梁、採鉱用の杭、木材パルプなどの需要も増加しているため、政府は乱伐防止に最善を尽くすと同時に、森林の保護を確実にする対策や、伐採された木の代わりとなる苗木の植林を進めている。

朝鮮半島の北と南では気候が大きく異なるため、多様な種類の樹木が分布している。北部の鴨緑江や豆満江の流域や高地帯では、ハリモミ、カラマツ、朝鮮マツ、カバなどが見られ、中部や南部の高地などの地域では、アカマツ、クロマツ、ナラ、クヌギ、ハンノキなどが見られる。そして、最南部の低地ではカシ、シイ、竹などを

486   ECONOMIC DEVELOPMENT OF KOREA

varieties of useful trees in Chosen shows how peculiarly it is suited for afforestation on the very widest scale.

Afforestation--

To carry on the afforestation undertakings conducted at national expense, the slopes of Hakuundo in Keijo and of Botandai in Heijo were utilized in 1907, and later on the cities of Suigen, Taikyu, and Kaijo offered lands for the same purpose. In recent years afforestation of hillsides and waste lands has been taken up to prevent sand-drifts and to afford a future supply of timber, this work for the most part falling to the Lumber Undertaking Station and the branch offices of the Forestry Section, and the area so covered between 1907 and 1922 totaled 13,230 acres, and the number of seedlings planted 16,160,000.

The first afforestation undertaking maintained at local expense was started in Kogen in 1911, and the example being followed, all the other provinces are now engaging in their own afforestation works, the total area of 6,453 acres afforested up to the end of 1921 increasing to 7,698 acres during the fiscal year 1922-3; and the number of seedlings planted from 11,320,000 to 14,229,000.

Plantations maintained by public bodies have made great progress in recent years, and, in addition to undertakings on a small scale by individual capitalists, the Oriental Development Company, and others are also engaging in the work on a large scale and undertaking the development of lands self-planted, and from 1911 to 1922 the area planted by private

目にすることが出来る。朝鮮には、700種もの有用な樹木があり、大規模な造林業に適した地であることが分かるだろう。

造林事業

国費事業としての造林を進めていくため、1907年に京城の白雲洞と平壌の牡丹台の傾斜地が利用されることとなった。その後、同様の目的で、水原、大邱、開城などの都市でも造林事業のための土地が提供された。近年では、傾斜地や荒地での造林に着手し、砂防および将来の木材供給に備えているが、それらは主に営林廠および山林課出張所によって進められており、1907年から1922年までの累積植栽面積は1万3230エーカーに達し、植栽された苗木の総数は1616万本にまでになっている。

地方財源によって賄われる模範造林事業が1911年に江原道で初めて実施され、その後、他の道政府もこれに倣い、現在では全ての道において造林事業が行われている。1921年末までの累計植林総面積が6453エーカーだったのに対し、1922年度中には7698エーカーにまで増えている。植栽された苗木の総数も1132万本から1422万9000本に増加している。

公共団体によって続けられている植林は近年非常な進展を見せており、個人資産による小規模な事業に加えて、東洋拓殖株式会社などの企業は大規模な事業を行い、さらに自生地の拡張という事業を進めている。1911年から1922年までに民間の事業によって植林が

488 ECONOMIC DEVELOPMENT OF KOREA

undertakings measured over 619,000 acres; and the trees planted numbered over 1,024,450,000, showing how energetically the work is being pursued.

Since 1911 the 3rd of April has been regarded as Arbor Day, and on that day trees are planted in commemoration of the Emperor Jimmu. The eleventh Arbor Day in 1921 saw over 16,790,000 trees planted, and the twelfth Arbor Day over 13,850,000, the grand total planted since its institution being over 188,285,000.

In 1907 three seedling plantations were established at national expense, and, following them, local nurseries were established to the number of 310 in all up to the end of 1912, when adjustment of them was effected. The seedlings raised are the Japanese red and black pine, acacia, alder, oak, larch, etc. In the fiscal year 1922-23 the plantations maintained at national expense raised 7,380,000 seedlings, and disposed of 1,730,000 young trees, while those maintained locally raised 26,450,000 seedlings, and disposed of 15,620,000 young trees. Private undertakings accounted for 168,810,000 seedlings and 104,000,000 young trees, those raising over 200,000 seedlings each for sale numbering 68. Of late years afforestation associations have started their own nurseries on a large scale.

Apart from the routine work of research, experimentation, regulation, and inspection, the Afforestation Section of the Industrial Bureau of the Government-General is occupied in carrying out a number of projects in different parts of the country having to do with the planting of forests as a measure of protection against extensive sand-drifting, and for the purpose of conserving the rainfall. As a matter of policy it was decided that work

行われた面積は 61 万 9000 エーカーを超え、植林された樹木の総数
は 10 億 2445 万本以上になり、造林事業がいかに精力的に行われて
いるかが分かる。

1911 年以降、4 月 3 日は植樹祭の日とされ、この日は神武天皇祭
の記念植樹が行われるようになった。1921 年の第 11 回目の植樹祭
には 1679 万本の木が植えられ、第 12 回の植樹祭には 1385 万本を
越える木が植えられた。植樹際が制定されてからの総計は 1 億 8828
万 5000 本以上になる。

1907 年には三カ所の樹苗園が国費で設立されたが、これに倣っ
て、各地で種苗場が設置されるようになり、1912 年末には種苗場の
数は 310 を数えた。種苗場で育てられる苗木は、アカマツ、クロマ
ツ、アカシア、ハンノキ、ナラ、カシ、カラマツなどである。1922
年度では、国費による事業で 738 万の苗木が育てられ、173 万の幼
木が譲渡された。一方、道の費用で経営されている事業では、2645
万本の苗木が育てられ、1562 万本の若木が譲渡された。民間の事業
では、1 億 6881 万本の苗木と 1 億 400 万本の若木を生産し、売却用
に 20 万本以上の苗木を育てているのは 68 カ所であった。近年、造
林組合が独自で大規模な種苗場の経営を開始している。

総督府殖産局山林課は、通常の調査や実験、規制、視察という業
務の他に、朝鮮の様々な地域で、大規模な砂防や、雨水の保水を
目的とした植林計画を実施していた。政府の方針として、こうした
内容の業務は国民の福利という点からも民間事業の手に委ねるより
も、政府主導にすべきであるとしているからである。

490 ECONOMIC DEVELOPMENT OF KOREA

of this character, beneficial as it is to all classes of the people, should be undertaken by Government instead of being left in the hands of private interests engaged in forest industries.

Accordingly an investigation was started in 1919 of the basins of all the larger Korean rivers, and the areas needing conservation works were definitely determined. Working plans have been prepared, calling for operations over a period of years. The financing of these projects is effected by means of subsidies granted by the Government-General to the Provincial bodies concerned, and to private enterprises engaged in the undertaking.

Fishery

The following account of the Korean fisheries is taken from the *Annual Report on Administration of Chosen, 1922-23.*

Chosen has a coast-line over 10,700 miles long, including islands, and her waters are full of life, and the Government-General, since its establishment, has done as much as possible for the development of the fishing industry, so that the value of marine products amounted to 73,960,000 yen in this year, or eight times that at the time of the annexation.

In 1909 laws and regulations relating to fishery were promulgated by the former Korean Government and were later adopted by the Government-General, but as they did not conform to existing conditions and the future prospects of the industry, new regulations were drawn up and put into practice in April, 1912, providing for the granting of permission for exclusive fishing rights over a certain area of water, the circumscription

1919 年、朝鮮の主要な河川の調査が始めて実施され、保全業務が必要とされる地域が確定した。数年に亘る工事を必要とする作業計画が準備され、計画の財源としては、總督府から道地方官庁および事業に参加する民間企業に交付する助成金という形で支給されることとなった。

水産業

　以下の報告は『朝鮮總督府施政年報　大正十一年度』から抜粋要約したものである。

　朝鮮はその属島を合わせての海岸線が 1 万 700 マイルに達し、水産資源も豊富ということで、併合後總督府は漁業の発展に力を注いできた。その結果 1922 年度の漁獲および水産製造高の累計は 7396 万円にもおよび、併合時の 8 倍に相当した。

　1909 年、大韓帝国政府は漁業法および規制を制定し、その後、總督府においても踏襲されたが、現状にも、将来の展望にも即さないということで新たに規制を制定し 1912 年 4 月より実施している。この規定により、一定範囲の漁業権を独占排他的に営むことが可能になり、加えてその隣接海域における漁業の妨害となる行為を制限

492   ECONOMIC DEVELOPMENT OF KOREA

or prohibition of certain acts likely to obstruct fishing in adjoining areas, the granting of permission to applicants according to ancient custom as far as possible, and the prevention of the exercise of a monopoly in any fishing place by a private individual, and their enforcement has checked the tendency for speculation while encouraging applications from such persons as are willing to pursue the work in a steady and progressive way.

For the protection and control of the fishing industry, regulations were promulgated at the same time as those relating to fishery, and placed some restrictions on the methods employed, the tackle used, and the season and place for fishing. Trawling is entirely prohibited in the seas surrounding Chosen, the number of whaling boats is limited, and the number of diving apparatus also. In the days of the former Korean Government Chinese ships frequented the western coasts of Chosen for the purpose of fishing, and occasionally do so now, even in the face of strict prohibition, but the vigilance of the local police and fishing associations has proved a check of late to the visits of these poachers.

In order to encourage development in fishing, as the industry was not carried on to any great extent by the local people, part of the interest derived from the Extraordinary Imperial Donation Funds, together with grants from the local revenues, was spent in giving special training to local fishermen and in providing educational organs for fishery by establishing a fishing school at Kunsan in 1915 and at Reisui in 1917.

As the quantity of aquatic products exported tended to increase year by year, and there was no uniformity in quality of the various products, while dishonest practices were rather common, regulations relating to the examination of aquatic products were promulgated and put into practice in

もしくは禁止することが出来る。免許漁業の出願者に関しては慣行を重んじ、なるべく従来の縁故者に許可する。いかなる魚場においても個人の独占を禁止し、また漁業出願者には投機的目的の傾向を禁止する、着実な漁業を奨励した。

　漁業の保護取り締まりに関しては漁業令の公布と同時に取り締り規制を公布し、漁法、漁具、魚場、漁期についていくつかの制限が設けられた。底引き漁法に関しては朝鮮海域では一切禁止し、捕鯨に関しては捕鯨船の数を、潜水漁業には潜水具の数を制限した。また併合前より中国船が朝鮮西海岸に出没し、厳重な取り締りにもかかわらず跡を絶たなかったが、最近では地方警察官および漁業組合による厳重な警戒が功を奏し密漁者が減っている。

　朝鮮人による水産業は未熟であったため、漁業の発展のために朝鮮漁民を訓練し漁業の知識を授けた。また教育機関として 1915 年に郡山に、1917 年には麗水に簡易水産学校を設立した。水産業教育は臨時恩賜金から得られる利息の一部と地方助成金を基に運営されている。

　水産製品の輸出が年々増加しているにも拘らず、製品の品質が統一されておらず、一方で不正手段が横行するという状況から、『水産製品検査規則』を公布し 1918 年 7 月より実施した。また日本と検査基準を同一にし、水産物の日本への輸出の円滑化を図った。

494 ECONOMIC DEVELOPMENT OF KOREA

July, 1918, and the standard for each grade was made the same as that in Japan proper, so that export to Japan might be carried on more smoothly. The regulations relating to markets promulgated in September, 1914, contained special provisions for fish markets as they were considered somewhat different from ordinary markets, while a government subsidy has annually been granted since the fiscal year 1912 to fishing ports and harbors, numbering about 300 in all, to effect various improvements in them. Of these ports, work on nine of the most important was finished by the end of the fiscal year 1920, and work on others is being taken up on a large scale.

Experiments in Aquatic Products--

In order to promote the development of the fishing industry, the Government-General has been engaging in aquatic experiments since 1912 under three heads: (1) study of the fish frequenting Korean waters with regard to varieties, distribution, coming and going, suitability of methods employed in catching them, and economic conditions; (2) experimental preparation since 1917 of salted and dried fish intended for China and America, and (3) artificial incubation of salmon at Kogen in South Kankyo since 1912 and naturalization of oysters at Koshin in South Zenra since 1918, together with experiments in raising fresh-water fish.

These experiments are still being carried on, and though some of them have already been productive of good results, further practical and scientific investigation and study is necessary for the future development of the fishing industry, so the establishment of an Experimental Fishing Station, as a central organ, was started at Fusan in 1920 and completed this

1914 年 9 月に市場規制を公布し、魚市場は普通市場と同一には扱えないという認識から、魚市場に対し特別な規定を設けた。その一方で 300 にも及ぶ港湾に対し、1912 年度以降、毎年總督府国庫から補助金を支出し状況の改善に努め、1920 年度末までには最も重要な 9 カ所の港について修築を終えている。その他の港に対しても大規模な修築工事を行う予定である。

水産試験

漁業の発展を目的として、總督府は 1912 年より次の 3 部門で水産試験を実施してきた。

（1）水産物の種類、分布状態、回遊状況、漁獲方法の安定性およびその経済性。

（2）1917 年より、中国とアメリカ向けの塩蔵干物の実験的製造。

（3）1912 年より咸鏡南道高原での鮭の人工孵化、1918 年より全羅南道康津でのカキの海水馴化、併せて淡水魚の養殖実験。

以上の実験は今なお続けられているが、すでに成功をおさめたものもある。漁業の今後の発展のためには実用的、科学的な調査研究の必要性が増しており、その中心母体として 1920 年釜山に朝鮮總督府立水産試験所が設立された。

496 ECONOMIC DEVELOPMENT OF KOREA

year.

Development of the Fishing Industry--

As Chosen is a peninsula it has great advantages in the pursuit of fishing, but in the days of the former Korean Government nothing was done to develop it, so progress in it was altogether wanting. This supineness on the part of the Government disappeared on the establishment of the present régime, and much has since been done to bring the industry into a more flourishing condition, so much so that the value of fishing products, which was only 8,100,000 yen at the time of the annexation, increased to 51,000,000 yen in the fiscal year 1923-24, while the value of prepared aquatic products increased from 2,650,000 yen in 1911 to 29,614,000 yen in the fiscal year 1922-23.

As for the fishing methods employed, they were of a most ancient and elementary character, and the Koreans engaged in fishing never ventured far from the coast, but seeing that the Japanese fishermen coming over made use of more profitable methods, they followed their example and gradually began to go farther and farther afield, with the result that steam and motor-boats for the transportation of fish came into use, and fishing was started on a large scale, especially for mackerel, the catch of which was worth over 5,800,000 yen in 1921.

In preparing aquatic products salting and drying were done in a very crude manner, as only the home market was served, but with the coming of Japanese fishermen new methods were introduced, while their more general use was quickened by the institution of the system of examination of fish for export in 1918.

水産業の発展

半島国である朝鮮は漁場としての有利な条件を兼ね備えているに
もかかわらず、以前の政府の無為無策が続き、水産業には進歩の跡
が全く見られなかった。しかし總督府設置によりこうした旧政府の
無関心な態度は消え去り、水産業は著しく発展をとげ、併合当時に
は810万円であった漁獲高が1923年度には5100万円に達した。ま
た1911年当時265万円であった水産製造高も1922年度には2961
万4000円に達した。

朝鮮人の漁法は極めて旧式で幼稚なものであり沿岸漁業の域を出
なかったが、日本人の通漁によりその漁法を目にするにつれて、そ
の有利性を模擬し、次第に沖合漁業に転じ発動機船および魚類運搬
用汽船の使用が増加した。漁業は大規模漁法へと変化し始め、特に
1921年度のサバの漁獲高は580万円に達した。

水産加工としては干物、塩漬けの加工法も粗雑なもので朝鮮内で
のみ販売されていたが、日本から入った最新の加工技術に加え1918
年に輸出製品審査が実施されたことにより、新しい加工法が急速に
広まった。

498   ECONOMIC DEVELOPMENT OF KOREA

The reason why the various aquatic products showed tendency to disappear from Korean waters in the days of the former Korean Government was that no control was exercised over the fishing industry, and it was carried on more or less regardless of time and seasons, in addition to which large sums must be locked up for many years in its pursuit before adequate returns begin to come in. The strenuous efforts of the Government-General, however, have resulted in many undertakings being started, among which the most flourishing is the cultivation of the laver in South Keisho and South Zenra.

As groups of Japanese fishermen were in the habit of coming over to fish in Korean waters, the Chosen Fishery Association League was established at Fusan in 1900 in order to offer convenience to these men, and this effected gradual enlargement in their fishing grounds, and induced more groups to come over. Japanese fishermen making permanent settlement here were found at first only on the coast of South Zenra and South Keisho, but they soon yearly increased in number through government help and gradually found a home in every maritime province. They now number more than 14,200 in all, and have founded forty fishing hamlets containing five or more families, and in conjunction with Korean fishermen are doing much to help on the development of the fishing industry.

Economic Progress of the Fishing Industry--

No phase of the economic development of Korea has shown a more remarkable rate of growth than the fishing industry. In 1912 the value of the catch was, in round figures, eight million yen, in 1923 it was fifty-two

以前の朝鮮政府は水産業に対する保護取り締まりをしなかったために、朝鮮沿海から水産資源が減少傾向にあった。また自然条件を無視した乱獲に加え、利潤を出すためには長期に亘り資金を固定する必要があったために事業が育たなかった。しかし總督府の精力的な努力の結果多くの事業が起業され、中でも慶尚南と全羅南の2道で始められた海苔の養殖は大成功を収めた。

　日本人漁師による朝鮮沿海での通漁が日常化したため、彼らに便宜を図るため1900年釜山に朝鮮通漁組合が設立された。それ以来日本人の漁場域が次第に拡大し、日本人漁師の数も増加した。朝鮮に永住する日本人漁師もおり、定住者は最初慶尚南および全羅南の沿岸に見られるだけだったが、政府の援助もあってその数は年々増加し、彼らは朝鮮沿海の各地に定住するようになった。その数1万4200人以上に達し、5世帯以上が暮らす漁村の数は40カ所にもなった。彼らは朝鮮人漁民と提携し水産業の発達に多大な貢献をしている。

水産業の経済成長
　水産業は朝鮮国内の産業中最も目覚ましい発展を遂げたと言える。1912年の漁獲高は概算で800万円、1923年の時点では5200万円に達した。同じ頃鮮魚の輸出額（90パーセントが日本への輸出で

500 ECONOMIC DEVELOPMENT OF KOREA

million. During the same period the value of fresh fish exported (about 90 per cent going to Japan) rose from 138,000 yen to nine million, the value of manufactured marine products from four million yen to twenty-nine million, and the value of manufactured marine products exported, chiefly to Japan, from 1,500,000 to 14,000,000.

In the order of their market value, as realized in 1923, the principal fish caught in Korean waters were mackerel, sardines and anchovies, pollock, several species of sciaena (known in the United States as redfish, red-horse, red-bass, and channel bass), herring, sea-bream, tunnyfish, cod, and plaice.

Mining

Historical--

The following account of the development of mining in Korea is condensed from pages 85 to 90 of *The Economic History of Chosen* compiled by Mr. T. Hoshino, Manager of the Research Department of the Bank of Chosen.

Precious metals and economically useful metals and minerals are well represented in Korea. The list includes gold, silver, copper, lead, zinc, tungsten, molybdenum, iron, graphite, coal, kaolinite, and siliceous sand.

Until comparatively recent times the mining industry in Korea was conducted on a very small scale. The first mining concession granted to a foreigner was one given to an American, Mr. James R. Morse, in 1896. Other concessions followed, almost all of them being for gold mining. The only other mining activities in the early days were connected with coal

あった）は 13 万 8000 円から 900 万円に跳ね上がり、水産加工品に至っては 400 万円から 2900 万円に達した。また加工品輸出額は 150 万円から 1400 万円に上昇した。

朝鮮沿岸で捕獲される魚の市場価格の順位は 1923 年現在サバを筆頭に、イワシ、カタクチイワシ、スケソウダラ、ニベ（米国では redfish, red-horse, red-bass, channel bass として知られる）、ニシン、タイ、マグロ、タラ、アカガレイの順となっている。

鉱業

鉱業の歴史

以下の朝鮮国内の工業の発展の歴史に関する記述は、朝鮮銀行調査部部長、星野徳治氏編纂の "The Economic History of Chosen" (pp.85-90) の内容を要約したものである。

朝鮮は貴金属類を始め鉱物資源に恵まれている。代表的なものとして、金、銀、銅、鉛、亜鉛、タングステン、モリブデン、鉄、グラファイト、石炭、高陵石、ケイ砂などである。

近年まで朝鮮の鉱業は小規模産業であった。外国人に採掘権が認められたのは 1896 年の米国人ジェイムズ・モルスが最初であるが、それを皮切りに採掘権が認められていった。殆どが金の採掘権であったが、石炭と鉄の採掘も早くから認められていた。採掘権を有

502   ECONOMIC DEVELOPMENT OF KOREA

and iron. These were conducted by a French company, a Korean-American Company, and a small group of Japanese, acting as agents for the Imperial Household.

The mining administration of Korea was extremely ill-managed, deeply corrupted by bribery, favoritism, and the overlapping of the functions of the Korean Court and of the Korean Government. In some cases a concession granted at one time was revoked at another without good reason or compensation, and wantonly bestowed upon a new concessionaire. The mining tax was not only collected by different departments of the government but also by the Korean Imperial Household itself, and often twice over, while the local authorities also imposed an arbitrary tariff. In such circumstances no healthy progress of the mining industry could be hoped for.

On the establishment of the Japanese protectorate in 1905, steps were taken to reform the abuses, and new laws were enacted and put in force in 1906. Enacted to meet urgent needs, these laws left much to be desired; and the mining regulations were amended from time to time until, in 1915, the last mining law was promulgated.

At the end of the protectorate régime (1910) the list of mining concessions showed the holders to be: American, 4 corporations and 4 individuals; English, 2 corporations and 1 individual; Italian, 1 individual. In addition there were several held by Japanese and Americans jointly, and by Koreans and Americans jointly.

Japanese activity in the Korean mining field—apart from a Government coal mine, and two Government iron mines—was unimportant prior to the annexation of 1910. In 1911, however, several important Japanese firms

していた企業はフランス、米韓合資会社がそれぞれ 1 社、皇室代理
人として数名の日本人のみである。

　大韓帝国の鉱業行政は極めて悪質で、賄賂、縁故主義が横行し腐
敗しきっており、裁判所や政府と権限が重複していた。許可された
採掘権が理由なく補償金なしで取り消されたり、新しい採掘者に気
まぐれに与えられてしまうこともあった。鉱業に関する税は、政府
の複数の役所に納税するだけでなく、朝鮮王室にも納税し、それだ
けで 2 度にわたって徴税されることも頻繁に起こった。その一方で
地方当局が独断で使用料も課していた。この様な状況では鉱業の健
全な発展は望むべくもなかった。
　1905 年、大韓帝国が日本の保護国になると、権力の濫用を阻止す
べく新しい法律を制定、翌年には施行され改革へと歩を進めた。し
かしこれらの法律は緊急の事態に応えるために制定されたもので
あったために改善の余地が残り、鉱業規制法は 1915 年に最終案が
制定公布されるまで幾度か修正されてきた。
　1910 年に保護国時代が終わった時点での採掘権所有者は次の通り
である。アメリカ：企業 4 社、個人所有者 4 名　イギリス：企業 2 社、
個人 1 名　イタリア：個人 1 名　加えて日米の共同、米韓の共同所
有が数社あった。
　朝鮮内の鉱業分野に対し、国営の石炭鉱・鉄鉱は別として、日本
はさほど重要視していなかったが、併合後の 1911 年より日本の主
要会社が参入し、それ以後参入する会社が続いた。彼らの関心も、

504   ECONOMIC DEVELOPMENT OF KOREA

entered the field, and in subsequent years they were followed by others. Their activities have been chiefly concerned with coal and iron.

Present State of the Mining Industry--

In order to obtain material for keeping the mining administration in touch with the times and to afford convenience to those operating mines, investigation of mineral deposits was begun as a continuing work for six years in the fiscal year 1911, and was all but completed in the time stated, the only part left undone being in the south, and there investigation was continued for another year and completed in the fiscal year 1917. Reports were published as the various provinces were investigated, much to the benefit of the mining industry in Chosen.

The investigation of mineral products being completed, the men charged with it were transferred in a body to the newly formed Geological Investigation Office in the fiscal year 1918. This office engages in the investigation of the nature of the soil, useful minerals and rocks, water utilization, civil engineering, and the making of maps. As it was estimated that it would take the office thirty years to complete this new work, the staff was increased in the fiscal year 1920 so that the work might be done in half the time, that is in fifteen years.

The post-war business depression seriously affected the mining industry in Korea. The Government-General has undertaken several measures designed to improve conditions. Among these are the encouragement of improved mining methods and of metallurgical technique, and the reduction of taxation on newly established mining rights.

For the past few years, mining products have been yearly on the

主に石炭、鉄に対するものであった。

鉱業の現状

　時代に即した鉱業行政の実施のため、また鉱山経営者への利便性を計るためにも鉱床に関する充分な資料が必要となり、1911年度より6年計画で調査を始めた。調査は南部地域を残して予定通り終了し、残った調査も引き続き行われ、翌年度には終了した。各地の鉱床に関する調査であったため、この報告書は出版され朝鮮鉱業の発展に大いに寄与した。

　鉱山資源に関する調査が終了した1918年度、その調査責任者は新設された地勢調査研究室に配属されたが、その研究所は土壌、鉱物、水資源の活用、土木に関する調査および地図作成を担うことになる。この新たな仕事の完了には30年要すると推定され、1920年度に職員が増員され、15年以内に調査研究を終了する予定である。

　戦後の経済不況は朝鮮鉱業に深刻な影響をもたらしたが、總督府はこの事態の改善にすでに対策を講じ、採掘技術および冶金技術の改善を奨励し、鉱業権の新設への減税を計った。

　この数年鉱業製品は年々増加し、1925年には総額1900万円にも

506 ECONOMIC DEVELOPMENT OF KOREA

increase, the total value reaching nineteen million yen in 1925. Owing to lower prices of commodities and labor on the one hand and to the rise in the market price of gold on the other, gold mining has been especially active of late. Coal mines are also in favorable condition. As a result of recent investigation of coal fields the state and volume of their deposits have been ascertained, and various experiments in the use of Korean coal have led to a wider use of it by the people, so it is expected that coal mining in Korea will make great strides in the future.

A new baryte mine recently discovered in Kogen Province is considered to be one of the greatest of its kind in the world.

The total value of the output of metals and minerals in Korea in 1910 was 6,000,000 yen. In 1918 the value rose to its highest point, of about 31,000,000 yen, reflecting the urgent demand and the high prices of the last year of the European War. In 1921 the value fell to 15,500,000 yen, which represents the normal growth of the industry since 1910.

Classified according to values the output in 1912, 1921, and 1923 was as follows:

VALUE OF THE METAL AND MINERAL OUTPUT IN KOREA

(In thousands of yen. 1 yen = 50 cents U. S.)

	1912	1921	1923
Gold....................	4,580	2,992	3,914
Alluvial gold............	670	359	336
Coal...................	546	3,192	2,750
Iron ore................	156	1,716	1,806
Pig iron................	....	4,829	5,684
Concentrates...........	275	1,489	1,626
Gold and Silver Ore......	3	587	590
Graphite...............	182	209	258
All others..............	228	214	362
Total..............	6,640	15,587	17,326

達した。安価な鉱物資源と労働力に加え金などの市場価格の高騰によるものであり、特に金鉱採掘は近年活発になっている。炭鉱も好調であり、最新の調査結果により石炭の状態と埋蔵量が確認された。また石炭の有効利用に関する実験によって人々の暮らしに様々な形で石炭が利用されるようになってきたため、国内の炭鉱事業は飛躍的発展を遂げるものと思われる。

また最近江原道で発掘されたバライト鉱脈は、世界有数の鉱脈であると思われる。

1910年に国内で産出された鉱物資源の総額は600万円であったが、1918年には最高値の3100万円に達した。これは先のヨーロッパ大戦による差し迫った需要と価格高騰によるものであった。1921年価格は1550万円まで下落したが、これは1910年以降の産業の正常な成長を反映した数値である。

次の表は、1912年、1921年、1923年における各鉱産物の価格を示したものである。

鉱産物の産出額（単位は千円　当時1円＝50セント）

	1912	1921	1923
金	4,580	2,992	3,914
砂金	670	359	336
石炭	546	3,192	2,750
鉄鉱石	156	1,716	1,806
銑鉄	-	4,829	5,684
精鉱	275	1,489	1,626
金銀鉱石	3	587	590
グラファイト	182	209	258
その他	228	214	362
合計	6,640	15,587	17,326

CHAPTER XIII

第十三章

CHAPTER XIII

ECONOMIC DEVELOPMENT OF KOREA

III. COMMERCE, MANUFACTURES, AND BANKING

Currency--

Under the native Korean Government the development of commerce and manufactures had been held back by a combination of adverse conditions. Of these the most important were the deplorable state of the Korean currency and the insecurity of life and property.

The old Korean currency was, in theory, based upon the silver standard; but in practice the Korean mint issued so few silver coins that practically all money transactions were carried out by the use either of copper cash, called *yupchun*, or of nickel coins named *tang-pak* and *tang-oh*, the former nominally worth one hundred cash, the latter worth five cash.

The copper cash were open to two serious objections, one that their actual exchange value against goods depended upon the intrinsic value of their copper content, and varied therefore with the market value of copper, the other that their value was so small that in large transactions the bulk and weight of the payment presented serious difficulties of transportation. Thus when the Japanese army bought timber in the interior of Korea, during the Chino-Japanese War, it had to charter a steamer and fill her completely with copper cash in order to finance the transaction.

第十三章

経済発展

Ⅲ 貿易，製造業，銀行業

貨幣

　かつての大韓帝国政府の下では、数々の悪条件が重なっていたため、貿易と製造業は停滞していた。中でも特に深刻だったのは酷い貨幣の流通状態と民衆の生命・財産の保護がないがしろにされていたことだった。

　古い貨幣は、理論上は銀本位制であった。しかし実際には大韓帝国の造幣局はほとんど銀硬貨を鋳造しなかったため、葉銭と呼ばれる銅貨か、当百銭と当五銭と呼ばれる白銅貨でほとんど全ての現金取引がなされた。当百銭は名目貨幣価値が100文で、当五銭は5文であった。

　銅貨には2つの大きな問題があった。1つは、物に対する実際の交換価値が本来の銅の価値によって決まるため、銅の市場価値次第で変化してしまうこと、もう1つは、銅貨の価値が非常に低かったため、大きな取引には重く大量の硬貨が必要となり、持ち運びが大変に不便だったことである。日清戦争中、日本軍が朝鮮半島の内陸部で木材を購入する際には、蒸気機関車を借り切り、銅貨でいっぱいに満たして取引したという。

The nickel coinage, on the other hand, was a token coinage, stamped with a nominal value. Originally minted by the Korean Government to serve as a currency auxiliary to the copper *yupchun* it circulated for a short time at its face value. But the difference between the intrinsic and the face value of these coins made their issue a very profitable business, so that finally the Royal Korean Mint issued them indiscriminately, with the result that their face value ceased to have any significance. The final abandonment of the old Korean nickels was hastened by the rapid growth of counterfeiting. A curious feature of this activity was that it was countenanced by the Korean officials, in consideration of bribes paid by the coiners, and that the official dies of the Royal Mint were sometimes rented to counterfeiters.

The following account of the Japanese reform of the Korean currency is condensed from the Government-General's *Annual Report for the Fiscal Year 1910-11.*When a Japanese financial adviser was engaged by the Korean Government in 1904, during the war with Russia, he caused the Korean Government to adopt the following measures of currency reform:

(1) The monetary standard of Korea was to be made identical with that of Japan. In order to effect this, the Currency Regulations, modeled on the Japanese Gold Standard Regulations and issued by the Korean Government in 1901, were to be put in operation.

(2) The old nickel coins were to be withdrawn from circulation, while the old copper cash were to remain in use for the time being.

(3) As soon as a sound subsidiary coinage was put in circulation the old copper cash were also to be withdrawn.

(4) The Dai-ichi Ginko (the First Bank, of Japan) which already enjoyed

第十三章　経済発展

一方、白銅貨は額面価格を刻印した代用硬貨であった。もともと李王朝が葉銭銅貨の補助的な貨幣として鋳造したもので、額面価値で短い間だけ流通していた。しかし銅本来の価値と額面価値に差があるため白銅貨の鋳造はとても収益が高く、そのため典圜局（てんかんきょく）は見境なく鋳造し、遂には額面価値を失うことになってしまった。大韓帝国では白銅貨は偽造の急増も後押しして、ついに破棄されるに到った。面白いことに、偽造は貨幣鋳造者から賄賂を受け取っていた朝鮮の役人から容認されており、また帝国鋳造機関の公認鋳型は時折偽造者に貸し出されていた。

下記の朝鮮貨幣に関する日本政府の改革は、『朝鮮總督府施政年報　明治四十三年』から要約したものだ。1904 年、日露戦争時に大韓帝国政府が雇用した日本人財務顧問により政府は以下の貨幣改革政策をとることとなった。

(1) 朝鮮の貨幣本位は日本と同じくすること。それには、日本の金本位制度に基づいて大韓帝国政府が 1901 年に発令した貨幣条例を実施すること。

(2) 旧白銅貨は流通から外し、旧銅貨は当分流通させる。

(3) 健全な補助硬貨が流通され次第、旧銅貨も廃止する。

(4) 朝鮮ですでに広く信頼されている第一銀行に、中央銀行として

514   ECONOMIC DEVELOPMENT OF KOREA

extensive credit in Korea, was to be allowed to discharge the functions
of a central bank, and its notes were to be recognized as legal tender in
all transactions, public or private. The currency of the Imperial Japanese
Government, whether coined money, or bank-notes, being identical in
quality with that provided for in the Currency Regulations of the Korean
Government, was to be legal tender throughout the Peninsula.

(5) The currency readjustment was to be carried out by the Dai-ichi
Ginko, under the supervision of the Minister of Finance of the Korean
Government.

As a first step toward currency reform, the Royal Korean Mint was
closed in November, 1904, and the work of issuing a new coinage for
Korea was entrusted to the Imperial Japanese Mint in Osaka.

The withdrawal of nickels and of copper cash began in July, 1905,
and by February, 1911, nearly four hundred million nickels had been
withdrawn, and copper cash to the value of about six million yen. The total
net cost of getting rid of the chaotic monetary system of the old Korean
Government and of replacing it with one identical with the gold-standard
system of Japan was less than eight million yen—an extremely small price
to pay for the manifold advantages of a stable currency.

At the beginning of 1918 it was estimated that the value of coinage in
circulation in Korea was 69,600,000 yen, of which less than three million
yen were represented by the old Korean coinage. On April 1, 1918, the
Coinage Law of Japan was enacted in Korea, and the circulation of Korean
coins was prohibited as from the first day of 1921, the Government
engaging to exchange them for Japanese coins during the five succeeding

第十三章　経済発展　　　　515

　の役割を許可し、その発行した紙幣は公的私的全ての取引に
　おいて法定通貨として認めること。大日本帝国政府の貨幣は
　硬貨も紙幣も、大韓帝国政府の貨幣法令の定める同等の質を
　保持していれば、朝鮮半島全土に於いて法定通貨とすること。
(5)　通貨再調整は政府の財務大臣の監督の下、第一銀行によって行
　われること。

　通貨改革の第一歩として、典圜局は 1904 年 11 月に閉鎖され、朝
鮮の新しい貨幣鋳造は大阪の日本帝国造幣局に委託された。
　白銅貨と銅貨の回収は 1905 年 7 月に始まり、1911 年 2 月には、
およそ 4 億個の白銅貨と、約 600 万円相当の銅貨が回収された。大
韓帝国政府の無秩序な貨幣制度を取り払い日本の金本位制度と同等
な制度に変えるのにかかった実費は 800 万円以下だった。これは安
定した通貨がもたらす種々の利点を考えれば、非常に小さなコスト
であった。

　1918 年の初め、朝鮮で流通していた貨幣は 6960 万円で、そのう
ち古い朝鮮貨幣が占めていたのは 300 万円以下と推定された。1918
年 4 月 1 日、日本の貨幣法が施行され、朝鮮貨幣の流通は 1921 年
元日から禁止されたが、政府はその後 5 年の間日本の貨幣と交換し
続けた。

516   ECONOMIC DEVELOPMENT OF KOREA

years.

Bank-notes were first issued in Korea in 1902 by the Dai-Ichi Ginko. Three years later these notes were made legal tender in the Peninsula. On the establishment of the Bank of Chosen in 1909 the note-issue privilege was transferred to it. In 1912 the value of Bank of Chosen Notes in circulation was approximately 25 million yen, and of metal currency four million yen. At the beginning of 1922 these values had risen, respectively, to 101 million yen and nine million yen.

With the settlement of the currency question and the rapid progress made after the annexation of 1910 in the suppression of banditry throughout the country, conditions speedily became such as to encourage the investment of Japanese capital in the Peninsula, and the planning of a general development of the country's resources.

第十三章　経済発展　　517

　銀行券は、朝鮮では1902年に初めて第一銀行によって発行された。これらは3年後には朝鮮半島の法定通貨となった。1909年、朝鮮銀行が設立され、紙幣発行権が朝鮮銀行に移された。1912年、流通していた朝鮮銀行の紙幣の価値は総額約2500万円で、硬貨は400万円であった。1922年の初めには、紙幣が1億100万円、硬貨が900万円に増えていた。

　通貨の問題が解決し、1910年の併合後に国中の匪賊が素早く鎮圧されると、朝鮮半島への日本からの投資と、半島の資源開発の計画が大きく促進されることとなった。

518   ECONOMIC DEVELOPMENT OF KOREA

Economic Development--

The broad features of this development, so far as they relate to commerce and manufactures are disclosed in the following table, in which banking statistics are included as an index to the volume of financing:

GROWTH OF COMMERCE, MANUFACTURES, AND BANKING IN KOREA, 1912–1923

(In thousands of yen. 1 yen = 50 cents U. S.)

	1912	1923
Commerce:		
Value of exports....................	20,985	261,665
Value of imports...................	67,115	265,790
Total foreign trade................	88,100	527,555
Manufactures:		
Factory products...................	29,362	242,788
Home products.....................	10,431	179,207
Banking:		
Paid-up capital....................	14,851	84,150
Reserve funds.....................	699	16,771
Deposits..........................	27,837	275,879
Loans.............................	58,070	409,302

Commerce

The Foreign Trade of Korea--

The geographical position of Korea as the close neighbor of the most advanced commercial nation in the Far East has led naturally to the predominance of Japan in the foreign trade of the country. It is interesting to note that the annexation of Korea by Japan in 1910 has not been followed by any striking increase in the proportion of Korea's foreign trade enjoyed by the sovereign power. In 1907 Japan's share of the foreign trade of Korea was 70.7 per cent; in 1921 it was 78.5 per cent. During that

経済開発

　貿易と製造業に関する経済開発の大まかな特徴は以下の表にまとめてある。この表には、融資額の指標として銀行業の統計が含まれている。

貿易・製造業・銀行業の発展 1912-1923
（単位は千円　当時 1 円＝ 50 セント）

	1912	1923
貿易		
輸出額	20,985	261,665
輸入額	67,115	265,790
対外貿易総額	88,100	527,555
製造業		
工場生産品	29,362	242,788
家内生産品	10,431	179,207
銀行業		
払込資本金	14,851	84,150
積立金	699	16,771
預金	27,837	275,879
貸付金	58,070	409,302

貿易

朝鮮の対外貿易

　極東で最も発達した工業国である日本の近隣国であったため、朝鮮の対外貿易相手は、自然と日本が主となることとなった。

　興味深いことに、1910 年の併合後、朝鮮の対日貿易の割合は大きく増えてはいない。1907 年度の大韓帝国の対外貿易では日本が全体に占める割合は 70.7 パーセントで、1921 年度は 78.5 パーセントであった。この 14 年間で、朝鮮の輸出に占める日本の割合は全体の

520   ECONOMIC DEVELOPMENT OF KOREA

fourteen-year period the value of Korean exports to Japan increased from a proportion of 76.3 per cent of the total to 90.4 per cent, and the proportion of Korean imports from Japan decreased from 68.4 per cent to 67.3 per cent of the total.

THE FOREIGN COMMERCE OF KOREA

Value of exports to and of imports from various countries

(Values in thousands of yen.   1 yen = 50 cents U. S.)

	1907	1912	1921
Japan:			
Exports...................	12,948	15,369	197,392
Imports...................	28,293	40,756	156,482
Total...................	41,241	56,125	353,874
China:			
Exports...................	3,220	4,058	19,223
Imports..................	5,577	7,027	50,188
Total...................	8,797	11,085	69,411
United States:			
Exports...................	2	95	302
Imports...................	2,919	6,460	14,374
Total...................	2,921	6,555	14,676
Great Britain:			
Exports...................	11	198	4
Imports...................	4,210	9,801	7,808
Total...................	4,221	9,999	7,812
All others:			
Exports...................	792	1,265	1,356
Imports...................	386	3,070	3,529
Total...................	1,178	4,335	4,885
Grand total:			
Exports...................	16,973	20,985	218,277
Imports...................	41,387	67,115	232,381
Total...................	58,360	88,100	450,658

76.3 パーセントから 90.4 パーセントに増え、朝鮮の輸入に占める日本の割合は全体の 68.4 パーセントから 67.3 パーセントに減っている。

朝鮮の外国貿易　各国に対する輸出入額
（単位は千円　1円＝50セント）

	1907	1912	1921
日本			
輸出額	12,948	15,369	197,392
輸入額	28,293	40,756	156,482
総　額	41,241	56,125	353,874
中国			
輸出額	3,220	4,058	19,223
輸入額	5,577	7,027	50,188
総　額	8,797	11,085	69,411
アメリカ			
輸出額	2	95	302
輸入額	2,919	6,460	14,374
総　額	2,921	6,555	14,676
イギリス			
輸出額	11	198	4
輸入額	4,210	9,801	7,808
総　額	4,221	9,999	7,812
その他			
輸出額	792	1,265	1,356
輸入額	386	3,070	3,529
総　額	1,178	4,335	4,885
合計			
輸出額	16,973	20,985	218,277
輸入額	41,387	67,115	232,381
総　額	58,360	88,100	450,658

522   ECONOMIC DEVELOPMENT OF KOREA

These contrary movements are to be explained as to exports by the heavy investment of Japanese capital in Korea and by the large demand in Japan for Korean products, whether for domestic consumption or for export. So far as Korean imports are concerned, the increase in non-Japanese imports reflects the increased demand in the Peninsula for commodities which Japan is not able to supply, particularly for Italian millet, wild cocoons, fertilizer, coal, petroleum and hemp cloth, most of which come from China.

Distribution of Foreign Trade--

The distribution of this commerce on the basis of the percentage of it carried out by the various countries trading with Korea is shown in the table on page 524.

Gold and Silver Bullion--

The following tables do not include the value of gold and of silver bullion. The export of the latter is insignificant, not having reached a value of 40,000 yen in any year since 1919.

The export of gold bullion reached a value every year from 1910 to 1916 second only to that of rice, rising from about nine million yen in the former year to over fifteen million in the latter.

Gold production was, however, seriously affected by the Great War, and the value of its export fell to six million yen in 1918.

During the years noted the value of the export of gold bullion has been as follows: 1919, 4,415,249 yen; 1920, 23,822,078 yen; 1921, 7,282,742 yen; 1922, 3,961,154 yen; 1923, 5,586,985 yen.

第十三章　経済発展　　　523

　このような相反する動きは、輸出に関しては、日本の資本による韓国への多額の投資と、国内消費用であれ輸出用であれ、韓国製品に対する日本での大きな需要によって説明される。朝鮮の輸入に関して言えば、日本以外からの輸入が増えたのは、日本が提供出来ない商品に対する需要が朝鮮半島で増えたためである。特に粟、野蚕繭、肥料、石炭、石油、麻布などが、主に中国から来ている。

対外貿易の割合
　様々な国との貿易の割合は 525 ページの表にまとめてある。

金と銀
　以降の表には金塊と銀塊の額は含まれていない。銀塊の輸出額はわずかで、1919 年より 4 万円に達した年はない。

　金塊の輸出額は 1910 年から 1916 年の間は米の輸出額に次ぎ 2 位を占め、1910 年の約 900 万円から 1916 年には 1500 万円以上に増えた。

　しかし、金の生産は第一次世界大戦によって深刻な影響を受け、1918 年には、輸出額が 600 万円に落ちている。

　金塊輸出額は以下のとおりである。

1919 年	441 万 5249 円
1920 年	2382 万 2078 円
1921 年	728 万 2742 円

524 ECONOMIC DEVELOPMENT OF KOREA

It may be noted that Korea furnishes nearly half of the total gold production of the Japanese Empire. The two largest gold mines in Korea are owned by American companies. They produce about 61 per cent of the total output.

PROPORTION OF KOREA'S FOREIGN COMMERCE CONDUCTED WITH VARIOUS COUNTRIES

(The figures refer to the percentage of the value of exports, of imports, and of the total foreign commerce)

	1907	1912	1921
Japan:			
Exports	76.3	73.2	90.4
Imports	68.4	60.8	67.3
Total	70.7	63.8	78.5
China:			
Exports	19.0	19.4	8.8
Imports	13.5	10.5	21.5
Total	15.1	12.6	15.4
United States:			
Exports	00.0	00.5	00.1
Imports	7.1	9.6	6.1
Total	5.0	7.4	3.2
Great Britain:			
Exports	00.1	1.0	00.0
Imports	10.2	14.7	3.3
Total	7.2	11.4	1.7
Other countries:			
Exports	4.6	5.9	00.7
Imports	00.8	4.4	1.8
Total	2.0	4.8	1.2

1922 年	396 万 1154 円
1923 年	558 万 6985 円

朝鮮が大日本帝国の金の生産の約半分を供給していることに注意したい。なお朝鮮の二大金山はアメリカの会社が所有するもので、そこで全体の約61パーセントを生産している。

朝鮮の貿易額に各国が占める割合
（数字は輸出、輸入、総額それぞれについてのパーセンテージ）

	1907	1912	1921
日本			
輸出額	76.3	73.2	90.4
輸入額	68.4	60.8	67.3
総　額	70.7	63.8	78.5
中国			
輸出額	19.0	19.4	8.8
輸入額	13.5	10.5	21.5
総　額	15.1	12.6	15.4
アメリカ			
輸出額	0.0	0.5	0.1
輸入額	7.1	9.6	6.1
総　額	5.0	7.4	3.2
イギリス			
輸出額	0.1	1.0	0.0
輸入額	10.2	14.7	3.3
総　額	7.2	11.4	1.7
その他			
輸出額	4.6	5.9	0.7
輸入額	0.8	4.4	1.8
総　額	2.0	4.8	1.2

526 ECONOMIC DEVELOPMENT OF KOREA

General Character of the Export Trade--

Considerably more than half of the value of Korean exports is represented by agricultural products, of which rice is more important than all the other items added together. The development of the various branches of the export trade is shown in the following table:

VALUE OF KOREAN EXPORTS
(In thousands of yen. 1 yen = 50 cents U. S.)

Products	1912	1917	1923
Agricultural............	14,758	50,048	160,378
Industrial..............	1,054	5,780	33,944
Fishery................	1,163	5,142	29,080
Mineral................	1,086	13,514	11,380
Forest.................	155	392	7,209
Miscellaneous...........	2,767	8,879	19,674
Total..............	20,985	83,755	261,665

The foregoing table covers a period of eleven years. It discloses an almost unparalleled record of economic development. I am by no means convinced that economic development is any criterion of the general advance of the society which has enjoyed, or suffered, from it. But, in respect of Korea, it may be said that, if we are to believe the boosters and rotarians, who form so large a proportion of the people who are giving its present tone to Western civilization, the Japanese administration in Korea has done more to advance the interests of Korea than any other government has done to advance the interests of any country in the world within the period with which the above table deals.

輸出貿易の一般的特徴

農作物は朝鮮の輸出額の半分を大幅に上回り、特に米の輸出額は、その他の農産物を全て合わせた額よりも重要である。様々な分野の輸出の進展は以下の表のとおりである。

朝鮮の分野別輸出額 (単位は千円　当時 1 円＝ 50 セント)

	1912	1917	1923
農業	14,758	50,048	160,378
工業	1,054	5,780	33,944
漁業	1,163	5,142	29,080
鉱業	1,086	13,514	11,380
林業	155	392	7,209
その他	2,767	8,879	19,674
合計	20,985	83,755	261,665

上記の表は 1912 年から 23 年までの 11 年間の統計であるが、他に例を見ないほどの経済発展を示している。私は経済発展が、それによって恩恵を受けようが受けまいが、社会の進歩を示す基準になるということに、決して納得しているわけではない。しかし朝鮮に関しては、西洋文明に現在の色合いを与えている人々のうち、非常に大きな割合を占める支援者やロータリークラブ会員を信じるならば、日本の朝鮮統治は、上記の表が扱っている期間中、他のどの政府が世界のいかなる国に対して行ったよりも、韓国の利益を増進させたと言える。

528   ECONOMIC DEVELOPMENT OF KOREA

That Korean agricultural exports should have increased in little more than a decade by more than a thousand per cent; industrial exports by more than three thousand per cent, fishery exports by nearly three thousand per cent, forestry exports by more than four thousand per cent, and mineral exports by more than a thousand per cent, would, if Korea were a selfgoverning country instead of a Japanese colonial dependency, be hailed throughout the Western world as an astounding example of national progress.

General Character of the Import Trade--

The total value of imports into Korea in 1923 was 265,790,000 yen. The following table shows the values of the imported articles which, individually, represented as large a proportion as 2 per cent of the total value of imports in any of the years covered by the table:

VALUE OF PRINCIPAL ARTICLES IMPORTED INTO KOREA

(In thousands of yen. 1 yen = 50 cents U. S.)

	1912	1917	1923
Cotton shirting, sheeting, and drill	9,744	14,459	23,616
Yarns and threads............	2,537	5,751	14,373
Italian millet.................	273	1,324	13,313
Clothing and accessories........	1,652	2,233	12,030
Coal........................	1,525	3,598	9,599
Lumber, various...............	2,263	1,803	7,905
Machinery....................	*	4,663	6,877
Chinese cloth.................	1,485	2,210	5,181
Silk tissue...................	1,383	841	7,742
Sugar........................	1,506	2,303	4,995
Medicines....................	336	1,048	4,198
Kerosene....................	1,770	2,651	4,171
Cement......................	659	1,685	4,147
Manure (bean-cake)...........	*	140	7,300

* Value too small to have separate item in import returns of 1912.

第十三章　経済発展　　529

　朝鮮の農業分野の輸出増加は 10 年強以内に 1000 パーセント以上
である。工業の輸出が 3000 パーセント以上、漁業の輸出が約 3000
パーセント、林業の輸出が 4000 パーセント、鉱業の輸出が 1000 パー
セント以上も増加したということは、もし朝鮮が日本への植民地的
依存ではなく独立した国であったならば、西洋の国々から驚異的な
国家発展の例として称賛されていただろう。

輸入貿易の一般的特徴

　1923 年の朝鮮への輸入総額は 2 億 6579 万円であった。以下の表
は記載してあるいずれかの年において、個々で総輸入額の 2 パーセ
ント以上を占めている品目の金額を示している。

朝鮮への主な輸入品の金額（単位は千円　1 円＝ 50 セント）

	1912	1917	1923
綿織物・敷布・亜麻布	9,774	14,459	23,616
織物用糸・縫い糸	2,537	5,751	14,373
粟	273	1,324	13,313
衣類・装飾品	1,652	2,233	12,030
石炭	1,525	3,598	9,599
木材（多種）	2,263	1,803	7,905
機械	＊	4,663	6,877
中国産の布	1,485	2,210	5,181
絹の薄い織物	1,383	841	7,742
砂糖	1,506	2,303	4,995
薬剤	336	1,048	4,198
灯油	1,770	2,651	4,171
セメント	659	1,685	4,147
肥料（豆かす）	＊	140	7,300

＊印は個別の項目にするには額が小さすぎるもの

530   ECONOMIC DEVELOPMENT OF KOREA

The contrasts between the figures for 1912 and those for 1923 disclose several interesting features of the general progress of the country. Especially noteworthy, as reflecting the improvement of agricultural methods, is the fifty-fold increase between 1917 and 1923 of the importation of bean-cake manure. The general economic advance of the Korean people is shown by the following increases in certain imports between 1912 and 1923: cotton shirting, etc., 260 per cent; yarns and threads, 470 per cent; clothing and accessories, 628 per cent; sugar, 233 per cent; kerosene, 135 per cent; medicines, 1,149 per cent. Of course these increases do not represent a net increase in Korean home consumption, as much of the material is used in manufactures of which the product is exported; and further, the general advance in prices means that the increases in volume are less than the increases in values. But, with such deductions made, the figures do unquestionably indicate a considerable general advance in the Korean standard of living.

第十三章　経済発展

　表の1912年と1923年の数値の違いは、朝鮮の全体的発展につい
ていくつかの興味深い特徴を表している。特に注目すべきは、1917
年から1923年の間に50倍も増加した豆かすの肥料の輸入である。
これは農業技術の進歩を反映している。

　朝鮮人の一般的経済発展は1912年から1923年の数項目に亘る輸
入の増加から見てとれる。綿織物など260パーセント、織物用糸と
縫い糸470パーセント、衣類と装飾品628パーセント、砂糖233パー
セント、灯油135パーセント、薬剤1149パーセント。もちろん、
これらの多くが製品を輸出する製造業者の製造材料として使われる
ので、その増加が朝鮮人家庭の消費の純増加を表すものではない。
さらに、物価の上昇を考慮すれば、価格の増加ほどには量が増加し
ているわけではないことを意味する。しかし、これらのことを差し
引いても、この数値は朝鮮の生活水準がかなりの全般的発展を遂げ
たことを疑いなく示している。

532   ECONOMIC DEVELOPMENT OF KOREA

Manufactures

As the relations between Japan and Korea became closer after the Chino-Japanese War, the question arose as to whether it was advisable to encourage the development of manufacturing industries in the Peninsula, Opinion was sharply divided on the matter. On the one hand were those who advocated every possible increase in the raw products, and especially of the agricultural products of Korea, and the continued dependence of the country upon the importation of manufactured products from Japan.

On the other hand there were many Japanese, of whom Count Terauchi, the first Governor-General of Korea, was the most prominent, who held the view that it was to the best interest of Korea that she should develop manufacturing industries of her own. The principal argument advanced on this side was that in the absence of manufacturing industries Korea would face a constant and increasing adverse trade balance.

This view prevailed. That it was amply justified is proved by the event. As the Korean manufacturing industries have grown, so the value of the excess imports has decreased, proportionately, in relation to the value of the total foreign trade. In 1912 the excess import-value over export-value was 46 million yen on a total foreign trade value of 88 million yen; in 1923 it was only 4 million yen on a total foreigntrade value of 527 million yen. In other words, the ratio of excess-import value to total foreign-trade value, fell during the ten-year period from 52 to 100 to less than 1 to 100. To the encouragement of manufacturing industry and of commerce in general the Government-General has devoted considerable sums of money. The expenditure falls under two heads—one including the salaries, traveling and other expenses of the personnel engaged in administrative

製造業

　日清戦争後、日本と朝鮮の関係がより近くなってから、朝鮮半島で製造業発展を促すことが妥当であるのかどうか、という疑問が浮上してきた。この点についての意見は明確に分かれた。一方は朝鮮の原産物、特に農作物を可能な限り増やし、製造品については、朝鮮は引き続き日本からの輸入に頼るべきだ、とする意見だ。

　他方で、製造業を自国で発達させることは朝鮮にとって得策であると考える日本人が多くおり、朝鮮の初代總督である寺内伯爵は最も顕著にこの考え方を支持していた。この考え方の主な論拠は、朝鮮は製造業がなければ絶えず貿易不均衡に直面し、それが大きくなっていく、ということだ。

　この考え方が優勢だったが、そこに充分な正当性があったということは次の事実によって裏付けされている。朝鮮の製造業が大きくなるにつれ、外国貿易総額に対する超過輸入額は比例的に減っていった。1912 年では外国貿易総額は 8800 万円で、貿易収支において輸入金額が輸出金額を 4600 万円上回っていたが、1923 年には外国貿易総額は 5 億 2700 万円で、貿易赤字はわずか 400 万円であった。言い換えると、過剰輸入の外国貿易総額に対する割合は、10 年で、52：100 から 1：100 以下に減ったのだ。

　製造業と貿易を全般的に促進させるため、朝鮮總督府は莫大な費用を注ぎこんだ。支出は 2 つのカテゴリーに分けられる。1 つは製造業と貿易活動に関連する管理事業や政府中央研究所で研究に従事

534   ECONOMIC DEVELOPMENT OF KOREA

business connected with manufacturing and commercial activities, and in

the research work of the Government Central Laboratory; the other grants-

in-aid, of various kinds. The expenditure on this acount is shown in the

following table:

GOVERNMENT EXPENDITURE TO FOSTER COMMERCE
AND MANUFACTURES
(Figures in yen. 1 yen=50 cents U. S.)

Year	Salaries and Expenses	Grants-in-Aid	Total
1912.	358,606	311,732	670,338
1913.	414,458	216,451	630,909
1914.	627,925	218,396	846,321
1915.	746,345	323,396	1,069,741
1916.	385,365	323,396	708,761
1917.	367,060	30,146	397,206
1918.	518,138	30,396	548,534
1919.	650,069	101,500	751,569
1920.	752,835	110,518	863,353
1921.	1,024,328	219,000	1,243,328
Total.	5,845,129	1,884,931	7,730,060

In 1912 there were in Korea 328 private manufacturing plants, equipped

with mechanical power and employing more than five hands as a daily

average. The capital invested in these factories was 13,000,000 yen, the

number of operatives 17,000, the total horse-power of the equipment was

8,000, and the value of the year's production was 29,000,000 yen. The

European War gave a great impetus to the local manufacturing industries.

In 1921 the number of factories had risen to 2,384, the invested capital to

179,000,000 yen, the number of operatives to 49,000, the horsepower to

86,000.

In order to get an accurate picture of the progress of manufactures in

Korea it is necessary to divide the industrial products into three classes

—home products, factory products, and factory-treated products. The

している職員の給料、旅費とその他の費用、もう1つは種々の補助金である。これらの支出は以下の表にまとめてある。

貿易と製造業発展のための政府支出
（単位は千円　1円=50セント）

	給料と諸費用	補助金	合計
1912	358,606	311,732	670,338
1913	414,458	216,451	630,909
1914	627,925	218,396	846,321
1915	746,345	323,396	1,069,741
1916	385,365	323,396	708,761
1917	367,060	30,146	397,206
1918	518,138	30,396	548,534
1919	650,069	101,500	751,569
1920	752,835	110,518	863,353
1921	1,024,328	219,000	1,243,328
合　計	5,845,129	1,884,931	7,730,060

　1912年、朝鮮には、機械を備え1日平均5人以上雇用している民間製造工場が328あった。これらの工場に投資された資金は1300万円、職人数は1万7000人、施設の総馬力は8000馬力、年間生産額は2900万円であった。ヨーロッパの戦争は現地の製造業に大きな弾みを与えた。1921年には、工場の数は2384に、投資資金は1億7900万円に、職人数は4万9000人に、総馬力は8万6000に増えた。

　朝鮮の製造業の発展を正確に理解するには、工業製品を3つのカテゴリーに分ける必要がある。それは、家内工業製品、工場生産品、工場加工生産品である。1番目の家内工業製品は家庭で作られた物

536 ECONOMIC DEVELOPMENT OF KOREA

first includes products made in the people's homes; the second, products in which the factory treatment to which they are subjected represents, as against the cost of the raw material, the principal item in determining the selling price, products such as fats and oils, straw and bamboo goods, liquors, and so on; the third, products where the cost of the factory process is small as against the cost of the raw material treated, processes such as rice-cleaning and polishing, the production of gas and electricity, the refining of various raw materials.

The value of home products rose from 10 million yen in 1912, reached a high point of 212 million in 1919, and fell to 179 million in 1923. The value of factory products rose from about 7 million yen in 1910 to 82 million in 1923. The value of factory-treated products rose from 29 million yen in 1910 to 242 million in 1923.

Taking these three classes of products and combining their values, the total value of manufactured products rose from about 40 million yen in 1912 to 421 million in 1923—an increase of 952 per cent. It is interesting to note that home products which in 1912 accounted for only about 25 per cent of the total value of manufactures, accounted for more than 40 per cent in 1923.

This reflects, no doubt, the influence of the industrial training schools and of the Government-General's encouragement of home industries.

In the order of their importance, as measured by the values in 1923, the principal home products were: liquors, 38 million yen; textiles, 23 million; straw articles, 20 million; tissue manufactures, 20 million; metal-ware, 8 million; flour, 8 million; fertilizers, 7 million; yeast, 5 million; wooden-

第十三章　経済発展　　537

を指す。2番目の工場生産品は、原料のコストそのものよりは工場
での処理が売値を決定する製品、例えば、油脂や石油、麦わらや竹
製品、酒などである。3番目の工場加工生産品は、原料のコストに
対して工場での処理費用が安いもの、例えば精米、ガスや電気生産、
種々原材料の精製などである。

　家内工業製品は1912年の1000万円から1919年の2億1200万円
の高額に上り、1923年には1億7900万円に下がった。
　工場生産品は1910年の700万円から1923年の8200万円に増えた。
　工場加工生産品は1910年の2900万円から1923年の2億4200万
円に増えた。
　これら3つのカテゴリーの生産品を全て合わせると、生産品の総
額は、1912年の4000万円から1923年の4億2100万円に増加して
いる。これは952パーセントの増加である。面白いのは、1912年に
生産品総額の25パーセントしかなかった家内工業製品が1923年に
は40パーセント以上を占めていたことだ。
　これは、疑いなく、工業訓練学校と總督府の家内工業促進の影響
を反映している。
　1923年の価値に基づく計算で重要な順に並べると、主な家内工業
製品は以下のようになる。酒3800万円、織物2300万円、麦わら製
品2000万円、薄い織物2000万円、金属製品800万円、小麦粉800
万円、肥料700万円、酵母500万円、木製品500万円、陶磁器400

538   ECONOMIC DEVELOPMENT OF KOREA

ware, 5 million; ceramics, 4 million; cakes, 4 million; silk cocoons, 3 million.

In the two categories of factory-products and factory-treated products the principal items were, in 1923, as follows: cleaned rice, 108 million; tobacco, 22 million; ginned cotton, 8 million; iron, 9 million; gas and electricity, 8 million; lumber, 7 million; sugar, 6 million; printed matter, 6 million; raw silk, 5 million; refined metals, 5 million; cotton-yarn, 5 million; machinery and implements, 5 million; drugs, 3 million; pottery, tiles, bricks, etc., 3 million.

Banking

Historical--

The first bank to be established in Korea was the Fusan branch of the Dai-Ichi Ginko (First Bank of Japan). This was opened in 1878 at the time when the ports of Gensan and Chemulpo were opened to foreign trade. Some years later two other Japanese banks, the Eighteenth Bank, and the Fifty-eighth Bank (now the One Hundred and Thirtieth Bank) opened branches in Korea.

It was not until 1899 that the first Korean bank was established, the Chyon-il, and a second, the Hansung Bank, opened its doors in 1901.

Prior to the opening of the banks referred to above there had been no banks in Korea, as we understand the term. What money-lending was done, apart from purely personal transactions, was in the hands of pawnbrokers, small loan associations called "Mutual Money Accommodation Societies," and inn-keepers. These agencies received money on deposit at interest,

万円、お菓子 400 万円、絹の繭 300 万円。

　工場生産品と工場加工生産品の 2 つのカテゴリーでは、1923 年の主な製品は以下の通りだ。精米 1 億 800 万円、煙草 2200 万円、綿繰り機で種を取った綿 800 万円、鉄 900 万円、ガスと電気 800 万円、木材 700 万円、砂糖 600 万円、印刷物 600 万円、生糸 500 万円、精製された金属 500 万円、綿糸 500 万円、機械・器具 500 万円、薬 300 万円、陶器・瓦・煉瓦など 300 万円。

銀行業

銀行業の歴史

　朝鮮半島で最初に設立された銀行は、第一銀行の釜山支店であった。これは 1878 年、元山と済物浦の港が外国貿易のために開港した時に出来た。

　数年後、他 2 つの日本の銀行、第十八銀行と第五十八銀行（後の第百三十銀行）がその支店を朝鮮半島に開いた。

　1899 年に、やっと朝鮮最初の銀行である大韓天一銀行が設立され、1901 年には 2 番目の銀行である漢城銀行が設立された。

　それらの銀行が開業する前は、我々が理解しているような銀行は朝鮮にはなかった。単なる個人的取引を除いては、貸金業は質屋や「相互資金融通組合」と呼ばれる小口貸付組合、あるいは宿の経営者によってなされていた。これらは利子付きで預入金を受け取って

made loans, and discounted promissory notes.

Bank notes were first issued in Korea in 1902 by the First Bank. At that time the general economic condition of the country was very unsatisfactory. This led to the appointment, in 1904, of a Japanese financial expert as adviser to the Korean Government. In the following year the First Bank was entrusted with the duty of adjusting the chaotic monetary system and of conducting the business of the national Korean treasury. This bank was also granted the privilege of issuing paper money, and it thus became the first central bank of Korea.

In the following years various steps were taken to improve credit and banking facilities.

Among these the more important were the establishment of agricultural and industrial banks in the provinces, the issuance of regulations for the formation of People's Banking Associations, and the creation of the Oriental Development Company.

This Company was formed as a joint-stock enterprise of which the shares could be held only by Japanese and Koreans. In its general character it was concerned chiefly with the agricultural development of the country and with securing suitable agricultural immigrants from Japan. It was specifically authorized by the Government of Korea to undertake the following forms of financial business: the loan of funds to Japanese and Korean agriculturists, on the instalment plan of repayment; making fixed-time loans on the security of immovable property; and loans to settlers and farmers in Korea on the security of their produce and their movable property.

The following account of banking in Korea from 1908 onwards is

貸付をし、約束手形を割り引いて売ったりした。

1902年に第一銀行によって初めて朝鮮で銀行券が発行された。その頃、一般経済の状況は大変不調であったため、1904年に日本人の金融専門家を大韓帝国政府の顧問として任命することになった。翌年、第一銀行は混乱した貨幣制度を調整し、大韓帝国国庫の業務を行う任務を与えられた。第一銀行は紙幣を発行する特権も与えられたので、朝鮮の最初の中央銀行ともなった。

その後数年は、貸付と銀行取引環境を向上させるために様々な措置がとられた。

その中でもより重要な措置は、地方での農工銀行の設立、金融組合設立のための法令の公布、東洋拓殖株式会社の創立であった。

東洋拓殖株式会社は、株式を日本人と朝鮮人のみが保有出来る共同資本事業として設立された。一般的特徴として、この会社は主に朝鮮半島の農業開発と日本からの適切な農業移民の確保を目的とした。特に大韓帝国政府から以下の金融事業を行うことを許可された。

・日本人と朝鮮人の農業経営者に返済の分割払いの計画の下に資金の貸付をすること

・不動産を担保に一定期間の貸付を提供すること

・農作物と動産を担保に移住者と農民に貸付を提供すること。

1908年以降の大韓帝国の銀行業務について次に説明する。これは

542 ECONOMIC DEVELOPMENT OF KOREA

condensed from a Government Report.

By 1908 the general economic and financial development of Korea had advanced to such an extent that it was found inconvenient to conduct the treasury business of the Korean Government, and the issue of paper money through an ordinary bank, even though it was *de facto* a central bank.

Accordingly in 1909 the Korean Government promulgated regulations under which late in the year the Bank of Korea (now called the Bank of Chosen) was established, as a de jure central bank, and assumed the duties and responsibilities which had formerly rested with the Dai-Ichi Ginko.

In 1910 Korea was annexed to Japan. This step affected the banking situation to the extent that whereas formerly the banking activities of Koreans had to be conducted under the local Korean laws and those of Japanese in the Peninsula under the Imperial Japanese laws, it now became possible, as it became also highly desirable, to make a single body of banking law for Korea.

Various laws and regulations were put in force from 1912 onward and they are now contained in four instruments—the Bank of Chosen Law, the Industrial Bank Ordinance, the Bank Ordinance, and the People's Banking Association Ordinance.

Encouraged by the financial expansion promoted by the industrial development, and especially influenced by the World War, many banks have been established in the provinces, but the existing agricultural and industrial banks were found much too weak to cope with the increasing demand for funds, their capital all told being only 2,600,000 yen, so to remedy this weakness the Chosen Industrial Bank Regulations were promulgated in 1918, and all the agricultural and industrial banks in the

政府の報告書からまとめたものである。

1908 年までには朝鮮の全般的経済・金融に発展が見られ、朝鮮政府の国庫事業並びに、紙幣の発行を一般銀行が行うことに不都合が生じてきた、たとえ事実上の中央銀行であってもである。

それ故、1909 年、大韓帝国政府は、韓国銀行（現在は朝鮮銀行と呼ばれる）を合法的な中央銀行として同年後半に設立し、以前第一銀行が担った義務と任務を担うことを定めた法令を公布した。

1910 年、大韓帝国は日本に併合された。以前は、朝鮮人の金融活動には現地の法律が、半島にいる日本人の金融活動には大日本帝国の法律が適用されていたが、併合により単一の銀行法によって規制されることが非常に望まれ、またそれが可能となった。

1912 年以降、様々な法律と法令が施行されたが、それらは現在 4 つの法律文書に含まれている。朝鮮銀行法、殖産銀行令、銀行令、金融組合令、である。

世界大戦による追い風の影響もあり、産業発展に伴う金融拡大により、地方に多くの銀行が設立されたが、既存の農工銀行は資本金の規模も 260 万円にすぎず、増え続ける資金需要には到底応じられそうもなかった。この問題を解決するため、1918 年に朝鮮殖産銀行令が公布され、朝鮮半島の全ての農工銀行が資本金 1000 万円の朝鮮殖産銀行に併合された。政府は工業事業への資金提供を促進する

544 ECONOMIC DEVELOPMENT OF KOREA

Peninsula were merged into the Industrial Bank of Chosen with a capital of 10,000,000 yen, and to this the Government is giving special protection and supervision with the object of facilitating the supply of funds for industrial undertakings.

The regulations concerning People's Banking Associations were revised in 1918 for the benefit of smaller banking organs established to meet the needs of the peasantry, and the wider establishment of such associations in villages was encouraged. In the towns, too, the establishment of associations of similar character for the benefit of small traders was encouraged.

These associations have formed federations according to their geographical distribution, so that any excess or deficiency of funds may be the more easily adjusted. Each federation supervises the business of the associations in the same province, and the Government has extended aid to them by lending each one a sum of 200,000 yen. They are required to maintain connection and co-operate with the Industrial Bank of Chosen in facilitating monetary circulation in the provinces.

Banking Statistics--

The banks included in the general banking statistics are the Bank of Chosen, the Chosen Industrial Bank, and Ordinary Banks (20 in number in 1923, with 64 branch offices in Korea) which operate under the terms of the Bank Ordinance. This law is, in respect of banking rules and Government supervision, based in the main on the banking regulations in force in Japan.

The following table shows the general condition of banking in Korea

目的で特別な保護と監督を行っている。

　金融組合に関する法令は、小作農のニーズに応えるための小規模銀行機関に便宜を図るため1918年に改正され、地方レベルで多くの金融組合を作ることを促した。都市部でも小規模商人たちに便宜を図るため、同じような組合を作ることが奨励された。

　これらの組合は地理的に近いもの同士で連合会を結成し、資金の過不足の調節がより簡単に出来るようにした。各連合会は同じ道にある組合の業務を監督し、政府は各連合会に20万円を貸し付けて支援した。連合会は地方での金融流通を円滑にするため、朝鮮殖産銀行との連携、協力関係を維持することが定められた。

銀行統計
　一般銀行統計には朝鮮銀行、朝鮮殖産銀行、そして銀行令に基づいて業務を遂行する普通銀行（1923年時点で朝鮮には20の普通銀行と64の支店がある）が含まれている。この銀行令は、銀行規律と政府の監督に関しては、主に日本で施行されている銀行法に基づいている。

　次の表は1924年までの10年間の朝鮮内の銀行の全般的状況を示

546   ECONOMIC DEVELOPMENT OF KOREA

during the ten years ending with 1924. The figures do not include the data in relation to the banking operations of the Oriental Development Company, or of the People's Banking Associations, to which reference will be found in later sections of this chapter.

BANKING STATISTICS OF KOREA
(In thousands of yen. 1 yen = 50 cents U. S.)

Year	Paid-up Capital	Reserve Funds	Deposits *	Loans	Net Profits
1910.....	7,080	362	18,355	40,912	540
1915.....	18,484	1,426	35,626	60,554	1,542
1916.....	17,545	1,621	43,716	69,364	1,858
1917.....	23,225	3,043	53,912	96,188	2,462
1918.....	38,066	3,796	84,649	140,338	5,193
1919.....	60,003	6,508	125,265	270,647	5,626
1920.....	83,050	10,083	139,357	230,696	10,253
1921.....	83,423	12,531	171,891	307,260	10,901
1922.....	84,650	14,145	168,171	301,393	9,542
1923.....	84,000	15,478	216,522	395,288	7,478
1924.....	84,150	16,771	275,879	409,302	7,666

* In Korea.

It will be noted that the ten-year period ending with 1924 showed an increase of approximately 370 per cent in paid-up banking capital, of 1,000 per cent in reserve funds, of 666 per cent in deposits, of 580 per cent in loans.

The Bank of Chosen--

This bank occupies a special position in Korea. It is the fiscal agent of the Government-General of Chosen, and enjoys the exclusive right of issuing bank notes. It was founded in 1909 under the name of The Korean

している。この数値には東洋拓殖株式会社と金融組合の銀行取引に関するデータは含まれていない。それについてはこの章の後半部分を参照されたい。

朝鮮の銀行統計
（単位は千円　1円＝50セント）

	払込資本金	支払準備金（積立金）	預金 *	貸付金	純利益
1910	7,080	362	18,355	40,912	540
1915	18,484	1,426	35,626	60,554	1,542
1916	17,545	1,621	43,716	69,364	1,858
1917	23,225	3,043	53,912	96,188	2,462
1918	38,066	3,796	84,649	140,338	5,193
1919	60,003	6,508	125,265	270,647	5,626
1920	83,050	10,083	139,357	230,696	10,253
1921	83,423	12,531	171,891	307,260	10,901
1922	84,650	14,145	168,171	301,393	9,542
1923	84,000	15,478	216,522	395,288	7,478
1924	84,150	16,771	275,879	409,302	7,666

＊ 朝鮮内

1924年までの10年間で、払込資本金は約370パーセント、支払準備金は1000パーセント、預金は666パーセント、貸付金は580パーセント増加したことに注目したい。

朝鮮銀行

朝鮮銀行は特別な位置にある。この銀行は朝鮮總督府の財務機関であり、銀行券の独占的発行権を持つ。朝鮮銀行は1909年に韓国

Bank. After the annexation of 1910 it was renamed the Bank of Chosen. The Governor and the Vice Governor of the Bank are appointed by the Imperial Japanese Government. Until September, 1924, the supervision of the Bank was in the hands of the Government-General of Chosen, and the directors were appointed by the Governor-General from among candidates elected at a general meeting of the shareholders, such candidates to be twice the number of directors to be appointed. On that date, however, the supervision was transferred to the Imperial Japanese Government, and the appointment of directors placed in the hands of the Japanese Finance Minister.

The main features of the bank's condition during the four years ending with 1923 are shown in the following table:

BUSINESS OF THE BANK OF CHOSEN

(In thousands of yen. 1 yen = 50 cents U. S.)

	1920	1921	1922	1923
Paid-up capital	50,000	50,000	50,000	50,000
Bank-notes issued...	114,034	137,611	101,658	110,750
Deposits:				
In Korea.........	46,920	39,028	42,036	95,586
In Japan.........	69,930	69,681	76,021	25,866
In Manchuria.....	28,129	34,005	32,518	31,487
Elsewhere........	15,642	19,777	9,835	9,891
Total..........	160,621	162,941	160,410	162,830
Loans:				
In Korea.........	77,232	90,183	66,581	134,895
In Japan.........	137,597	54,605	136,416	122,699
In Manchuria.....	72,573	118,357	107,547	115,110
Elsewhere........	6,863	10,599	8,413	10,352
Total..........	294,265	373,744	321,357	383,056

銀行という名で設立され、1910年の併合後に朝鮮銀行と改名された。総裁と副総裁は大日本帝国政府が任命する。

1924年9月までは、總督府がこの銀行を監督し、理事たちは株主総会で選ばれた候補者の中から總督によって任命された。候補者の数は実際に任命される理事の数の2倍必要とされた。しかし、1924年9月以降、監督任務は大日本帝国政府に移され、理事の任命は、日本の大蔵大臣が行うことになった。

1923年までの4年間における朝鮮銀行の主な業務状況は、次の表に示されている。

朝鮮銀行の業務状況（単位は千円　当時1円＝50セント）

	1920	1921	1922	1923
払込資本金	50,000	50,000	50,000	50,000
発行した銀行券	114,034	137,611	101,658	110,750
預金				
朝鮮	46,920	39,028	42,036	95,586
日本	69,930	69,681	76,021	25,866
満州	28,129	34,005	32,518	31,487
その他地域	15,642	19,777	9,835	9,891
合計	160,621	162,941	160,410	162,830
貸出金				
朝鮮	77,232	90,183	66,581	134,895
日本	137,597	54,605	136,416	122,699
満州	72,573	118,357	107,547	115,110
その他地域	6,863	10,599	8,413	10,352
合計	294,265	373,744	321,357	383,056

550   ECONOMIC DEVELOPMENT OF KOREA

Comparing the above figures with those given on page 548 it is seen that the Bank of Chosen had, in 1923, about one-third of the bank deposits in Korea, and put out about one-third of the banking loans in Korea.

During the past few years the Bank of Chosen has been embarrassed owing to bad loans made outside of Korea. The matter came to a head in 1925; and at a general meeting of the shareholders held in August of that year, a resolution was passed to reduce the capital of the bank by one-half, and the number of its shares in the same proportion.

The Chosen Industrial Bank--

This bank has a paid-up capital of 15 million yen. During the past few years it has experienced a great expansion in its business. Between 1918 and 1923 its issue of debentures increased from 3,000,000 to 100,000,000 in the year, its reserve fund from 600,000 to 2,000,000, its deposits from 15,000,000 to 48,000,000, and its loans from 30,000,000 to 172,000,000. Its net profits increased from 400,000 yen in 1919 to nearly 2,000,000 in 1923.

Ordinary Banks--

These banks had in 1923 an aggregate capital of 19 million yen, with reserve funds of about 2,500,000. Their deposits amounted to 73 million, their loans to 88 million, and their net profits to something over two million. Their business has shown a steady development year by year.

前出の「朝鮮の銀行統計」の表と比べると、朝鮮銀行は1923年に朝鮮内で約3分の1の預金を保持し、約3分の1の貸付を行ったことが分かる。

ここ数年、朝鮮銀行は朝鮮外で発生した不良債権のせいで憂慮すべき状況に追い込まれた。1925年には危機的状況に陥り、同年8月に開かれた株主総会で、資本金を2分の1に、株式も同じ比率で減らす決議案が通過した。

朝鮮殖産銀行

朝鮮殖産銀行は払込資本金1500万円を持つ。ここ数年で事業を非常に大きく拡大している。1918年から1923年の間に、債券発行規模は300万円から1億円に、準備金は60万円から200万円に、預金は1500万円から4800万円に、貸付金は3000万円から1億7200万円に増えた。純利益は1919年の40万円から1923年には200万円に増えている。

普通銀行

1923年の全ての普通銀行の資本金総額は1900万円、準備金が約250万円だった。預金は7300万円、貸付金8800万円、純利益はおよそ200万円強であった。普通銀行の事業は毎年順調に拡大している。

552   ECONOMIC DEVELOPMENT OF KOREA

People's Banking Associations--

These were first organized in 1907, and are modeled on the best features of the Reifeisen and Schulze systems. They resemble the People's Credit Associations of Japan, but are better managed than the latter. The system is considered one of the most useful measures ever adopted in Korea, and it is fully appreciated by the people, as is proved by the rapid expansion of their business. In the ten years ending with 1924 the number of these Associations increased from 240 to 509, the number of members from 66 thousand to 375 thousand, the capital subscribed by members from 786 thousand yen to nearly eight million, the reserve funds from 529 thousand to nearly five million, the deposits from 197 thousand yen to nearly 38 million, loans from about two million to more than 58 million, and the net profits from 64 thousand to nearly two million.

These banks are grouped in thirteen Federations of People's Banking Associations, which co-operate with the Provincial Governors and with the Governor-General of Chosen in supervising the operations of the various Associations in their respective districts.

The Oriental Development Company--

This Company, which was organized in 1908 engages in agricultural and industrial undertakings and participates with the Government-General in the development of the natural resources of the Peninsula. One of its main functions is to furnish the funds necessary for agricultural and other activities of the population.

Up to the year 1917 the O.D.C. limited its undertakings to Korea, but in the following year extended its sphere of operations to Manchuria, North

金融組合

　金融組合は 1907 年に初めて結成され、ライファイゼン制度とシュルツェ制度の優れた特徴に基づき作られた。金融組合は日本の相互信用組合と似ているが、それよりもうまく管理されている。金融組合は朝鮮史上行われた措置の中で最も有益とされ、人々に高く評価されており、金融組合の急速な事業拡大もそのことを証明している。

　1924 年までの 10 年間で、金融組合の数は 240 から 509 へ、組合員数は 6 万 6000 人から 37 万 5000 人に、組合員が出資した資本金も 78 万 6000 円から 800 万円近くへ、支払予備金は 52 万 9000 円から約 500 万円へ、預金は 19 万 7000 円から約 3800 万円近くへ、貸付金は約 200 万円から 5800 万円以上に、純利益は 6 万 4000 円から 200 万円近くまで増加した。これら金融組合は 13 の金融組合連合会に分けられ、連合会は道知事と總督に協力して、各地域の金融組合の営業を監督している。

東洋拓殖株式会社

　東洋拓殖株式会社は 1908 年に設立された。農工業に携わり、總督府とともに朝鮮半島の資源開発も行っている。主な役割の 1 つは、人々の農業活動やその他の事業活動のために必要な資金を提供することだ。1917 年までは東洋拓殖株式会社は朝鮮内でのみ事業を行っていたが、翌年、満州、北中国、南太平洋諸島まで拡大した。

　東洋拓殖株式会社の授権資本額は 5000 万円だ。その事業拡大は、

554 ECONOMIC DEVELOPMENT OF KOREA

China, and the South Sea Islands. The Company's authorized capital is 50 million yen. The increase in its activities may be measured by the fact that it issued debentures to the value of 36 million yen in 1917, and to the value of 182 million in 1924, while the total amount of its loans grew during the same period from 12 million yen to 148 million. These loans were distributed as follows in the year 1924: in Korea 55 million yen, in Manchuria 72 million, in Northern China 10 million, and in the South Sea Islands 12 million, the figures being those of the nearest million.

Mutual Credit Associations (Mujin-Ko)--

Apart from the regular finance organs in Korea there exists a system of mutual credit transactions on a small scale, known as *Mujin*. Persons associated together for the purpose of forming and operating a credit unit of this character are known collectively as *Mujin-ko*. The system originated in Japan about the year 1387, and it is one of the earliest known instances of mutual credit societies.

Within the past few years the operations of *Mujin-ko* have extended rapidly in Korea; and in order to insure proper supervision of these activities the Chosen Mutual Credit Business Ordinance (*Mujin rei*) was promulgated in 1922. The following table shows the principal features of the condition and transactions of the *Mujin-ko* during the years indicated. The statistics are based upon an annual return which divides the year into two six-month terms. The figures are to the nearest thousand.

債券発行額が1917年に3600万円だったのが1924年には1億8200万円に増え、また貸付金額も同時期1200万円から1億4800万円に増えたという事実からも分かる。1924年の貸付状況は次の通りだ。

朝鮮……………………　5500万円

満州……………………　7200万円

北中国…………………　1000万円

南太平洋諸島…………　1200万円

なお、この数値は100万円単位の近似値である。

相互信用組合（無盡講）

朝鮮では正規の金融機関の他にも、無盡（むじん）と呼ばれる小規模相互信用組合が存在している。このような性質の信用団体をともに構成・運営するために集まった人々を無盡講と呼ぶ。この制度は1387年頃に日本で始まったもので、相互信用組合の最も古い例の1つである。

ここ数年で無盡講の活動は朝鮮で急速に広まり、その適切な監督のために朝鮮無盡業令が1922年に公布された。

次の表は、無盡講の該当年度に於ける営業や取引状況の主な数値を示している。なお、この統計は一年を6カ月単位に分けており、数値は千円単位の近似値である。

ECONOMIC DEVELOPMENT OF KOREA

CONDITION AND BUSINESS OF THE MUTUAL CREDIT ASSOCIATIONS

(In thousands of yen. 1 yen = 50 cents U. S.)

Year and Term		Paid-up Capital	Re-serve	Loans	Number of Repayment Contracts		
					Com-pleted	Incom-plete	Total
1922..	2nd Term.	280	6	171	2,037	7,007	9,044
1923..	1st Term..	430	10	395	3,316	8,630	11,946
	2nd Term.	531	16	554	4,264	8,410	12,673
1924..	1st Term..	759	31	702	6,161	12,070	18,230
	2nd Term.	840	51	931	8,040	12,542	20,583
1925..	1st Term..	857	87	1,088	9,479	13,452	23,021

I am indebted to Professor Kiyoshi Ogata for the following brief account of the *Mujin* system, which is taken *verbatim* from pages 14 and 15 of his elaborate volume, *The Co-operative Movement in Japan*.

In the course of its growth, the *Mujin* system blossomed forth in many directions. Before I give a detailed explanation of how the *Mujin* is carried on in practice at present, it is necessary to make a few preliminary remarks on its various aspects:

(1) *Mujins* are usually formed for raising capital sums required for business or for private expenditure. By the term private expenditure, we are to understand household expenses (which include taxes, marriage expenses, social gatherings, school expenses, etc.), repayment of old debts, pilgrimages to temples, and holiday trips, etc.

However, some *Mujins* are started to raise funds for particular public purposes, such as the repair of school or temple buildings, bridges

相互信用組合の営業状況
（単位は千円　1円 =50 セント）

期間	払込資本金	支払準備金	貸付金	貸出償還		
				償還完了	償還中	合計
1922 下半期	280	6	171	2,037	7,007	9,044
1923 上半期	430	10	395	3,316	8,630	11,946
1923 下半期	531	16	554	4,264	8,410	12,673
1924 上半期	759	31	702	6,161	12,070	18,230
1924 下半期	840	51	931	8,040	12,542	20,583
1925 上半期	857	87	1,088	9,479	13,452	23,021

　以下の無盡についての説明は、緒方清教授によって入念に書かれた " *The Co-operative Movement in Japan*" の 14 〜 15 ページから、そのまま引用したものである。

　無盡制度はその成長過程で、様々な方面へと発展していった。現在無盡が実際にどのように行われているかの詳細を説明する前に、そのいろいろな特徴についていくつか述べておく必要がある。

(1)　無盡は通常、事業や個人的支出に必要な資金を集めるために作られる。ここで言う個人的支出とは家計支出（税金、結婚費用、社交費用、学費など）、借金の返済、お寺への巡礼、休暇旅行などである。しかし、無盡の中には、学校、寺院、橋や道路の修繕などの特定の公共の目的や、慈善機関のための資金集めに設立されるものもある。また、貯蓄を積み立てるためや、

or roads, or for some charitable institution. Others are formed for furthering thrift, and others again for purchasing houses or land. We shall see that most of these objects are the same as those pursued by the modern credit societies.

(2) Most of the *Mujins* aim at providing their members with cash advances, but some aim at providing their members with goods, such as clothing. In the latter case the *Mujin* is a form of purchase by easy instalments.

(3) In *Mujins* there is sometimes a first beneficiary, for whose special benefit the society is formed, and who receives the subscription at the first meeting, as an advance without interest, or even as a free gift, in return for which he must undertake the collection and administration of subscriptions while the *Mujin* continues in existence. This means, in effect, that the subscriptions of one meeting are given to him to alleviate his distress. On the other hand many *Mujins* are purely mutual finance organizations, without any special beneficiary.

(4) The *Mujin* is also limited in duration. The length of one series of *Mujin* varies from ten months to fifty years, according to the membership and the frequency of the meetings, three to six years being the most usual, but each series may be repeated when the first one is ended.

(5) Subscriptions are usually paid in cash, but sometimes in kind, or even in labor.

(6) One of two forms of security is required in cases where the *Mujin* makes advances; either personal guarantors or the mortgage of real property.

第十三章　経済発展　　　559

家や土地を買うために設立されるものもある。これらの目的の
ほとんどは、現代の信用組合が達成しようとするものと同じで
あることを認識する必要がある。

(2)　ほとんどの無盡は加入者に現金の前貸しを行うことを目的
とするが、衣服などのものを提供するところもある。後者の場
合は、無盡は簡単な分割払いでの物品の購入ということになる。

(3)　無盡には、時には目的をもって講を設立して最初に益を受
ける人がいて、その人が最初の会合で、利子なしの前借、また
は無償の贈与として給付金を受け取り、その代わりに、無盡が
存続する間ずっと払込金・貸出金の集金と運営を行わなくては
ならない。これは事実上、最初の会合で集められた給付金は彼
の経済的困窮を和らげるために提供されたことを意味する。他
方で、多くの無盡は特定の受益者のいない、純粋な相互扶助機
関である。

(4)　無盡には期限もある。無盡が一周するには、組合員数と会
合の頻度によるが、10 カ月から 50 年かかるところもある。大
体 3 〜 6 年が通例で、一周すると、また次の周へと繰り返され
ることもある。

(5)　払込金は普通現金で払われるが、時には物や労働で支払わ
れることもある。

(6)　無盡が貸出を行うときは、個人の保証人か不動産の担保の

(7) One share in a *Mujin* may be in the names of two or more persons, or one member may hold more than one share.

(8) The total amount to be drawn usually ranges from 100 yen to 300 yen, but it may be sometimes as little as 5 yen, and sometimes as much as 10,000 yen.

(9) The amount of one share usually ranges from 5 yen to 30 yen, but sometimes subscriptions are as low as 10 *sen* and sometimes as high as 100 yen. When the subscriptions in *Mujins* are rather high, payment may be arranged by instalments, in which case a special collector is employed to go round and collect such instalments.

The *Mujin-Ko* is usually formed by from thirty to fifty persons (sometimes by less than ten, sometimes by more than five hundred), living in the same street, or following the same trade, or worshiping at the same temple or shrine. The meetings are usually held at a beneficiary's or founder's house, or at the temple, or at a restaurant, such meetings taking place as frequently as twice a month or as rarely as twice a year.

第十三章　経済発展　561

どちらか1つによる保証が必要である。

(7) 無盡の配当（株）は2人以上の名で受け取ることが可能で、また1人の組合員が1つ以上の株を保有することも出来る。

(8) 引き出される総額は普通100円から300円の間であるが、時には5円程度の少額、または1万円ほどの高額に上ることもある。

(9) 一配当（株）の額は普通5円から30円だが、払込金が10銭と低かったり、または100円と高かったりすることもある。無盡の払込金がやや高い時は、分割で払うことも出来、その場合は特別集金人が雇われ集金に回る。

　無盡講は普通、同じ地域に住んでいたり、同じ職業に従事していたり、同じ寺院や神社にお参りしていたりする30人から50人で構成される（時には10人以下や500人以上のこともある）。会合は通常、組合員か「親」の家、寺院、または食堂などで行われ、月に2回行われるところもあれば、1年に2回と極めて少ないところもある。

APPENDICES

附録

564

APPENDICES

A   Treaty of Annexation, Signed on August 22, 1910, and Promulgated on August 29th.

B   The Imperial Rescript on Annexation, Promulgated on August 29, 1910.

C   The Korean Emperor's Rescript on Cession of Sovereignty, Promulgated on August 29, 1910.

D   The Imperial Rescript Concerning the Reorganization of the Government-General of Chosen, Promulgated on August 19, 1919.

E   The Governor-General's Instructions to High Officials Concerning Administrative Reforms. Issued on September 3, 1919.

F   The Governor-General's Proclamation to the People of Chosen. Issued on September 10, 1919.

G   The Governor-General's Address to Provincial Governors. Delivered on October 3, 1919.

H   The Administrative Superintendent's Instructions to Provincial Governors. Delivered on October 3, 1919.

I   Rules for Teachers. Notification No. 11, issued January 4, 1916.

附録

A 1910 年 韓国併合に関する条約（明治四十三年八月二十九日）

B 1910 年 韓国併合に付下し給える詔書
（明治四十三年八月二十九日）

C 1910 年 日韓併合に関する旧韓国皇帝の勅諭
（明治四十三年八月二十九日）

D 1919 年 朝鮮總督府官制改正の詔書（大正八年八月十九日）

E 1919 年 總督府および所属官署に対する總督の施政方針訓示
（大正八年九月三日）

F 1919 年 總督による朝鮮人民への声明（大正八年九月十日）

G 1919 年 總督による道知事への演説（大正八年十月十三日）

H 1919 年 道知事会議に於ける政務総監の訓示要旨
（大正八年十月十三日）

I 1916 年 朝鮮總督府訓令　教員心得（大正五年一月四日）

※附録に掲載した日本語資料は、英文からの翻訳ではなく、日本語原典の資料を掲載している。また、原書の英文では省略されている部分についても掲載しているため、対応する英文がない部分もある。

※附録資料については、原文のカナは平仮名に直し、一部の旧字を新字に改め、適宜句読点を加えた。

566   APPENDICES

APPENDIX A

Treaty of Annexation, Signed on August 22, 1910 and

Promulgated on the 29 of August

His Majesty the Emperor of Japan and His Majesty the Emperor of Korea, having in view the special and close relations between Their respective countries, desiring to promote the common weal of the two nations and to assure permanent peace in the Extreme East, and being convinced that these objects can be best attained by the annexation of Korea to the Empire of Japan, have resolved to conclude a Treaty of such annexation, and have for that purpose appointed as Their Plenipotentiaries, that is to say:—

His Majesty the Emperor of Japan, Viscount Masakata Terauchi, His Resident-General;

And His Majesty the Emperor of Korea, Yi Wan Yong, His Minister President of State;

Who, upon mutual conference and deliberation, have agreed to the following Articles.

Article I. His Majesty the Emperor of Korea makes complete and permanent cession to His Majesty the Emperor of Japan of all rights of sovereignty over the whole of Korea.

Article II. His Majesty the Emperor of Japan accepts the cession mentioned in the preceding Article, and consents to the complete annexation of Korea to the Empire of Japan.

Article III. His Majesty the Emperor of Japan will accord to Their Majesties the Emperor and ex-Emperor and His Imperial Highness the

附録　A
韓国併合に関する条約
（明治四十三年八月二十九日公布）

日本国皇帝陛下 及 韓国皇帝陛下は、両国間の特殊にして親密なる関係を顧い、相互の幸福を増進し、東洋の平和を永久に確保せんことを欲し、此の目的を達せんが為には韓国を日本帝国に併合するに如かざることを確信し、茲に両国間に併合条約を締結することに決し、之が為日本国皇帝陛下は統監子爵寺内正毅を、韓国皇帝陛下は内閣総理大臣李完用を、各 其の全権委員に任命せり。因て右全権委員は会同協議の上左の諸条を協定せり。

第一条　韓国皇帝陛下は韓国全部に関する一切の統治権を完全且永久に日本国皇帝陛下に譲与す

第二条　日本国皇帝陛下は前条に掲げたる譲与を受諾し且全然韓国を日本帝国に併合することを承諾す

第三条　日本国皇帝陛下は韓国皇帝陛下太皇帝陛下皇太子殿下

568   APPENDICES

Crown Prince of Korea and Their Consorts and Heirs such titles, dignity, and honor as are appropriate to Their respective ranks, and sufficient annual grants will be made for the maintenance of such titles, dignity, and honor.

Article IV. His Majesty the Emperor of Japan will also accord appropriate honor and treatment to the members of the Imperial House of Korea and their heirs other than those mentioned in the preceding Article, and the funds necessary for the maintenance of such honor and treatment will be granted.

Article V. His Majesty the Emperor of Japan will confer peerages and monetary grants upon those Koreans who, on account of meritorious services, are regarded as deserving such special recognition.

Article VI. In consequence of the aforesaid annexation, the Government of Japan assumes the entire government and administration of Korea and undertakes to afford full protection for the persons and property of Koreans obeying the laws there in force, and to promote the welfare of all such Koreans.

Article VII. The Government of Japan will, so far as circumstances permit, employ in the public service of Japan in Korea those Koreans who accept the new régime loyally and in good faith and who are duly. qualified for such service.

Article VIII. This Treaty, having been approved by His Majesty the Emperor of Japan and His Majesty the Emperor of Korea, shall take effect from the date of its promulgation.

In faith whereof, the respective Plenipotentiaries have signed this Treaty, and have affixed thereto their seals.

並<ruby>並<rt>ならび</rt></ruby> 其の后妃 及<ruby>及<rt>および</rt></ruby> 後裔をして各其の地位に応じ相当なる尊称威厳 及<ruby>及<rt>および</rt></ruby> 名誉を享有せしめ且之を保持するに十分なる歳費を供給すべきことを約す

第四条　日本国皇帝陛下は前条以外の韓国皇族及其の後裔に対し各相当の名誉及待遇を享有せしめ且之を維持するに必要なる資金を供与することを約す

第五条　日本国皇帝陛下は勲功ある韓人にして特に表彰を為すを適当なりと認めたる者に対し栄爵を授け且恩金を与ふべし

第六条　日本国政府は前記併合の結果として全然韓国の施政を担任し同地に施行する法規を遵守する韓人の身体及財産に対し十分なる保護を与へ且其の福利の増進を図るべし

第七条　日本国政府は誠意忠実に新制度を尊重する韓人にして相当の資格ある者を事情の許す限り韓国に於ける帝国官吏に登用すべし

第八条　本条約は日本国皇帝陛下及韓国皇帝陛下の裁可を経たるものにして公布の日より之を施行す

右証拠として両全権委員は本条約に記名調印するものなり

570 APPENDICES

APPENDIX B
Imperial Rescript on Annexation

We, attaching the highest importance to the maintenance of permanent peace in the Orient and the consolidation of lasting security to Our Empire and finding in Korea constant and fruitful sources of complication, caused Our Government to conclude in 1905 an Agreement with the Korean Government by which Korea was placed under the protection of Japan in the hope that all disturbing elements might thereby be removed and peace assured for ever.

For the four years and over which have since elapsed, Our Government have exerted themselves with unwearied attention to promote reforms in the administration of Korea, and their efforts have, in a degree, been attended with success. But, at the same time, the existing régime of government in that country has shown itself hardly effective to preserve peace and stability, and, in addition, a spirit of suspicion and misgiving dominates the whole Peninsula. In order to maintain public order and security and to advance the happiness and well-being of the people, it has become manifest that fundamental changes in the present system of government are inevitable.

We, in concert with His Majesty the Emperor of Korea, having in view this condition of affairs and being equally persuaded of the necessity of annexing the whole of Korea to the Empire of Japan in response to the actual requirements of the situation, have now arrived at an arrangement for such permanent annexation.

His Majesty the Emperor of Korea and the members of His Imperial

附録　B
韓国併合に付下し給える詔書
（明治四十三年八月二十九日）

朕東洋の平和を永遠に維持し、帝国の安全を将来に保障するの必要なるを念い、又常に韓国が禍乱の淵源たるに顧み、曩に朕の政府をして韓国政府と協定せしめ、韓国を帝国の保護の下に置き、以て禍源を杜絶し、平和を確保せしめんことを期せり。

爾来時を経ること四年有余、其の間朕の政府は鋭意韓国施政の改善に努め、其の成績亦見るべきものありと雖、韓国の現政は尚未だ治安の保持を完するに足らず。疑懼の念毎に国内に充溢し、民其の堵に安ぜず。公共の安寧を維持し、民衆の福利を増進せむが為には、革新を現制に加ふるの避く可らざること瞭然たるに至れり。

朕は韓国皇帝陛下と与に此の事態に鑑み、韓国を挙て日本帝国に併合し、以て時勢の要求に応ずるの已むを得ざるものあるを念い、茲に永久に韓国を帝国に併合することとなせり。

韓国皇帝陛下及 其の皇室各員は、併合の後と雖、相当の優遇を受くべく、民衆は直接朕か綏撫の下に立ちて、其の康福を増進す

572   APPENDICES

House will, notwithstanding the annexation, be accorded due and appropriate treatment. All Koreans, being under Our direct sway, will enjoy growing prosperity and welfare, and with assured repose and security will come a marked expansion in industry and trade. We confidently believe that the new order of things now inaugurated will serve as a fresh guarantee of enduring peace in the Orient.

We order the establishment of the office of Governor- General of Korea. The Governor-General will, under our direction, exercise the command of the army and navy, and a general control over all administrative functions in Korea. We call upon all of Our officials and authorities to fulfil their respective duties in appreciation of Our will, and to conduct the various branches of administration in consonance with the requirements of the occasion, to the end that Our subjects may long enjoy the blessings of peace and tranquillity.

The 29th day of the 8th month of the 43rd year of Meiji (1910).

べし。産業及貿易は治平の下に顕著なる発達を見るに至るべし。而して東洋の平和は之に依りて愈其の基礎を鞏固にすべきは、朕の信じて疑わざる所なり。

朕は特に朝鮮總督を置き、之をして朕の命を承けて陸海軍を統率し、諸般の政務を総轄せしむ。百官有司克く朕の意を体して事に従い、施設の緩急其の宜きを得、以て衆庶をして永く治平の慶に頼らしむることを期せよ。

574   APPENDICES

APPENDIX C
The Late Korean Emperor's Rescript on Cession of Sovereignty
(Promulgated on August 29, 1910)

Notwithstanding Our unworthiness We succeeded to a great and arduous task, and from Our accession to the Throne down to the present time We have used Our utmost efforts to follow the modern principles of administration. In view, however, of the long-standing weakness and deep rooted evils, We are convinced that it would be beyond Our power to effect reforms within a measurable length of time. Day and night We have been deeply concerned about it, and have been at a loss to find the means how to rectify the lamentable state of things. Should it be left as it goes on, allowing the situation to assume more serious phase, We fear that We will finally find it impossible to adjust it in any way. Under these circumstances We feel constrained to believe it wise to entrust Our great task to abler hands than Ours, so that efficient measures may be carried out and satisfactory results obtained therefrom. Having taken the matter into Our serious consideration and firmly believing that this is an opportune time for immediate decision, We have ceded all the rights of sovereignty over Korea to His Majesty the Emperor of Japan in whom we have placed implicit confidence and with whom we have shared joy and sorrow from long time since, in order to consolidate the peace of the Extreme East and ensure the welfare of our people.

You, all the people, are expected not to give yourselves up to commotion, appreciating the present national situation as well as the trend of the times, but to enjoy the happiness and blessings by pursuing your

附録C
日韓併合に関する旧韓国皇帝の勅諭
（明治四十三年八月二十九日）

皇帝若く曰く朕否徳にして艱大なる業を承け、臨御以後今日に至るまで維新政令に関し丞図し備試し用力未だ嘗て至らずんばあらずと雖も、由来積弱痼を成し疲弊極処に到り時日間に挽回するの施措望無し。中夜憂慮善後の策茫然たり。此に任し支離 益 甚しければ終局に収拾し得ざるに底らん。寧ろ大任を人に託し完全なる方法と革新なる功効を奏せしむるに如かず。故に朕是に於て瞿然として内に省み、廓然として自ら断じ、茲に韓国の統治権を縦前より親信依仰したる隣国の日本皇帝陛下に譲与し、外東洋の平和を鞏固ならしめ内八域の民生を保全ならしめんとす。惟 爾 大小臣民は国勢と時宜を深察し煩擾する勿く各其の業に安んじ、日本帝国の文明の新政に服従し、幸福を共受せよ。朕が今日の此の挙は爾有衆を忘れたるにあらず。亶に 爾 有衆を救活せんとするの至意に出づ。爾臣民等は克く朕の此の意を体せよ。

※『朝鮮總督府施政年報 自大正七年度 至大正九年度』より引用。
　原文は漢文で記されている。

occupations in peace and obeying the enlightened new administration of the Empire of Japan. We have decided to take this step by no means disregarding your interest but in our eagerness to relieve you of this deplorable situation. We command you, therefore, to take due cognizance of our wishes.

附録

578   APPENDICES

APPENDIX D

Imperial Rescript Concerning the Reorganization of the

Government-General of Chosen

(Promulgated on August 19, 1919)

We have ever made it Our aim to promote the security and welfare of Our territory of Korea, and to extend to the native population of that territory as Our beloved subjects a fair and impartial treatment in all respects, to the end that they may without distinction of persons lead their lives in peace and contentment. We are persuaded that the state of development at which the general situation has now arrived calls for certain reforms in the administrative organization of the Government-General of Korea, and We issue Our Imperial command that such reforms be put into operation. The measures thus taken are solely designed to facilitate the working of administration and to secure good and enlightened government in pursuance of Our settled policy, and in fulfilment of the altered requirements of the country. Specially in view of the termination of the war in Europe and of the rapid changes in the conditions of the world do We consider it highly desirable that every effort should be made for the advancement of the national resources and the well-being of the people. We call upon all public functionaries concerned to exercise their best endeavors in obedience to Our wishes in order that a benign rule may be assured to Korea, and that the people, diligent and happy in attending to their respective vocations, may enjoy the blessing of peace and contribute to the growing prosperity of the country.

附録 D

朝鮮總督府官制改正の詔書
（大正八年八月十九日）

朕夙に朝鮮の康寧を以て念と為し、其の民衆を愛撫すること一視同仁、朕が臣民として秋毫の差異あることなく、各其の所を得、其の生に聊し、齊しく休明の澤を享けしむことを期せり。今や世局の進運に従い總督府官制改革の必要を認め、茲に之を施行す。是従来の廟謨に基き、時に應じ宜を制し、以て施政の便に資し、治化の普及を謀るに外ならず、方今、欧州の戦乱新に息み世態の変遷、殊に激し朕深く茲に鑑みる所あり。益民力の発達に努め、其の福利を増進せしめんことを念う。百官有司、克く朕が意を体して事に当り、徳化を宣布し、民衆をして各職に励み、業を楽しみ永く昇平の恵澤に浴し、共に邦家の隆運を扶翼せしむことを勗めよ。

580   APPENDICES

APPENDIX E

Governor-General's Instruction to High Officials Concerning

Administrative Reforms

(Issued on Sept. 3, 1919)

The main policy of the administration of Chosen is clearly embodied in the Imperial rescript issued on the occasion of the annexation of Chosen in 1910. The progress made by Chosen since she was brought under Japanese rule, in education, industry, communications, sanitation, and other directions, has been remarkable, thanks to the efforts of those who have been responsible for the administration of the country. It cannot be denied, however, that during the ten years that have elapsed since the annexation of Chosen the general affairs in the Peninsula have undergone such change that the Government has thought it advisable to frame and. promulgate a new organization of the Government. General of Chosen.

The purport of the revised official organization is to enlarge the application of the principle of universal brotherhood, which is the keynote of the Imperial rescript recently issued. The official organization has been altered in such a way that either a civil or military man may be appointed at the head of the administration in Chosen. The gendarmerie system has been abolished and replaced by the ordinary police system. Further, an improvement has been introduced in the matter of the eligibility for appointment of Koreans as officials. The whole aim and object of the revised organization is, in short, to give more happiness and satisfaction than is the case at present by bringing their treatment socially and politically on the same footing as the Japanese.

附録E
總督府および所属官署に対する總督の施政方針訓示
（大正八年九月三日）

国家重大の時局に際し、朝鮮總督の大命を拝受し恐懼措く所を知らず。短才微力、能く此の大任を完うし得るや否や、衷心安きを得ざるもの多しと雖各位の協翼に依り、日夜精励を以て大命に奉答せんことを期す。

朝鮮統治の大方針は、明治四十三年、日韓併合の際下し賜える、明治天皇の勅書に昭にして、従来の總督府官制ならび其の下に行われたる各般の行政施設は皆此の聖旨の実現を企図したるものに外ならず。而して、各先任者の努力と国民の奮励とに依り、克く和平を維持し、民衆の福利を増進し、教育、産業、交通、衛生、社会救済、其の他各方面に亙り頗る其の面目を一新したるものあるは、中外の均しく認むる所なり。然りと雖、今や併合行われてより既に約十星霜を経過し、其の当時に於いて適切有効なりし制度ならび施設にして、往々時勢の進運と朝鮮の実情とに適合せざるものなきに非ず。ここにおいて政府は、今回新たに官制を改正し、客月二十日、其の公布を見るに至りたり。官制改正の主旨は、今上陛下の優詔に示す如く、日韓併合の本旨に基き、一視同仁、各其の所を得、其の生に聊んじ、休明の澤を享けしめんが為、時に応じ宜を制し、施政の便に資せしめらるるに在り。即ち總督は文武官の何れよりも任用し得るの途を啓き更に憲兵に依る警察

I am not well conversant with all the phases of affairs in Chosen and will have to depend on your guidance and suggestions in carrying out the object of the Imperial rescript. At the same time, I would like to call your attention to the following points in regard to the administration of Chosen.

All officials of the Government-General should do their best to discharge their duties in a conscientious and impartial manner, so that the public may be induced to rely on them. All official routine should be simplified and made easier, avoiding red-tape as far as possible. The rights of the people should be respected, and the freedom of press and speech should not be interfered with unless it is distinctly calculated to be inimical to the preservation of peace. Special attention should be paid to the improvement in education, industry, communications, police, sanitation, and social works, as well as in general administrative and judicial matters, so that the welfare of the Koreans may be advanced with the ultimate object of the establishment of local autonomous government.

What is required of the officials who are charged with the administration of Chosen is that they should acquaint themselves with the general trend of ideas among the Koreans and adopt a method of administration which will be in keeping with the requirements of the times. In other words, efforts should be made so that the political foundations may be placed on a firm, secure basis. The Koreans and Japanese must be treated alike as members of the same family. If the officials in Chosen try to live up to the ideals set forth in the Imperial rescript, there is no doubt that the Koreans will be induced to recognize the benefit of Japanese rule.

制度に代うるに普通警察官に依る警察制度を以てし、尚服制に改正を為し、一般官吏教員等の制服帯剣を廃止し、朝鮮人の任用待遇等に考慮を加えんとす。要之文化的制度の革新に依り朝鮮人を誘導提撕（ていせい）し以て其の幸福利益の増進を計り将来文化の発達と民力の充実とに応じ政治上、社会上の待遇に於ても内地人と同一の取扱を為すべき究極の目的を達せんことを庶幾（しょき）するものに外ならず。聖恩宏大誰か感孚（かんぷ）せざらんや。

不肖官制改正と相前後して新に大命を拝す。只如上の大詔を奉戴し制度改正の趣旨に則り（のっとり）誠心誠意献身的努力を為し、聖旨の普及を計らんとするの外（ほか）他意なし。赴任日尚浅く未だ朝鮮の実情を審（つまびらか）にせず、施政の具体的方針に至りては更に査覈（さかく）を加え各位の啓沃に待ちて徐に決定する所あるべしと雖、茲（ここ）に二三の根本方針（いえど）に就き留意を乞う所あらんとす。

官吏は一心同体を旨とし、上下四方共同戮力（りくりょく）し公明正大なる政治を為すべし。總督府内の各局課 及（および）總督府と地方庁との間に於て努めて意思の疎通を図り、各一貫したる意気を以て互に連絡を取り、最善の努力を為すべきは勿論、身を持する謹厳、正直、不党不（ふとうふ）偏（へん）、各種の情弊を芟除（せんじょ）し、専ら（もっぱら）正理公道に就き民衆をして施政に信頼せしめんことを期すべし。

時代の進運と民心の帰嚮（ききょう）とに鑑み、行政、司法事務の各般に互り（わたり）左の改善を加えんことを期す。

一、形式的政治の弊を打破し法令は成るべく簡約に従い誠意国民を誘掖して其の精神の徹底を図り、行政処分は事態民情に顧みて

584   APPENDICES

適切なる措置を執り努めて被処分者の諒解を得しむべし

一、事務の整理簡捷に努め民衆の便益を計り官庁の威信を保持すべし

一、言論、集会、出版等に対しては秩序及公安の維持に妨げなき限り相当考慮を加え民意の暢達を計るべし

一、教育、産業、交通、警察、衛生、社会救済其の他各般の行政に刷新を加え国民生活の安定を図り一般の福利を増進するに於て新に一生面を開かんことを期す。殊に地方に於ける民風の涵養ならびに民力の作興は地方団体の力に待つことを便とすべきが故に将来時期を見て地方自治制度を施行するの目的を以て速に之が調査研究に着手せんとす。

如上の改善刷新は只徒に新奇を衒い時流を追わんとするものに非ず。成るべく朝鮮の文化と旧慣とを尊重して其の善を長じ其の弊を除き以て時勢の進軍に順応せんことを期するに在り。換言すれば民生民風を啓発し以て文明的政治の基礎を確立せんとするの趣旨に外ならず。

制度改正と共に人心の一新を要するは固より言を俟たざる所なり。各位は須く聖旨を奉じて率先躬行、其の範を示さんことを期し、内鮮人をして常に一家の親、同胞の愛を以て相接し、共同輯睦の実を挙げしむべく殊に朝鮮人をして心身を研磨し其の文化と民力とを向上して愈、聖代の徳澤に浴せんことを期せしめらるべし。各位希くば此機会に於て協力一致益朝鮮統治の刷新を図り、聖明の宏謨に副い奉らんことを。

APPENDIX F

Governor-General's Proclamation to the People of Chosen

(Issued on September 10, 1919)

On my assumption of duty as Governor-General, the organization of the Government-General was revised. Accordingly, I desire to address a few words to the people at large.

That the administrative policy of Chosen should be based on the great principle of placing the Japanese and Korean peoples on an equal footing and should aim at promoting their interests and happiness, as well as at securing the permanent peace of the Far East, was determined upon at the very beginning. Those successively charged with the administration of this Peninsula duly appreciated its meaning and strove to improve and develop its people and resources. The people, too, diligently engaged in their business. It is now recognized at home and abroad that the present development of Chosen came as the result of their joint efforts. It goes without saying, however, that all administrative institutions must be planned and executed in conformity with the standard of popular living and the progress of the times, so that appropriate measures may be carried out and popular desires prevented from taking a wrong course. The times have progressed so much and civilization too that it is difficult to draw a comparison between this and former days. Since the great European War was brought to an end, moreover, the condition of the world and human psychology have undergone a marked change. In deference to this hard fact, His Majesty's Government, through a revision in the Organic Regulations, enlarged the sphere of appointment for the Governor-

附録 F

總督による朝鮮人民への声明
（大正八年九月十日）

不肖、茲に朝鮮統治の任に就くに方り、朝鮮總督府の官制亦改正せらる。乃ち一言以て民衆に告ぐ。

朝鮮統治の方針たる一視同仁の大義に遵い、民衆の福利を増進し、東洋の平和を確保するに在るは、宏謨の夙に定まる所にして、累代統治の任に膺れる者、克く此の意を体して斯土の開発に従い、国民亦拮据其の業に励み、以て今日の発達を致したるは中外の齊しく認むる所なり。然れども百般の施設は之を民度に徴し、時世に考え、以て其の宜を制し、人心の適帰を愆らしめざるべきは固より言を俟たず。今や時運の推移、文物の進歩亦曩日の比に非ず。加うるに欧州の戦乱新に熄み、世態人心の変遷特に著しきものあり。是に於てか政府は官制を改革して總督任用の範囲を拡張し、警察制度を改正し、以て時代の進運に順応して施政の簡捷と治化の普及とを図れり。不肖、大命を奉じ任に就くに当り、亦偏に宏謨を紹述し、併合の精神を発揚せんことを期し、自今部下を督励して 益 公明正大の政治を施し、形式に拘泥することなく、輿衆の便益と民意の暢達とを図り、朝鮮人の任用待遇等に関し、亦考慮を加えて、各 其の所を得しめ、又朝鮮の文化及び旧慣にして 苟 も採るべきものあれば之れを採りて統治の資に供し、更に各

588 APPENDICES

General, reformed the police system, and made such provision for simplification and prompt transaction of state business and the diffusion of enlightened administration as to bring them in perfect accord with the forward movement of this age. On assuming my present duty by Imperial order I determined in my own mind to pursue faithfully the State policy and vindicate the spirit of annexation. I am determined to superintend officials under my control and encourage them to put forth greater efforts to act in a fairer and juster way, and promote the facilities of the people and the unhindered attainment of the people's desires by dispensing with all formality. Full consideration will be given to the appointment and treatment of Koreans so as to secure the right men for the right places, and what in Korean institutions and old customs is worthy of adoption will be adopted as a means of government. I also hope to introduce reform in the different branches of administrative activity, and to enforce local self-government at the proper opportunity, and thereby ensure stability for the people and enhance their general well-being. It is most desirable that the government and governed throw open their hearts and minds to each other and combine their efforts to advance civilization in Chosen, solidify its foundation of enlightened government, and thus answer His Majesty's benevolent solicitude. If anybody is found guilty of unwarrantably refractory language or action, of misleading the popular mind, and of impeding the maintenance of public peace, he will be met with relentless justice. May it be that the people at large will place reliance on all this.

September 10, 1919.

BARON MAKOTO SAITO,

Governor-General of Chosen.

般の行政に刷新を加え、且将来機を見て地方自治制度を実施し、以て国民の生活を安定し一般の福利を増進せんことを期す。冀くは官民互に胸襟を披きて、協力一致、朝鮮の文化を向上せしめ、文明的政治の基礎を確立し、以て聖明に奉答せんことを。若し濫に不逞の言動を為し、人心を惑乱し公安を阻害するが如き者あらんか、将に法に照して寸毫も仮借する所なからんとす。一般民衆、其れ之を諒せよ。

APPENDIX G
Governor-General's Address to Provincial Governors
(Delivered on October 3, 1919)

Gentlemen:—I am very glad to have opportunity at this meeting of Provincial Governors to speak to you of my policy and to listen to your opinions concerning the administration of Chosen.

When I assumed my duty last month, I made up my mind to establish in this country a civilized administration by conforming my policy to the idea of His Majesty that both Koreans and Japanese should be treated as equals. As you are already well aware, I issued some time ago an instruction to all the officials serving in the Government-General and its affiliated offices. Since that time the Government-General itself has been, and is, endeavoring to carry out various important measures. Gentlemen, I do not doubt that you also have carried out or are intending to carry out these reforms, and are leading your subordinates in the same spirit as myself. I earnestly desire you to realize the administrative reforms by entering into the spirit of my instruction more thoroughly than ever. As to concrete plans and measures to be followed for effecting the reforms, the Administrative Superintendent will separately give you instructions. By observing these instructions you are expected to introduce a new spirit and new life into the government of this country and attain good results.

The most important task to be accomplished today is the adjustment and completion of the police organs and the maintenance of public peace and order. However, at this transition time, when the replacement of gendarmes with ordinary police is being effected, it is very difficult to expand the

附録G
總督による道知事への演説
（大正八年十月十三日）

茲に道知事会議を招集し、朝鮮統治の方針に関し、親しく各位に告ぐる所あり、且各位の意見を聴取するを得るは予の頗る欣幸とする所なり。

前月就任の初に当り予は一視同仁の聖意を遵奉して文明的政治の確立を期し、曩に訓示を発し、本府及所属官署の職員に告ぐる所ありたるは既に各位の諒知せらるるが如し。爾来總督府内に於ても、鋭意各要項の実現に努力しつつあり。各位に於ても或は既に之を実施し、或は近く実施せんことを計画し、予と心を一にして部下を督励しつつあることを信じて疑わず。冀くは将来益訓示の精神を拡充して施政の改善を図らんことを。其の具体的方針並び施設に至りては別に政務総監より訓示する所あるべし。各位は宜しく之に準拠して庶政を刷新し著著実績を挙げんことを期すべし。

警察機関を整備し治安の維持を計るは目下喫緊の要務に属す。然れども時恰も憲兵と更迭の過渡期に際し、警察官の補充頗る容易ならず。各種警察の設備も亦未だ完きを見るに至らざるを以て、

police force. Besides, arrangements for various police organs have not as yet been completed. I can well sympathize with you in your anxiety and trouble, standing, as you do, in this difficult situation, but I ask you to ensure the peace of the localities under your jurisdiction and make the people under your administration repose full confidence in the authorities, by maintaining satisfactory and smooth relations with all the public offices interested in this task, and by checkmating the activities of agitators through taking the best possible measures.

This year's drought in places north of the central part of this Peninsula was so severe as to be unprecedented in recent years. In consequence, in these places only very poor crops have been obtained and many people are suffering from scarcity of food. To study measures for relieving them, a committee has been specially organized and general plans for doing so have been decided on. Gentlemen, you are asked to follow these plans in the main and leave no room for criticism in assuring the sufferers in affected localities of safe living by taking such measures as are appropriate to local conditions.

The world's thoughts and ideas are in an unsettled state due to the great European War. In these days it is of the utmost importance to restrain our people from resorting to thoughtless and harmful acts, to induce them calmly to pursue their respective occupations, and to allow them freedom to make orderly progress, for all this is the way by which the State can attain a healthy development. Especially is it important in Chosen, where disturbances have broken out one after another since March last, where wild rumors still continue to be in the air, and where the popular mind is still disturbed, to free the people from anxiety and lead them in a right

此間に処する各位の苦心は、之を諒とせざるを得ずと雖、各位は克く関係官署と円満なる協調を保持し、最善の方法を講じて不逞者を鎮圧し、以て地方の寧謐を確保し、民衆をして深く当局に依頼する所あらしめんことを期せよ。

中部以北に於ける今歳の旱害は、近年其の比を見ざる所にして、秋收減少し、人民の窮乏、殊に甚し。之が賑恤に関しては既に旱害救済委員会を開きて、其の大綱の決定を見るに至りたり。各位は之に基き、更に地方の状況に応じて適切なる措置を講じ、罹災地方民の生活を安定するに於て遺憾なきを期すべし。

今や世界の思潮は欧州戦争の影響を受けて動揺不定の情勢に在り。此の秋に際し我が国民をして軽挙妄動を慎み、平静其の業に精励し、以て秩序ある進歩を図らしむるは、即ち国家をして健全なる発達を得しむる所以にして、洵に刻下の緊急時たり。特に朝鮮に於ては本年三月以降騒擾続発し流言蜚語徒に伝えられて、民心未だ安静を見るに至らず。各位は特に意を民心の綏撫と善導とに致されんことを望む。

direction.

I hope and desire that, together with your subordinates, you will put forth greater efforts than hitherto to open up a new and happy era in the administration of this Peninsula by adapting your course to the progress of the times.

附録

希くば各位 益 部下を率いて奮励努力し、時勢の進運に順応して、
半島統治の上に新生面を開かんことを。

APPENDIX H

Administrative Superintendent's Instructions to Provincial

Governors

(Delivered on October 3, 1919)

Gentlemen:—With regard to the reform of the administration of Chosen, the Governor-General, on the assumption of his duty, showed in his instruction to the officials of the Government-General and its affiliated offices the fundamental points in his policy. So I trust that you are already endeavoring steadily to put them into practice. I now desire to call your attention to the essential measures, which the Government-General has already carried out since its reorganization or is about to carry out.

In order to realize the Imperial idea of placing Japanese and Koreans on the footing of equality and reap the fruit of fair and enlightened administration by the co-operation of the Government and people, the Government-General has considered it urgently necessary to abolish the discrimination hitherto existing between Japanese and Korean officials in their treatment, and to open the way for the appointment to official posts of men of talent and ability by giving them very good treatment. The Government-General has accordingly decided to make the salaries of Korean officials equal to those of Japanese officials. Regulations concerning this measure will shortly be published. Also, the power of Korean judges and public procurators has been extended to the same degree as that of their Japanese colleagues, while the posts of principals of common schools hitherto exclusively given to Japanese will hereafter be given to Koreans too. For officials in general, in view of the present

附録 H
道知事会議に於ける政務総監の訓示要旨
（大正八年十月十三日）

朝鮮施政の刷新に関しては、總督就任の初に当り、本府 及 所属官署の職員に対し其の根本要綱を訓示せられたるを以て、各位に於ても著 著 之が実施に努力せられつつあるは予の深く信じて疑わざる所なり。仍て予は茲に各位の会同を機とし、官制改正以来、行政各般の刷新上本府に於て既に施設し、若は近く施設せんとする要項を挙げ以て各位の注意を請う所あらんとす。

一視同仁の聖旨を奉戴し上下協心戮力して公明正大なる政治の実績を挙げんが為には、先ず内鮮人官吏（註：日本人と朝鮮人の役人）の差別待遇を撤廃すると同時に、人材登用の門戸を開放し、其の待遇を改善するを以て急務なりと認め、本府は既に朝鮮人たる官吏の俸給を内地人と同一制度の下に置くの方針を採り、近く之に関する法令の発布を見るに至らんとす。又朝鮮人たる判検事（註：判事と検事）の権限は之を内地人と同一たらしめ、従来 殆ど内地人に限りたる普通学校長の任用は自今朝鮮人に対しても亦之を行うことと為せり。更に一般官吏に対しては、現下社会の実情に鑑み、財政の範囲内に於て待遇上の改善を為し、煩雑なる任用制限、昇給内規等を廃止し、適材を適所に置き、以て能率を増進し、清新なる意気を以て国務に当らしめんことを期せんとす。

598   APPENDICES

state of society, the Government is prepared to give them better treatment as far as its finances will allow. The Government is also prepared to abolish complicated restrictions concerning appointments, and regulations concerning promotions, so that the right men may be found in the right posts and all officials may serve the State with increased efficiency and in a spirit of fresh vigor.

One way of promoting the welfare of the governed is to eradicate the evil of formality and simplify the transaction of official business. In this respect it is regrettable that there was something needing improvement in the administration of Chosen. In addition, due to the progress of the times and the economic development of the Peninsula, the business of government offices has been rapidly augmenting, strengthening the desire for its prompt handling and settlement. In view of this, the Government has recognized the necessity of speedily introducing improvement in the transaction of official business. To do so, the Government has set aside the principle hitherto pursued of centralizing power in the Government-General in favor of that of distributing it among local offices. In conformity with this idea the Government-General will shortly adjust itself and extend as far as possible the power entrusted to local officials. For instance, the transaction of affairs relating to the appointment of retirement of lower class officials in local offices and the distribution of bonuses among them, as well as of affairs relating to traveling by subordinates on official business, has already been entrusted to Provincial Governors. Rules relating to the enforcement of the Myen (village) system have been revised and nearly all business concerning it has also been transferred to their hands. Further, Provincial Governors have been given the power of

形式的政治の弊害を打破し、事務の簡捷刷新を計るは、被治者の福利を増進するの途なるに拘らず、朝鮮に於ける行政に就きて之を見れば、此事たる従来頗る閑却されたるやの感なき能わず。加うるに時勢の進運と経済界の発展に伴い、官庁の事務は愈激増すると同時に、之が処理の敏活を要望すること益緊切を加えつつあるが故に、事務の整理刷新に就ては特に速に改善を加うるの必要なるを認め、従来の中央集注の主義に換うるに分任主義を以てし、近く本府に於ても此の旨趣を以て之が整理を行い、又地方官の権限に関しては努めて之を拡張し、地方庁判任官及判任官待遇職員の進退及賞与ならび部下職員の出張に関する事項の如きは既に之を道知事の職権に委ね、而制施行心得を改正して其の殆ど全部を地方官の権限に移し、参事の任命の如きも之を大体道知事をして専決施行せしむることとせり。尚近き将来に於て驛屯土、小作料及使用料の減免の如きも、道知事の承認を得て府尹、郡守、又は島司をして之を処分せしむるの途を開き、間接国税犯則処分法第十四条第一項の通知の如きも道知事の承認を要せず、郡守をして直に之を専行せしむることに改むる所あらんとする等努めて繁縟の弊を芟除し煩瑣なる法令を整理し事務の簡約

appointing Councillors. Besides, it is the intention of the Government-General to empower Prefects and District Magistrates to deal with matters relating to the exemption or reduction of ground-rent for State lands after they have obtained the approval of the Provincial Governor of their localities. The authorities also intend to give District Magistrates certain power to deal with offences relating to the payment of indirect taxes without taking the trouble of obtaining the approval of their superiors to do so. All these measures already taken or about to be taken are aimed at the elimination of red-tapeism, the adjustment of complicated laws and regulations, and the simplification of business transaction, so as to lessen as far as possible the inconvenience felt by the people at large. You are asked, therefore, gentlemen, to appreciate this idea, and, in dealing with affairs coming under your domain, give to them due deliberation and transact them in a spirit of responsibility.

It is essential for a government to establish a thorough understanding between the government and the people governed, and to carry out such administration as is suitable to local conditions. Gentlemen, you should endeavor, by directing your subordinates in a proper way, to make the people under you thoroughly understand the ideas of the Government and appreciate the motives of the law and administrative measures adopted. At the same time you should not neglect to know what the people desire or complain of and inform the Government of what they think. This is a matter, the importance of which is self-evident. Nevertheless, it is an evil common to all ages that this is not well done in practice. Now let us consider how it was in Chosen. As a matter of fact, there was something lacking in this respect. People did not fully understand and appreciate

を期し、以て国民の不利不便を少なからしむる所存なるを以て、各位に於ても此の主旨を諒し、其の主管する事項に就き適当に考慮を加え且つ充分なる責任観念を以て事に当られんことを望む。

凡そ政治は官民意思の疎通を図り、克く地方の状勢に適合することを必要とす。各位は宜しく部下を督励して常に上意の下達に勗め、被治者をして制度並びに施政の本旨を了得するに至らんことを期すると同時に、克く下意在る所を明察し民意を暢達するに於て遺憾なきを期すべし。然るに此の事たるや事理頗る明白なるに反して、実行頗る挙らざるは古今の通弊なり。朝鮮の情勢に於て之を見るも、従来法令の趣旨訓示の精神の如き又各般行政上の施設の如き其の克く民衆の脳裡に徹底し、其の理解を得る能わざるが為行政の円満なる施行を阻害し、国民の怨嗟を来したるの嫌なきにあらず。本府に於て曩に各位の推薦に係る地方有志を京城に招集して施政更新の趣旨を宣明し、又總督の諭告及び訓示を印

602   APPENDICES

the aims and motives of the laws and regulations enacted, or the spirit of
the proclamations and instructions issued. For this reason, in not a few
instances the enforcement of administrative measures was much hampered
and excited the ill-feeling of the people in general. Gentlemen, it was
in order to avoid the repetition of such blunders that the Government-
General convened to a meeting here some days ago leading Koreans in the
provinces recommended by yourselves, and explained to them the motives
and aims of the administrative reforms undertaken. The distribution
throughout the country of the Governor-General's proclamation and
instruction, the dispatch of a number of high officials to the provinces on a
mission of inspection of popular conditions, and the invitation of opinion
by the Government from the Central Council, which hitherto existed as
a nominal advisory body only —all these were done by the Government
with the purpose of realizing the idea mentioned. Gentlemen, I ask you to
convey this idea to your subordinates, to guide and help the people under
your administration, and to make them thoroughly understand the policy
of the Government. I also ask you to learn clearly and fully their mental
condition and endeavor to take fitting measures to give them satisfaction.

    In order to advance the capabilities of the people in the provinces,
improve their habits, and enable them to take part in the Government, the
Government recognizes the necessity of carrying out a system of local self-
government. The Director of the Internal Affairs Bureau is investigating
and studying the subject, so that some time in the future the Government
will announce a concrete plan thereanent. You are requested to submit to
me your views, if you have any, without the least reservation.

    The police system has been reformed with the reorganization of the

行して洽く各地に配布したるが如き、又近く事務官を各道に分派して親しく民情を観察せしめたるが如き、或は従来諮詢機関たるの名ありて其の実なかりし中枢院の会議を開きて意見を徴したるが如き、其の帰する所、此の趣旨の実現を企図せるものに外ならず。各位に於ても克く部下に此の旨を伝え被治者を誘掖指導して施政方針の徹底を期すると同時に、親しく民情を洞察し之に順応する施設を講ずるに努められんことを望む。

　地方の民力を作興し民風を涵養し、国民をして政治に参与せしむるが為には、地方自治制を施行することを必要と認め、現に主管局長をして調査研究せしめつつあるが故に、具体的成案を発表するの機あるべし。各位に於て之に関し意見あらば遠慮なく申出られんことを望む。

　警察制度は今次の官制改正に依りて一新生面を開き、憲兵と警

Government-General, the police and gendarmes being now separated, each having its own proper duties. The police power is now in your hands. Accordingly you must remember that you have now greater responsibility than hitherto in maintaining peace and order in the localities under your jurisdiction. I desire that, by encouraging your subordinates, you will achieve great improvement in the administration of police affairs. The police being in direct contact with the people, and having as their duty their protection and control, their acts and behavior not only concern the interests of the people to a large extent, but often become the cause of criticism against the Government-General regime. I desire you, gentlemen, to be careful in the direction of the police officers under you, so that they may commit no blunders but uphold their prestige.

The popular mind is still disturbed in Chosen and it is not impossible that the situation may take on a serious aspect. Taking advantage of this state of things, wicked men are secretly at work endeavoring to incite the masses and disturb the order of society by spreading wild and seditious rumors. In consequence, law- abiding people are menaced in regard to life and property, suffering therefrom much loss. Gentlemen, you should exercise strict control over those wicked men, and endeavor to free peaceful people from the fear of groundless rumors, give them assurance of the security of life and property, and set the popular mind at ease.

With regard to the control of disturbances and similar occurrences, you should try to, use the police organs to the best advantage, and, by paying the most circumspect attention, should try to prevent such from taking place. You should, however, be fully prepared promptly to suppress any untoward occurrence that may take place.

察官と相分離して各自本来の職責に其の力を専にすることとなり、警察の実権は各位の掌握する所となれり。従て各位は管下治安維持上、一層重大なる責任を負うに至れることを思い、克く部下を督励して警察事務の刷新改善を図られんことを望む。而して警察官は直接民衆に接触し、其の保護と取締との任務を有するものなるを以て、其の行動は民衆の利害に関すること至大なるのみならず、動もすれば其の一挙一動が總督政治の良否を批判するの因となるが故に、各位は部下の警察官を督励し、其の過誤なきを期すると同時に、其の威信を失墜せしめざるに留意せられんことを望む。

　方今朝鮮に於ける人心未だ安定せず、情勢の転変測り知るべからざるものあり。不逞の徒、亦巧に其の間に跳梁し、動もすれば流言蜚語を以て民衆を扇動蠱惑して社会の秩序を紊さんとす。之が為に良民は財産生命の脅威を受け、損害を受くること勘少にあらず。各位は克く此の状勢を察し、不逞の徒に対しては極力取締を厳にし、良民をして無根の流言に畏怖せずして生命財産の安固を保持し、人心の安定を得しむることに努力せられんことを望む。尚、騒擾等取締に就いては、特に意を警察機能の活用に注ぎ、予め周到なる注意を傾倒して事を未発に防ぐに努むべく、若一旦事端の発生するあらば、迅速之を制圧するの準備に遺算なきを期せられんことを望む。

606   APPENDICES

It is necessary to extend medical and sanitary organs and to complete their equipments in order to prevent the outbreak of epidemics and to give people suffering from diseases prompt and efficient medical attention. It is a measure calculated to give assurance to the popular mind. In this branch of the Government work, thanks to the splendid efforts put forth by our predecessors, some excellent arrangements have already been made in this country, there being in existence nineteen charity hospitals and more than one hundred public doctors. Nevertheless, in consideration of the progress of the times, the Government has recognized the necessity of introducing improvement in the work as far as its finances allow. The authorities are now deliberating plans to establish more charity hospitals, appoint more public doctors, and increase the force of sanitary experts attached to provincial governments. You are asked to enter into this idea of the Government and leave no room for criticism in promoting the hygienic welfare of the general public and spreading the benefit of medical relief.

The method of punishment by flogging has long been practised in Chosen and was considered a measure suitable to the standard of the people as a preventive of minor offences. SD the Government has continued it against Koreans only. It is, however, a method of punishment at variance with the modern idea aiming at the reformation of erring people. For this reason, the Government will shortly abolish it, substituting for it imprisonment with labor or fines, so as to conform to the progress of the times.

The Government-General since its establishment has earnestly encouraged industry in this country with the result that a fine development has been attained. The development of industry is to be achieved on the

医療衛生機関を普及し其の内容の整備を図るは、疾患を防止し救療を敏速にし民心を安ずる所以なり。而して此の方面に対しては先任者の努力に依り、既に相当の施設を加え慈恵医院十九、公医百有余名を算すと雖時勢の進運に伴い、尚改善を為すの必要を認め、財政の許す範囲に於いて慈恵医院及び公医等を増加し且各道にも衛生に関する技術員を増置するの計画に付考慮しつつあり。各位宜しく此の趣旨を体し一般公衆の衛生を進め救療の恵澤を普及するに於て遺憾なきを期せよ。

笞刑は古来朝鮮に於て一般に施用せられ、軽微なる犯罪の制裁として民度に恰適する刑罰なりしを以て、朝鮮人に限り之を襲用し来りしも、元来現代思想に基く刑罰の性質に背馳するものなるを以て、近く之を廃止し、基本刑たる懲役又は罰金を以て之に代え、時代の進歩に順応せしめんとす。

朝鮮の産業は、總督府施政以来鋭意之が奨励に努め、大に成績の見るべきものあり。元来産業の事たる地方多年の経験と民族習慣を基礎として其の進歩を講すべきものにして、漫に新奇の施設

basis of experience as well as of manners and customs. Its pace should not be forcibly accelerated by the launching of novel ventures or by the introduction of sudden changes. So, in improving industrial undertakings and institutions already under way, you should be very careful in selecting what is good and rejecting what is bad, so as to assure their healthy progress.

Education is the means by which the human intellect is developed and a virtuous character built up. In view of the present condition of this country, the Government recognizes the urgent necessity of spreading education among the people by advancing the standard of educational organs and enriching their equipment. Accordingly, the Government is now deliberating plans for the extension of the school course for Korean children, improvement of school curriculums, increase in schools, and the establishment of new organs for higher education, as well as the improvement of those already existing. But no good result in education can be achieved through the completion of its system and arrangement, unless it is reformed and improved in spirit and conduct. I desire you, gentlemen, to be very careful in the selection and superintendence of teachers, and to endeavor to improve the method of teaching.

It is scarcely necessary to say that the knowledge of the Korean language is very important to officials in discharging their duties. Accordingly, in order to encourage the study of the language by them, the Government-General intends to find a way for granting special liberal allowances to those mastering it. Especially great is the importance of the mastery of the language by police officers and officials serving in provincial governments, as they daily come in contact with the Korean

を試み或は急劇なる改良を強い、以て事功を急ぐかの如きは固より戒慎すべき所なり。故に既往の計画制度等を改良するに際しては最慎重の考慮を加え取捨宜しきを制し、以て其の進歩を期すべし。

　人智を啓発し徳器を成就するは一に教育の力に俟たざるべからず。朝鮮の現状に鑑みるに、教育の施設を普及し其の程度を昇進せしめ、之が内容を充実するの必要は最切なるものあるを認む。仍て朝鮮人に対する普通教育の修業年限延長、内容の改善、学校の増設、高等教育機関の新設並に改善等に付、目下企画を進めつつあり。然れども教育の効果は単に制度と設備との完成のみを以て足れりとすべきにあらず。其の内容の刷新改善を最必要とす。各位は宜しく教員の人選監督を周到にし、且つ教授方法の改善に努めしめられんことを望む。

　朝鮮語学の研究は官吏の職務遂行上に於て最必要なるは言を俟たざる所なり。依て本府に於ては、之が奨励の為、将来相当高額の手当を支給するの途を開かんとす。殊に警察官及び地方官吏に在りては、日常民衆に直接するを以て、朝鮮語に通達するの要一層其の切実なるものあるを感ず。各位は克く部下の官吏をして此の趣旨を諒し朝鮮語の練習に努めしめられんことを望む。

people. I ask you to communicate this idea of the Government to your subordinates and induce them to take up the study of Korean in earnest.

With regard to the maintenance of official discipline, the preceding heads of the Government-General frequently issued instructions, so that I do not doubt that you are always paying due attention to the subject. I see, however, that the morality of society is very loose of late, and there is a tendency for its bad effects to appear among Government officials in general. I regret that I frequently hear of various unpleasant affairs taking place among them. I ask you to drive home in the minds of officials under you that they are expected to be examples for the people at large and to maintain the dignity and prestige due to their positions.

Since my arrival here, I have been working hard, together with gentlemen under me, with a view to obtaining some good results from the new régime. It is, however, less than two months since it was inaugurated. The new policy of the Governor-General is not as yet thoroughly realized, and those measures already taken for its realization have not as yet borne fruit. All this I regret very much, but I shall continue to put forth my best efforts in the discharge of my duty with the purpose of bringing into the administration of this country a new and happy feature. Gentlemen, I beseech you to remember the great responsibility reposed in you, to appreciate the motives and ideas of the new regime, and to discharge your duty with courage and without flinching. The administrative reform we have taken up, however, must be preceded by circumspect deliberation and study, as well as by the amendment of existing institutions. In addition, funds must be provided. Unless we are given time, it is impossible for us to achieve our desired end. Together with you I wish to go on our work

官規の振粛に関しては従来屢次訓示せられたる所あり。各位に於ても常に之が振張に留意せらるるを疑わずと雖、近時社会の風紀弛廃して一般官吏の風尚亦其の余波を受くるの傾向あり。屢各種の不祥事を耳にするは、予の頗る遺憾とする所なるを以て、各位は宜しく部下を戒飭し、克く民衆の儀表と為り、官吏の威信を保持せしめんことを期すべし。

予は着任以来部下と共に夙夜励精治務を挙げんことを期せざるに非ずと雖、時日を閲すること未だ二月に足らず。總督の施政方針尚未だ徹せず、之に伴う施設の如きも未だ克く其の効果を発現する能わざるは、遺憾に堪えざる所なり。予は今後一層施政の新生面を開くが為に努力せんことを期す。希くは各位に於ても其の責任の重且つ大なるを自覚し、新政の趣旨を体して勇往邁進、克く其の職務を遂行せられんことを。然れども施政の革新は慎重の調査と制度の改正を要し、且つ費用の之に伴うものあり。仮すに時日を以てするにあらざれば、万全の効果を見得べきにあらず。予は各位と共に深く慮り、遠く察し、漸を追うて確実に効果を収むることを欲し、往々世評に拘泥して事功を収むるに急にして軽挙事を誤るなからんことを期す。尚各位の多くは永く朝鮮に在住し地方の事情に精通せらるるを以て此の機会に於て忌憚なく其の

slowly but steadily, thinking deeply of the present and the future. Above all, I am determined not to be swayed by the superficial criticism of the public, and not to be too hasty in endeavoring to reap the fruit of our labor, so that we may not commit blunders by acting thoughtlessly. Gentlemen, many of you have lived long in Chosen and are well versed in affairs and in the conditions in your localities. I desire you to take the present opportunity to submit to me your views without the least reservation, and thereby contribute to the reform of the administration of this country.

抱懐する意見を吐露せられ、施政の改善に資せらるるならば幸甚なり。

APPENDIX I

Rules for Teachers

(Notification No. 11, January 4, 1916)

I. The fostering of loyalty and filial piety shall be made the radical principle of education, and the cultivation of moral sentiments shall be given special attention. Loyalty and filial piety form the basis of moral principle and are the natural sentiments of subjects and sons. Acting on this basic principle and natural sentiment, the actions of all will be restrained within the bounds of propriety. It is only what may be expected of a loyal and dutiful man, who knows what is demanded of a subject and a son that he should be faithful to his duties, and manage his household with thrift and diligence, thus enabling him to establish himself in society, succeed in business, and contribute to the enhancement of the prosperity of the country. It is, therefore, required of persons in education that they train

附録 I

朝鮮總督府訓令　教員心得
（大正五年一月四日）

　帝国教育の本旨は夙に教育に関する勅語に明示せらるる所、其の内地人に対すると朝鮮人に対するとを問わず均しく聖慮に基き忠良なる国民を育成せざるべからず。蓋し我が帝国は開闢以来、万世一系、君臣一体、世界に比類なき国体を有す故に、帝国臣民たるものは協心戮力祖先の美風を継承し以て天壌無窮の皇運を扶翼せざるべからず。是れ実に教育の大本にして又国家が特に教育を布く所以なり。故に教育の任に当たる者は、常に国民教育の大本に思を致し、特に左の三箇条に留意して努力奮励せんことを要す。

第一条　忠孝を本とし徳性を涵養すべし

　　忠孝は人倫の大本にして臣子の至情に出づ。此の大本に基き此の至情に出でて始めて百行其の軌を誤らざるを得べし。忠誠孝順能く臣子の本分を知るものは日常其の業を執ること忠実に其の産を治むること勤倹に以て身を立て世に処し国運の発展に貢献するの人たるを得べし。故に教育の任に当たるものは忠孝を本として徳性を涵養し以て帝国の臣民として其の本分を完うし得るの人物を教養せんことを期すべし。

the moral sentiments of their pupils on the basis of loyalty and filial piety, so that they may grow up imbued with the desire and power to meet the requirements of their country.

II. Practical use shall be made the aim in imparting knowledge and art. The object of education is to raise up practical men able to meet the requirements of the State. How can it be expected that a man will establish himself and succeed in business, thus advancing the national interests, and do that which the State requires of him, if he gives himself to vain argument and becomes thereby of little use to the world, or if he is averse to industry and labor and neglects the practice thereof? It is therefore, required of persons engaged in education that they pay their primary attention to the principle of utilization of knowledge, the promotion of the national welfare, and to the imparting of useful knowledge, so that practical persons to meet the national requirements will be found to be the rule, not the exception, in the Empire.

III. Robust physical development shall be striven for. Robust physical development is necessary in order to carry through undertakings, while the development of the national strength also depends much upon the exertions of the people constituting the country. How can it be expected of a person of weak physique and unfit for work, to get along in the world, carry on business, and thereby contribute to the development of the country? It is, therefore, required of persons engaged in education always to bear this in mind, so that their pupils may be brought up strong and healthy.

The above-mentioned three items are the essential principles of education. The fate of a country depends upon the quality of the people constituting it; and the quality of the people depends upon the morality,

附録

第二条　実用を旨として知識技能を教授すべし

教育の要は実用的人材を育成し国家の需要に応ぜしめんとするに在り。若し国民にして徒に空論に走りて世用に遠ざかり勤労を厭いて実行を忽にするが如きことあらば何ぞ能く身を立て産を興し国益を増進し以て其の本分を完うすることを得んや。故に教育の任に当る者は須らく利用厚生の道に着眼し、有用なる知能の啓沃に務め以て国家の需要に適応する実用的人材を育成せんことを期すべし。

第三条　強健なる身体を育成すべし

凡百の事業を遂行するには強健なる体力を要し、国家の富強も亦強健なる国民の努力に待つこと大なり。身体脆弱にして用に耐えずんば、何ぞ能く世に処し業に服し以て帝国の進運に貢献することを得んや。故に教育の任に当る者は此に留意し強健なる国民を育成せんことを期すべし。

以上の三箇条は教育の大綱なり。凡そ邦家の隆替は之を構成する人民の良否に由り、人民の良否は其の徳操智能体力の如何に存す。故に、苟も教育に従事する者は其の初等教育たると高等教育たる

ability, and physique possessed by them. Whether the education being given is elementary or higher, common or special, persons engaging in it shall always bear these principles in mind, and give their whole energy to the realization of them, so that the object of education may be attained. With regard to the ways and means by which these principles are to be realized: special attention shall be paid to the following nine rules:

(1) Education shall be adapted to the characteristics of the pupils and to the circumstances in which they are placed. It is necessary for teachers to make themselves acquainted with the characteristics of their pupils and with the circumstances in which they are placed, so that they may give suitable education adapted thereto. Education desultorily given without first studying such characteristics and circumstances, will not only fall short of attaining its object, but sometimes may even prove harmful. It is, therefore, required of teachers that they make themselves well acquainted with the age, physique, disposition and habits of the pupils under them, thereby deriving suggestions as to the method of imparting education to them. Besides the disposition and circumstances of the pupils, teachers shall also make themselves acquainted with their individual personality, so that they may give to each the education exactly needed by them, just as a physician gives his patients those medicines required for curing their disease. Education limited to classrooms, where it is given in common, neglecting the special direction and assistance required by pupils, whether in common or individually, leaves much to be desired.

(2) Education shall aim at adapting itself to the needs of the times and to the conditions of the people. The object of education is not to be attained by being restrained within conventional forms, or given in a careless

とを問わず、普通教育たると専門教育たるとを論ぜず、常に此の大綱を念頭に置き、全力を挙げて其の実現を期し、以て教育の本旨を達せざるべからず。而して之が実現の方法につきては、特に左の九項に注意するを要す。

一　生徒の性質境遇に順応して教育を施すべし

　　教師は先ず生徒一般の性質境遇を明かにし、之に順応して適当なる教育を施さざるべからず。生徒の性質及び境遇の如何を究めずして漫然教育を為すが如きことあらば、教育の効果を収める能わざるのみならず、或は有害なる結果に陥るべし。故に教師は予め生徒の年齢体質気風習慣等を知悉して教育の資となさんことを要す。又教師は生徒一般の性質境遇の外に各生徒の個性を知り、之に応じて善導すること猶お良医の応病施薬の工夫をなすがごとくなるべし。若し夫れ教室に於ける一般教育のみを以て能事畢れりとなし、一般生徒に対しても個人に対しても特別の指導扶掖を怠るが如きことあらば、未だ以て周到切実なる教育と言うこと能はず。

二　時勢と民度とに適合する教育を施すべし

　　教育は時勢と民度とを稽え、之に適合せんことを務めざるべからず。徒らに因襲の形式に拘束せられ、或は漫然事を処

manner. Teachers are, therefore, required first to lay down established plans and arrangements with regard to the training of their pupils, whether moral,intellectual, or physical, so that nothing is left undone in devising methods of education.

(3) Instruction shall be given so that the national characteristics are fostered. In imparting education, the developing of the national characteristics shall be made the object, and the cultivation of virtue be striven for, by paying special attention to instruction given. Not to mention hours for lessons, or for practical training, every opportunity that may present itself shall be seized by teachers to give their pupils suitable instruction, so that pupils may be brought up to behave themselves leniently towards others, but strictly towards themselves, to value order and to observe discipline, to be thrifty and industrious, and honest and trustworthy. In this way, these qualities may become their second nature, so that when grown up they may discharge in full their duties as people of the Empire.

(4) Education given shall be uniform in system, and practice shall be repeated, so that pupils may grasp what they have learned. In order to make secure the efforts of teaching, the object of each lesson shall be made clear, a system followed, and proper order observed. At the same time, care must be taken to establish connection and unity between the lessons, so that each shall be dependent on, and not counteract the other. In case different teachers give different branches of a lesson, attention shall be especially given to this point, and conference between them held, so that connection is established between them, and the pupils enabled to receive thoroughly connected teaching. It shall not be the aim to impart

するが如きは、教育の功を収むる所以にあらず。故に教師は徳育に智育に体育に各一定の計画を立て、周密なる予定を案じ、以て教育の方法を校量するに於て遺算なからんことを要す。

三　訓育に留意し国民的性格の養成に力むべし

　教育に於ては国民的性格の養成を期し、特に訓育に力を用い、徳性の涵養を務めざるべからず。されば学科を授くる間にも実習を課する間にも其の他機会のある毎に訓育に留意して訓誨に勉め、生徒をして日常人に接するに寛容己れを持するに謹恪秩序を重んじ、規律を守り、力行業励み、倹素身を奉じ、著実敦厚習い性となり、能く国民たるの本分を完うすべき人物を教養せんことを期すべし。

四　統一ある教授を行い練磨の効を積ましめ生徒をして其の学ぶ所を確実ならしむべし

　教授を的確ならしむが為には、各教科目の教授の目的を明かにし、系統を追い秩序を正すと共に、各教科目の間に連絡統一あらしめ、散漫孤立に陥り扞格矛盾するが如きことなきを要す。各教師、科目を分ちて業を授くる場合には、特に此の点に注意し、互に連絡を保ち、協議を怠らず、生徒をして首尾相応し脈絡貫通する教授を受けしめんことを期すべし。生徒に授くる知識技能の分量は必ずしも多きを貪るべから

622   APPENDICES

a great deal of knowledge or art, as it is essential that the pupils be made fully to understand and make their own that which they are taught. It is, therefore, required that they be given as ample opportunity as possible for repetition of, and exercise in, what they are taught. In this way, it is hoped the knowledge imparted to them may be firmly implanted in their minds, a perfect system established, and free use of that knowledge made by the pupils with promptitude.

(5)   Education shall be given so as to arouse the interest of pupils in their studies and thus induce in them the habit of voluntarily pursuing them. On the occasion of giving a lesson, it is necessary to use suitable methods, so that pupils may be interested, and brought thoroughly to understand what they are taught, and thus be led to enjoy their studies. In teaching, pupils shall not only have knowledge and art imparted to them, but they shall also be taught the method of study. Besides, in teaching the practical side of subjects, endeavor shall be made to induce pupils to feel an interest in it and to pursue it with pleasure, so that they may acquire the habit of industry and the taste for labor. In this way, it is hoped from the oversight of teachers, they will not lapse into idleness, but keep up the habit of self-training and push onward in their calling.

(6) Attention shall be paid to physical development, and along with gymnastics suitable athletic sports shall be encouraged. It is necessary for a person to have a strong physique in order to get on in the world and succeed in business. Gymnastics well adapted to the stages of physical development shall, therefore, be practised, and exercises or pastimes for the seasons and locality encouraged, so that the body of the pupils may be hardened, their mental strength invigorated and they may be the possessors

ず。要は生徒をして十分に理會習熟せしむるにあり。故に一旦授けたる知識技能は、機に触れ物に応じて反復練磨の効を積ましむべし。此の如くにして始めて生徒の修得せる智能は確実なる根蔕を具え、円熟なる統一を保ち、自由に敏活に運用せらるるに至るものなり。

五　学習に興味を感じ自学自習の習慣を得しむべし

　教授の際は適当なる方案により興味を感ぜしめ、理會の透徹を図り、生徒の向学心を振起すること肝要なり。又生徒を教授するに当りては、単に知識技能の授与を為すのみならず、兼て学習の方法をも指導せんことを要す。其の他実科教育に於ては実習に対して興味を感ぜしめ、生徒をして欣んで之に服せしめ、勤勉の習慣と労作の趣味とを養成すべし。斯くて生徒が他日業を卒え、師を離るるも、遊衣徒食に安んぜず、尚お能く自学自習の習慣を保持し、又各自の業務に奮励するの気風を養成せんことを要す。

六　身体の鍛錬に留意し情操と共に適当なる運動を奨励すべし

　人の世に処し事を成すや強健なる体力に待たざるべからず。故に身体の発育に伴い適度の情操を課し、又季節に応じ土地の状況に従い、適当なる運動、遊戯を奨励し、以て身体を鍛錬し、気力を旺盛にし、寒暑風雪を冒し、困苦欠乏に耐え得るの体質を養成すべし。尚お生徒をして修学中は勿論、

624   APPENDICES

of physique able to stand the changes of the seasons, and rise superior to the hardships they may experience. It shall also be an object to induce pupils to volunteer for physical training, not only during their school life, but also after that is over, so that their physique may continually develop.

(7) Teachers shall exhibit to their pupils love and dignity, and make themselves models for them. Dignity is necessary for a teacher in facing his pupils, because with it he is able to give life to his teaching and training, and thereby attain the objects of education. At the same time there must be warm love and deep affection to enable teachers to maintain friendly relations with their pupils, and thus exercise sufficient influence over them and bring them up satisfactorily. What they desire of their pupils, teachers shall show by their own example and by acting up to their words will make themselves fit models for imitation.

(8) Teachers shall have a firm purpose, and always strive after mental cultivation. Education does not look for immediate results, as its aim is far-reaching. Teachers shall, therefore, regard education as an honorable profession, and become firmly attached to it, so that they may strive always for its final aim and be ready to die, if needed, martyrs for that profession. Teachers shall also endeavor to comprehend the seriousness of their duties, so that they may experience a sense of failure if they find the culture possessed by them falling short of their high calling, and they will be urged thereby to faithful prosecution of their studies and to the proper application of experience, and to strive for the expansion of their acquirements, and so to attain the desired improvement and progress in themselves and the faithful execution of the duties expected of them.

卒業後と雖自ら進んで運動を務むるの風を養成し、その体質を強健にせんことを期すべし。

七　教師は親愛と威重とを以て生徒に臨み常に率先して模範を示すべし

　　教師の生徒に臨むや威重なかるべからず。之によりて教授訓練共に凛として生気あり。以て教育の効力を生ず。然れども一面には温情春の如く、慈愛海の如きものありて、以て師弟間の親和を繋ぎ、感化薫陶の実を挙げざるべからず。而して教師の生徒に求る所のものは、必ず自ら率先して躬行し、言行一致、以て生徒の儀表たらんことを期すべし。

八　教師は志操を堅実にし常に自己の修養に力むべし

　　教育の事業たる功を日前に求めずして、之を永遠に期するものなれば、教師たるものは教育を以て名誉ある天職とし、屈せず撓まず終局の目的に向って勇往邁進し、斯業に殉ずるの操守なかるべからず。又教師は其の任務の重大なる所以を自覚し、修行の足らざるを以て憂とし、益進みて事業を研究し、経験を積み、常に意を人格の修養と学芸の研鑽とに用い、以て向上進歩に務め、其の責務を完うせんことを期すべし。

APPENDICES

(9) Teachers shall be ready to keep on friendly terms with one another, and, further, to extend their friendship to elders of the local community, so that they may exert a good influence over them. Education is closely related to social matters, so that it is difficult to attain its objects by school education alone. It, therefore, follows that teachers must keep on friendly terms with one another, and advise each other with will, so that all may be kept from swerving from the path of duty, a good esprit de corps established among the schools, and pupils surrounded with the best possible influence. They shall also keep on good terms with elders of the local community, and acting, in concert with them, endeavor to accomplish the object of education. At the same time, they shall keep in view the fact that they are leaders of the community, and so endeavor to influence and reform it.

In short, teachers shall thoroughly master the fundamental principles of the education of the Empire, and endeavor to bring that education into realization, putting forth their strength in all sincerity, and by gaining the fruitful result of education contribute to the desired development of the Empire. All conduct in life is to be based on sincerity and endeavor. It is only by acting with sincerity and endeavor that pupils can be trained to be loyal, and the Imperial behest be obeyed. With regard to education in Chosen, I, the Governor-General, depend greatly upon those in responsible positions, and so lay down herewith the daily rules for teachers, so that what is desired of them shall be quite clearly set out before them.

九　教師は同僚相親<ruby>和<rt>あい</rt></ruby>し進んで父兄郷党に親み之を教化するの覚悟あるべし

　　教育の事業たる、関係する所大にして独力其の効果を挙げ<ruby>難<rt>がた</rt></ruby>きものなれば、教師は同僚<ruby>互<rt>たがい</rt></ruby>に親和一致し、好意を以て忠告善導し、優良なる校風を<ruby>扶植<rt>ふしょく</rt></ruby>し、最善の訓化を生徒に及ぼさんことを期すべし。其の他教師は父兄<ruby>郷党<rt>きょうとう</rt></ruby>と親睦提携し、<ruby>相<rt>あい</rt></ruby>呼応して教育の事業を成就せんことを<ruby>計<rt>はか</rt></ruby>ると共に、社会の先学を以て自ら任じ、之を教化誘導するの覚悟あるを要す。

　　之を要するに、教師たるものは帝国教育の本旨を体し、之を実現する所以の方法を講じ至誠を<ruby>基<rt>もと</rt></ruby>とし努力<ruby>之<rt>これ</rt></ruby>を遂行し、以て教育の実績を挙げ、帝国の<ruby>進運<rt>しんうん</rt></ruby>に貢献せんことを期すべし。<ruby>蓋<rt>けだ</rt></ruby>し人生凡百の行為<ruby>一<rt>ひとつ</rt></ruby>として至誠に<ruby>基<rt>もとづ</rt></ruby>かざるはなく、努力に待たざるはなし。此の至誠、此の努力ありて始めて能く忠良なる国民を育成し、聖旨に奉答することを<ruby>得<rt>う</rt></ruby>べし。本總督、朝鮮の教育に関し其の職に当る者に<ruby>望<rt>のぞみ</rt></ruby>を<ruby>属<rt>しょく</rt></ruby>するや切なり。<ruby>茲<rt>ここ</rt></ruby>に教師の日常<ruby>心<rt>こころ</rt></ruby><ruby>得<rt>う</rt></ruby>べきものを示し、其の<ruby>帰嚮<rt>ききょう</rt></ruby>する所を知らしむ。

APPENDICES

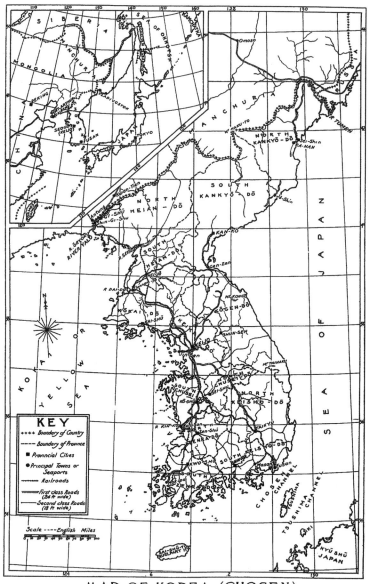

MAP OF KOREA (CHOSEN)

編集部翻訳方針について

本書は、アメリカ合衆国で E.P.Dutton & Company により出版された Alleyne Ireland, F.R.G.S.; The New Korea, 1926 に基づいている。

※原書中の"KOREA"という単語の訳は史実に従って、名目上独立している期間は「大韓帝国」とし、それ以外は「朝鮮」とした。尚、人種を指す場合はどの時代であっても「朝鮮人」で統一した。

※読者の便宜のため原文に改行を追加した箇所があるが、内容については原書のままである。

※日本文中あえて一部にふり仮名を附しているのは一般読者の便に資する為である。

※日本文中、ある特定の固有名詞については当時の漢字をあえて用いている（例　総督府→總督府）

※原文中の註は、原文と同様に＊で示して脚註を附した。

※原書の目次には、一部、本文中の小見出しと厳密に対応しないものもあるが、原書目次をそのまま生かした。

※本文中の教育勅語の現代訳は、文部省による教育勅語の全文通釈による。

翻訳協力：飯塚涼子、高野三峰子、武井優子、森田亨、安田京子、Rena Narita

著者：アレン・アイルランド（1871-1951）

イギリス生まれ。王立地理学会特別会員（F.R.G.S.）。植民地運営
に関する専門家。アメリカの雑誌などに広く執筆活動を行なって
いた氏は、1901 年、米シカゴ大学の招きにより、植民地運営研究
の委員に任命され、3 年間極東に派遣され、イギリス、フランス、
オランダ、そして日本による植民地経営のシステムを研究、また
フィリピンに 6 カ月間滞在した。コーネル大学、シカゴ大学、ロ
ーウェル・インスティテュートなどで教鞭を執った。

Author: Alleyne Ireland (1871-1951)

Born and raised in England, Mr. Ireland was a leading authority
on Colonial Administration and a F.R.G.S. (Fellow of the Royal
Geographical Society). While he wrote largely for American
magazines, he was appointed Colonial Commissioner of the
University of Chicago, U.S.A. in 1901, and was sent to the Far
East where he spent three years studying the British, French,
Dutch and Japanese systems, and stayed six months in the
Philippines. During his career, he served as a lecturer at Cornell
University, the University of Chicago and the Lowell Institute.

著書に以下がある。
The followings are some of his books:

Tropical Colonization (1899)

China and the Powers: Chapters in the History of Chinese
Intercourse with Western Nations (1902)

The Far Eastern Tropics; Studies in the Administration of Tropical
Dependencies Hong Kong, British North Borneo, Sarawak, Burma,
the Federated Malay States, the Straits Settelements, French Indo-
China, Java, the Phillipine Islands (1905)

The province of Burma; a report prepared on behalf of the University
of Chicago Volume 1, Volume 2 (1907)

改訂版　**THE NEW KOREA**
朝鮮が劇的に豊かになった時代

2025 年 4 月 3 日　初版　第 1 刷発行

著　者　アレン・アイルランド

編　者　桜の花出版編集部

発行者　山口春嶽

発行所　桜の花出版株式会社
　　　　〒 194-0021　東京都町田市中町 1-12-16-401
　　　　電話 042-785-4442

発売元　株式会社星雲社（共同出版社・流通責任出版社）
　　　　〒 112-0005　東京都文京区水道 1-3-30
　　　　電話 03-3868-3275

印刷製本　株式会社シナノ

本書の内容の一部あるいは全部を無断で複写（コピー）すること
は、著作権上認められている場合を除き、禁じられています。
万一、落丁、乱丁本がありましたらお取り替え致します。

©Sakuranohana Shuppan Inc.　2025　Printed in Japan
ISBN978-4-434-35298-0 C0095

〈表紙写真〉
著者アレン・アイルランド：Print Collection, Miriam and Ira D.Wallach Division of Art, Prints
and Photographs, The New York Public Library, Astor, Lenox and Tilden Foundations

〈表紙装丁〉：A. WAKAMATSU

本書は、2013 年 8 月 14 日刊行の『The New Korea　朝鮮が劇的に豊かになった時代』から、
編集部の付した「写真で見る朝鮮の変化」「朝鮮略史」などを削除し註釈を最低限にして、でき
るだけ原著に近い形で改訂版として刊行したものです。